The Book of Books

The Book of Books

by

ANNALEE SKARIN

DeVorss & Co., Publishers
1641 Lincoln Blvd.
Santa Monica, Calif. 90404

THE BOOK OF BOOKS

by

ANNALEE SKARIN

Vol. VIII.
© 1972
by
ANNALEE SKARIN

All Rights Reserved

Printed in the United States of America by—
DeVorss & Co., Publishers, 1641 Lincoln Blvd.,
Santa Monica, Calif. 90404

Quotations from THE LOST BOOKS OF THE BIBLE AND THE FORGOTTEN BOOKS OF EDEN are reprinted by permission from The World Publishing Company; © 1926-27 by Alpha House, Inc.

The APPENDIX contained in this work pertains to the preceding book, BEYOND MORTAL BOUNDARIES.

BOOKS BY ANNALEE SKARIN

I. "YE ARE GODS," published by the Philosophical Library, Inc., 15 East 40th Street, New York City, N.Y. 10016.

II. TO GOD THE GLORY, published by DeVorss and Co., 1641 Lincoln Boulevard, Santa Monica, Calif. 90404.

III. THE TEMPLE OF GOD, published by DeVorss.

IV. SECRETS OF ETERNITY, published by DeVorss.

V. THE CELESTIAL SONG OF CREATION, published by DeVorss.

VI. MAN TRIUMPHANT, published by DeVorss.

VII. BEYOND MORTAL BOUNDARIES, published by DeVorss.

There have been many editions or printings of the above list of books.

Christine Mercie's little book SONS OF GOD belongs also with the above collection.

THIS IS AN APPENDIX TO THE BOOK, BEYOND MORTAL BOUNDARIES, RECENTLY PUBLISHED BY DEVORSS AND CO.

By Annalee Skarin

In the book, "Beyond Mortal Boundaries" are countless misprints and innumerable errors, but the truths are mostly apparent and will remain unchanged except for the chapter on THE THREE DEGREES OF GLORY. There must be a correction made to that which has been printed.

On page 239, of the above mentioned volume is described the TELESTIAL DEGREE OF GLORY, which is likened to the brilliance of the stars and with as great a variety of intensity. For as one star differs from another in glory so are the different degrees of existence for those who are assigned to this lesser realm of rewards or states of lower, "telestial" existence.

The realm of the pickpockets is described. And the liars and the braggarts are mentioned along with the selfish and profane who will inherit some degree in these *telestial*, inferior realms, according to that which they merit. Those who have developed only their physical or animal traits, indulging in the mortal cravings will have nothing to look forward to later.

The lesser degrees are for those of lesser qualifications.

And this inferior, "TELESTIAL DEGREE OF GLORY" IS NOT "CELESTIAL GLORY!" as has been written into the volume "Beyond Mortal Boundaries." This correction must be made and forever established.

The Telestial degree of glory is the least of the three degrees of glory or eternal inheritances awaiting man in his future existence, according to his own qualifications—or lack of them.

The second degree of glory is the "TERRESTRIAL." And it is likened unto the moon, whose light far exceeds the light of the stars from our earth view. The stars vary in brilliance to dim, pin-points of light or radiance. The Terrestrial glory, which is likened to the brilliance of the moon, is for those who are honorable and honest and who are successful to a certain degree in their affairs and with their dealings with their fellowman. This realm requires a degree of integrity and honesty and understanding above and beyond the requisites of the Telestial realms. In this higher degree, the Golden Rule is accepted as one fulfills the admonition "to do unto others as he would be done by."

The "CELESTIAL" glory is the very highest and is likened in brilliance to the sun in its radiance. This glory is not for the dishonest, the cheats, the thieves or pickpockets, the sex-perverts, the liars or the unclean. Nor is it for the successful ones who have lived on a mere mortal plane of striving always "TO GET AHEAD!" as they labor for the things that perish.

This Celestial glory is for those who have obeyed the injunctions of the Lord Jesus Christ. It is for those who LOVE the Lord and who obey His Commandments. It is for those who have developed the power and the strength of their souls or spirits instead of just their physical traits.

And even in this Celestial Realm there are three degrees or levels. The highest in this realm is for those who OVERCOME!

Such is the information I have been instructed to impart in order to correct some of the gross errors contained in the printing of the volume preceding this one. With this correction made I am permitted to continue with the information which God has instructed me to share with the world at this time to further reveal the path that leads back into His Presence.

However there is one more correction that must be made. This one is placed in the jacket of the before mentioned book, and is also repeated in their printed folder. This is the statement in its gross error of misquotation: "This record also reveals the glorious, triumphant march of man toward Godhood and the breathtaking wonder of his divine lineage, the dynamic race of Gods, his (ONLY ANCESTRY)." This statement is a gross falsehood. My words in the Preface of the book are thus: "the breathtaking wonder of his divine lineage, the dynamic race of Gods, his *"HOLY* ANCESTRY." To call this man's ONLY ancestry is a contradiction to all truth.

"We have fathers of our flesh" who corrected us and we gave them reverence, how much more should we be in subjection to the Father of Spirits and live!" To claim that our ONLY HERITAGE is the lineage of God is ridiculous and absurd and a misquotation. We most assuredly do have the HOLY HERITAGE OR LINEAGE, but it is NOT the ONLY ONE. Each individual has a mortal lineage, fathers and mothers of our flesh—and their fathers and their mothers, generations of them—back to the very beginning of time.

So much for two of the NUMEROUS ERRORS contained in the printing of the book "Beyond Mortal Boundaries." And yet, all the forces and powers of darkness could not possibly destroy the dynamic truths and the glory contained in it. That book was not merely written! It was thundered out of eternity! And "Was wholly written by the finger of God," as the writer of the Odes of Solomon foretold. The errors are man's mistakes. The truths are God's and will remain forever.

There is also another point that must be corrected here. A misguided person proclaimed that I had given her the information that "the most genteel way to obtain translation is through the grave." This blessed woman, with the best intentions in the world, knows nothing whatsoever of the divine, holy law of translation, or transfiguration or ascension, which ever you choose to call it. Bless her, she is speaking her own words, not mine. Her knowledge does not go beyond death and the resurrection to the complete purification and perfection of one's body that "one can change his carnal flesh to flesh divine, without descending through the gates of death!"

This unenlightened sister, this beautiful teacher of half truths claimed that I had informed her that at last I had to admit that the ability to just disappear would be "too great a shock." God bless her, everything which God has placed in my hands to reveal and to prove is that holy information of how DEATH IS TO BE OVERCOME. Nothing on earth is a greater shock than death itself, either to the one passing through it or the loved ones left behind.

Everything God has commanded me to write has been to show the error of death, the needless indignity of this shameful experience and the repulsiveness of so wasteful a process as going down into the grave to moulder and rot! *This is the great shock!* But for those who are carnally minded it is impossible for them to change their carnal flesh to flesh divine and so they deny that it is possible for anyone to do so.

Neither have I ever been contacted by, nor have I communed with those who go into trances. My work has been in the open and with those in full control of all their God-given faculties. There has been nothing of darkness in my work, no "familiar spirits," no soothsaying and none of the forbidden things.

And so I earnestly entreat you to pray that God will reveal to you, individually, by the power of the Holy Ghost, the truth of every statement He has instructed me to write.

Test everything you hear by this method and you will never judge wrongfully, for God Himself will become your teacher. Learn to listen to His Voice and you will KNOW THE TRUTH when it is placed before you. You will never need to reject TRUTH because of fear engendered by ignorance. Neither will you ever accept falsehoods as TRUTH. And only "The Truth will make you free!" Contained in this Spirit of Truth is the Spirit of Discernment and he who possesses this gift cannot possibly be deceived for through his own humble contact with God he is indeed one of the elect.

Test everything you hear by this method of prayer, "ASK" and "SEEK" and "KNOCK" and above all "LEARN TO LISTEN!" As you learn to trust in God with all your hearts, and lean not to your own understandings or (in the arm of flesh) you will never need to doubt truth or to reject it. And in like manner the falsehood of all evil doctrines will be made manifest unto you by the power of the Holy Ghost.

And God bless you forever, for I lie not! Neither have I taught you falsely.

Preface

This volume contains the laws of complete fulfillment for any individual who will fulfill them. It reveals the way by which one can literally "change his carnal flesh to flesh divine without descending through the gates of death," even as Enoch of old did.

Man, as a rule tries to set his own terms of fulfillment and that is the reason for the delay or failure of many who undertake this journey into the higher realms of achievement. As man insists upon his own rules, according to his understanding or lack of it, he rejects the idea that God has His own terms. And God's terms are definite and as exacting as the laws of mathematics and as unfailing when one is willing to familiarize himself with them.

One beautiful woman began teaching, after reading the last volume published, that only those who had talked in tongues or prophesied could have any part in this divine work of glory. Bless her! She did not realize that her terms were not God's terms. There is not one of the Holy Promises of Almighty God that is based upon speaking in tongues or upon prophesying. Each Promise is based, it is true, upon certain requirements and these requirements are strictly upon God's terms. They are unmistakable and most plain and precious. There need be no haggling over them or false assuming of their true meaning.

Vain man, in adding his own interpretations only dulls the glory of God's great and dynamic TRUTHS.

DEATH, man's greatest enemy, can be conquered, not just forestalled in the weak accomplishment of longevity. Prolonged life, without purpose or meaning, would be stupid and gruesome. Only vibrant, glorious life could possibly justify the OVERCOMING OF DEATH and fulfill the Promise of "LIFE EVERLASTING!" "LIFE MORE ABUNDANT!" "LIFE ETERNAL!"

FAITH is composed of the highest vibrations released from a human heart. *Faith* in action IS *belief* held forth on a high level of anticipation as doubts are banished.

FAITH is power! It is the exerted energy of THOUGHTS and FEELINGS as one goes beyond thought into the realm of true reality.

"LOVE casts out all fear!" And FAITH banishes darkness and conquers doubting. FAITH builds bridges across the deepest chasms and scales the highest mountains in existence. FAITH IS the material which constructs highways to the very stars!

And "without FAITH it is impossible to please God!"

FAITH is not only the substance, material, element or essence of things hoped for—FAITH IS things HOPED FOR. FAITH IS THE DREAM, THE DESIRE, THE HOPE ITSELF. And man is the creator of dreams. Man was formed and fashioned with the divine capacity with which to dream, to imagine and to visualize as he conjures his mental images from the pure, perfect elements of creation.

When FAITH is completed it no longer embraces an intangible dream or desire of invisible hope. It is established in the realm of tangible substance or material matter and becomes forever the reality.

The great change in man comes when he becomes a translated being, "BEING BORN OF THE SPIRIT," as Christ informed Nicodemus, so that he can henceforth come and go as the wind and no one will know from whence he came or whither he goeth.

And as FAITH IS PERFECTED BY USE so is it transformed into KNOWLEDGE. FAITH evolves into KNOWLEDGE as surely as the butterfly evolves from the worm.

"KNOW THE TRUTH AND THE TRUTH WILL MAKE YOU FREE!"

This life experience is the greatest privilege man has ever received. This earth is the school for Gods but not all will fulfill so great an assignment, *but many will.* Those who assume the responsibility of living up to their highest, inborn instincts will evolve into Godhood. Each individual selects his own goal and reaches it according to his own desiring.

Devils seek only to destroy. Gods are Creators. And men are Gods in the making. This volume contains fully and completely the laws of Creation and man's power to use them.

This work contains the truths which Christ so earnestly wished to share with His apostles on that last night, at the Feast of the Passover.

If you are prepared to receive them you are chosen indeed.

Contents

Chapter		Page
I.	"Live the Teachings and You Will Know"	1
II.	God's Terms of Fulfillment	8
III.	Man's Terms of Fulfillment Inadequate	16
IV.	Do You Desire to Please God?	23
V.	The Dynamic Power of TRUTH	39
VI.	The Keys of All-Knowing	50
VII.	The Odes of Solomon	60
VIII.	Life! Life More Abundant!	76
IX.	Why and What Is Death?	88
X.	The Everlasting Power of Love	102
XI.	The Chief Corner Stone	114
XII.	The Caterpillar and the Butterfly	125
XIII.	"Health in the Navel"	132
XIV.	The Love for God	145
XV.	The Fullness of the Gospel of Jesus Christ	150
XVI.	"All the Laws Fulfilled"	161
XVII.	The Primal Substance of All Existing Things	172
XVIII.	The Cosmic Power of Light Generated by Faith	182
XIX.	True Prayer is Faith in Action	194

Chapter		Page
XX.	The Treasure House of God	203
XXI.	The Magic Switch or Button	216
XXII.	"Ye Are Gods!"	226
XXIII.	"All That the Father Has Is Yours"	236
XXIV.	The Day the Foundations of the Earth Were Laid	247
XXV.	The Promises of God	264
XXVI.	The Glorified Road to Zion	281
XXVII.	The Three Gifts of a Wise Man	299
XXVIII.	The Message and Seal of Jesus Christ	315
XXIX.	The Holy Spirit of Promise	321

CHAPTER I.

"Live the Teachings and You Will Know"

"Yes, he that repenteth and *exerciseth* FAITH and bringeth forth good works, and *prayeth continually without ceasing* unto such is given to know the mysteries of God; yea, unto such it shall be given to reveal things which never have been revealed; yea, and it shall be given unto such to bring thousands of souls to repentance." This glorious Promise was revealed centuries ago and it still stands in all the power of everlasting fulfilling and eternal PROMISE.

And, it is right here that I would like to share some very sacred information. The knowledge contained in the books I have been called to write was given because I had fulfilled the Promise pertaining to them. I would like to explain it more fully. Years ago a very noble *"Man of God"* gave me this Promise, "Dear Sister, the blessings which God has in store for you are unspeakable, in the fact that we cannot comprehend them at this time!" And my mind and heart and soul opened wide to try and comprehend what these promised blessings would be. And as my life became more and more attuned to prayer and the adoration of God, the knowledge contained in the books I have been instructed to write was unfolded. And these hitherto "unspeakable truths" have not only been "SPOKEN" they have been written and sent forth upon the wind to encompass the earth—to be shared with anyone who wishes to have a part in these "unspeakable" Promises and blessings. And in the privilege of sharing, my heart melts in a love and humility that is almost overpowering. I have no desire for fame or credits or rewards. I melt with love as my hand reaches out to touch your fingertips with the contact of eternal TRUTH. And God bless you! And may God give you understanding to comprehend His mighty wonders and to accept *"His unspeakable blessings"* for they are yours.

This particular book is the record that will unfold the dynamic way of fulfilling every Promise of God and every righteous desire of the human heart. This is the great volume promised long ago and which God has been preparing His chosen ones to receive from the very beginning of time. This record contains those "great and marvelous things which have been hid up from the foundations of the world because of the blindness of men's eyes, and the hardness of their hearts, and because of the gross wickedness of unbelief!" And because there are those, who like Columbus, can no longer be shut out from KNOWING, that great, dense, dark veil of unbelief is beginning to be pulled aside.

Within this work is unveiled some of the hitherto "unspeakable, incomprehensible things which eyes have never seen, nor ears heard, nor yet has entered into the heart of man—those things which God has prepared for THOSE WHO LOVE HIM!"

This sacred Path of fulfilling and of unfolding glory is so clearly revealed and its powers made so plain, that as Isaiah declared, "A FOOL NEED NOT ERR THEREIN, though the wicked can never cross over."

And so, this book is not written for the unbelievers or for those who love not God, or for those who are so sealed in their present beliefs that even God cannot teach them. This work is for the PURE IN HEART, the humble, the teachable, the gracious, evolving sons of God. "It is for those who are hungering and thirsting after righteousness."

This record completely glorifies that "Straight and Narrow Path that leads to Life Eternal!" It is the road to glorious perfection. And every step of this Way is a joy beyond measure.

"But no man is possessor of all things except he be purified and cleansed from all sin.

"And if you are purified and cleansed from all sin, ye shall ask whatsoever you will in the Name of Jesus and it shall be done!"

The word "ZION" remember, means "THE PURE IN HEART!" The road to Zion is the road of the purification of the heart. And only by the purification of the heart can one ever travel it, though a fool need not err therein. This is the Pathway of LOVE in which one practices and learns to love God with all his heart. This is the road of fulfilling. And as one's heart is purified by such dynamic love in action, he will automatically be cleansed from all sin. The very forgiveness of sin can only be accomplished through love as one forgives all who have ever trespassed against him. This is love in action. This contains the power to be cleansed (or forgiven) for all sins. It is beautiful! It is unfailing! It is truth eternal! If you wish to be cleansed from all sin, then love until it reaches out to enfold your trespassers in the glory of your own divine forgiveness. Let old grudges melt away. Let present hurts be dissipated in compassionate understanding. Let mercy caress and enfold all whom your thoughts touch. This is the power to be cleansed from all sin. And with this power all things will become subject unto you—and you can ask what you will and it will be granted. For in this great outpouring of your love "your minds and lips will have lost the power to hurt or wound and your voice will be heard among the Gods," for you will have joined them in the upward trend of your own divinity.

Yes, "The nearer man approaches perfection the clearer are his views and the greater are his enjoyments, till he has OVERCOME the evils of his life and lost every desire for sin, and like the ancients, arrives at the point of FAITH where he is wrapped in the power and glory of his Maker and is caught up to dwell with Him!"

You say you do not believe this?

Then, my friend, do not continue with the reading of this record for it is not for you.

These "Wayfaring men," which Isaiah speaks of in his thirty-fifth chapter and eighth verse, are those who are traveling onward along a continual pathway of growth and perfecting. And this glorious Pathway is a lighted, Holy trail of ever increasing brilliance. Along its walls are mirrors, magic mirrors, which reveal continually the unfolding light and glory being developed within the individual, not to increase his pride, but to enhance his joy as he draws ever nearer to perfection, in a devotion of love that becomes unutterable in its great outflowing glory. And the man himself becomes perfect as his inward traits are purified.

The door to this glorious Path of joy and gladness and increasing enlightenment and understanding is contained fully in that divine, First, Great Commandment of all power—LOVE!

"LIVE the laws and you will KNOW!" So said Christ. And no one can possibly KNOW anything unless he himself experiences it. To hear about things and conditions, or of God may become part of one's *beliefs*, but never becomes a part of his own actual KNOWLEDGE until he experiences it for himself.

Yes, "LIVE that First and Great Commandment and you will KNOW!" And "you will need none to teach you for God Himself will be your teacher!" And to LIVE it does not mean to merely nod one's head over it in an inactive affirmation or a casual acceptance of the idea. To fulfill it requires that every cell and fibre and atom of one's being be imbued with it. Only then does it become a part of one's own experience, hence his KNOWLEDGE.

This "LIVING" requires that one embeds those instructions into the living tissues of his heart, his soul and his mind until they not only become a very part of his being, THEY BECOME HIM! And HE BECOMES THAT LOVE! "For he who would interpret the wonders of the Lord would be dissolved and become that which is interpreted."

LIVE that First and Great Commandment and the Second One will follow naturally, without effort or striving. The developing and releasing of LOVE from the heart, soul and mind overcomes all negation, dislikes, fears, ugliness, weaknesses and human, mortal grubbiness, for these traits will be dissolved. And such a one will automatically become that LOVE! "Live the laws!" admonished Christ; "And you will KNOW!" And to KNOW requires the experience of receiving all the knowledge and the PROMISES AND POWERS pertaining to that information.

Man has never accepted the dynamic challenge to LIVE CHRIST'S teaching. Man has only weakly affirmed his inactive endorsement of those teachings as a fullness of acceptance. And many think they are proving their belief by going forth and hammering others with their interpretations as they send forth their haranguements in discordant, sanctimonious self-righteousness. Yet Christ's actual teachings have never been acknowledged as a Way of Life and of fulfillment or an everlasting privilege of stupendous accomplishment, crowned with every reward contained in every Promise ever given since time began.

That First and Great Commandment, when LIVED contains the breathtaking fulfillment of every PROMISE God ever gave, plus all perfection and all power. Within it is held forever the fulfilling of the LOVE which brings into one's life a complete knowledge of the things which "Eyes have never seen, nor ears heard, neither hath entered into the heart of man—those unspeakable glories, which God has PREPARED FOR THOSE WHO LOVE HIM— and prove it by their living of that law pertaining to it.

This fulfilling is not something which can be boasted about, shouted about in worldly sermons or declarations, nor is it fulfilled by a silent nod of approval. This commandment must be LIVED! This requires an exerted effort of constant desire and application until the very cells of the body and brain and heart sing together in a glory of joyous response at the slightest suggestion or thought of God, or of His blessings. It is as that LOVE is developed that it will finally take over in every cell and fibre and tissue that one *"Transforms his carnal flesh to flesh divine without descending through the gates of death!"* Even as Enoch of old accomplished.

It is as one, like Enoch, "transforms the carnal flesh to flesh divine, without descending through the gates of death," that he arrays himself in the white raiment of eternal glory and is truly *"Born of the Spirit!"* And the shame of his mortal nakedness, whatever its cause, will be OVERCOME and one will be clothed in Light and will "COMPREHEND ALL THINGS." He will be robed in Light and Love and eternal, everlasting power. And this is the glory of it!

And this is God's plan! And it has always been His plan! And this is the Way Christ traveled. It is the Path He mapped for all mankind to follow if so be they wished to rise above dreary mortality and its consequent evils and dismays and vicissitudes.

Chapter II.

God's Terms of Fulfillment

There are many who would have already fulfilled the great and mighty Promises of God if they had realized that their error has been the cause of their failure or delay. They have failed to realize that their restraint has been in expecting God to fulfill His Promises on their own mortal terms.

God does not and will not fulfill His most holy, almost unspeakable Promises upon any man's terms. Man must fulfill them upon God's Terms. And HIS terms are most explicit and plain to understand unless one's mind is sealed with his own orthodoxed ideas or pride in his own self-importance. It may be that this very pride has so sealed one's mind that unconsciously he refuses to relinquish any preconceived belief he may be harboring. Man's terms are the individual beliefs, his personal ideas, opinions or set notions, or theories.

Such may read the Promises of God and for a flashing moment comprehend them and desire them greatly, so greatly that he becomes blinded by the very brilliance insomuch he fails to see the price that is required for their fulfillment. However, even that price becomes a glorious, divine challenge of everlasting glory and enjoyment before this record is ended.

In the Book of Revelations, chapter three, Christ declared, "Because thou sayest I am rich and increased with goods and have need of nothing and knowest not that thou art poor and wretched and miserable and blind and naked.

"I counsel thee to buy of me gold tried in the fire that thou mayest be rich; and white raiment that thou mayest be clothed that the shame of thy nakedness may not appear."

How is it possible to purchase or *buy* anything except by paying a price for it? "Buy of me gold that is tried in the fire" of your own souls. This gold, tried in the fire is but the purification of your own hearts as they are cleansed by love and devotion. Only this purified offering is acceptable, for Christ proclaimed that the only acceptable sacrifice or offering or payment that God would henceforth acknowledge would be the offering or sacrifice of a broken, or open heart and a contrite spirit. If that is the only offering acceptable to God then it alone could be the payment for the gold that is tried in the fire—the very gold that would make one rich indeed.

Then is given the information in Isaiah, that the glorified road to Zion over which a fool need not err therein, but over which the wicked can never travel, is the road of the purification of the heart.

Then is given that dynamic command to LOVE, which reveals just how the heart is cleansed and not only purified but spiritualized, softened, opened and perfected.

Along with this glorious Commandment is the Promise that in LIVING this one great law one automatically FULFILLS ALL THE LAWS AND THE PROPHETS. By purifying the heart with this love one can purchase the fulfilling of every Promise. Then it is that one is able to *comprehend all things,* and have all power, and behold the "things which eyes have never seen nor ears heard, neither has entered into the heart of man—THE THINGS WHICH GOD HAS PREPARED FOR THOSE WHO LOVE HIM!"

This is how the promise is given in its fullness: "Man is Spirit. The elements are eternal, and spirit and element, inseparably connected receiveth a fullness of joy.

"And great shall be their reward and eternal shall be their glory.

"And to them I will reveal all mysteries, yea, all the hidden mysteries of my kingdom from days of old, and for ages to come I will make known unto them the good pleasure of my will concerning all things pertaining to my kingdom.

"Yea, even the wonders of eternity shall they know, and things to come will I show them, even the things of many generations.

"And their wisdom shall be great, AND THEIR UNDERSTANDING REACH INTO HEAVEN, and before them the wisdom of the wise shall perish, and the understanding of the prudent shall come to naught.

"For by my Spirit will I enlighten them and by my power will I make known unto them the secrets of my will—yea, even those things which eye hath not seen nor ear heard nor yet has entered into the heart of man * * *

"These great and unspeakable things can only be seen and understood by the Power of the Holy Ghost, which *God bestows on* THOSE WHO LOVE HIM AND PURIFY THEMSELVES BEFORE HIM.

"TO WHICH HE GRANTS THE PRIVILEGE OF SEEING AND KNOWING FOR THEMSELVES.

"That through the power and manifestation of the Spirit WHILE IN THE FLESH they may be able to bear His Presence in the World of Glory." (Page 251 of "Ye Are Gods.")

Only by loving God with all the heart can the heart be opened and purified and made acceptable.

As one learns to love God with ALL his heart the little egoself with its false beliefs and erroneous, creeded indoctrinations will be relinquished. Then only can one be prepared to be taught of God. In this holy cleansing old beliefs drop away like ugly, worn-out rags and are discarded and left behind.

And here are the terms which God places upon the fulfilling of His Promises and the glory of receiving the rewards pertaining thereto.

"If ye do as *I* say then am I bound; but if you do not as I say then you have no Promise!" In other words, the Promises are not yours, nor can you claim them.

Isaiah informs us that "The fear (awe, love) toward God is taught by the precepts of men. And that they draw near to Him with their lips and with their tongues do honor Him, BUT THEIR HEARTS ARE FAR FROM HIM!"

Here is His own verification of the need to LOVE GOD WITH ALL THE HEART! No words are sufficient! No phrases are great enough! Only THROUGH THE VERY HEART ITSELF CAN THE TRUE LOVE FOR GOD BE RELEASED. And this cannot be taught by the precepts of men. It is only achieved by the actual LIVING of that First and Great Commandment of Almighty God.

Now, the true baptism of water, of which the earthly ordinance is but the symbol, is also contained in that requirement of loving God with ALL THE HEART.

Notice these words recorded in St. John 4:10 and verses 13 and 14, as follows: "And Jesus saith unto the woman of Samaria; If thou knewest the gift of God, and who it is that saith to thee, Give me to drink: Thou wouldst have asked him, and he would have given thee living water * * *

"Whosoever drinketh of this water shall thirst again. But whosoever drinketh of the water that I shall give him shall never thirst; but the water that I shall give him shall be in him a well of water springing up into everlasting life."

Then check the following from John seven and verse thirty-eight: "He that believeth on me, as the scripture hath said, out of his belly shall flow rivers of living water."

The "belly" signifies the whole living heart-center of man. This is the center from which LOVE is generated and shed forth to permeate every living cell and atom and tissue of the body with its cleansing, purifying glory of perfect washing and renewing. It is the true baptism of the water in its fullness and complete power and divine purity. It is the true reality which the symbol of baptism has only indicated. The one is the symbol, the other, the complete fulfillment.

Revelations 21:6-7: "And he said unto me, I am Alpha and Omega, the beginning and the end. I will give unto him that is athirst of the fountain of the waters of life freely. He that OVERCOMETH shall inherit all things; and I will be his God, and he shall be my son."

The waters of life are the "living waters" that flow forth through a heart filled with LOVE. These waters cleanse, purify and glorify the gift of life right within man.

"And I am come that they might have life, and have it more abundantly."

"Behold, I give no commandment or PROMISE save I prepare the way of its fulfillment." Every Promise is based definitely upon the perfect conditions of its complete accomplishment. And those conditions are upon God's terms. His terms contain the perfect pattern, the absolute conditions of the exquisite realization and full completion.

Notice the following: "And no man receiveth a fullness unless he keepeth His commandments * * * And if he keep that First and Greatest Commandment he has fulfilled ALL THE LAWS AND THE COMMANDMENTS AND THE PROPHETS!"

"He that keepeth His commandments (of perfect love) *receiveth Truth and Light, until he is* GLORIFIED IN TRUTH and KNOWETH ALL THINGS!"

Can you imagine being "GLORIFIED IN TRUTH" insomuch that you would COMPREHEND ALL THINGS? Such would KNOW THE TRUTH! And he would be free! Free Indeed! Free from all the burdens and strains and negations of mortality. "He could truly be BORN OF THE SPIRIT!"

God's terms are not difficult when one is sincere and determined and filled with love. His terms are perfect and sure, and the results of fulfilling them, as God gave them, contain the keys of everlasting glory!

And His PROMISES are offered to every living soul upon this earth, to every layman, to every minister and every member of every church and to those without any church affiliation whatsoever. They pertain to all mankind. They have not been fulfilled because self-righteous leaders have assumed that their congregations or followers can only go to God throgh THEIR mediating, which is the great error. This is the error of "Trusting in the arm of flesh," which in itself is damnation. Every living soul has the right and the invitation standing forth to "KNOW GOD" for themselves. And to KNOW GOD is life eternal!

The gift of life is stressed in the words: "THE FRUIT OF THE TREE OF LIFE IS THE LOVE OF GOD which is shed forth through the hearts of the children of men."

As one loves God with all his heart that love, of necessity, must go out through the living cells and atoms of his entire being and thus will the tissues and cells be cleansed and quickened and renewed and made alive. And this is the "PROMISE OF LIFE"—"LIFE EVERLASTING"—"LIFE MORE ABUNDANT!"

This is also the only method by which one can possibly travel that glorified ROAD TO ZION, or that Straight and Narrow Path, which is the road of the "PURIFICATION OF THE HEART," the Way to Life Eternal, as Christ designated it. Remember always, "Zion" means "THE PURE IN HEART!" And only LOVE CAN POSSIBLY PURIFY THE HEART!

I. John 2:3-5: "And hereby we KNOW that we *know Him*, if we *keep* HIS COMMANDMENTS. ("And this is Life Eternal to KNOW THEE the only true and living God and Jesus Christ Whom thou hast sent.")

"He that saith, I know HIM, and keepeth not his commandments is a liar, and the truth is not in him.

"But whoso keepeth HIS WORD, in him verily IS THE LOVE OF GOD PERFECTED."

Chapter III.

Man's Terms of Fulfillment Inadequate

I have met many who have accepted of God's Promises with all their minds while their hearts have been far from Him, except for their desire to receive the unutterable fullness of His Promised Powers.

There are those, many of them, who would have already proved and fulfilled all things had they accepted the Promises upon God's terms instead of upon their own.

"If ye do as I say, then am I bound, but if you do not as I say then you have no Promise." In other words, the Promise you demand, without fulfilling the requirements is not yours. You have no claim upon it. Unless you accept God's terms for the fulfilling you have no Promise.

The volume preceding this one, "Beyond Mortal Boundaries" contains the unfolding of the most famous and the most important parts of scripture, excepting Psalms 23 and 91. These have not been included for they need no explanation in order to be lived for they are based on fact not on PROMISE.

These books open with the Power of the PROMISES. Then the glory and power of the First and Great Commandment and the wonder contained within its actual LIVING is made apparent.

MAN'S TERMS OF FULFILLMENT INADEQUATE   17

Next there is the unveiling of that most famous chapter of I. Corinthians and the thirteenth chapter and the marvel of its hitherto unrealized truths.

In that divine volume, *"Beyond Mortal Boundaries,"* is revealed the wonder of the ancient Patriarchal Order and how, in olden times, they did not live under the law, but lived by the PROMISES, *according to Faith*. There is a partial unveiling of their hopes and their individual Promises. And there is also recorded their failure to fulfill the fullness of the PROMISES because they placed them in the "AFAR-OFF," in the great "SOMETIME OF THE FUTURE" instead of in the NOW!

And the same is true today, everything has been placed in the days of expected glory when Christ will come and exalt everyone without them fulfilling one single observance of His divine counseling. To bring forth the wonder of His instructions the unfolding of that Sermon on the Mount is plainly given. In fact, the whole volume has been more or less a stressing and explaining of that most famous of all Sermons ever given on the earth.

And in the last chapter of that Sermon on the Mount, Matthew seven, is given the record of Christ's rebuke to those who would prophesy in His Name, cast out devils in His Name and perform many miracles, to whom he declares: "Depart from me, ye that work iniquity. I know you not!" And to make this scripture perfectly clear God required that a complete explanation on demonstrating be included, "THAT ALL MEN MIGHT BE LEFT WITHOUT EXCUSE."

This was written according to God's command. And no man's opinion can change it. But there are those who still insist that only through their own personal demonstrating can the divine, dynamic Promises of God be fulfilled. And they err greatly. And worlds without end they will not be able to receive the glory of His Promises until they accept His Promises upon His Terms—AND NOT UPON THEIR OWN.

God's Promises are not fulfilled through outward show, through the gifts or through prophesying or speaking in tongues or in outward "UNSEEMINGLY" demonstrating. They are fulfilled when one has learned to "BE STILL" and KNOWS that God is God, as they contact Him and obey His Voice and Keep His Commandments that they might be taught of Him, IN HIS WAY!

There are His definite terms upon which every PROMISE can be fulfilled. And not one of them is based on the Speaking in tongues, or in Prophesying—or in any outward show.

"There is a law irrevocably decreed in heaven, before the foundations of the world, upon which all blessings are predicated, and if we obtain any Promise or blessing from God it is upon obedience to the laws upon which it is predicated," or promised.

"He who is thankful in all things shall be made glorious. And when one is MADE GLORIOUS he will "BE BORN OF THE SPIRIT!" This promise to be made glorious says nothing at all about speaking in tongues or prophesying or of any of the other gifts. It is based entirely upon GRATITUDE, or BEING THANKFUL!

"If YOUR MINDS BE SINGLE TO THE GLORY OF GOD, your whole bodies shall be filled with light and there will be no darkness in you. And that person who is filled with light shall comprehend all things * * * and God will unveil his face unto him," etc. This glorious fulfilling is based on the complete LOVE of God filling the mind of man until his thoughts BECOME SINGLE TO THE GLORY OF GOD. These are God's terms and no personal beliefs are included or accepted.

Another Promise: *"He who prayeth continually without ceasing* shall be given to understand the mysteries of God (or as the other promise declares, shall *comprehend all things*) and shall reveal things which have never been revealed," etc. This praying continually, without ceasing includes the releasing, through the heart center, that New Song, that Celestial Song of Praise and Love and Gratitude in living vibrations of eternal rhythm and glory, not in shouting or through any *unseemly* action. True adoration is always from within, not demonstrated on the outside. "Self-righteousness" is always worn on the outside to be seen of men. "RIGHTEOUSNESS" is manifested deep within the soul of man and is a part of his innermost being and cannot be put on display.

"And no man receiveth a fulness unless he keepeth His Commandments (of LOVE). *He that keepeth His commandments receiveth Truth and Light until he is glorified in Truth and* KNOWETH ALL THINGS!" Yes! He who fulfills that great law of LOVE shall be glorified in TRUTH and shall KNOW all things! And in KNOWING the TRUTH he shall become free. He shall be "Born of the Spirit" and be able to come and go as the wind in a service as yet unimagined.

Thus each Promise carries with it God's terms of fulfilling. They have nothing to do with man's little personal beliefs or ideas. They are without flaw and need no individual interpretation to make their meaning clear.

Yet they all lead to the PROMISE of the great, complete fulfilling as the Power of Almighty God is vested in man and he enters into a higher phase of existence, beyond anything mortal mind has ever before envisioned.

"Cast out the darkness from among you and you will be ordained (commissioned) of God (not man) * * * and all things will become subject unto you both in heaven and on earth; the light and the life; the Spirit and the Power sent forth by the will of the Father through Jesus Christ, His Son.

Such are a portion of God's Promises which I have been commissioned to hold forth. The Promises are not mine! They are God's Promises and they are based upon His terms.

Learn to Praise and give Thanks continually and light and love will be generated out through you. And as you learn to generate light the darkness will be banished from you and you yourself will be filled with Light and comprehend all things! This is not accomplished by any outward demonstrating, but by learning "to hear the Voice of God" and in following His instructions and fulfilling His terms. Then only is it possible to actually KNOW GOD! And this is LIFE ETERNAL, TO KNOW THEE, THE ONLY TRUE AND LIVING GOD AND JESUS CHRIST WHOM THOU HAST SENT!"

And regardless of which of God's Promises one might rejoice in most, as he lays hold upon it with the intensity of his own desiring, they all lead to the same fulfilling glory.

For instance: "The nearer man approaches perfection, the clearer are his views and the greater are his enjoyments, until *he overcomes* the evils of his life and loses every desire for sin, and like the ancients, arrives at the point of Faith where he is wrapped in the power and glory of his Maker and is caught up to dwell with Him!"

This is the fulness of the Power and reality of TRANSLATION and the very terms of God's upon which it is predicated.

Remember: "After one has been tested and tried in all things and when the Lord has thoroughly proved him, and finds that he is determined to serve God at all HAZARDS, then he will find his calling and his election made sure. Then it will be that the Lord Himself will appear unto him," etc. (AND THIS IS LIFE ETERNAL!)

These are the Promises of Almighty God—and each contains the exact TERMS of its fulfilling. And though they all do lead to the great dynamic fulfilling of man's own glorified OVERCOMING, nevertheless they are predicated upon certain terms. And those terms are God's terms, just as the Promises are God's Promises. They are irrevocably decreed before the foundations of the world. "And if you receive any blessing from God it is by obedience to the laws upon which it is predicated."

There are no man-made beliefs or ideas or substitutes acceptable, as man seeks to put forth his own terms. And there is no mention ever made to any outside witnessing—but only to the inward LIVING of that which is required.

"If you do as I say, then am I bound. But if you do not as I say, (but as you say) then you have no Promise."

Such are God's terms! And only by His terms can one possibly receive the fulness of His dynamic Promises and the powers thereof.

I. John 2:3-5: "And hereby we KNOW that we *Know HIM*, if we keep HIS Commandments. ("And this is Life Eternal to KNOW Thee the only True and Living God and Jesus Christ, whom thou hast sent.")

"He that saith, I know Him, and keepeth not his commandments is a liar, and the truth is not in him.

"But whoso keepeth *His Word*, in him verily is the Love of God perfected."

CHAPTER IV.

Do You Desire to Please God?

"Without FAITH it is impossible to please God." So says the scriptures and our ears have grown dull of hearing and our minds have ceased to respond to the wonder and truth of these words.

We are told that "FAITH IS THE SUBSTANCE OF THINGS HOPED FOR." It is the essence, the material, the element of things "hoped for" according to this definition. Then there is another record, very ancient, which declares: "FAITH *IS* THINGS HOPED FOR!" With this definition we understand that anything that one can possibly hope for *is* faith. This is beautiful!

And then again we are told that "without hope or the substance or material of things hoped for it is impossible to please God." "He who is without HOPE (or faith) must needs be in despair. And despair cometh because of iniquity." And, according to the dictionary, "iniquity is a grievous violation of right or justice. It is gross wickedness. It is sin." It is from a Latin word meaning "inquiet" or "unquiet," or "not quiet." It even suggests meaning, in-equal or unworthy; not up to par or standard.

This lack of inner quiet is the full indication of lack of contact with God. Only by *"being still"* can one possibly KNOW or contact God—and receive His help.

So truly, without FAITH it is indeed impossible to please God. "For he that cometh to God must BELIEVE that He is, and that He is a rewarder of all who diligently seek Him." In the first place one could not even attempt to approach God unless he believed that "God did exist and is a rewarder of all those who diligently seek Him." Without this awakened ability to BELIEVE or to try to PROVE there can be no possible contact with God.

"THE VERY FIRST REQUISITE TO KNOWLEDGE (of any kind) IS THE ABILITY TO BELIEVE." Without this ability to believe, to test, to seek or to prove, a man is no better than a beast of the field, a dead stump, a lifeless, mediocre, unalerted, unawakened clod.

Enthusiasm, which is the spark of God in action in the soul of man, is based entirely on faith. Without enthusiasm there can be no faith. Enthusiasm is the kindled spark of Faith that lights the pathway to the fulfilling of the hopes of man. Show me any individual who cannot experience enthsuiasm and I will show you a person whose soul has departed from him or who has permitted himself to become not much more than a vegetable.

Enthusiasm is a mental or spiritual *force* which has always been regarded by mankind with approval and more often with a deep respect, mingled with awe. To the ancients it was assumed to be a special gift of the gods, and by them it was regarded as animating the individual with almost divine attributes of power. And surely enthusiasm is a part of the divine nature within man.

Without enthusiasm it is impossible to please God. Enthusiasm is the living spark of the soul that lights the Path of progress. It is the breath and life of incentive. It is FAITH in action.

Incentive is the first step toward unfoldment. Incentive awakens the desire to "KNOW!" The desire to KNOW leads into the Pathway of searching, which fulfills the command to "Ask, to seek and to knock!" And the Promise is: "That EVERY ONE WHO ASKS RECEIVES! AND HE WHO SEEKS FINDS! AND UNTO HIM WHO KNOCKS IT SHALL BE OPENED," or revealed.

Without the incentive to ask comes the inability to receive.

As one follows the incentive to ask, to seek and to knock, one's mind will be opened to the gift of anticipation, which will lead into the vibrant wonder of enthusiasm, which contains the very power of developing and releasing FAITH. And in this progress one can and does please God. And "God is a rewarder of all those who diligently seek Him."

One's requests may not be answered in a moment, or a day, or a week, or even a year. Some answers take longer to grow into their own fulfillment. Or as Abraham Lincoln once said, "An answer to prayer comes sometimes with a demand for sacrifice." The sacrifice may be the shouldering of responsibilities in order to live up to the new knowledge. It may require the sacrifice of old, threadbare, outmoded, personal opinions; the relinquishing of pet erroneous ideas. But whatever the fulfilling of one's request may entail the very acceptance of it will produce the fires of enthusiasm that change the individual from a common, mediocre individual into one who has been inflamed or animated by the gods.

Also it is possible that one's requests may be so "AMISS" that the pray-er himself will need time to grow into the answer. But the answer will be given and when it does come the one who has continued to ASK, TO SEEK AND TO KNOCK *without* wavering, will himself have grown into a dynamic person—one who truly PLEASES GOD and becomes acceptable to Him.

Anyone, no matter what his level of intelligence, goodness, badness or mediocrity will be acknowledged who continues to "ask, to seek and to knock." This is how FAITH GROWS. And how any individual can be lifted above mediocrity or inferiority.

One's prayers may not be answered in the way he had hoped. But as the individual grows in faith and understanding he will begin to develop the power to "ask in Spirit" and he will no longer ask "amiss," but will place himself in tune with the mind and will of God. He will make that inner contact where iniquity, or that lack of inner quiet has been banished from his life. "And he will ask in spirit, or ask according to the will of God, and he shall have whatsoever he asketh." And his very desires will have been purified and expanded into glorious requests, worthy of the full attention of God, as they are fulfilled by Him. And in this method of "asking" the individual will himself become glorious!

Prayer itself and the divine invitation to pray is an eternal gift offered by God to man. In distress and misery or dismay or in hardships or troubles of any kind man is invited to go to God—and to "talk to Him as one man talks to another!" And since God is All-Powerful, beyond any potentate or Ruler or King or Magistrate upon the earth it is a wonderful experience and indeed a privilege to be invited into His Presence to talk over one's difficulties, problems or overwhelming disasters. In such a process there will be the instantaneous help of the Holy Comforter, which establishes the quiet and peace necessary for the vibrations and powers of God to begin their unfolding, their healing and their straightening out of all errors and mistakes.

But this access to God is not just a privilege offered under great stress. It is an eternal privilege. And as one keeps this daily tryst and turns it into a sacred appointment with God his love and faith will increase until he will reach the very "point of Faith where he will be wrapped in the Power and glory of his Maker."

This going to God in prayer is something quite different from anything most mortals have ever considered. Most prayers are an insult to God, the FATHER. Assume that you are a father—or a mother, very busy, but that on each evening, or morning, or both, you open up the doors of your sacred study and invite your children to enter into your Presence and have a visit. You love them greatly. You wish intensely to hold them close in your arms, to talk to them individually, but they will have none of it. They stand or kneel in your presence unprepared to listen, unanimated and bored to recite some dreary little, memorized piece, without either thought or feeling. There would be no need for you to give ear. You had heard that same soulless recitation so many many times repeated in the same childish manner as they remain frozen and unapproachable before you and unheeding.

Just listen to the *habitual* prayers of anyone and you will know what I mean. And after the stupid recitation the child turns and walks out of your presence to never give you another thought. So have the prayers of mankind been laid barren and worthless on the altar of our Almighty, Loving Father.

My blessed grandmother made a ritual of prayer, every morning. It was a long prayer offered every morning in a sanctimonious tone implying devotion. It was the same every day without variation and lasted about twenty minutes in its painstaking recital, that required no thought or expenditure of energy. She had crossed the continent with the Pioneers—and her prayer had not changed or varied in one single word, I am sure since the days of her youth, though she lived into her nineties. It began something like this: "OOOOH, Lord, bless our flocks and our herds—" (and she had probably four or five hens). "Protect us from the inclemencies of the weather," and she neglected to thank God for her snug home of comfort and peace. She was still crossing the continent as she looked backward, expressing the old sing-song phrases she had practiced for a lifetime. This is *not Praying!* This is vain repetition!

When you pray realize that you are fulfilling a very righteous, divine invitation to "talk with God as one person talks with another!" Let no two prayers be identical any more than you would permit your conversation with your neighbor to be exactly as it was yesterday and the day before, word for word. *Talk to Him!* Glory in the privilege of such a sacred opportunity. And do not feel that you have been unburdening yourself in dutiful OBLIGATION of devotion. You are not giving any devotion or love to God! You are merely insulting Him.

Learn to talk to God, not at Him. Learn to glory in the sacred, divine privilege of so sacred an opportunity. Let your love flow out. Let your requests be added after your thanks and gratitude and praise have been expressed in every increasing wonder and joy in the privilege of living on this wonderful earth. And as you rejoice and give thanks your happiness will grow and increase to match your blessings. Learn to look forward to those moments you spend with Him and you will begin to know that He hears and approves of you.

It is so much easier to PROVE that God does live and that He does hear and answers prayers than it is to disprove Him, for He is truly a rewarder of all who DILIGENTLY seek Him!

Those who seek only to disprove that God does not exist are only proving that they have not made any effort to really reach Him. And they are actually closing the great door into His presence against themselves. And in so doing they have lost the purpose and the meaning and the unspeakable joy of existence. God is not in the least affected by any individual's actions or resentments or evils —but man himself is the loser, the releaser of the boundless ills that are gathering, according to the unfulfilled laws of righteousness. Not that God is going to punish man. Man creates his own punishments and releases them as he brings them to pass.

And this fact must be stated and magnified. No one has ever DISPROVED that there is a God, except to those who have never sought to KNOW for themselves. For His invitation has stood down the timeless ages of existence: "Seek me early and you shall find me!" Or "Seek me diligently and you shall KNOW me!"

While these UNBELIEVING ONES have failed to make the least effort to KNOW THE TRUTH, there are thousands upon thousands who have proved, in their lives, the great reality of a True and Living God and who KNOW of His mercies and His powers because they have become daily more aware of His blessings as they have been multiplied unto them.

This is the day of which Daniel spoke, when he stated: "Go thy way, Daniel: for the words are closed up and sealed till the time of the end."

"Many shall be purified, and made white, and tried; but the wicked shall do wickedly; and none of the wicked shall understand."

Then in Daniel 12:3-4 is revealed the exact time of the fulfilling of this scripture. "And they that be wise shall shine as the brightness of the firmament; and they that turn many to righteousness as the stars forever and ever.

"But thou, O Daniel, shut up the words, and seal the book, even to the time of the end: MANY SHALL RUN TO AND FRO, AND KNOWLEDGE SHALL BE INCREASED!" This is the day when they are "running to and fro" to the extent that great freeways have cobwebbed the nation with their lanes of traffic.

This is "the time of the end" and it is the time when God has declared that He will do His strange work, "That all men will be left without excuse" (for not knowing)—and then it will be too late to graduate from this earth plane with honors. In THIS DAY it will be an unholy condition to be "A drop-out" when every atom and leaf and bird and cloud and blade of grass testifies continually of the Great Creator of all that is—and the man who fails finds he has no part in it. Such will fulfill Daniel's words, revealed in chapter 12:2, thus: "Some will stand forth to receive everlasting life, and some to shame and everlasting contempt."

This glorious record of Paul to the Romans 8:24-27: "For we are saved by HOPE: But HOPE *that is seen is not hope:* for what a man seeth, why doth he yet hope for?"

Likewise the Spirit also helpeth our infirmities; for we know not what we should pray for as we ought; but the Spirit itself maketh intercession for us with groanings which cannot be uttered.

"And he that searcheth the hearts knoweth what is in the mind of the Spirit, because he maketh intercession for the Saints according to the will of God.

"And we knoweth that all things work together for good to them that love God, to them who are called according to his purpose.

"For whom he did foreknow, he also did foreordain to be conformed to the image of his Son, that he might be the firstborn among *many* brethren.

"Moreover whom he did foreordain, them he also called and whom he called, them he also justified; and whom he justified, them he also glorified."

As the foregoing scripture is read and re-read it will continue to expand in meaning and in power. It is beautiful, but I am informed that the fulness of its glory will be unfolded to each individual as he seeks to receive the full measure of its promise.

And so again I am told to stress the truth and the power of prayer as one uses it as a means of communication with God, instead of as a dreary, boring time of dull, stupid, childish recitals, or memorized complaints, of unfelt, unanimated words linked together like beads on a chain to be used for the sake of convenience and by force of habit to avoid thought or true participation in a privilege so great and so divine.

If you wish to TALK with God NEVER LET TWO PRAYERS BE THE SAME. LEARN TO SPEAK *TO* GOD AND WITH HIM! And soon your words will flow from your heart in the power of exquisite revealing.

Now, if you wish to please God and to perfect your gift of LOVE speedily, remember, "HE WHO IS THANKFUL IN ALL THINGS SHALL BE MADE GLORIOUS! *And the things of this earth shall be added unto him a hundred-fold; Yea,* MORE!"

To develop the gift of gratitude until one's entire being is rejoicing in God's blessings, whether many or few, large or small, apparent or so negligible only a grateful heart would be able to discern them is the law of plenty being brought into action. And it is the releasing of gratitude that opens the windows of heaven, so that the blessings of God can begin to be poured out without measure, insomuch there will not be room enough to receive them.

He who is thankful in all things, could not possibly feel sorry for himself. He could not wallow in self-pity, nor enter through the gates of despair. He could not feel pinched or skimped or destitute. He could not be clothed in the desolating bleakness of want or poverty.

The fulness of the vibration of appreciation, along with the praise that goes with it, will clothe one in a radiance that will demand respect wherever he goes. Among the mighty and kings and rulers he will be so clothed in the vibrations of Light and abundance that millionaires will envy him, and the successful and the learned and the wealthy will seek his companionship.

Gratitude, or thanks, or the holy gift of appreciation is the spiritual law of increase and of the glorious multiplication of substance. "And with the use and development of gratitude ALL THINGS WILL BE TURNED INTO BLESSINGS!"

Appreciate the old, shall we say, rags you resent and the living atoms in them will so rejoice they will array you in singing glory. It matters not in the least what you wear, it is how you wear it.

No one is clothed so much in his earthly apparel as in the vibrations of his own released joyous radiance or in his own carnal resentments of self-pity. There is the glorious apparel of heaven or the repulsive rags of the beggar, but the great difference is in the attitude of him who wears it. Yes, "Buy of me the white raiment that thou mayest be clothed!"

Look at the bleak, desolate little individual who resents everything—and everyone—and you will behold a person clothed in the ugly desolation of his own resentful attitudes while his very possessions begin to shrivel in his hands. The atoms, which compose his apparel will lose their joy and their buoyancy and turn into a repellent substance as repulsive as the physical body of the being who sends out his destructive resentments.

"He who is thankful in ALL THINGS WILL BE MADE GLORIOUS!"

No one on the face of the earth can disprove this statement. But everyone who desires can put it to the test and so prove the power and truth of it. All it takes is a little mental adjusting from the standpoint of mortal thinking into the higher thinking which transforms the thinker into a radiant person of glorious Light—and delight!

And in this gratitude, when put to the test, every seeming calamity, every distress and every imagined misfortune can be transmuted into blessings. This power is an almost unspeakable reality as one takes hold of it and uses it. "ALL THINGS WORK TOGETHER FOR GOOD TO THOSE WHO LOVE GOD!" And no one can truly love God without rejoicing continually in His blessings.

Do you wish to KNOW GOD? Do you wish to please God? Then begin to live by His Promises and you will KNOW—HIM—and this is Life Eternal!

No girl is ever unpopular because of the inadequacy of her clothing. It is only her reactions to her clothing that can cause her to become unpopular as she sends out her own desolating, negative thoughts and vibrations. Her very resentments transform her into an unattractive individual.

One's physical clothing is enhanced or ugly according to the attitude of the one wearing it. One's attitude is the reality.

Yes! *"He who is thankful in all things will be made glorious!"*

The very glory of his gratitude not only clothes him in a glowing radiance, but actually transforms the individual into that sublime radiance. He becomes so vibrantly radiant that no misfit, ugly apparel can possibly hide it.

The PROMISE of glory is guaranteed to those "WHO BECOME THANKFUL IN ALL THINGS!" It is not a hit and miss bit of instruction. And this degree of gratitude is the point of complete fulfillment as one rises above the hurts, the wounds, the negative conditions, the lacks and anguishes of life by focusing his attention upon the blessings. And no one can possibly be thankful without "lifting his eyes to behold the glory of God!"

"APPRECIATION" is even more special. It is gratitude enfolded in all the love one can possibly generate. It is a song carried on the wings of Light to the very throne of God.

In the attitude of appreciation or gratitude all blessings are increased, all poverty and lacks are overcome; all negation is transformed into beauty and loveliness and plenty. And truly, one becomes glorious!

Then, as one is made glorious, the things of this world are added unto him a hundred-fold; yea, MORE! The law of increase and of multiplication is fulfilled and nothing will be withheld. One will have reached that "Kingdom of God" (within). It is not a releasing of words generated from the lips which brings this great fulfilling. It is only powerful and glorious because it is generated from the heart.

When Christ tried to explain the glory and marvel of this spiritual radiance, he spoke of the lilies of the field, and how "Solomon, even in all his glory, was not arrayed like one of these." This is the reality of the spiritual beauty and radiance of the glowing vibrations and the exotic personality one carries who is THANKFUL IN ALL THINGS.

It is this law of glory that lifts one from mediocrity— or from the mental, unappreciative attitude of dull unawareness as he resentfully or grudgingly takes all blessings for granted with no recognition of the boon they carry. There is no sparkle or radiance in such a person, no enthusiasm, no joy. Such an individual is just a drab, earthy mortal, unanimated and uninteresting.

Gratitude is the greatest of all attitudes. Gratitude—the great BE-ATTITUDE. It is always enhanced and clothed in love. It opens the gates within man as the essence of spiritual power flows out from him who carries it in a stream of healing, joyous blessing. "Be the attitude"—*always* and life will lay her treasures at your feet. Yes, "Be that Attitude" and all else will fall into place in your life in a great miracle of divine OVERCOMING as the evils of your life melt away.

In developing the use of this divine and holy law of gratitude and appreciation, which is the law of plenty and glory, one reaches the point where he no longer needs to ask or to even think of his desires. At first it is necessary for one to take hold of that select law of creation and by concentrated thought and love and belief that reaches beyond doubts, hold forth the pattern of his needs or desires in a glowing reverence, as he gathers from the universe, the very substance or material of "those things *hoped* for" to fulfill or fill full the pattern he holds forth. But as one continues in this work, it becomes KNOWING and then comes the completion of the PROMISE: "BEFORE THEY ASK I WILL ANSWER," saith God. (More will be given on this later as God will unfold the glory of all fulfilling).

As one holds his mind upon his blessings they increase and become ever more beautiful. His mind, enlightened, will begin to behold through his spiritual eyes and in such beholding new gifts and new blessings will meet his vision. His conscious mind will expand above the worm consciousness for he himself will begin to evolve.

He will no longer be a warped little mortal of lack and destitution and suffering and anguish. He becomes clothed in light. And in that higher attitude he will begin "TO COMPREHEND ALL THINGS!" He will comprehend the very laws of creation and be able to use them. He will understand the exquisite wonder of holding forth a thought—a wish—a desire and watch it take form as he holds it forth in a loving, singing radiance of gratitude. It is then the very eternal elements begin to fulfill the patterns which he holds forth, "WITHOUT DOUBTING!" "For he who asks without doubting in his heart shall have whatsoever he asks."

As one "comprehends all things" he will KNOW that all things are composed of the spiritual substance of those divine, cosmic rays that can be, and are transformed into atoms, for "They are but waiting to become!" (See page 331 of "Ye Are Gods.")

He will comprehend that all substance and all tangible objects and elements are formed of these elements waiting to be formed into atoms, and hence he learns to manipulate and to fashion the very substance or material of FAITH into the things for which he *hopes*.

Thus were the five thousand fed, the Red Sea divided, the sick healed, mountains removed and the dead restored to life.

In this radiant song of singing gratitude all doubts are conquered, all darkness is banished and all lacks are supplied.

These dynamic blessings have been awaiting man's acceptance of them from the very beginning of time.

To use these powers and lay hold of these truths, that one might actually KNOW is the greatest method of all in which to please God. "For without FAITH it is impossible to please Him!" And without the gift of gratitude in action there is no approach into His presence.

FAITH is developed through an incentive to KNOW or to experience TRUTH. Incentive will bring forth the glorious quality of enthusiasm, which is the activating of the element of FAITH. And FAITH and GRATITUDE work together to fulfill all needs and he who uses them pleases God indeed!

CHAPTER V.

The Dynamic Power of TRUTH

At first there will be only one's own little trickle of love as he exerts himself to generate this dynamic life force of eternal power. However, as one continues to hold forth love in every thought and action and released vibration the love of God will soon be added to his own meager little supply. And as the "love of God is shed forth through the hearts of the children of men they begin to partake of the *Fruit of the Tree of Life!*"

The very atoms of one's body, which were composed of the cosmic rays direct from the throne of God, holding within their central nucleus, the spiritual substance of all creation, will become converted or reverted back into their pure spiritual essence and one will become spiritualized.

"Man is spirit! The elements are eternal (or spiritual when understood), and spirit and element, inseparably connected (or when one becomes "Born of the Spirit" or translated) he receives a fulness of joy!

"And great shall be their reward and eternal shall be their glory!"

The only possible way for spirit and element to become inseparably connected is through this spiritualization of the flesh. The spirit and the elements are separated when one descends into the grave, or "GIVES UP THE GHOST" or Spirit as the Bible describes it. And even the resurrection is not the inseparable connection of which the aforementioned scripture speaks, for the body and the spirit have already been separated. Death is the separation. And only as one is truly *"Born of the Spirit"* can this inseparable condition be achieved.

In being "Born of the Spirit," as Christ explained to Nicodemus, in John's record, chapter three, verses five to eight, one's physical body is transposed, translated or converted into its pure spiritual elements. Or as was said of Enoch, "Write the works of Enoch as a prophet, priest and seer; write of his life of purity and love, and how he changed his carnal flesh to flesh divine without descending through the gates of death."

The elements of which man is composed is not only spirit, as is revealed in the statement: "Man is spirit," "Man was that TRUTH in the beginning."

If the *great* TRUTH is that man was that TRUTH or SPIRIT in the beginning, then surely that Holy Spirit of Truth is the foundation of man's being and existence, only he has been completely unaware of his own divine nature.

"KNOW THE TRUTH! AND THE TRUTH WILL MAKE YOU FREE! AND HE WHO IS FREE SHALL BE FREE INDEED!"

Yes, KNOW that you are Spirit. In other words, EXPERIENCE THIS KNOWLEDGE as "you OVERCOME all the evils of your life." KNOW or EXPERIENCE the boundless, breathtaking fact that you can be transformed into your own true spirit nature and essence. KNOW or EXPERIENCE the fact that your spirit and the elements of your physical body can become inseparably connected! And when that is achieved death cannot touch you! You can actually KNOW this as the EXPERIENCE of fulfilling becomes your own.

"Nothing is impossible!" And only SIN can possibly bring death! "The wages of sin is death!" "OVERCOME all sin and death will have to back down for it will have no claim," so declared the ancients.

Or accept this glorious PROMISE of Almighty God, "who is a God of truth and cannot lie," "The nearer man approaches perfection the clearer are his views and the greater his enjoyments until he OVERCOMES THE EVILS OF HIS LIFE and loses every desire for sin, and like the ancients, arrives at the point of FAITH where he is wrapped in the power and glory of his Maker and is caught up to dwell with HIM!" This is translation. And it has been an open invitation to man from the beginning. It is for those who will use the gift of FAITH and fulfill God's terms in receiving it.

Remember, the only way one can possibly KNOW ANYTHING, is to EXPERIENCE IT!

And Christ left these words to verify this fact: "LIVE THE LAWS AND YOU WILL KNOW!"

Yes, "KNOW THE TRUTH! EXPERIENCE it for yourselves by living the laws pertaining to it. LIVE THE LAW OF LOVE and receive the fulness of its boundless, everlasting Promises for it is as far-reaching as eternity— and yet so very near at hand.

"KNOW THE TRUTH" and be free from all little narrow-minded, cramped ideas and orthodoxed doctrines. "KNOW THE TRUTH and YOU WILL BE FREE! AND HE WHO IS FREE SHALL BE FREE INDEED!" Yes! For he will "BE BORN OF THE SPIRIT AND WILL

BE ABLE TO COME AND GO AS THE WIND AND NO ONE WILL KNOW FROM WHENCE HE CAME OR WHITHER HE GOETH," as he is ordained and sent forth to accomplish the *greater works* of which Christ spoke.

"And so is everyone that is born of the Spirit," Christ imparted to Nicodemus. Then He added this information: "If I have told you earthly things and you could not believe, how could you believe if I told you heavenly things?" Poor Nicodemus could not believe in the great glory enfolded within this information. Neither have the rest of mankind ever been able to BELIEVE in the literal TRUTH of His Words. Nor have they realized that they were for the EARTH condition, for the here and now!

This divine ordinance or accomplishment of "Being Born of the Spirit" is definitely something that must be accomplished while in the flesh. It is an earthly experience and pertains to mankind while clothed in mortal form. "IF I HAVE TOLD YOU *EARTHLY THINGS*, and you could not believe, how could you possibly believe if I told you heavenly things?"

"KNOW THE TRUTH!" KNOW it by EXPERIENCING it! And you will become again that TRUTH!

Yes, "He who would interpret the wonders of the Lord will be dissolved and will become that which is interpreted." (26th Ode of Solomon, verse eleven and twelve).

LOVE is the key for he who lives those two Great and Wonderful Commandments" will have FULFILLED ALL THE LAWS AND THE PROPHETS." In other words, every divine PROMISE and PROPHECY OF THE SCRIPTURES will be fulfilled in him. And the rewards of the prophets will be his own.

Impossible, you say? You may say so, but you are not infallible! Your words and ideas and thoughts have been brought to naught before. But "TO GOD NOTHING IS IMPOSSIBLE!" And "NOTHING IS IMPOSSIBLE TO HIM WHO BELIEVES!"

Nicodemus did not believe the things Christ told. Neither has any man believed them since that day, except a very few chosen ones.

As one works upon himself instead of upon others, to fulfill and to perfect that great law of complete LOVE HE WILL BE DISSOLVED AND WILL BECOME THAT LOVE. As he sends that love through his own heart center God's love will join with his, and that love will go first through the living cells and atoms and tissues of his own body to renew, spiritualize and perfect and glorify it. And only in this way can his carnal flesh be transformed into flesh divine without descending through the gates of death. This glory is a spiritual EXPERIENCE in which the FULL KNOWING IS ACHIEVED.

Yes, "Write the works of Enoch as a prophet, priest and seer; write of his life of purity and love, and how he changed his carnal flesh to flesh divine without descending through the gates of death!" Yes, write it upon the tissues and fibers of your soul and you will become as Enoch.

Then go beyond that! Write the record of your own OVERCOMING!" And let that record be written and engraved upon your own soul for you yourself will be the living record to endure forever. And on that record will be the enhancing glory of "yourself made perfect even as the Father in heaven is perfect" for you will become the LOVE! You will KNOW THE TRUTH and you will become the TRUTH. You will be filled with Light as you become the glory of eternal LIGHT. Yes! You will become humble, glorious and divine, the very record of the very highest things possible to think and be and exalt.

Read Paul's words in Romans chapter three and verse twenty-three. Read then let the fullness of their power sink into the depths of your own soul as you ponder them in your heart: *"We* have all fallen short of the glory of God!" If we have fallen short it is our fault and not God's. He gave us the capacity to reach up and fulfill His glory right within ourselves. And the invitation to become perfect even as our Father in Heaven is perfect still stands.

The baptism of water precedes the baptism of Spirit, or "BEING BORN OF THE SPIRIT!" Baptism means literally to be *"immersed in."* This true immersion is perfected and completed as one brings forth and then holds himself in that River of Living Water that is to be poured forth through his "BELLY" or through his entire heart center and on out through the atoms and cells and tissues of his entire being. These are the literal "waters of life," which Christ promised. John 7:38: "He that believeth on me, as the scripture hath said, out of his belly shall flow rivers of living water." And the "Belly" signifies the whole living heart center as those waters of life are shed forth, from within, through every cell of the physical body. This is the real cleansing, the true purification.

Romans 5:21: "That as sin hath reigned unto death, even so might grace reign through righteousness unto eternal life, by Jesus Christ our Lord."

II. Peter 1:3-4: "According as His divine power hath given unto us all things that pertain unto LIFE and GOD-

LINESS, through the knowledge of Him that hath called us to glory and virtue.

"Whereby are given unto us exceeding great and precious Promises, that by these ye might be partakers of the divine nature, HAVING ESCAPED CORRUPTION, *that is in the world through lust."*

After the complete purification of the physical body comes the baptism of the Spirit or that sacred wonder of "BEING BORN OF THE SPIRIT," in which one becomes a full partaker of divine nature, having escaped corruption, as the foregoing scripture testifies. In this glorious process one becomes immersed in spirit and thus his carnel flesh is changed to flesh divine without descending through the gates of death.

This is the great TRUTH, which to KNOW sets one forever free. And to KNOW necessitates that one actually EXPERIENCE this glorious breathtaking achievement.

It is the fulness of this EXPERIENCE that reveals the great TRUTH or KNOWLEDGE in which one becomes free indeed! Eternally free! Free from mortality and all its earthly claims of sin and sickness and ignorance and DEATH.

And like the writer of the Odes of Solomon experienced, one acquires a body free from sorrow or affliction or pain and becomes clothed in light. (21st Ode of Solomon, from the Lost Books of the Bible).

Such are some of the Promises of Almighty God! And such are the PROMISES of those *Two Great Commandments,* WHEN LIVED.

Remember, that to begin to EXPERIENCE the breathtaking wonder of this great power of LOVE one must begin to work upon himself—not upon others! It is his own thoughts and vibrations that must be trained and purified. And "When his mind and lips have lost the power to hurt and wound his voice will be heard among the Gods!"

As one begins to generate LOVE through his divine heart center he will feel his heart soften and compassion take the place of wrath and anger. He will begin to feel mercy flow through when others fail or make mistakes instead of condemnation and criticism. And as the divine power of one's own forgiveness is developed he is automatically being forgiven for all his past mistakes and errors and weaknesses he himself has carried. And as one revels in this power he can use it ever more freely. He can send it back along the pathway of his past life. And he can use it in a double portion for the present, in which he lives. And soon he *will be interpreting the very wonder of God's* LOVE *and will be* dissolved as he becomes the very essence and light and glory of the healing, perfecting power of LOVE.

As one works upon himself he will soon become aware of God's divine powerful LOVE being added to his own. And as he makes use of this everlasting power of healing and refining glory his supply will continually increase according to his need and his own capacity to send it forth. And then, without knowing or being aware of just when it happened, he will find that the Love he generates will go forth to vibrate across the universe and play new melodies upon the stars.

Such a one will be able to send this love into the far-flung realms of eternity and out to enfold the universe. And he will be able to concentrate it upon those who know not these higher laws. And then, reaching into the realms of the damned he will be able to light up the very confines of hell.

Power? It is limitless! It is unspeakable in the degree of its full accomplishments! And as one rejoices in the privilege of being invited to LOVE God with all his heart, soul, mind and strength he will comprehend fully the magnificent privilege and wonder of an invitation so great. For then one will realize that it is not God who needs his love. It is he who needs to GIVE IT. The blessings and the rewards and the joys and the powers are forever his own.

As one loves with all his heart, with all his entire being and with all the powers of his mind he will experience the wonder of all his dislikes and all the bitterness and the evils of his life being dissolved and transformed into glory.

As one opens wide his soul to the love of God it flows through his own heart and he will experience the breathtaking wonder of having the physical cells transformed into their true spirit essence and his carnel flesh will be changed to flesh divine without descending through the gates of death.

This great love will flow out through one's hands to heal and bless! It will flow through his eyes to give comfort and understanding. And that one will become a lighted magnet of released power of healing and joy and beauty.

Yes, all are invited to "KNOW THE TRUTH" and to become that TRUTH! And he who is prepared to know the TRUTH will become free from every evil, mortal weakness and inclination and vicissitude and pain and anguished suffering. He will become divine, "For his mind and lips will have lost the power to hurt and wound and thus will his voice be heard among the Gods!"

Such are the PROMISES of Almighty God, our Divine, Heavenly Father! And such is our right to receive as we live up to His everlasting invitation to fulfill.

Man was created to be a generator of LOVE and LIGHT and in fulfilling his divine destiny of eternal, everlasting glory he will no longer "FALL SHORT OF THE GLORY OF GOD."

John 16:13; "Howbeit when he, the Spirit of TRUTH is come, He will guide you into all truth, for he shall not speak of himself; but whatsoever he shall hear that shall he speak; and he will show you things to come.

"And no man receiveth a fulness unless he keepeth His commandments." (And "If he keeps that First and Great Commandment he will have fulfilled ALL the laws and the commandments and the PROPHETS.)

"He that keepeth His commandments RECEIVETH TRUTH AND LIGHT, UNTIL HE IS GLORIFIED IN LIGHT AND KNOWETH ALL THINGS!"

This is verified in the following quotation: "And if your eyes be single to my glory your whole bodies shall be filled with Light and there shall be no darkness in you. And that body which is filled with Light shall comprehend all things!"

"And this is the confidence that we have in him, that, if we ask anything according to his will, he heareth us;

"And if we know that He heareth us; whatsoever we ask, we know that we have the petitions that we desired of him." (I. John 5:14-15.)

And "If we are led by the Spirit YE ARE NOT UNDER THE LAW." (Gal. 5:18). In other words he will have fulfilled all the laws and the commandments, for this is the perfection of living that First and Great Commandment.

Chapter VI.

The Keys of All-Knowing

Man is a marvel and a wonder beyond anything he has ever thought or dreamed. Man has locked within himself the realms of the three degrees of glory, the telestial, the terrestrial and the celestial. And he has the capacity to select the level of his own existence. He will most assuredly inherit whichever one he chooses to abide in mentally while here on this earth for it is here where the selection is made.

There is the outside, emotional man, consisting of his carnel flesh and its attributes, subject to pain and vicissitudes, rocked by his hates, devastated by his mortal conflicts and frustrations as he is carried along the pathway of his own lusts and physical desires and unproved beliefs.

Any who dwell only on the outside, emotional level of their natures, riding the ferris-wheel of life in an up and down state of uncontrolled exuberance to the low depths of anguish and despair are being cheated. These unstable ones, are like ships without rudders. These can hate harder, dislike more violently and judge more harshly than any others.

The scholar, the true seeker, the sincere searcher may each ride his own smaller, controlled ferris-wheel from the lesser heights to the depths and up again, yet not at such a great variance. They are more or less aware of a hungering for answers to satisfy their thirst for knowledge. The tragic thing is that far too many are satisfied with only a small portion of knowledge, or just half-truths. If one does not go far enough he may often assume that every thought or idea he chances to hear, or is willing to accept, is the ultimate TRUTH of ALL-TRUTH!

I knew a woman once who believed there could be no truth or fact unless she had hatched the idea in her own mind, or unless her own selected leader imparted it to her. And bless her, she was completely carried away with just slight unveilings of truth or with partial truths and so she stood still while TRUTH passed her by.

It must be remembered always, NO ONE PERSON HAS A MONOPOLY UPON TRUTH! Truth will be revealed to anyone who will seek for it or ask for it! Truth belongs to God—and is awaiting the discovery of every individual on the earth who will only "ask and seek and knock!" "FOR EVERYONE WHO ASKS RECEIVES! AND HE WHO SEEKS FINDS! AND UNTO HIM WHO KNOCKS IT SHALL BE OPENED!" This is the most perfect assurance anyone can possibly have on this earth that his search TO KNOW (*for himself*) will not be in vain.

And so man is the great marvel and wonder who has remained unfulfilled as he has been satisfied with the outside, emotional, every-day, carnal level of his being.

Then there is the mental being of man, who too few have ever really associated with at all. *Few really think!* Modern education is more or less a cramming process as the thoughts and ideas of others become stashed and crowded into the minds of the students. Thinking involves a process of choosing and eliminating and of PROVING. Thinking requires that the mind be harnessed and placed under control as one learns to concentrate upon the subject of his inquiry until he has tested and proved his idea or solution.

The mind must become the servant. It must learn to obey. It must accept and reject as it PROVES ALL THINGS. This is required if one is to fully KNOW THE TRUTH. And in this training even the mind evolves into a higher capacity of functioning.

So is man endowed. And so is man's capacity to KNOW for himself. And the full KNOWING can only be established as one PROVES or EXPERIENCES any TRUTH.

When one finally enters the realm of KNOWING, his emotions will have been brought under control, the powers of his mind will have developed the marvel of their full functioning, and he will be prepared to be "TAUGHT OF GOD!" And by his own developing he will be prepared "TO COMPREHEND ALL THINGS!" This is the condition in which he will have developed the ability TO ACTUALLY KNOW! "Nothing will remain closed to him, for he will have discovered that he is truly the door to everything," as the writer of the Odes of Solomon testified.

This realm of "All-knowing" goes beyond the mental realm. Or rather, it is reached when the mind itself has evolved into its highest point of functioning. Or when the conscious mind has joined with the super-conscious mind in a divine contact of development. It is the realm where PEACE abides—"THE PEACE THAT PASSETH UNDERSTANDING!" This realm where love goes beyond thought. Then it is that one can KNOW TRUTH FOR HE

WILL BE ABLE TO EXPERIENCE IT, not just hear or read about it.

And there are many in this precious day and age who will never be satisfied with anything short of the full TRUTH. For these are the promises given: "Seek me early and you shall find me!" Or, "Seek me diligently and you shall KNOW me!" Yes, "Blessed are those who hunger and thirst after righteousness for they shall be filled with the fulness of God." Or to express it in another way: "THEY SHALL KNOW THE TRUTH" fully and completely.

This inner realm of glorious KNOWING is difficult to describe. It is so far beyond emotions and even beyond thought and the carnal existence there seems to be no terms available with which to make it KNOWN or comprehensible. It is the realm of deep, inner stillness.

The contact with the TRUTH or understanding or divine knowledge that goes beyond thought or feeling is an inner discernment that was implanted in every living soul from the beginning. It has become a dormant faculty in most because it has been neglected and unused.

"Therefore it is given to abide in you as the record of heaven; The Comforter; the peaceable things of immortal glory; the truth of all things; that which KNOWETH all things, and hath all power, according to wisdom, mercy, truth, justice and judgment."

This is one of the great revelations which God has given to man. But its full impact and power can only be comprehended by those whose hearts are softened by love and devotion and whose minds are opened to receive, and who have OVERCOME the great evil of UNBELIEF. To them this scripture, given originally to blessed Enoch of old, will become their own. And all the promised wonders of it will be fulfilled in them—the complete all-knowing, the all-power of accomplishment, the memory of that pre-existent experience and their own individual assignment and the way of its unfolding.

When I used to teach classes questions would sometimes arise which I had never before heard or thought of —and many of them pertained to points to which no answers had hitherto been recorded, I learned, during those experiences, that there is no question without an answer. And the true answer will be given if one does not pretend or assume that he already knows everything. If one makes such pretentions he will begin to teach false doctrine and give out unproved theories. He will be *"trusting in the arm of flesh"*—his own weak arm of uncomprehension.

In every such emergency it is possible to stand perfectly still for a moment, to weigh and measure the question asked, for no question must be slighted or ignored, and in that momentary stillness one's mind will automatically reach down into the depths of his own soul and there will be the answer. It will be direct and true and beyond controversy. It will be infallible and carry its own weight of authority.

As I learned to use this method I learned that I did not even have to search for the answers, or rack my brain for them. And when an answer came forth to fill my conscious mind with its infallible truth it was clothed in the everlasting perfection, direct from the sources of all-knowing. Those answers had the divine power sealed upon them. They would be clothed in the plainness and TRUTH of uncontradictable substance around them.

Thus I used this source of *all-knowing* for years to answer the questions and to solve the problems of others. And my own problem went unsolved.

I stood alone upon the mountain with my own desire and fulfilling unfulfilled. How was I to have that great PROMISE of my earlier years granted—that PROMISE that *"My life would be sanctified unto God fully and completely, for His service, insomuch that saints and angels would rejoice and KNOW that a renewed strength and assurance would be injected into HIS work as I would become a servant in HIS hands in very deed!"*

That question became the uppermost concern of my life. How was I to go about *sanctifying* my life to such an extent? The need was so great and the fulfilling became so urgent I felt overwhelmed with the burden of it. In my own great intensity I forgot the unfailing power of God's PROMISES AND POWERS, if we would only ASK. And it was in my ASKING and humble willingness to accept completely His answer that the great enlightenment of eternal TRUTH was poured out upon me.

"The Holy Spirit of Promise, which the Father sheds forth upon all who are JUST and TRUE" is a wonder almost incomprehensible. But as one opens his mind to comprehend it holds a satisfaction and enlightenment in an unfailing power of ever unfolding glory as one becomes TRUE to its infallible Witness of Truth.

And there is no soul who has not been given or who will not be given the Witness or Testimony of Truth if he asks to KNOW the TRUTH about any information, condition or fact, being truly sincere in his asking and humble in his receiving. This Holy Witness or Spirit, when verifying TRUTH or revealing knowledge is like a living flame of glory being lighted in the center of one's soul. It carries a singing vibration of exquisite, eternal radiance and marvelous, divine assurance and power which is undeniable at the time of its Witnessing.

It is only later, when one opens up his heart and mind to doubting that he loses that Testimony or Witness and fails to be TRUE to TRUTH. As he encourages his own unbelief and doubting he closes the door to the "Light communicated to his intellect from heaven" and so goes even deeper into the darkness than he was before.

There is always a burning Witness in the soul to the very TRUTH OF ALL THINGS if one is JUST and TRUE in his desire to KNOW TRUTH, and then is willing to remain TRUE to that TRUTH.

As one opens his mind to receive enlightenment, in humble requesting, he will assuredly be given the outflowing Witness to TRUTH upon every occasion *until he is led into all truth!* This ability to be TRUE to that Holy Spirit makes one ELECT! And the scripture states that "Lucifer will deceive even the very ELECT, *if possible.*" This is only possible when one has not "Made his calling and his election sure." And this *election* is achieved if one does not fail to give heed to the Light communicated from heaven to his intellect.

This developed ability to be TRUE to the divine Witness of that Holy Spirit makes one's calling and election sure! And he who achieves this status can never be deceived or left comfortless or alone in his journey to glory or into the realms of TRUTH! And only those who are JUST and TRUE can ever know the TRUTH!

This being TRUE to this divine Holy Witness of Truth and Promise is that which is required to make one's calling and election sure and permanent as the Holy Spirit becomes his eternal Companion. And as this is accomplished one will be led into ALL TRUTH and will receive the fulfilling of every PROMISE ever given by God until he himself is perfected and glorified and exalted.

This statement must be made clear and plain at this point. It is stated in the scripture and those "who sin against the Holy Ghost (or Spirit) will not be forgiven in this world—or in the WORLD TO COME!" To deny the Testimony or instructions or Witness of that Holy Spirit of Promise is that unforgivable sin that takes a lifetime and a world beyond to atone for. This unpardonable sin or unforgivable sin is when one rejects or denies or defies God in a rebellious effort to make HIM adhere to one's own erroneous beliefs and accept them. Thus they reject LIGHT and TRUTH and become ever more unjust. Such have sinned indeed! They have shut themselves out from TRUTH and LIGHT and progress for their entire lives. And because they have so retarded their own progress, rejecting the Pathway of advancement and enlightenment and glory they have condemned their own souls to a lower, inferior status in that world which is to come.

And may God have mercy on them! So that when this world and the world to come have passed on these retarded ones will be able at last to pick up again where they failed. But in this retardation they will perhaps be ages even eons behind where they could have been had they not been UNTRUE.

Oh gracious, wonderful, Holy Spirit of Promise, I shall sing to Thy praise! I shall worship and adore and thank God continually for a blessing so great and so divine as Thy eternal, unfailing Companionship, for Thou hast led me along the Pathway of TRUTH! I rejoice in Thee always for thou hast never failed or forsaken me from the first moment of my awareness of Thy glory and the wonder of Thy infallibility and unspeakable TRUTH! For Thou hast indeed made me free! Eternally Free!

This is glory beyond thought! It is power beyond man's greatest dreams. It is the ultimate in all wonders and achievements. And the privilege of this marvelous Witness belongs to all who will only believe and who will "ASK and SEEK and KNOCK!" For everyone who asks receives! And he who seeks will find, the answers. And to him who KNOCKS the door to that Kingdom of Heaven will be opened wide. This is God's personal, indvidiual Promise to you and is eternally Witnessed by that Holy Spirit of Promise if you are willing to receive.

It is there for everyone. Yet none can ever KNOW this TRUTH or EXPERIENCE IT WHO ARE SATISFIED WITH THEMSELVES and with their present, inadequate, powerless beliefs. Neither can they be satisfied with the outward show of things, or who are carried away with pride in their own understandings. This realm is reached only as man opens up his soul and heart to receive that Holy Witness of God. It is for those who are JUST and TRUE!

As one learns to associate with that Holy Spirit of Promise he begins to abide in higher realms. It is not only the realm of PROMISE, but the realm where Promises are fulfilled and made eternally sure. This is the Kingdom which man was instructed to seek for first and above all else. It is the Kingdom of ALL-TRUTH and ALL-POWER! One enters it by desiring and then by asking and finally by being TRUE to the PROMISES vouchsafed to his own soul in the flaming power of God's eternal Witness of TRUTH.

As one uses his mind and soul to explore, to weigh and to measure and to PROVE or to LIVE BY the PROMISES, he enters the realm of the Patriarchs. These are no longer under the law but LIVE BY THE PROMISES, at first through FAITH and then through KNOWLEDGE. As one lives true to the PROMISES he begins to exert his own ability to PROVE THEM. In this Proving one enters the realm beyond thought. This is the realm of Spirit where one can actually behold the mighty forces of God take hold of the elements of Creation as they fashion requests and desires into the things "WAITING TO BECOME!" Here one views the wonder of the Holy Spirit of Promise solidifying *the substance of things hoped for* into tangible reality. This is glory indeed!

THIS IS THE LAND OF PROMISE! This is where the great and Holy Promises of God take form and solidify into supreme fulfillment. This is the realm of the Holy Spirit of Promise as it fulfills all things! This is the realm in which one comprehends all things! This is the realm of the "HOLY OF HOLIES!" This is the "SECRET PLACE OF THE MOST HIGH!" This is the realm in which one can comprehend all things. It is the realm in which all evils and ugliness and falsehoods and doubts are eliminated. It is that Kingdom of HEAVEN (within) as one reaches it—his own PROMISED LAND!

Chapter VII.

The Odes of Solomon

(From the Lost Books of the Bible)

Now, I am instructed to introduce you to my wonderful friend, the writer of those precious, sacred "Odes of Solomon." This writer was not King Solomon. King Solomon lived over one thousand years before Christ. The writer of the Odes of Solomon was a near contemporary of the Lord Jesus Christ. He was a convert to Christianity shortly after the advent of Christ. He states in the forty-first Ode: "All those will be astonished that see me, for from another race (than Judah) am I; For the Father of Truth remembered me: He who possessed me from the beginning."

In order to give a more complete introduction to this marvelous individual's works I shall quote part of the explanations concerning his writings as reported by the translators of his words. They are as follows: "Here are some of the most beautiful songs of peace and joy that the world possesses. Yet their origin, the date of their writing, and the exact meaning of many of the verses remain one of the great literary mysteries.

"They have come down to us in a single and very ancient document in Syriac language. Evidently that document is a translation from the original Greek * * *.

They are strangely lacking in historical allusions. Their radiance is no reflection of other days. They do not borrow from either the Old Testament or the Gospels. The inspiration of these verses is first-hand * * *. There does not seem to be anything about which everyone seems to agree unless it be that the Odes are of singular beauty and high spiritual value."

So much for the introduction to these precious Odes by the scholars and the translator of "THESE DAZZLING MYSTERY ODES," J. Rendel Harris, M.A., Hon. Fellow of Clare College, Cambridge.

And now, let me introduce the writer of these sacred Odes to you, in the glory of his meekness. He was too humble to use his own name, so he 'titled them "The Odes of Solomon," or to unfold the meaning fully, "The Odes of Wisdom."

The love of this man became so great he was given the laws of "translation" and of perfection, and he fulfilled them. And then, in the mercy of God, he was shown how, at the end of time, these great truths of OVERCOMING DEATH would be made known to the world.

Quoting from Ode 3:3-5: "For I should not have known how to love the Lord, if He had not loved me.

"For who is able to distinguish love, except the one that is loved?

"I love the Beloved and my soul loves Him."

Then in verses nine to thirteen it states: "And because I shall love Him that is the Son, I shall become a son;

"For he that is joined to Him that is immortal, will also himself become immortal;

"And he who has pleasure in the Living One, will become living.

"This is the Spirit of the Lord, which doth not lie, which teacheth the sons of men to know His ways.

"Be wise and understanding and diligent. Halleulujah!"

And now, in order to reveal a more complete appreciation of the writings of these beautiful Odes I shall have to share with you my own introduction to this glorious writer.

I was fulfilling the command of God to write the book, *"Ye Are Gods,"* which I had been informed was to be A GREAT VOLUME and was to go forth to the whole world. I was copying a quotation from Nicodemus when the pages slipped away from me and my eyes came to rest upon these words: "THE HEAD WENT DOWN TO THE FEET, FOR DOWN TO THE FEET RAN THE WHEEL, AND THAT WHICH WAS A SIGN UPON IT—"

These words, as I glanced at them, went through me like a two-edged sword. "Oh, my God!" I exclaimed in awed wonder for they were as familiar to me as the palms of my own hands. They were more familiar to me than the words of the language I had been taught from childhood. They were a part of my very self. Excitedly I read that twenty-third Ode through to the end and then I read it through from the beginning. I shall introduce it here with the translators words sealed upon it: "THE REFERENCE TO THE SEALED DOCUMENT SENT BY GOD IS ONE OF THE GREAT MYSTERIES OF THE COLLECTION."

After I had read that Ode through I was told: "The mystery of that sealed document" is contained in the great wonder of God's KNOWING. It is a mystery because it pertains to the bringing forth of this document I have commanded you to write. This will be the GREAT VOLUME, WHOLLY WRITTEN BY THE FINGER OF GOD. And the mystery is that the earth has never before contained it.

And I wept in the wonder of it and in my own feeling of deep humility.

I marveled even more as the words of that foretelling were verified and fulfilled later in the release of that first volume which God commanded me to write, the book *"Ye Are Gods."*

23 Ode of Solomon

1. "Joy is of the saints! And who shall put it on but they alone?

2. "Grace is of the elect! And who shall receive it except those who have possessed it from the beginning?

3. "LOVE is of the elect! And who shall put it on except those who have possessed it from the beginning?

4. "Walk ye in the knowledge of the Most High without grudging: to His exultation (praise) and to the perfection of His knowledge (or to the complete knowing of God).

5. "And His thought was like a letter; His will descended from on high, and it was like an arrow which is violently shot from a bow:

6. "And many hands rushed to the letter to seize it and take it and read it.

7. "And it escaped their fingers and they were affrighted at it and at the seal that was upon it.

8. "Because it was not permitted to them to loose its seal; for the power that was over the seal was greater than they.

9. "But those who saw it went after it that they might know where it would alight and who would hear it;"

This prophecy, given nearly two thousand years ago was most literally fulfilled. The head authorities of the church to which I then belonged watched to see which of its members would receive this great book or who would have copies of it in their homes. Homes were investigated and if those books were visible on the shelves or on tables the members of that home would be informed that if they did not get those books out of sight they would be excommunicated, "Or cast out of the synagogue," as it was expressed in the days of Christ.

Later, when I realized that Christ Himself had been cast out of the synagogue of Capernaum, or excommunicated, my sorrow became a very humble satisfaction to me. It was however, as I grieved with a sorrow too great to express that I was tenderly informed that the Son of God had sustained that same devastating experience.

And now, to continue with that twenty-third Ode.

10. "But a wheel received it (the great letter) and came over it." (A wheel is the movement of the power of God in action.) And it was so. These books, which God instructed me to write, have never been advertised or pushed forward by any publisher, or group or denomination or club or church yet they have gone forth to the ends of the earth.

"This wheel" which received this work or rolled it forth has been the wheel and the power of God's great love. Each individual who has received this work has felt the great urge to share it with his own special loved ones and friends. And only through this great sharing and this expressed love in action has it gone forth. It was this very love of God in the hearts of the children of men which has sent it forth and kept it going.

11. "And there was with it (the wheel) the sign of the Kingdom and of the Government;

12. "And everything which tried to move the wheel it mowed and cut down:

13. "And it gathered the multitude of adversaries, and bridged the rivers and crossed over and rooted up many forests (old ideas and beliefs) and made a broad path.

14. "The head went down to the feet, for down to the feet ran the wheel, and that which was a sign upon it."

(The great sign is LOVE! The books were all written and published through LOVE. No royalties were ever charged, only the price the publishers have required to pay for the printing expenses of these volumes has ever been required. And only a growing circle of love, as the wheel has enlarged, has been the means of their increasing popularity.)

Now, back to that 23rd Ode.

15. "The letter (or volume) was one of command, for there were included in it all districts: (physical, mental, moral and spiritual, along with a record of pre-existence, earth life and the knowledge of being able to step across into the higher dimensions without going through "THE GATES OF DEATH.")

16. "And there was seen at its head, the head which was revealed even the Son of Truth from the Most High Father.

17. "And He inherited and took possession of everything. And the thought of many was brought to nought.

18. "All the apostates hasted and fled away. And those who persecuted and were enraged became extinct.

19. "AND THE LETTER WAS A GREAT VOLUME, WHICH WAS WHOLLY WRITTEN BY THE FINGER OF GOD.

20. "And the name of the Father was on it, and of the Son and of the Holy Spirit, to rule for ever and ever. Hallelujah!"

So much for the sealed document for it was the first book which God requested me to write and I wrote it in fire and tears.

And that volume was written in thirty days, under the hand of the Almighty—or as he "wrote it with His finger!" Take an outstretched finger and you will behold a finger pointing out the way or the direction or the correct road to travel.

While that book was being poured out through me, for I was only the humble scribe, I begged God to get someone important to write it. I pleaded with Him in these words: "Dear God, please get someone in authority or someone important to write this book. I would love it if I found it scribbled on scratch paper, lying in the gutter and soiled with sewer dirt and wrapped in slime."

"That is why you were called to write it!" came the answer powerful beyond all argument and all doubting.

I wrote that book in fire and tears for I wept almost all the way through it as light poured down through my being and out through my fingertips onto the pages in my typewriter.

At times I would be almost blinded by the glory and I would ask: "Dear God, how can I write these things? They have never even been thought before. And who will be able to receive them? And who read them?"

"It is no concern of yours who will read them or who will receive them," I was told; "you are to write!"

And so I wrote.

Later, to my great amazement, that 26th Ode came to my attention.

1. "I poured out praise to the Lord, for I am His;

2. "And I will speak His holy song, for my heart is with Him.

3. "For His harp is in my hands, and the Odes of His rest shall not be silent.

4. "I will cry unto Him from my whole heart; I will praise and exalt Him with all my members (my whole being).

5. "From the east even to the west is His Praise;

6. "And from the south and even to the north is the confession of Him:

7. "And from the top of the hills to their utmost bound is His perfection.

8. "WHO CAN WRITE THE PSALMS OF THE LORD OR WHO READ THEM?" And so my prayer was understood and foretold two thousand years ago. The very

words I prayed had been written down by the writer of those Odes so long ago.

And now, I must share with you that precious sixth Ode, for it is very sacred, and is as follows:

1. "As the hand moves over the harp, and the strings speak.

2. "So speaks in my members the Spirit of the Lord, and I speak by His love.

3. "For it (*love*) destroys what is foreign, and everything that is bitter.

4. "For thus it was from the beginning and will be to the end, that nothing should stand up against Him. (For those who fight against Him shall be destroyed).

5. "The Lord has multiplied the knowledge of Himself, and is zealous that these things should be known, which by His grace hath been given to us.

6. "The praise of His name He gave us; for our Spirits praise His Holy Spirit.

7. "For there went forth a stream and BECAME A RIVER GREAT AND BROAD";

(This stream that went forth and became a "RIVER GREAT AND BROAD" is this work God has brought forth in this day. The first volume, *"Ye Are Gods"* was only a stream in comparison to that which has followed, even to this last volume. With this record added, which is the eighth book, it has indeed become a RIVER GREAT AND BROAD).

8. "For it flooded and broke up everything and it brought water (or life) to the Temple:

9. "And the restrainers of the children of men were not able to restrain it, nor the arts of those whose business it is to restrain waters;

10. "For it spread over the face of the whole earth, and filled everything: and all the thirsty upon earth were given to drink of it;

11. And thirst was relieved and quenched; from the Most High the draught was given.

12. "Blessed then are the ministers of that draught who are entrusted with that water of His;" (The ministers of that draught are the blessed, glorious ones, who through their LOVE, have shared these books or truths with others. God bless them forever!)

13. "They have assuaged the dry lips, and the will that had fainted they have raised up;

14. "AND SOULS THAT WERE NEAR DEPARTING THEY HAVE CAUGHT BACK FROM DEATH:

15. "And limbs that had fallen they straightened and set up;

16. "They gave strength for their feebleness and light to their eyes:

17. "For everyone knew them in the Lord, and they lived by the WATERS OF LIFE for ever. Hallelujah!"

From here on I shall quote only portions of these great and holy writings, that I might give you a more clear picture of the man who wrote them.

Ode 12:11-12: "For the dwelling-place of the WORD is man; and its Truth is LOVE.

"Blessed are they who by means thereof have understood everything, and have known the Lord in His Truth!"

Ode 13.

1. "Behold! The Lord is our mirror: open the eyes and see them in Him; and learn the manner of your face:

2. "And tell forth praise to His Spirit; and wipe off the filth from your face; and love His holiness, and clothe yourself therewith.

3. "And be without stain at all times before Him. Hallelujah!"

Ode 15.

8. "I have put on *incorruption* through His name; and HAVE PUT OFF CORRUPTION by His grace.

9. "DEATH HATH BEEN DESTROYED BEFORE MY FACE; and Sheol hath been abolished by my word;

10. "AND THERE HATH GONE UP DEATHLESS LIFE IN THE LORD'S LAND.

11. "AND IT HATH BEEN MADE KNOWN TO HIS FAITHFUL ONES, AND HATH BEEN GIVEN WITHOUT STINT TO ALL THOSE THAT TRUST IN HIM! Hallelujah!"

The holy writer of the Odes of Solomon (I am not yet permitted to reveal his name) is the first and only one, until now, who has been permitted to write a record of his life and of His progress and of his achievement.

Enoch was permitted to leave no such record, or Moses or Elijah or any of the many others who reached out with their perfected LOVE to bridge that chasm of death.

Ode 17.

1. "I was crowned (ordained) by my God; my crown is living;

2. "And I was justified in my Lord; my incorruptible salvation is He.

3. "I was loosed from vanity, and I was not condemned.

4. "The choking bonds (of mortality) were cut off by her hands; I received the face and fashion of a new person:

5. "And the thought of Truth led me on. And I walked after it and did not wander;

6. "And all that have seen me were amazed, and I was regarded by them as a strange person;

7. "And He who knew and brought me up is the Most High in all His perfection. And He glorified me by His kindness, and raised my thoughts to the height of His truth.

8. "And from thence He gave me the way of His precepts (teachings). And I opened the doors that were closed.

9. "And break in pieces the bars of iron; and my iron melted and dissolved before me;

10. "And nothing appeared closed to me; because I was the door to everything." And so it is!

Ode 18.

1. "My heart was lifted up in the love of the Most High and was enlarged; that I might praise Him for His name's sake.

2. "My members were strengthened that they might not fall from His Strength.

3. "SICKNESS REMOVED FROM MY BODY AND IT STOOD TO THE LORD BY HIS WILL. For His Kingdom is true!"

The testimony and the witness of this gracious, saintly writer is entirely of LIFE EVERLASTING—and he has testified of the truth of this work and of the books which God has called me to write. In prophecy he has testified of them and of their coming forth in this day and age. Each volume God has instructed me to write has made that RIVER *become more great and broad* as it has increased in power and size and momentum. Then in the thirty-ninth Ode it states: *"Great Rivers are the power of the Lord;*

2. "And they carry headlong those who despise Him; and who entangle their paths."

Ode 30.

1. "Fill ye waters for yourselves from the living fountain of the Lord, for it is opened to you!

5. "For it flows from the lips of the Lord and from the heart of the Lord is its name.

6. "And it came infinitely and invisibly; and until it was set in the midst they did not know it;

7. "Blessed are they who have drunk therefrom and have found rest thereby. Hallelujah!"

Ode 34.

1. "No way is hard where there is a simple heart.

2. "Nor is there any wound where the thoughts are upright.

3. "Nor is there any storm in the depth of the illuminated thought."

Ode 38.

1. "I went up to the light of truth as if into a chariot;

2. "And Truth took me and led me; and carried me across pits and gullies; and from the rocks and the waves it preserved me;

3. "And it became to me a haven of salvation; *and set me on the arms of immortal life;*

4. "And it went with me and made me rest, and suffered me not to wander, because it was the Truth;

5. "And I ran no risk, because I walked with Him;

6. "And I did not make an error in anything because I obeyed the truth.

7. "For error flees away from it, and meets it not; but Truth proceeds in the right Path, and

8. "Whatever I did not know, it made clear to me, all the poisons of error, and THE PLAGUES OF DEATH WHICH THEY THINK TO BE SWEETNESS."

Ode 41.

11. "And His Word is with us in all our ways;

12. "The Savior who makes alive and does not reject our souls;

13. "The man who was humbled, and exalted by His own righteousness.

14. "The Son of the Most High appeared in the perfection of His Father;

15. "And the light dawned from the Word that was beforetime in Him;

74 THE BOOK OF BOOKS

16. "The Messiah is truly one; and He was known before the foundation of the world.

17. "That He might save souls for ever by the Truth of His Name: A NEW SONG ARISES FROM THOSE WHO LOVE HIM! Hallelujah!"

I shall not quote more from the glorious record of that inspired, saintly writer of long ago. His message has come down to us in this day and age for this is the time scheduled for the fulfilling. These sacred words have been brought forth in the Lost Books of the Bible by the World Publishing Company and copyrighted 1926 by Alpha House, Inc. Rejoice in them.

Not everything written in the Lost Books of the Bible are true or trustworthy. Many of them are. Read them with an open, prayerful heart and that which is authentic will find a place in your own soul. Otherwise lay it aside. However, this record of the Odes is true and authentic. It is sacred indeed. Read it with prayer and you will receive not only a full understanding of its truths but a blessing from the writer thereof.

And here is the special message given to us in our time:

"Beloved ones of this later generation, Greetings!

"It was to you I spoke in the days of my writings. It was of these truths and of their coming forth that I engraved my ancient record with such infinite care.

"And again I say, Joy is of the Saints and none can put it on but they alone!"

"There is no living soul who cannot cast out the darkness of his own doubts and fears and discords. Anyone in existence, if he so chooses, can walk in the realms of glory at all times as he holds his mind single to glory and gladness and thankfulness. Thus he clothes himself in Light and will acquire a body free from sorrow or affliction or pain. It is True that, the nearer man approaches perfection the clearer are his views and the greater are his enjoyments until he *overcomes* the evils of his life and loses every desire for sin in the joy of everlasting mastery. And like the ancients, or patriarchs, he arrives at *the point of faith* where he is wrapped in the power and glory of his Maker and is caught up to dwell with Him. This is accomplished by applying these higher, glorious principles of joy and rejoicing and eternal gladness and thankfulness in his life. This is how one becomes the joy and the gladness and the Master, with limitless Power.

"Make this practice of rejoicing the constant purpose of your existence and you will become the master of love and harmony and joyous, powerful living. This can be done by any living soul who desires to overcome the evils of his life, as self-pity is exalted into power and glory and understanding and strength.

"In this method are the keys of OVERCOMING contained. And any who lives by them cannot possibly be OVERCOME by the vicissitudes of life. And all things become subject unto him, for he is the MASTER."

Chapter VIII.

Life! Life More Abundant!

"Forasmuch as this people draw near me with their mouth and with their lips do honor me, but HAVE REMOVED THEIR HEARTS FAR FROM ME: and their fear (or love) toward me is TAUGHT BY THE PRECEPTS OF MEN * * *" Etc. (Isaiah 29:13).

The above scripture is most startling. "The precepts of men" are the teachings of the creeds and churches and the various denominations of Christendom that exist upon this earth today.

How do we know that this prophecy of Isaiah was for *this day?* Because there is no prophecy in the scripture that does not give a key to the time of its fulfilling. This scripture from the twenty-ninth chapter of Isaiah, contains its own complete key. In verses seventeen to twenty-one it reveals the time element. It is to be when "Lebanon shall be turned into a fruitful field and the fruitfield shall be esteemed as a forest—when the deaf shall hear the words of the book and the eyes of the blind shall see out of obscurity and *the meek shall increase their joy in the Lord and the poor among men shall rejoice in the Holy One of Israel."*

The land of Israel, cursed and barren and uninhabited by her natural sons for centuries is now being turned into a fruitful field. Thirty-five years ago a man could not make a living on sixty acres for a wife and one child. Now, on two acres he can produce an abundance for himself and a family. The ancient curse is indeed being lifted from the land and it is turning into a fruitful field. And the great miracle of the other promises and the essence of the time involved is already at our doors. The deaf are being given small, electronic devices with which to hear. The blind are being able to read Braille that they can see out of obscurity.

There is no question as to the time.

And it is the precepts of men or the teachings of the orthodoxed groups and churches that have been responsible for powerless lip service as their members draw near to HIM with their mouths and honor HIM with their lips, WHILE THEIR HEARTS have remained cold and barren and unawakened. This is because none of the creeds or denominations or churches have comprehended or known how to fulfill those TWO GREAT COMMANDMENTS OF LOVE. Neither have they lived by such teachings. *Their love toward God has indeed been taught by the precepts of men*, which hold forth the idea of attendance at church meetings, paying of contributions or tithes and offerings and the filling of a seat in the assembly as they give lip service as their show of devotion.

That First and Great Commandment has never been taught! Nor the second one in a manner that would make it a privilege and a living power of divine glory. These divine, holy Commandments of Love have never been fully accepted. Congregations have nodded their heads in a weak acclaim and that is as far as it has ever gone. These divine laws of LOVE have never been made a living issue or a divine privilege of everlasting glory and power. While many believe their own little pet road to heaven is paved with their individual selected passages of scripture, unlived and unfulfilled. The necessity or the method of LOVING GOD WITH ALL THE HEART, SOUL, MIND AND STRENGTH has never been considered.

"God is in the midst of all things!" He is in the center of every atom, the living nucleus in every infinitesimal, tiny organism. It is God's living intelligence and power around which the atom is formed and consists. And as one learns to LOVE God with his entire being those spiritual centers, "In the midst of every living cell and fibre of his own body "begin to be quickened" and expanded into a knowing or a recollection of their true, divine functioning. This quickening or awakening is the most glorious experience possible to realize as one holds his mind in a control of singing splendor and radiant majesty. With this accomplishment the power of LOVE will begin to be released throughout that individual's entire being. And this very LOVE will renovate those physical cells into a renewed vigor and awareness of LIFE—YES! "LIFE MORE ABUNDANT!"

"It is given to abide in you the record of heaven; the Comforter; the peaceable things of immortal glory; the truth of all things; that which quickeneth all things, which maketh alive all things; and hath all power."

As this LOVE FOR GOD is comprehended the cells and atoms will begin to yield up their dead component parts and the entire being of man will turn from its half-dead, mortal functioning of being but a repository of dying materials, or the sepulcher of them, into living tissues as they become filled with Light and Life. In this process the Christ Light will be released from its tomb, right within man, into a radiant existence of complete fulfillment as it fills one full with its own fulfilling glory. Then it is that the Light or Spirit, centered in every atom will be glorified and will unite and become ONE. And in that spiritual renewing of the individual cells and atoms one is prepared to "BE BORN OF THE SPIRIT and henceforth will have the power to come and go as the wind, and no one will know from whence he came or whither he goeth" as he gives his strength and intelligence in a joy of service beyond all mortal men to comprehend. This is joy beyond understanding. This is fulfillment!

"Without vision the people perish!" Vision is an awakening, or an alerting of the soul as one's understanding expands. With this visioning desires and yearnings unfold to reveal new and living possibilities. And it is true, that without vision or HOPE one is already trudging that pathway of death or destruction.

A man is but a seed in which the living life germ of divinity is dormant and unfulfilled until awakened. So is every atom of the body but an unfulfilled glory, waiting to "BECOME—GLORIOUS!" A man or an atom, for that matter, can remain like a seed, a mere kernel of grain, unawakened and inactive and insignificant, just filling some infinitesimal place, some unimportant niche as it continues in a dead state of existence. Or the atoms and cells and man himself can, with the right conditions, and with his own choosing and intense desiring, or awakening vision quicken that life germ within as he begins to envision the glory of perfection and the fulfilling of the PROMISES OF ALMIGHTY GOD in his life.

As that inner germ is awakened, through visioning, it

begins to reach toward heaven. The very desiring that is expanded by a new awareness generates the heat of its own germinating as it begins to evolve toward its own divine fulfillment. Thus it is within the power of every individual to fulfill all things!—To "BECOME PERFECT EVEN AS THE FATHER IN HEAVEN IS PERFECT!" And each atom and cell will in like manner begin to generate the Spirit Light of their primal existence and to fulfill the full measure of their divine quickening until the Spirit within each minute fibre and tissue is renovated, transformed and prepared to "BE BORN OF THE SPIRIT." In this fulfilling is contained the full measure of man and every PROMISE EVER GIVEN!"

One cannot possibly LOVE GOD *with all his mind* without developing a mind single to the glory of God. And in doing this he will become filled with Light. With the awakening of that spiritual intelligence and life within the very atoms and cells of his entire being they will be alerted and quickened as they begin to fulfill their own glorious functioning. Then the individual will complete his inborn assignment, whatever it may be. He will not only *"be filled with Light but will* COMPREHEND ALL THINGS!" FOR THIS IS ACCORDING TO GOD'S OWN PROMISE!

> Breathes there a man with soul so dead
> Who never to himself has said,
> I am a son, a child of God?
> I can from grubby earth arise
> And tread the Pathway of the Skies!
> Within me is the seed of God
> And I can tread where He has trod!

This inner purification of the HEART, through LOVE, as it is cleansed from all unrighteousness and evils is truly the divine "ROAD TO ZION," of which Isaiah spoke in his thirty-fifth chapter. "ZION IS THE REALM OR ABODE OF THE PURE IN HEART!"

And as the heart is purified and cleansed so is the entire body and the cells and the atoms thereof spiritualized and exalted as they are transformed into their true spiritual counterparts. And this is "THE LIFE MORE ABUNDANT" which Christ came to give. And it is awaiting each individual's acceptance of it. In this divine process, which is the OVERCOMING, every cell and atom and tissue puts off the darkness of mortality and vibrates in a newness of quickened, glorious, radiant LIFE. This is Christ's gift to the world. It is for everyone who desires it, and who will prepare themselves to receive it.

Christ never once spoke of death nor sought to prepare man to accept it. Christ spoke always of LIFE! "LIFE MORE ABUNDANT!" Or LIFE ETERNAL, in which a man need never die!

And those who profess to be followers of Christ, and yet accept not of His teachings are professing in vain.

And it is along that "ROAD TO ZION" or the complete purification of the heart, that one has the power to "cross over" the bridge from mortality into immortality. Again, we shall quote from that most sacred twenty-third Ode of Solomon, who told of this work in detail, starting with verse ten, as follows: "But a wheel (which means the power of God in action), received the great volume (see verse 19), and came over it;

"And there was with it a sign of the Kingdom and of the Government (of God);

"And it gathered the multitude of adversaries, and BRIDGED THE RIVERS AND CROSSED OVER AND ROOTED UP MANY FORESTS AND MADE A BROAD PATH.

"The head went down to the feet (the authorities descended below the laymen), for down to the feet ran the wheel and that which was a sign upon it."

This glorious, ancient record of that venerable, inspired Saint, goes on to tell that *Christ is the HEAD of this work and that none can stop it, even those who make it their business to restrain waters."* (See 6th Ode).

This power to "CROSS OVER" is the *ability to cross over from mortality into immortality, without dying.*

This is verified in the ancient record of Enoch, who overcame death and was translated. It is as follows: "Write the works of Enoch as a prophet, priest and seer; write of his life of purity and love, and how he changed his carnal flesh to flesh divine without descending through the gates of death." Yes, write the works of Enoch upon the fibres of your own soul. And know that whatever Enoch accomplished you too can accomplish. There are no monopolies in the realms of our Almighty Creator.

Then we have this glorious record in II. Peter 1:3-4: "According as His (Christ's) *divine power hath given unto us all things that pertain unto LIFE and Godliness, through the knowledge of Him that hath called us to glory and virtue.*

"WHEREBY ARE GIVEN UNTO US EXCEEDING GREAT AND PRECIOUS PROMISES, THAT BY THESE YE MIGHT BE PARTAKERS OF THE DIVINE NATURE, HAVING ESCAPED CORRUPTION, THAT IS IN THE WORLD THROUGH LUSTS!"

The only possible meaning of the foregoing quotation is the promise to escape death. Corruption is death! Death is corruption! And nothing else could express it so completely and so fully in so few words.

This power or ability to *bridge the rivers and cross over* is the Straight and Narrow Path that leads to LIFE ETERNAL—which is reached THROUGH THE PURIFICATION OF THE HEART. And this condition of perfection can only be accomplished through the transcendant excellence of LOVE! This very "BRIDGING OF THE RIVERS" is the method by which that glorious ROAD TO ZION is traveled.

Christ never spoke of death. He did however, speak of the *Broad Open Way that leads to* DESTRUCTION. DEATH was always expressed as DESTRUCTION, by Jesus. While His message was always of LIFE. And any individual who has that "LIFE MORE ABUNDANT" is a vivacious person, alive, exuberant, vital, not a mere clod, unanimated, dull or a deadly bore.

The sacred writer of those inspired Odes of Solomon explained it thus: "And I put off darkness and clothed myself in Light and acquired a body free from sorrow or affliction or pain."

Such a person is one who has put off mortality and in so doing has OVERCOME DEATH—THE LAST ENEMY.

This Road to Zion, in which a fool need not err therein, but over which the wicked can never cross, according to Isaiah, is that Straight and Narrow Path in which one "Evolves from the man Kingdom into the God Kingdom." He passes from mortality into immortality without descending through the gates of death, by living a life of

PURITY AND LOVE, by which his carnal flesh is changed to flesh divine. It is the point where one can fulfill Christ's most beloved teachings as He gave them to Nicodemus that night he conversed with him. "And he who is born of the Spirit can come and go as the wind and no one will know from whence he came or whither he goeth; so is *everyone* who is born of the Spirit," or who spiritualizes himself thrugh the perfecting of LOVE right within himself.

This Straight and Narrow Path does most assuredly lead literally INTO LIFE ETERNAL. It is the Straight and Narrow Path which Christ endeavored to reveal, in "WHICH A MAN NEED NEVER DIE!" It is the "Road to Zion!" It is the Way of the complete purification of the heart in which one evolves from grubby mortality into that divine, holy, exquisite realm of the OVERCOMERS. It is the Road which Enoch traveled, and which all who desire to do so are invited to follow. And the way of its glory is fulfilled in the LIVING OF THAT FIRST AND GREAT COMMANDMENT OF LOVE, not as it is taught by the precepts of men, but by Christ Himself.

Love is a vibration of infinite power. Love is a force that surmounts all obstacles. Love removes all negation. Love casts out all fear. Love is energy in its highest, purest, spiritual essence of renewing, invigorating, exalted, healing power. Pure love is completely freed from selfishness or self-seeking. "It seeketh not its own." Love flows ever outward, from those who possess it, in a giving glory of benediction. Love is the spirit of sharing. Love never turns inward to hold, to clutch, to grab or to seek for credits and rewards. Love is never self-indulgent. It never demands. It is not possessive. Love gives! Love blesses! Love sacrifices as it rejoices in the great privilege of sacrificing.

This LOVE is divine and it is the bridge across the chasm or gulf between mortality and that realm of immortality. And "through it one changes his carnal flesh to flesh divine without descending through the gates of death."

And there is one more point I am instructed to clarify here. When Christ warned of "The dogs that would return to their vomit" he was speaking of those who would receive these more glorious teachings, then looking back to the false teachings that required no self-discipline or effort, would return again to their old pattern of effortless acceptance—or vomit. There are so many who are unwilling to exert themselves in the least to fulfill or PROVE the Promises of God. And so they quite willingly accept the defiled food offered to them—the teaching declaring they need do nothing at all, but that Christ is to come and He will lift them into the highest degree of glory. And they are being fed the filth of Devil Doctrine! And it is a lie! Christ informed all men that only as they *DID WHAT HE SAID*, could they be saved. And "IF YE BELIEVE ON ME THE WORKS THAT I DO SHALL YOU DO ALSO, AND GREATER WORKS THAN THESE SHALL YE DO!" There is nothing in the scriptures to indicate that any soul will be exalted without effort and the exercising of faith. The command is to "ASK, TO SEEK AND TO KNOCK!" And this requires effort and must be followed through until the answer is received.

And without the attribute of LOVE being developed all is but sounding brass and clanging symbols. To develop love requires the exerted effort of casting out the negations, the fears, the doubts and the evils of one's life as FAITH is exercised and perfected.

The "vomit" mentioned is first given in Isaiah. And vomit is but undigested, unassimilated food that is spewed out without the individual preacher having fulfilled the things he teaches or having received the value of its divine nourishment. This is VOMIT. Those who preach without having fulfilled first the things of which they speak are but "spewing out vomit to defile the banquet tables of the Lord!"

And so, the dogs are the ones to whom Christ referred who will return to such vomit, being unwilling to make any effort to change themselves, but who adhere to the devil-doctrine of waiting for Christ to come and to exalt them into glory. They forget that when He comes "WE ARE TO BE PURIFIED EVEN AS HE IS PURE!" And that "WE ARE TO PURIFY OURSELVES!" "WE ARE TO SANCTIFY OURSELVES!"

The "Swine that will return to their wallow" are those who, having received these precious, glorious truths of enlightenment, and had the Pathway of OVERCOMING revealed, will be drawn back into the darkness of their fears and doubting and negation and will wallow in the mud of their encouraged self-pity and despairing despondency. This is for those who love the darkness more than they love the Light. They will make no effort to "OVERCOME THE DARKNESS, the self-pity or the unbelief which they permit to blot out their goal. Wallowing in their encouraged negation and doubting they are henceforth designated as "Swine that returned to their wallow!"

This "STRAIGHT AND NARROW WAY," this Pathway of the Patriarchs is truly the Pathway of OVERCOMING in a glory of praise and love and joyous gratitude. This Pathway is for the strong! And any who persistently travel it will become strong and mighty and glorious. "I GAVE MEN WEAKNESS THAT THEY MIGHT BECOME STRONG" in the glory of OVERCOMING. The very overcoming of any weakness contains the elements of which strength is generated and perfected.

Any who undertake to travel this Straight and Narrow Path, and look back, "Is not fit for the Kingdom." But the power to look ahead and to fulfill is within every man's reach, for this is the gift Christ came to give— LIFE! LIFE MORE ABUNDANT! LIFE ETERNAL! Life without descending through the gates of death.

Daniel 12:9-10 is as follows: "And he (the angel) said, Go thy way, Daniel: for the words are closed up and sealed till the time of the end.

"Many shall be purified and made white and tried; but the wicked shall do wickedly; and none of the wicked shall understand; but the wise shall understand."

Then in Daniel 12:3-4 is given this wonderful Promise: "And they that be wise shall shine as the brightness of the firmament; and they that turn many to righteousness as the stars for ever and ever.

"But thou, O Daniel, shut up the words, and seal the book, even to the time of the end; many shall run to and fro, and knowledge shall be increased."

Pray that your understanding will be fully opened to comprehend the glory of the above scripture, for it is yours.

CHAPTER IX.

Why and What Is Death?

When Satan boasted to the Prince of Hell that he had overcome the Son of God and had him hanging on a cross, the Prince of Hell drew back in horror exclaiming: "O thou Prince of destruction, author of Beelzebub's defeat and banishment, the scorn of God's Angels and loathed by all the righteous persons, what inclined thee to act thus?

"Thou wouldst crucify the KING OF GLORY, and by his destruction, has made us promises of very large advantage, but as a fool wert ignorant of what thou wast about." (From the Lost Books of the Bible; Nicodemus XVIII).

Now to quote from verses one and two and verses nine and ten and verses twelve and thirteen, I am instructed to share the following:

"O Prince Satan, thou great keeper of the infernal regions, all thy advantages which thou didst acquire by the forbidden tree, and the loss of Paradise, thou has now lost by the wood of the cross;

"And thy happiness all then expired, when thou didst crucify Jesus Christ the King of Glory.

"O Satan, Prince of all evil, AUTHOR OF DEATH, and source of all pride, thou shouldst first have inquired into the evil crimes of Jesus of Nazareth, and THEN

THOU WOULDST HAVE FOUND THAT HE WAS GUILTY OF NO CRIME WORTHY OF DEATH.

"Why didst thou venture, without either reason or justice, to crucify him, and hast brought down to our regions a person innocent and righteous, and therefore hast lost all the sinners, impious and unrighteous in the whole world?

Christ's trip into Hell is verified in the teachings of Saint Peter. That the gates of Hell were opened is true. And the prisoners were set free, but they were not exalted. Each soul was released from the bonds of Hell, but each was only placed on the level where he could begin to transform his life and make amends for his failures in the past as his own development began.

There is also the record of the ancients which acclaims: "On him who OVERCOMES sin DEATH HAS NO CLAIM."

Satan was the author of death! Not God!

God permitted death to be established as a way of release for those who would continue to sin throughout their mortal lives, with no desire to overcome their weaknesses.

"THE WAGES OF SIN IS DEATH!" Then is given this information, in the day when man was driven from Paradise. Genesis three, verse twenty-four: "So God drove out the man; and he placed at the east of the Garden of Eden, Cherubim, and a flaming sword which turned every way, to keep the way of the tree of life—(Lest Adam, or man, put forth his hand and LIVE FOREVER in his sins). This is the fullness of that ancient record.

That Straight and Narrow Way back into Eden, the realm of Life was guarded and is still guarded so that man cannot partake of the Fruit of the Tree of Life—AND LIVE FOREVER IN HIS SINS.

And as sin is the cause of death, so is it the cause of every condition leading to death, all the deterioration, the pain and anguish, the misery and old age and the intense suffering that accompanies death.

Therefore if man was permitted to put forth his hand and partake of the precious Fruit of the Tree of Life, without first OVERCOMING sin he would go on living forever in his sin. And in such an existence his miseries and distresses would not only continue to increase, but would intensify until the lot of man would be utterly impossible to endure. And so it was that God permitted death to remain on the earth until man himself OVERCAME THE CAUSE OF IT—which cause is Sin. Death itself is a back-door release from the distressed, agonized tortures of the physical ills and sufferings brought on by sin. So it is through the very evils of one's own transgressions man is required to relinquish the body or temple, which God bestowed upon him in order to endure the low grade of mortality which he brought upon himself.

And it is true, "That through one man death came into the world," each man since that day has brought on his own death. For each man is punished for his own sins and not for Adam's transgression. We have been born into this lowest realm of mortality and are forced to remain here because of our own failure to rise up and OVERCOME THE EVILS OF OUR LIVES.

But death, seen from this angle, as a means of release from suffering, old age and helplessness is a mercy. And so God has permitted it to remain. Yet death is not necessary. It may be a privilege to the wicked and ungodly and sinners, but there is no glory in it. Man was not ordained to die. Man has only to OVERCOME SIN and Death will have to back down and all the inherent ills thereof.

This is verified in Hebrews 11:13-15. This scripture is speaking of the ancient Patriarchs who never lived under the laws (for the law was given because of sin, according to Galatians). However, before the sins of the people, under Moses, the ancient Patriarchs lived not under the law, but under THE PROMISES THROUGH FAITH."

In this chapter of Hebrews is mentioned some of the Patriarchs, the first one named is "Enoch, who was translated that he should not see death; and was not found because God translated him; for before his translation he had this testimony, that he pleased God." So it was through his righteousness that Enoch overcame death.

This chapter in Hebrews also mentions Noah, Abraham, Sarah and Moses, then in verses thirteen to fifteen it states that these Patriarchs all died in the faith (not having overcome completely and thereby had failed to turn FAITH INTO KNOWLEDGE).

Verse thirteen reads thus: "These all died in the faith, NOT HAVING RECEIVED THE PROMISES, BUT HAVING SEEN THEM AFAR OFF. They were persuaded of them, and embraced them, and confessed that they were pilgrims on the earth.

"For they that say such things declare plainly that they seek a country.

"AND TRULY, IF THEY HAD BEEN MINDFUL OF THAT COUNTRY FROM WHENCE THEY CAME OUT, THEY MIGHT HAVE HAD OPPORTUNITY TO

HAVE RETURNED," without dying or relinquishing the body for had they exercised that gift of FAITH fully they would have been able to OVERCOME all sin and advanced into the state of "ALL-KNOWING!" This condition contains the PROMISE that "If your eyes be single to the glory of God you shall be filled with Light and there shall be no darkness in you (no negation, no doubts, no evil, no jealousies or fears or DEATH). And he who is filled with Light shall COMPREHEND ALL THINGS and GOD WILL UNVEIL HIS FACE UNTO HIM!" WHICH IS LIFE ETERNAL!

Such are the Promises of Almighty God. And His Promises cannot return unto Him unfulfilled or void. And the Promises of God can only be returned to Him as man lays hold of them and fulfills them. The PROMISES are in the hands of man. They were meant to be fulfilled in the eternal NOW! Not in "The afar-off!" God gives no commandment or law save He prepared the way of their fulfillment. And man is the Way. As man fulfills the Promises he automatically has the power to return to God for God's face will be unveiled to such.

In Rev. 21:4, is given this pertinent passage of scripture: "THERE SHALL NOT BE ANY MORE DEATH!"

Proverbs 13:14: "The law of the wise is a fountain of life, *to depart from the* SNARES OF DEATH." Chapter fourteen, verse twenty-nine proclaims: "The fear (awe or LOVE) of the Lord, is a FOUNTAIN OF LIFE, TO DEPART FROM THE SNARES OF DEATH!"

The foregoing scripture declares plainly that death is accomplished by ENSNARING mankind. What are the snares? They are often so subtle and so camouflaged as ordinary human traits we accept them whole-heartedly.

WHY AND WHAT IS DEATH? 93

These SNARES are all negative thoughts. Hate, discords, selfishness, jealousy, greed or any of the multiple, ordinary human traits. These are the SNARES. These are the cleverly planned traps that bring on old age, ugliness, sickness and finally DEATH.

A woman I once knew, when the thought of perfection was mentioned, declared emphatically, "Why I wouldn't give up one of my faults or weaknesses for the glories of heaven!" And she meant it. And so do most people feel who have not learned to look with the eyes of loving understanding.

It is only as one looks closely at the ills and evils and the desolating vicissitudes of mortal life and begins to wonder about the why and the wherefore as he begins to contemplate the possibility of a higher way that it is possible to begin to direct one's destiny, and the possibility of escape from those SNARES OF DEATH. Then is it possible to find a way of escape from that "Broad Open Path that leads to destruction" by entering into THE STRAIGHT AND NARROW WAY, *which is difficult to find* but not at all difficult to travel for it is a way of joy and increasing happiness. It is the Pathway of the Patriarchs, who traveled it through FAITH IN THE PROMISES. And anyone on this earth, who so desires can enter into the status of the Patriarchs. He can pass beyond the laws and enter into the glory of the PROMISES through developing his own attribute of LOVE.

Anyone who will take hold of that First and Great Commandment of LOVE and apply it in his life will no longer be under the law. He will have fulfilled all the laws and the prophets. He will have entered the Way of the Patriarchs, which is the contact with God, in which one will be instructed in his actions and in his life and will be directed in the unfolding and perfection of his own individual destiny, and often to foresee God's perfect plan for others. It is a great and holy calling, the calling of the Patriarchs.

The Way of the Patriarchs, that "Straight and Narrow Way, that leads to Life Eternal," is the Way Christ traveled and left the map for. This higher Way is the Way of the Patriarchs, those who LIVED BY FAITH IN THE PROMISES. And this Way has been awaiting every individual on the earth who will only lay claim to it through desire and through BELIEVING—or FAITH.

The law of the Patriarchs is to live by the Promises in a dynamic FAITH in their fulfillment.

In Isaiah, chapter twenty-five and verse eight, this great prophet foretells of Christ in these words: "He who would swallow up death." And this great privilege was offered to all who will only accept it. As the following testifies: "If a man keep (LIVE) my sayings; he shall never see death." (John 8:51). The more perfect translation states it thus: "He shall never see or experience death."

Romans 6:16: "Know ye not, that to whom ye yield yourselves servants to obey, his servant ye are to whom ye obey; whether of sin unto death, or of obedience unto righteousness."

Verses twenty-one to twenty-three continues thus: "What fruit had ye then in those things whereof ye are now ashamed? For the end of those things is death.

"But now, being made free from sin, and become servants of God, ye have your fruit unto holiness and the end—EVERLASTING LIFE.

"For the wages of sin is DEATH: but the gift of God is Eternal Life through Jesus Christ our Lord."

This gift of Eternal Life is offered to all, by God, through Jesus Christ, His Son, to all who would exercise their FAITH to the point where faith would become KNOWLEDGE. FAITH WILL AUTOMATICALLY GROW OR DEVELOP INTO KNOWLEDGE if man will only fulfill the PROMISE of its power. And in the fulfilling of FAITH in the Promises one can become the master of himself and OVERCOME sin and the tendency to accept mortal inclinations and weaknesses as his only heritage.

The ordinary mortal traits are the SNARES that lead to DEATH. But all the powers of Hell cannot force any living soul into these SNARES unless he willingly yields himself to follow the low, human path of least resistance. But man can resist and he can conquer! Man was created in the image and likeness of God. Whenever he rises up and begins to give battle or to exert himself to fulfill his divine heritage the SNARES of Satan crumble into nothingness. Man *can* "OVERCOME the evils of his life and lose every desire for sin!" And Satan, the enemy of man, has to back down. This is how DEATH IS CONQUERED.

I. Cor. 15:26: "The last enemy that shall be destroyed (in any man's life) IS DEATH!"

Romans 7:5: "For when we were in the flesh, the motions of sin, which were by the law, did work in our members (or bodies) to bring forth fruit unto death."

Romans 8:6: "For to be carnally minded is death; but to be spiritually minded is life and peace."

James I: 12-15: "Blessed is the man that endureth temptation (such a one is literally destroying the SNARES which Satan instigated to entrap him into the grave) for when he is tried; he shall receive the crown of life, which the Lord hath promised to them THAT LOVE HIM.

"Let no man say when he is tempted, I am tempted of God; for God cannot be tempted with evil, neither tempteth he any man.

"But every man is tempted, when he is drawn away of HIS OWN LUSTS AND ENTICED. (Or ensnared).

"Then when lust hath conceived, it bringeth forth sin; and sin, when it is finished, bringeth forth death."

Death itself is corruption! And Death is the fulfilling of Satan's plan in which the body and the Spirit are separated. This body is Lucifer's greatest envy. He does not possess one, nor can he except through possessing the bodies of the weak and the wicked who yield themselves into his hands. But as man dies his body is left uninhabited to go down into the grave to fulfill Lucifer's triumphant plan of full corruption and decay and foulness.

The scriptures speak of DEATH in these terms: "And they gave up the Ghost (OR SPIRIT)." Yes! THEY GAVE IT UP! They yielded it up—the gift of life was relinquished because of the ills and ignorance and misfortunes that had accumulated by yielding to the SNARES that had been placed along their paths.

There is no honor or glory in such a relinquishing. One turns his God-given gift over to Lucifer, that the forces of evil might fulfill the completion of destruction to this sacred temple, or body, which man came to earth to gain.

It is true, there will be a resurrection, but the power of OVERCOMING is relinquished when one goes down into the grave.

And there are many in this day who believe that astral projection is the greatest achievement possible to attain. In astral projection the body and the spirit are *separated*. Astral projection is not the great aim or accomplishment. At best it is only a partial, inferior achievement.

In "BEING BORN OF THE SPIRIT" of which Christ spoke, the body becomes completely purified and spiritualized so that it goes along with the spirit. When the pure perfection is fulfilled, or when one is truly "BORN OF THE SPIRIT" the body and the spirit thereafter become inseparably united and only then can one receive a "FULNESS OF JOY!" And only then is his life completely sanctified as he is given the full power of service in the hands of God.

Now, to give the full unfolding glory of man as he was intended to be.

"MAN IS SPIRIT. THE ELEMENTS ARE ETERNAL, AND SPIRIT AND ELEMENT, INSEPARABLY CONNECTED (without death or a need for resurrection) *receiveth a fulness of joy.*

"AND GREAT SHALL BE THEIR REWARD AND ETTRNAL SHALL BE THEIR GLORY.

"And to them I will reveal all mysteries, yea, all the hidden mysteries of my kingdom from days of old, and for ages to come, will I make known unto them the good pleasure of my will concerning all things pertaining to my kingdom.

"Yea, even the wonders of eternity shall they know, and things to come will I show them, even the things of many generations.

"And *their wisdom shall be great,* and THEIR UNDERSTANDING REACH INTO HEAVEN, and before them the wisdom of the wise shall perish, and the understanding of the prudent shall come to naught.

"For by my Spirit will I enlighten them and by my power will I make known unto them the secrets of my will * * * yea, even those things which eye hath not seen, nor ear heard, nor yet has entered into the heart of man."

Then we are told that, "These great and unspeakable things can only be seen and understood by the power of the Holy Spirit, which God bestows on those who LOVE HIM AND PURIFY THEMSELVES BEFORE HIM.

"TO WHICH HE GRANTS THIS PRIVILEGE OF SEEING AND KNOWING FOR THEMSELVES.

"That through the Power and manifestation of the Spirit WHILE IN THE FLESH they may be able to bear His Presence in the world of glory." (Page 251 *"Ye Are Gods."*)

In Isaiah is mentioned those great and unspeakable things which neither eye hath seen, ear heard and which has never entered into the heart of man—THE THINGS WHICH GOD HAS PREPARED FOR THOSE WHO LOVE HIM.

Paul was given a partial understanding of these great and almost unspeakable things as recorded in I. Cor. 2:5-11 as follows: "That your faith should not stand in the wisdom of men, but in the power of God.

"Howbeit we speak wisdom among them that are perfect; yet not the wisdom of this world, nor of the princes of this world, that come to naught.

"But we speak the wisdom of God in a mystery, even the hidden wisdom, which God ordained before the world unto our glory;

"Which none of the princes of this world knew; for had they known it, they would not have crucified the Lord of Glory.

"But as it is written, Eye hath not seen, nor ear heard, neither have entered into the heart of man, the things which God hath prepared for them that LOVE HIM.

"But God hath revealed them to us by his Spirit; for the Spirit searcheth all things; yea, the deep things of God.

"For what man knoweth the things of man, save the spirit of man which is in him: Even so the things of God knoweth no man, but by the Spirit of God."

So it is that these great Promises can only be given to those who fulfill that First and Great Commandment of LOVE! And in fulfilling it they will have fulfilled all the other laws of perfection—and so will receive THE PROMISE OF THE FULNESS OF TRUTH.

II. Peter I:3-4: "According as His divine power hath given unto us all things that pertain to LIFE and Godliness, through the knowledge of Him that hath called us to glory and virtue.

Whereby are given unto us exceeding great and precious PROMISES, that by these ye might be partakers of the DIVINE NATURE, HAVING ESCAPED CORRUPTION, that is in the world through lust."

Death is the great enemy of man and of life! Death is the destroyer of man, his plans and his body. "Death IS the wages of sin, but the gift of God is Life Eternal, through Jesus Christ, His Son."

The gift of TRANSLATION or "BEING BORN OF THE SPIRIT" or the great glory of TRANSFIGURATION, which Christ received on the Mount of Transfiguration, is the reward for those who OVERCOME! The body becomes so purified and so spiritualized, through the perfecting of LOVE and hence in the relinquishing of one's weaknesses insomuch that *Satan Snares* have no power whatsoever. And as one grows and waxes strong in Spirit he is prepared fully and completely to "BE BORN OF THE SPIRIT" if so be he is willing to fulfill the laws of his own coming forth.

This condition of being "BORN OF THE SPIRIT" or TRANSLATED is not only a possibility but an eternal truth.

In the days of Christ this law of translation was understood. Luke 9:27. "But I tell you a truth, there be SOME (which is plural) standing here, which shall not taste of death, till they see the Kingdom of God."

Matt. 16:28 reveals it thus: "Verily I say unto you, There be SOME standing here, which shall not taste death, till they see the Son of Man coming in His Kingdom."

In the Lost Books of the Bible, there is a record of Tecla, a convert of Paul's who was TRANSLATED.

Then, of course, there is the recorded testimony of the writer of those sacred Odes of Solomon, who bore witness of his own experience.

On the evening of November first, 1950, the Pope gave out the information that the Catholics had accepted or adopted the New Doctrine, that the Virgin Mary took her body with her into heaven, even as Elijah and Moses had —and many others. This (New) Doctrine was accepted and acclaimed because there are many records in the treasure house of the Vatican to prove it, besides the many instances of the Virgin's appearances to chosen ones of this earth in recent years.

And so death is the great enemy of life—the accepted lie of the ages. AND DEATH IS TO BE OVERCOME by all who put forth the effort to fulfill the PROMISES of Almighty God and so RECEIVE THE GIFT OF LIFE EVERLASTING!

"Write the works of Enoch as Prophet, priest and seer. Write of his works of purity and love and *how he changed his carnal flesh to flesh divine without descending through the gates of death.*"

"For to be *carnally minded* is death; but to be spiritually minded is life and peace."

Thus it is given that only in the control and the exalting of one's thoughts can the *carnal thoughts* and habits be OVERCOME *and the carnal flesh be changed to flesh divine.*

Christ included among the dead those who had never become animated or quickened by the divine power and love of God.

Matt. 8:21; "And another of his disciples said unto him, Lord, suffer me first to go and bury my father.

Verse 22: But Jesus said unto him, "FOLLOW ME: AND LET THE DEAD BURY THEIR DEAD."

Chapter X.

The Everlasting Power of Love

As one offers his LOVE to God, through that powerful instrument, the heart, he is offering to God the only acceptable sacrifice.

This glorious sacrifice, or offering, is the price that is required in the payment for "THE GOLD THAT IS TRIED IN THE FIRE * * * AND THE WHITE RAIMENT," so that one can be clothed in Light that the shame of his mortal nakedness will never appear. This price or offering is the only price acceptable or required for any of the special blessings of Almighty God.

Then follow the admonition to LOVE with all the soul! The soul is the spirit and the body of man. It is his entire being. The concentration of generated love being directed into the cells and atoms and fibres and tissues and sinews and bones of one's body prepares and alerts the carnal flesh into a higher functioning as it begins to take on "THE LIFE MORE ABUNDANT," which Christ Promised. In this manner the very glory of life itself is increased in its power and effulgence.

As the cells become more aware of this increasing glory of LIFE that power of LIFE and LOVE penetrates into the cells and tissues and fibres and atoms and glands with a quickening, glorified renewing process. "This is the method used by Enoch as he changed his carnal flesh to flesh divine without descending through the gates of death."

As the reality of this process is comprehended and accepted an entirely new phase of existence begins to take place. Each living cell, as a distinct brain cell of intelligence, awakens and begins to also generate LOVE AND LIGHT and thus are they quickened and renewed. "It is given to abide in you, the record of heaven, The Comforter, the Truth of all things: that which QUICKENETH ALL THINGS, and MAKETH ALIVE ALL THINGS; that which KNOWETH ALL THINGS AND HATH ALL POWER!" This holy, divine transformation is accompanied from within, not from without. The power to "QUICKEN AND MAKE ALIVE *is given to abide in man.*" This must be acknowledged and accepted. This great spiritual change is man's to accomplish! It is in his hands! It has always been! Yes! "ALL THAT THE FATHER HAS IS YOURS!"

In this manner of learning to generate LOVE in every cell and fibre and atom and tissue and sinew the body will begin to take on the properties of the Spirit and will gradually be transformed into "FLESH DIVINE." And then one will "BE BORN OF THE SPIRIT!"

This whole glorious process is achieved through the mind being trained to yield its powers to the control of the Spirit, even as a wild horse is harnessed and trained to obey the will of man.

Learn to hold the mind steady. This is most easily accomplished by getting it focused on ONE great desire. As one holds his mind to a one-pointedness his divine energies are no longer dissipated or squandered. It is in this one-pointedness that all desires are fulfilled. As the mind clarifies the hopes or desires and holds to them, without wavering, they are imprinted on the emotions and become engraved upon the very fibre of one's being. And in this method they are "held forth," in the very secret depths of one's closet—"AND GOD WILL FULFILL THEM OPENLY," *or bring them into* OPEN *tangible reality*. This is the spiritual method of creation, whether it be the material things of this earth or the Divine Spiritual PROMISES of everlasting perfection.

If you wish to "BE BORN OF THE SPIRIT" then that desire must become your greatest concern and most glorious HOPE as you yourself begin to transform the cells of your body into a higher quality of spiritual substance. Only in this manner can "carnal flesh be changed into flesh divine." It is not accomplished in a day, not any more than the body of an embryonic infant fills the measure of its forming in an instant or a day or a month. Each tiny tissue and cell must grow and increase in its forming. So is the spiritual form divine brought forth in its growth until it reaches the full developing of its own maturity. Then will one be "BORN OF THE SPIRIT!" The method is perfect and cannot fail. Man can fail, but not the perfection of God's plan of bringing forth.

It is as the mind "lays hold of the best gifts" that they begin to take form in the heart. Then conception takes place. It is as the soul or cells of the body, both physical and spiritual, begin to unite in the generating of compassionate, joyous LOVE that the great accomplishment be achieved. It is in this way that the powers of God are released throughout one's entire being to fulfill all righteousness and to become powerful in the fulness of God's great plan of perfection.

This must be remembered always: It is man who is to "PURIFY HIMSELF EVEN AS HE (CHRIST) IS PURE." And thus also is it man who "is TO SANCTIFY HIMSELF!"

Perfect that Great Commandment of LOVE and you will have fulfilled all the laws—of purification and sanctification and Spiritual perfection.

Heb. 13:15-16: "By him therefore let us offer sacrifices to God continually, that in, the fruit of our lips, giving thanks to his name * * * with such thanks God is well pleased."

Send this LOVE AND PRAISE out through your mind, out to bless and heal. Send it into your heart center as you concentrate that flow or current of LOVE into the great living center, the "Holy of Holies," the "Secret Place of the MOST HIGH," and feel the powers of God sanctify your offering as it is accepted. Only through the releasing of this divine LOVE, through the heart can the heart be opened and its hardened seals be broken. And let me remind you that it has been because of the blindness of men's minds, the *hardness of their hearts* and because of the gross wickedness of unbelief that these great and unspeakable truths have been "Hid up from the foundations of the world." And the powers of them have lain dormant within each man as he had trudged along his grubby, mortal road to the grave. God never intended it to be thus. But God permitted it that man could have his own choice and not be forced back into His presence. "But it is true, that *all that the Father has is yours!*"

As your mind takes hold of your desire it becomes a dynamic blueprint held forth for its own fulfilling. It is within the secret closet of your own soul as you close the door to hold forth the pattern of your request that God will reward you openly as the very SUBSTANCE OF THINGS HOPED FOR" is called forth to fulfill the pattern. And thus "God will reward you openly," or in the full manifestation of tangible accomplishment or materialization. This is the plan and the pattern. And by your FAITH is it achieved, and all righteousness brought forth—or all righteous desires fulfilled.

Practice daily sending LOVE through the fibres and tissues of your body. Practice feeling this LOVE being generated first through your mind and then through your heart, as you concentrate upon that divine center of your soul. Then train your cells to respond in an ecstasy of singing glory and peace and power as you alert them to take up that divine symphony of LOVE. Learn to hold your entire being in this vibrating essence of LOVE AND LIGHT for at least one half hour each day, preferably fifteen minutes in the morning and another fifteen minutes at night. Make it a reality in your daily living even as a musician learns to master his instrument. And know fully, that you are transforming your "carnal flesh into flesh divine!"

This glorious privilege, for so it is, was not meant to be a dull, dead, burdensome ordeal. It is the very power of your own spiritual perfecting as you are not only filled with the Spirit of the Lord, but become increasingly responsive to this divine substance of perfection. As you "hunger and thirst after righteousness" so will your supply be increased until you yourself are prepared to *"come forth full formed,"* "BORN OF THE SPIRIT" and gloriged in truth.

All the hosts of heaven are anxiously awaiting your coming forth as you are released or freed from all mortal restrictions and foul weaknesses and failings. This is the great TRUTH, which one can only KNOW BY EXPERIENCING IT. *"Know* the Truth and the Truth will make you free," from all the sorrows of the flesh! "And he who is free shall be free indeed!" Such is the Promise!

In order to make the foregoing just a little more comprehensible I am instructed to include the following information: The commandment to LOVE GOD with all the mind must be fully considered as the first step toward divine achievement.

The subconscious mind has been named and described in the volume *"Beyond Mortal Boundaries"* which precedes this one. But it has not been fully examined as the realm of the Divine or Holy Helper, the great and Glorious One, endowed with the KNOWLEDGE OF ALL TRUTH, and with the perfect memory and all the facts one has ever learned, gleaned or experienced in the past. In the realm of the subconscious mind is the pituitary gland, which more or less is in charge or governs all the other glands of the body.

The physical body is ruled and governed from the realm of the subconscious mind. When the subconscious mind becomes too clogged or defiled by evil so that the glorious Holy Helper is restricted in Its work of functioning, the body itself begins to pay the price. Ill health, deterioration of the organs and the tissues commence to be made manifest and old age and senility and physical suffering become apparent as death begins to drag upon one's heels.

If one LOVES GOD WITH ALL HIS MIND then the subconscious realm, being cleansed and renovated, the Holy Helper is given full power to function in Its own great capacity of loving service. And the body cannot then possibly grow old, or ugly or ill—or DIE! Thus the physical, mortal body begins to take on immortality—and "the carnal flesh *can be* transformed into flesh divine, without descending through the gates of death."

Every unhappy thought of the past, every bleak, hateful memory, every discordant happening must be blessed —and *forgiven* and *forgotten* and *erased*. Thus the subconscious mind is cleansed and purified and exalted into the true functioning of everlasting glorious power. This is a joy beyond all mortal joys! This is the glory of God in action! This is the point of power in which one forgives all who have dispitefully used him and he prays for all those who have persecuted or misused him and he begins to take on "the perfection of his FATHER WHICH IS IN HEAVEN!" (Matt. 5:48).

IMPOSSIBLE? Try it and see!

LOVE with all the conscious mind and "Your minds and lips will lose the power to hurt and wound!" LOVE with all the great conscious mind and *"You will think only the most beautiful things possible!"* LOVE *with all the great, living, conscious mind and* you will begin to think only the most POWERFUL THINGS POSSIBLE! *And the most beautiful and the most powerful things to* THINK *is to have one's mind open to the power of* "BEING BORN OF THE SPIRIT!"

This holds the keys of all fulfilling! This is the BEST GIFT! This is the most glorious gift possible to receive in mortality for it exalts one beyond mortality!

THE EVERLASTING POWER OF LOVE 109

"LAY HOLD OF THIS GIFT, FOR THIS IS THE BEST GIFT" and this is what the GIFT OF FAITH WAS ESTABLISHED FOR.

As one fulfills that First, Glorious Commandment of LOVE he becomes purified. This is the road of purification, which leads to *Zion, the pure in heart!* And in that state of exalted thinking one truly begins to "COMPREHEND ALL THINGS! HE IS FILLED WITH LIGHT! And HE ENTERS THAT SUPERCONSCIOUS REALM OF "ALL-KNOWING!" And God will unveil His Face unto him! And THIS IS LIFE ETERNAL!

"With God all things are possible!" (Matt. 19:26 and Mark 10:27).

"And Jesus said unto him, If thou canst believe all things are possible to him that believeth." (Mark 9:2-3).

The renovating of the subconscious mind prepares for the full functioning of the *conscious mind.* Often the *conscious mind is* designated as the *mental mind.* It is used for the NOW and everyday living. It is the realm where one is privileged to select his thoughts and the caliber of them. In this selecting is the power of his own advancing, growth and fulfilling. This is the glory of God's great gift of choice, or "free-agency" in which all rewards are held, and honors bestowed. Everything of value must be earned. This power of choice holds all the indescribable glory of man's divine heritage of everlasting splendor. Without it there is no honor or credit or rewards, just existence as one relinquishes his divine prerogative of choice. This realm of reason and choice is also the realm of rejection and selection and of achieving. It is the heritage of divinity.

As one perfects LOVE and holds only kind, gracious thoughts forth his comprehension of joy and understanding begin to expand or to grow and evolve. As one uses his conscious mind to "think only the most beautiful things possible" he becomes as beautiful as his thoughts—or as "powerful as his thoughts" according to the use he makes of his mind.

In ancient times this sacred mind was known by the name of PYMANDER! And man can be its commander or its slave. It is powerful beyond the comprehension of unthinking mortals. It holds the keys of control, of choice, of selection and of progression—or of retrogression, according as a man uses it or permits it to use him. It holds the keys of rulership and within it is the fate, the life, the misery or the *death* of each individual. Also within it is contained the magnificent powers of one's own ability to OVERCOME!

Anyone who permits his mind to dwell in the realm of hate with nothing but the vibrations of discords, fears, self-pity, jealousies or resentments or with his thoughts centered upon sex is generating through his own being the powers of his own destruction. Sex is not only physical IT IS ANIMAL.

In ruling one's mind man becomes the Master! And mastery is the first step beyond mortality. It opens the doors to divinity.

As one learns to control the conscious mind by the caliber and selection of thoughts, that are true and powerful, he leaves the carnal, craven, unclean realms of existence behind. He is no longer just a mere mortal.

In using the conscious mind thus the subconscious mind is released to function in the full power and the

Holy Helper is able to direct and assist one to Its fullest capacity of willing, glorious service. With Its complete co-operation one will be directed into the paths of fulfillment, without errors or mistakes or bitterness or misfortune shrieking out their deriding accusations.

Thus, without heartbreaking effort one can open the SUPERCONSCIOUS MIND, which is the realm of "ALL-KNOWING" or full Comprehension. It is this glorious SUPERCONSCIOUS MIND which rules the Spirit, and is in constant contact with the divine realms of glory and power and perfection. It is as one LOVES GOD WITH ALL HIS MINDS that they become united in a power of full perfection and one reaches the point where *"He comprehends all things."* *"And there shall be no darkness in him,"* no failures, no sorrows or dismays and like the writer of the Odes of Solomon, he will be "Clothed in Light and acquire a body free from suffering or affliction or pain."

Thus the three minds are all part of man's being and when united by LOVE man truly "Evolves from the man kingdom into the God Kingdom!"

It is through this uniting, by LOVE, of the three minds that one achieves the fulness of God's PROMISE; "IF YOUR MINDS (all three of them) *become single* (or as one) *to the glory of God your whole body shall be filled with Light and there shall be no darkness in you. And that body which is filled with Light shall comprehend all things—And God will unveil His Face unto you!"* Which is LIFE ETERNAL!

We are informed that the unveiling of God's Face will be in God's own time, and in His own way and according to His Will. To be exact, it will be upon God's terms and that will be when the individual is prepared and ready.

This accomplishment will be when the mind turns inward with an increasing awareness of the LOVE man himself is generating right within himself. And in that generating every cell and atom and tissue of his being will become filled with the glory and the magnificent power of a complete awareness of his own evolving divinity.

This very training, this evolving, this developing is greater than any experience ever imagined by man. It is the TRUTH of the unveiling of that which man has never before seen, nor heard from any preacher's lips, nor yet has entered into his heart.

And it must be remembered that these great and unspeakable Truths are RESERVED FOR THOSE WHO LOVE GOD! This is the only possible way they can be received. And this LOVE must go beyond words. It must contain the fulfilling power of the great vibrating glory of generated LOVE being actually released. As one practices sending forth this LOVE through his entire being he opens the very channels of his own soul to God and henceforth *God's own great* LOVE *begins to be generated through his heart and this is the FRUIT OF THE TREE OF LIFE!"* And the Fruit of The Tree of Life contains the full power and essence of Everlasting Life!

Only by developing this great LOVE can one possibly KNOW or EXPERIENCE the glory of God's fulfilling. And to KNOW is to EXPERIENCE IT FULLY AND COMPLETELY FOR ONE'S SELF. And the *promise* is that those who fulfill this great LOVE will "SEE AND KNOW FOR THEMSELVES!" This is God's own Eternal

Promise to those who perfect the gift of LOVE. And the Promise cannot be broken, neither can it return to HIM unfulfilled or void! This fulfilling alone can bring the great power of Its glory or actual experiencing. There is no other way to actually KNOW!

Yes, KNOW THE TRUTH and the TRUTH will make you free from all earthly harassments and mortal bondage. "And he who is free shall be free indeed!" He will "Be Born of the Spirit and will henceforth be able to come and go as the wind and no one will know from whence he came or whither he goeth!"

This is the true reality of righteousness. It has nothing to do with self-righteousness. It completely by-passes all fanaticism and the bigoted claims of the orthodoxed, creeded conformists which have drawn near to God with their lips and with their tongues *confessed Him as their LOVE has been taught by the precepts of men!"* The LOVE of which Christ spoke, in reference to that First and Great Commandment, when fulfilled, is unspeakable in its divine powers of utter glory as it fulfills all laws ever given or imagined or taught. IN IT IS MAN'S OWN COMPLETE FULFILMENT AND GLORY!

CHAPTER XI.

The Chief Corner Stone

"And if your MINDS be single to the glory of God your whole bodies shall be filled with Light and there shall be no darkness in you. And that body which is filled with Light shall COMPREHEND ALL THINGS!" Such is the PROMISE. And the minds mentioned are the three minds belonging to each individual.

The subconscious mind, as stated before, is the mind or the realm which governs the physical body and its functioning. It keeps the heart beats measured, the breath controlled, the liver working and all the rest of the magnificent structure of man operating in rhythm and perfection. It controls the pituitary gland which is more or less the master gland which supervises the adrenals and pancreas and the other glands of the body. It also contains the archives of memory and the power of proficiency in all skills, which are the keys of mastery in any profession.

Also within the realms of the subconscious mind is held the keys of one's destruction when misused. This subconscious mind is fed and trained by the conscious mind and it accepts the thoughts that are sent into it— GOOD or BAD. And it acts accordingly for the glory and benefit of each individual or for his destruction, according to his thinking habits. If it is fed nothing but jealousy and hate and filth one will assuredly "reap the whirlwind." For those thoughts and vibrations he releases become himself. "As a man thinketh so is he!" If one's subconscious mind is fed on the vibrations of love and joy and confidence and gratitude his very life will be filled with the wonder of that which he has planted within the depths of his own mind. And the result will be vibrant health and Light and understanding and eventually perfection. James Allen expressed it perfectly in his little book, AS A MAN THINKETH. "Man is made or unmade by himself; in the armoury of thought he forges the weapons by which he destroys himself; he also fashions the tools with which he builds for himself heavenly mansions of joy and strength and peace. By the right choice and true application of thought, man ascends to the Divine Perfection; by the abuse and wrong application of thought, he descends below the level of the beast. Between these two extremes are all the grades of character and man is their maker and master."

The CONSCIOUS mind is the mind in charge of everyday living, of choosing and rejecting, of thinking really. For it is the realm that makes choices and decisions. It is the realm which rules man's conscious actions and decisions. It is the realm which rules man's conscious actions and persuasions. It is the conscious mind that sends all the materials or elements of his own building into the subconscious to be used for his "weals or his woes." "Men imagine that thought can be kept secret, but it cannot; it rapidly crystallizes into habit and habit solidifies into circumstance." (James Allen).

The SUPERCONSCIOUS MIND is the Spiritual mind or the one in contact with the Spirit of Almighty God and the higher functioning of man. It can only be contacted and used by those of pure thought and high devotion. Its powers are manifested in life as hunches at first. It is the source of inspiration and of superhuman strength or ability when called upon in emergencies. It is the source of miracles, delivered upon those rare occasions when it is a matter of life or death, failure or victory when they hang in the balance. But as one "asks or seeks or knocks" this divine SUPERCONSCIOUS MIND is opened to bestow its choicest blessings of understanding and divine powers. And this realm is always there for man to use. "Call and I will answer, saith your God!" "For EVERYONE WHO ASKS RECEIVES: AND HE WHO SEEKS FINDS! AND TO HIM WHO KNOCKS (on the door of the SUPERCONSCIOUS) it shall be opened!"

This Superconscious Mind is mentioned in the scripture as the "CHIEF CORNER STONE, which was rejected by the builders."

This "chief corner stone" is the one Christ was referring to when he spoke these words: "Therefore whosoever heareth these sayings of mine, and DOETH THEM, I will liken him unto a wise man, which buildeth his house upon a rock." (Matt. 7:24-25). The information is given in the *Sermon on the Mount,* for it is at the end of this most famous of all sermons that Christ reveals the reality of the ROCK on which one must build in order to stand firm against the storms of life.

Yes, "Whosoever cometh to me, and heareth my sayings and *doeth them,* I will show you to whom he is like:

"He is like a man which built an house, and digged deep, and laid the foundation on a rock; and the flood arose, the storm beat vehemently upon that house, and could not shake it; for it was founded upon a rock.

"But he that heareth, and doeth not, is like a man that without a foundation built an house upon the earth; against which the storms did beat vehemently, and immediately it fell; and the ruin of that house was great."

And Christ also said, "And why call ye me, Lord, Lord, and do not the things which I say?"

"If ye love me ye will keep my commandments." And these HIGHER LAWS ARE HIS COMMANDMENTS. These are the Spiritual laws by which one gains access to the higher superconscious mind. And if ye keep my commandments "Ye need never die!" When one has gained access to that higher mind he will become spiritualized and be prepared to be "BORN OF THE SPIRIT" and will never die. This is the PROMISE.

Few have ever accepted these higher, glorious revelations as a way of life. Few have ever applied them in their everyday living. And only by the LIVING of them can they be PROVED and their unspeakable powers be placed in man's hands.

This "chief corner stone" this "capstone" that has been rejected by the builders is that divine contact with God through the Superconscious mind. When this Super conscious mind is permitted to function its power is impelling and all-knowing. And it is as one makes contact with that mind that he "COMPREHENDETH ALL THINGS!" Yet man has ignored and rejected this glorious seat of all-knowing from the beginning.

Each individual has built his physical body from the elements of the earth as day by day he has partaken of the foods which mother earth has supplied. He has thus built his body of the temporal foods and elements as he has constructed for himself a physical body. From the day of one's birth the physical being of every individual is stressed as one learns to focus his eyes, manipulate his hands, train his feet to walk and all the other conscious functions of mortal life. The subconscious remains in charge of the growth and inside functioning. But the spiritual part of the child is ignored. Many foolish parents think that filling the children's minds with dead scripture, and orthodoxing them into narrowed conformity stilted by sectarian ideas that they are developing the souls of their off-spring.

The soul is not developed by this demanding, not any more than the physical body will develop and grow by rubbing the food on the outside. Growth is always from within. And if a child can be trained in the principles of LOVE and kindness and appreciation and service as it is taught to worship God in a glory of vibrating nearness then that "Chief Corner Stone" will no longer be a rejected factor in his life.

That Chief Corner Stone is portrayed in all the inspired drawings of that Great Pyramid of Gezeh, in Egypt. Its chief corner stone, or cap stone was truly REJECTED BY THE BUILDERS, even as man's has been. That great edifice of stone is symbolic of man himself. It is a temple of unimaginable wonder. There are hidden, sacred rooms, sealed up and waiting for a generation that will be willing to live the higher laws of Jesus Christ and who are worthy to receive the unspeakable truths through the purification and sanctification of their lives.

The chief cornerstone of that sacred monument of stone was rejected by the builders in the true symbology of man's individual rejection of the revelations of truth and power as he fails to open up the Superconscious mind to that divine contact with God. Yet under the inspiration of the Almighty God, that sacred symbol was selected as one side of the seal of this great nation, which is meant to stand forth as a democracy of freedom and hope and Light to the whole world.

That glorious seal of the United States of America was chosen under the direct hand of God and is engraved to be placed upon all official documents of this land. In the seal, as in the ancient records that rejected capstone is suspended just above the pyramid, with an eye—"THE ALL-SEEING EYE" of everlasting Truth and Knowledge and Power suspended above it, waiting to be accepted and put into place.

The other side of that seal is the Eagle—symbol of everlasting life. Or as Isaiah said: "They who wait upon the Lord shall renew their strength; they shall mount up with wings as eagles: they shall run, and not be weary; and they shall walk and not faint."

Or as Christ said, "Those Saints who keep their bodies (or temples undefiled and pure), walking in obedience to the Commandments (The Sermon on the Mount and the Two Great Commandments of LOVE) shall receive wisdom and great treasures of knowledge, even hidden treasures. They shall run and not be weary and walk and not faint, and I, the Lord, give unto them a PROMISE, that the destroying angel shall pass them by as the children of Israel and not slay them." Which is the Promise to "BE BORN OF THE SPIRIT, that they can come and go as the wind and no one will know from whence they cometh or whither they go."

Anyone who builds his life (or house) upon the Revelations of the Lord Jesus Christ, not just upon narrowed portions of accepted conformity, but upon HIS full teachings or His Revelations, will continue to receive revelations for his own life and time and all the evils of life and the falsehoods of hell will not be able to prevail against him for he will have placed that chief corner stone upon its proper place as a source of divine contact with God for every moment of living.

Yes, "Live my words and you will KNOW OF THEIR TRUTH AND THEIR POWER." For the very power of them will be released into your lives and the gates of hell cannot prevail against them.

"Trust not in the arm of flesh, for cursed is he that trusteth in the arm of flesh," for he is built upon a sandy foundation and will fall.

"Trust in the Lord with all thine heart—and *lean not to* thy own understanding." Bring forth that divine contact with Almighty God and you will be directed in all your ways. And in this way only can you "purify and sanctify yourselves before Him, even as He is pure!" For when He appears it will not be to purify us, as the false teachers proclaim. "When He appears WE ARE TO BE LIKE HIM!" We are to be purified in order to meet Him. We are to be already sanctified and completely prepared!

Within the laws of that divine Sermon on the Mount and those Two glorious Commandments of *Love is the fulness of the power of All-knowing, and All-fulfilling and All-glory!*

Rev. 2:17, is given this glorious Promise: "To him that OVERCOMETH will I give to eat of the hidden manna (which is the bread of life that a man need not die) and

I will give him a white stone (THAT "CHIEF CORNER STONE" OR ROCK OF REVELATION OR contact with the realm of COMPLETE KNOWING and he will be able to COMPREHEND ALL THINGS). And in the stone a new name written, which no man knoweth saving he that receiveth it."

There have been boasting, blasphemous ones who have testified that they have received that glorious stone and that New Name though they have not OVERCOME one single, tiny flaw of their ugly, mortal personalities or traits. By this you may know they testify falsely, no one ever goes forth proclaiming that he has received that sacred experience. His very boasting would disqualify him.

This precious stone, this Rock of Revelation, can be claimed and used by those who purify themselves before Him, and this is done by LIVING HIS laws, not by outward show or boasting. But it is possible for every child of God to begin to use that precious stone or superconscious, divine spiritual mind through LOVE and obedience. That contact has been made temporarily by athletes, under great stress. By them it is called "THE SECOND WIND." It has manifested as *super strength* upon occasions of great necessity. But it is available AT ALL TIMES to those who will only BELIEVE AND PREPARE THEMSELVES TO USE IT.

The contact with this superconscious, or spiritual mind is possible for every child of God as he uses it to grow into the Spirit of Revelation.

"The Spirit of Revelation is in connection with obedience to the great laws and commandments of Jesus Christ. Yes, "The Spirit of Revelation is in connection with the promised blessings. A person may profit by noticing the first intimation of the Spirit of Revelation: for instance, when you feel pure intelligence flow into you, it may give you sudden strokes of ideas so that by noticing it, you will find it fulfilled the same day or soon. Those things that were presented unto your minds by the Spirit of God, will come to pass; and thus by learning the Spirit of God and understanding it, you may grow into the principle of revelation, UNTIL YOU BECOME PERFECT IN JESUS CHRIST!" And this is of God! And it belongs to all mankind if so be they will humble themselves in purity before Him.

This glorious principle of revelation is not the wild, abandoned statements made by the self-righteous seeking acclaim, or by those only mouthing their own personal, vain-glorious desires. This principle of revelation belongs only to those who have practiced and fulfilled that First and Great Commandment in its fulness. Or until they themselves can vibrate and generate love. Only then, is the braggadocia-self set aside. And only then can God's words come through pure and undefiled as one receives the crowning marvel of that precious, sacred capstone—that "NEW STONE" of Revelation in which that "ALL-SEEING EYE" is opened fully to behold the great wonders of Almighty God. Then one comprehends all things.

This is the complete contact with God in which one actually KNOWS or EXPERIENCES those most holy things which eyes have never seen nor ears heard, nor yet has entered into the heart of man.

And anyone who boasts that he alone has the gift of Revelation is struggling under the veil of gross darkness and self-deception. And he may even deceive multitudes by his self-acclaim but his condemnation will be only the greater, for God has given the keys by which anyone can grow into the Spirit of Revelation, until he becomes perfect in the Lord Jesus Christ, as he continues to receive Truth upon Truth until he KNOWS ALL-TRUTH.

And unto such "NOTHING IS IMPOSSIBLE!"

This glorious stone, which the builders rejected, this great capstone of complete understanding contains the very seal of God which will be placed in the foreheads of those who OVERCOME. And the destroying angels have been commanded to hold back their harvest of destruction until "THE SAINTS ARE SEALED IN THEIR FOREHEADS!" They are commanded not to hurt the grass, the shrubs or any green thing until this great, glorious promise is fulfilled upon the Saints.

And the time is NOW! There will be famine over the whole earth shortly! Very shortly! And famine can only reach its full peak of devastation when it blights and destroys the "growing things," the herbs, the grasses and the trees. And that time is at hand. Therefore is the time NOW for man to prepare to receive that divine seal in his forehead as he opens his own superconscious mind to the spiritual glories of that contact with God.

There is still another bit of information that must be shared with the unfolding of the three minds and the power of their functioning; the *subconscious mind*, the *conscious mind* and the *superconscious mind*. They are all necessary and most precious.

The *subconscious* mind is the receptacle of the experiences of the past. Glorify it and the errors and the mistakes of the yesterdays can be cleansed and renovated into their qualified redemption. This mind is also the abode or ruling realm of the Comforter or Holy Helper. In it is contained the "record of heaven" which is given to abide in man. (More will be given on this later).

The *conscious* mind is of and for the present. It is for the NOW! As one begins to become the chooser and t*h*e master of the thoughts he harbors he selects the road he will travel in this life. And he will travel it in honor and majesty.

The *superconscious* mind is for the future in which the great fulfilling and perfection is achieved. And these three minds can be brought into their full functioning NOW as one loves with all his MIND. When these three minds are thus developed and brought into their full spiritualization and functioning, through love, "One becomes filled with Light and comprehends all things!" He becomes "glorious" for his minds "become single to the glory of God" and he will be enfolded in that glory.

CHAPTER XII.

The Caterpillar and the Butterfly

Scientists have discovered an infinitesimal gland in the brain of a caterpillar, that if removed or injured, the worm can never develop into a butterfly. It may go into its cocoon and fulfill the outside laws of its own perfecting yet fail to bring forth the actual inside achievement. In order to fulfill its promised destiny it has to put the outside flesh aside and let that inner-knowing take over. And only as that tiny gland is developed can that full functioning take over. And only as that tiny gland is developed can the full functioning of a brilliant, evolved caterpillar be accomplished.

This should become the knowledge of every living soul, for without that chief cornerstone being used, as the pineal gland is developed and opened one will remain but a worm, a grubby mortal in comparison to the promised possibilities of his full, divine accomplishments.

There is also within the caterpillar another gland, infinitely tiny, located in the center of its body. And man has both of these glands also. They are right within himself. The one in the brain changes the thinking, being personality of the worm conscious, which transforms the mortal conscious man into a new being as far above his mere human condition as the butterfly is above the worm. The change in the caterpillar lifts it above the drab, ugly earth into new heights and realms of vision and grandeur. It has a new heightened awareness of itself and its surroundings.

The central gland develops the very wings needed to match the advancement in thought and comprehension. The caterpillar is no longer a crawling insect pushing and dragging itself along over every obstacle in its path. It can fly above the clods and sticks and stones and mountains of grass. It can travel in a minute the distance that would have required a full day of grinding effort in its previous condition.

The caterpillar is the perfect symbology of man in his unawakened state of mortal, worm consciousness.

And Christ declared: "I am come that ye might have LIFE and have it more abundantly! Even Life Eternal!" This information is glorious indeed!

"Man is that he might have joy!" Joy in his life! Joy in every moment of his living and his being! Joy in the new-found glory of "BEING BORN OF THE SPIRIT" for the transition is literally an advancement from that worm or mortal consciousness of man into the Christ consciousness, with the "power to come and go as the wind!" "Life more abundant!" It is that and more! It is life glorious, beautiful and in its full complete functioning. It is man evolving into a higher state of existence without descending through the gates of death.

That divine capstone—the superconscious mind within man, when developed, perfects that pineal gland and opens that "ALL-SEEING EYE" of divine understanding so that *"he is able to comprehend all things!"*

This holy, spiritual center in the brain is the realm of the superconscious or divine mind in which one gains contact with God. It is the realm of super-understanding, super achievement and super or *full knowing!* It is a realm and a condition as far above the worm, or mortal consciousness of man, as the brilliant colored, soaring butterfly is above its former inclinations and thoughts.

And within that middle gland, located within the great, living heart center, is the one that can help transform the physical cells of man's being into their required perfection that he might "BE BORN OF THE SPIRIT!" as Christ explained to Nicodemus.

This is the true heritage of man. This is the purpose and the plan for man's true existence, that he might OVERCOME mortality. And "If your mind and lips lose the power to hurt and wound your voice will be heard among the gods," and you will henceforth associate with the higher beings.

"The wages of sin is death. But if one OVERCOMES ALL SIN, THEN DEATH HAS NO CLAIM," so declared the ancients in their divine knowledge as they were "taught of God!"

"And they are called gods unto whom the word of God comes!" The "Word of God" can only come (direct) to those who have learned to make contact with that higher, spiritual mind of all-glory as they begin to walk in majesty. There can be no sloppiness either in attitude or habits as one steps into this higher functioning. One's very vibrations must be kept on that highest level of expectancy and joy.

"And in that day they shall all be taught of God * * * and they will need no man to teach them!"

The teachers, mentioned, will not be needed except to instruct others in how to open up their own individual minds and hearts so that each will be able to receive that divine instruction direct from the Father of Spirits—"AND LIVE!" This will be the only function of any teacher. No preaching or haranguements will be accepted.

That seal, or pineal gland, or ALL-SEEING EYE must now be comprehended and OPENED. This opening can only be accomplished through the natural process of developing divine LOVE. It cannot be achieved through force or violent exercising. This sensitized jewel, this precious gem is so delicate and so divinely exquisite it can only be used as it is polished with LOVE. And to be useful it must be held in more gentle tenderness than any infant wrapped in swaddling clothes. This sacred gift is attained through humble devotion and love exercised in the fingers of perfect FAITH. And the time for the worthy ones to begin to comprehend and to gain access to this most sacred gift is NOW, for the time is at hand.

Already the destroying angels are seething in impatience under the command which restrains them from going forth to destroy the green vegetation on the earth. They are put under a definite restraint "to hurt not the grass, or the shrubs or the trees, or any green thing UNTIL THE SAINTS ARE SEALED IN THEIR FOREHEADS!" And that seal in the forehead is the sacred bestowal of man's own crown, the fullness of the gift of the "Chief Cornerstone" with its power of ALL-KNOWING. This contains the power of man's contact with God. It contains the divine honor of man's graduation from mortality.

Everyone of intelligence and foresight realizes that famine is approaching and is already at our very doors. Yet, this devastating evil of destruction can only be poured out or released WHEN THE SAINTS HAVE BEEN

SEALED IN THEIR FOREHEADS. Thus all the forces of both good and evil are awaiting man's reception of that holy seal, which is his guarantee against death and destruction. For the powers of destruction are commanded to "hurt not those who have the seal of God in their foreheads!"

Those days of famine are already at hand. They are no longer IN THE AFAR-OFF. The warning from the beginning being that one "seek first that Kingdom of Heaven (within) so that he will need to take no thought about what he shall eat, drink or wear, FOR ALL THESE THINGS WILL BE ADDED UNTO HIM!"

It is not for me to go into this at the present time. Now my work is to prepare the Saints speedily to receive that glorious *seal* that they might know fully—and understand—AND BE SPARED! And the time is NOW!

Self-righteousness will not fulfill the divine wonder of this holy accomplishment. This is the super-condition of being prepared to actually KNOW GOD! Not just know about Him. And only by loving God with all the heart can one possibly open the heart wide, as the only acceptable sacrifice offered to God in the vibrations of true devotion. And the loving of God with all the minds alone can possibly prepare one to receive that contact with the superconscious or divine mind of God and open that "ALL-SEEING EYE" of full comprehension—"that they might comprehend all things" according to the PROMISE.

Self-righteousness is worn on the outside. It is a robe of display and self-acclaim. It is a garment of deception and darkness. For the one who wears it is deceived, and those without the Spirit of discernment will sometimes be lead astray by those wearing it.

Righteousness is worn on the inside. It is powerful in its fulfilling, though it may be silent in the fullness of its strength. *It is only recognized by its fruits*, not by the gifts put on display. It is all a matter of inward LIVING— not in outward professing or loud acclamations.

We are informed that "God is love!" This is true! But love is not God! Also, "God is Spirit!" This also is true. But Spirit is not God! Love is an attribute of God. It is His greatest, eternal, unfailing attribute. And Spirit is the essence and the power of His complete awareness and the means of His All-Knowing contact with His creations in divine assistance and knowledge of their fulfilling perfection, AS THEY PERMIT.

Again we are told that "IN HIM WE LIVE AND MOVE AND HAVE OUR BEING!" This is also true, but to understand it fully this information must be added. The embryonic infant in the mother's womb has its being in her. It lives and moves in her. But it is not her. And the mother is not it. There are those who foolishly, even blasphemously claim that they are God, because of this scripture. They realize not that they are only held in the womb of Light and Spirit until they themselves can come forth full-formed, as sons and daughters of God—not as God! But as themselves evolved into perfection. And "as man is God once was! And as God is man may become!" This is the eternal TRUTH that man must begin to comprehend.

The fish lives and moves and has its being in the ocean but the fish is not the ocean.

As one loves God with all his mind, that superconscious mind, which is the point of contact with All-Mighty God, "he will be filled with Light and COMPREHEND ALL THINGS * * * AND GOD will unveil His face unto him!" And "HE WILL BE BORN OF THE SPIRIT!" He will come forth full formed, evolved from the worm state of grubby mortality.

And as your LOVE for GOD is perfected you will emerge from your confined state of dreary mortality as painlessly and smoothly as the worm ascends above the flowers and the fields into the radiance of a superb existence as it accomplishes the full measure of its creation.

This is the symbology of man, evolving into his own perfection. And "MAN IS THAT HE MIGHT HAVE JOY!" And joy itself is a spiritual condition and cannot possibly be understood or received or expressed on any mere physical plane of demonstrating hilarity. It is an entirely spiritual condition, and belongs to those who OVERCOME. Or as the writer of the Odes of Solomon expressed it: "Joy is of the Saints and none can put it on but they alone!"

Chapter XIII.

"Health in the Navel"

(Isaiah, chapter thirty-eight and verses seventeen to nineteen). "Behold, for peace I had bitterness; But thou hast in love to my soul delivered it from the pit of corruption; for thou hast cast all my sins behind my back.

"For the grave cannot praise thee, death can not celebrate thee; they that go down into the pit cannot hope for the truth.

"THE LIVING, THE LIVING, he shall praise thee, as I do this day; the father to the children shall make known the Truth!"

Then in Isaiah, chapter forty and verses twenty-eight to thirty-one, is given this information: "Hast thou not known: hast thou not heard, that the everlasting God, the Lord, the Creator of the ends of the earth, fainteth not, neither is weary? There is no searching of his understanding.

"He giveth power to the faint; and to them that have no might he increaseth strength.

"Even the youths shall faint and be weary, and the young men shall utterly fall:

"But *they that wait upon the Lord shall renew their* strength; THEY SHALL MOUNT UP WITH WINGS AS

EAGLES; they shall run and not be weary; and they shall walk and not faint."

This power to *mount up with wings as eagles* is the pledge for the complete renewal of the body as it receives the PROMISED *"Birth of the Spirit,"* even as Christ explained to Nicodemus, in the third chapter of St. John.

In Proverbs 3:3-8, is given this beautiful information: "Let not mercy and truth forsake thee; bind them about thy neck; *write them upon the tablets of thine heart;*

"So shalt thou find favor and good understanding in the sight of God and man.

"Trust in the Lord with all thine heart; and lean not to thine own understanding. ("Cursed is he who puts his trust in man or maketh flesh his arm.")

"In thy ways acknowledge HIM, and he shall direct thy paths.

"Be not wise in thy own eyes; fear the Lord, and depart from evil.

"It shall be health to thy navel, and marrow to thy bones."

This promise of health in the navel is most remarkable. Health in the navel is the actual promise of that spiritual contact in which one receives continual nourishment and instruction from God. As one has health in his navel he can fulfill that wonderful pledge of the Almighty, *"Blessed is he who hungers and thirsts after righteousness* —for he shall be filled with the very fullness of God," which was left out of the Bible scripture.

This health in the navel reaches out for the appeasement of this spiritual hungering within the soul of man as that umbilical cord to God's supply is opened to him. The physical navel has no meaning or use in the life of any living individual after it completes its physical function of feeding the infant body in its preparation for birth into this world. And from all accepted knowledge that was the end of its functioning and use. However, as one begins to "hunger and thirst after righteousness," the spiritual umbilical cord is established and one begins to receive the divine nourishment necessary for the growth and complete development of his soul.

Yes, *"Blessed is he who hungers and thirsts after righteousness!"* And blessed is he who has health in the navel for only through that inner hungering can the purpose and functioning of the spiritual navel be established. The mother does not push the food into the embryonic infant within her womb. It draws its nourishment, as needed, through the umbilical cord. And so it is in the spiritual growth and maturing of every child of God. He must "Hunger and Thirst" in order to develop that contact with the umbilical cord that draws from the spiritual supply of divinity. It is only through this health in the navel and the hungering and thirsting after righteousness that can possibly open up the channel of supply that one can be prepared to "BE BORN OF THE SPIRIT!"

This navel is the point where one's deepest emotions are generated and, shall we say, appeased by the nourishment which God Himself supplies as new truths and knowledge is given to the individual. This is the center gland so necessary for the changing of the physical body from its worm estate into its divine counterpart. And it is true that the "Father will lead you to the Christ (or this Christ center), and then the Christ will reveal the FATHER," which lifts one's attention to the superconscious Mind and its All-Knowing powers.

This promise of "health in the navel" is also given in the eighty-ninth section of the D. & C., which reveals the wisdom of purifying the body as the living temple of God, and the laws that will help to maintain that physical health. Then it states: "And all who remember to keep and do these sayings: WALKING IN OBEDIENCE TO THE COMMANDMENTS, *shall receive health in the navel,* marrow in the bones (which is the regenerating substance that restores the worn out cells to life). They shall receive wisdom, and great treasures of knowledge; even hidden treasures. They shall run and not be weary and walk and not faint (as promised also in Isaiah). And I, the Lord, give unto them a promise that the destroying angel shall pass by them as the children of Israel and not slay them."

This promise of "treasures of knowledge," is the verification of that other divine scripture, which Promise is: *"They shall comprehend all things!"*

The Promise that the destroying angel shall pass them by is the promise of EVERLASTING LIFE—the Promise that Death cannot claim them. In the next chapter will be given the full information of just what those divine *commandments* consist of and the glory and the power of them.

Man is truly the temple of the living God. And as he travels that "Straight and Narrow Path that leads to Life Eternal," he begins his journey along that secret, inner path, toward that Kingdom of Heaven, which is within— where all else is added. We are told, by Christ, that the Straight and Narrow Path, which so few find, leads to LIFE ETERNAL. As one travels this Path, seeking that Kingdom and its Righteousness, he establishes every righteous principle in existence right within his own being. And these holy principles become himself—his very flesh. And when this is accomplished God will truly unveil His Face to that individual.

Yes, "Blessed is he who hungers and thirsts after righteousness!" Anyone who is completely satisfied with what he has and with what he has been taught, and is being taught, will have no "hungering" whatsoever. This dull state of satisfaction is the sure witness against them. For such there is no more growth or maturing or progress. These are the ones who never "ask or seek or knock." They accept. And that which they accept is usually only vomit that is spewed out second-handed.

In one's very "hungering" he expresses an inner desire to KNOW GOD! And in that "hungering" he will receive according to the intensity of his need. Thus he commences his search to actually KNOW FOR HIMSELF. He is perhaps, unconsciously at first, seeking for that holy Kingdom of God, within, in which all else will be added. And in his own searching desire to KNOW he will eventually receive a knowledge of the full TRUTH which includes the renewal of his body so that he will be able "TO MOUNT UP WITH WINGS AS EAGLES!" His very body will become spiritualized and he will be prepared to "BE BORN OF THE SPIRIT, insomuch that he will be able to come and go as the wind and no one will know from whence he came or whither he goeth." He will have OVERCOME *Death*, for this is "Life Eternal to KNOW THEE, the only True and Living God and Jesus Christ, Whom Thou hast sent!"

And here I am instructed to include a small word of warning: There are those who, through their searching or hungering have been given some small portion of Truth and henceforth believe they KNOW ALL TRUTH. But according to Isaiah, chapter twenty-nine, we are told that truth is revealed "line upon line, precept upon precept; here a little and there a little," until one comes to a full KNOWLEDGE OF THE TRUTH, or becomes perfect in Jesus Christ, or in His divine Light. "And no man receiveth a fulness unless he keepeth His commandments. He that keepeth His commandments RECEIVETH TRUTH AND LIGHT, UNTIL HE IS GLORIFIED IN TRUTH AND KNOWETH ALL THINGS." Such are the instructions of the Lord Jesus Christ.

Yet there are thousands who seek to come into the grand Spiritual estate prematurely. They are therefore inadequately prepared for the fulness of Life. Such usually come forth inept, even stillborn as far as spiritual functioning is concerned. They remain immature and never achieve the full power of their own undeveloped, divine faculties.

To those who complete their growth and maturing, as they continue to "hunger and thirst" until they actually KNOW GOD and establish within themselves the very power of LIFE ETERNAL will be prepared to "BE BORN OF THE SPIRIT!" They will "COMPREHEND ALL THINGS, AND KNOW ALL TRUTH"—THE FULL TRUTH and will be endowed with Power from on High as they go forth to do the greater works.

These divinely prepared ones will never be braggarts nor self-righteous, nor go forth spewing out their vomit to feed all who will only give ear to their impotent, immature, inadequate teachings. Those who have ceased to "hunger or thirst," believing they have already received all-truth and a complete knowledge of TRUTH, and therefore are no longer interested in "asking, seeking or finding" are DAMNED! Their progress has stopped. *Damnation* is but the stopping of one's own journey toward perfection and complete fulfillment. It is a defiled condition of unwholesomeness.

Such believe they are doing the works of Christ and that they are serving Him! They are in truth only loving what they do because they love to listen to their own words and their own ideas. But they have never learned to listen to anything but their own voices, therefore they can never hear the words of TRUTH, for their ears and hearts are sealed. It is to such as these, who will proclaim "Lord, Lord!" and demand a great reward for their services and Christ will "profess, depart from me ye that work iniquity; I know ye not!"

To receive the fullness of TRUTH and the powers thereof one must live by the PROMISES, or according to them and the terms upon which they are based. At first this journey along that Straight and Narrow Way is based entirely upon Faith and the diligent practice of those TWO GREAT COMMANDMENTS OF LOVE! This lifts one beyond the mortal laws, which were given because of the gross wickedness of the people, and exalts one into the high realm of the PATRIARCHS, which were known of old. And only then can one be prepared to be taught of God and to KNOW THE TRUTH, and "BE FILLED WITH LIGHT and COMPREHEND ALL THINGS!"

FULFILL THESE HIGHER LAWS AND YOU WILL KNOW!

The Promises have always been there for men to fulfill. Man has failed to see them because of "the blindness of his eyes and the hardness of his heart; and because of the gross wickedness of unbelief." But more often because of his own satisfaction in his condition of self-righteousness.

Centuries ago, the ancient Prophet Ammon gave this sacred information: "Yes, he that repenteth (which means to turn from the outside path to that divine inward path of purification), and exerciseth FAITH and bringeth forth good works, and PRAYETH CONTINUALLY WITHOUT CEASING unto such it shall be given to KNOW the mysteries of God; Yea, unto such it shall be given to reveal things which never have been revealed; yea, and it shall be given unto such to bring thousands of souls unto repentance." So stands the Promise of the Lord. And so shall it be fulfilled unto all those who fulfill the conditions pertaining unto it.

This PRAYING CONTINUALLY WITHOUT CEASING does not mean a fanatical spewing out of words, especially in public places. It includes the releasing of that NEW SONG of inner praise and love and gratitude that flows forth from a gracious heart as it generates and releases LOVE and *gratitude and praise* in silent vibrations of everlasting joy and eternal power that go direct to the throne of God. And along these opened channels will one's blessings flow back to him, until he will not have room enough to receive them.

It is in the releasing of these inner vibrations that the soul is nourished and developed and prepared to hold the full measure of these "unspeakable blessings of knowledge and joy and power" in the great enfolding of everlasting LOVE!

There is another mystery connected with this "Health in the navel" that is now permitted to be unfolded.

There are TWO special, spiritual centers located within the sacred being or temple of man. The first one is that "Chief Cornerstone that has been rejected by the builders."

In Psalms one-hundred and eighteenth chapter, verses fifteen to twenty-two is given this enlightening information: "The voice of rejoicing and salvation is in the tabernacles of the righteous; The right hand of the Lord doeth valiantly.

"The right hand of the Lord is exalted; the right hand of the Lord doeth valiantly.

"I SHALL NOT DIE, but live, and declare the works of the Lord.

"The Lord hath chastened me sore; but he hath not given me over to death.

"Open to me the gates of righteousness; I will go into them, and I will praise the Lord:

"This gate of the Lord, unto which the righteous shall enter.

"I will praise thee, for thou hast heard me, and art become my salvation.

"THE STONE WHICH THE BUILDERS REFUSED is become THE HEAD STONE OF THE CORNER.

"This is the Lord's doing; it is marvelous in our eyes."

Now as one LOVES WITH ALL HIS HEART, the health in the navel is established and that central gland of physical change is opened to function in its full measure of transforming the carnal flesh into flesh divine.

When one LOVES WITH ALL HIS SOUL the cells and tissues and atoms of his mortal body become renovated and renewed.

When one LOVES WITH ALL HIS MIND, he is prepared to receive the crowning glory of that rejected capstone. And that supreme gland of complete understanding and KNOWING is opened as that "ALL-SEEING EYE" unveils and bestows the unspeakable gifts of its functioning. It is then the ability to COMPREHEND ALL THINGS is bestowed. That chief cornerstone is representative of the SUPERCONSCIOUS MIND, which so few have ever used, or even suspected they possessed. And though man has built his physical body that glorious capstone *has been rejected* as it has remained unused. The most brilliant men only use about one tenth their brain power. That Super Conscious Mind, that Spiritual part of the brain has been totally rejected by the builders of these physical temples.

When man learns to LOVE GOD with All his MINDS, that divine, spiritual part of his being, the chief corner stone will no longer be a rejected factor in his life. It will connect with the conscious mind—and "one's minds will become single to the glory of God, and he will be filled With Light, and there will be no darkness in him, and that person who is filled with Light shall COMPREHEND ALL THINGS—and GOD WILL UNVEIL HIS FACE TO HIM!"

That "all-seeing eye" and the spiritual gland of understanding and comprehension is one and the same thing. But it has truly been rejected. Man has built his body from the elements of the earth. He has developed the physical body—but that chief capstone he has ignored and rejected. For the keys to its opening and use is in learning TO LOVE GOD WITH ALL THE MIND!"

It is time for that superconscious mind to be accepted and used, that those who are worthy might receive that precious "Seal of God in their foreheads!" This information must be comprehended NOW for it is time for the Destroying Angels to be released, but are being restrained until the "Righteous are sealed in their foreheads!"

The world is growing daily more wicked, and only by the removal of the most wicked can the earth itself be spared. It is being spared as the very heavens are awaiting the full preparation of the righteous to receive that most sacred seal of escape and approval and KNOWLEDGE AND UNDERSTANDING, and contact with the LIVING GOD. These are the ones who will do the very works which Christ did, namely, OVERCOME THE WORLD, and its wickedness as they themselves OVERCOME MORTALITY and all earthly conditions. And though all the vegetation on the earth is destroyed and there is complete famine upon the face thereof, they will need to take no thought as to what they shall EAT, or DRINK or wear, for all these things will be brought forth from the universal substance according to their needs.

Remember, Christ's last witness and testimony was: "I HAVE OVERCOME THE WORLD!" And *the works which He did we are to do also.*

These glorious OVERCOMERS will have fulfilled the righteousness of Enoch of old. Yes. "Write the works of Enoch as a Prophet, Priest and Seer; write of his life of purity and love, and how he changed his carnal flesh to flesh divine without descending through the gates of death!"

The keys of perfection, which Enoch used have now been placed in your hands. And the great accomplishments which Enoch achieved can now be fulfilled in you.

Scientists have discovered that within the brain of a grubby, crawling caterpillar is that tiny, minute cell or gland, that develops while the insect is dormant in its cocoon. There is also that other cell in the center of its body which is awakened to transform the body of the worm to bring forth its beautiful wings. That cell in the brain is awakened to new dimensions in which the worm mind is exalted and geared to soar above the earth and its searing difficulties.

These cells are also contained right within man himself. The "All-Seeing Eye" is a part of man's very mind substance, though dormant and unused. The Navel is the realm of that second cell that prepares the body for its transforming into the pure spiritual substance—or LIFE ETERNAL, without descending through the gates of death.

It is through the exercising and developing of these two sacred centers within the heart and the mind of man that one can become purified and conditioned to "Change his carnel flesh to flesh divine, without descending into death and the grave and corruption—or "destruction" as Christ designated it.

These sacred keys which Enoch used have never before been revealed. And the great accomplishment which Enoch achieved is now opened up for man to fulfill also. But each individual must fulfill it for himself. He must work upon himself—not upon others in this glorious work of transition. Each individual must become the master of his own inclinations, his emotions and his thoughts. And each individual must purify his own being through the perfecting of that redeeming gift of love. Man transforms his carnal flesh to flesh divine as each cell and atom and tissue is renewed and restored through the perfecting of LOVE.

Christ promised that those who "asked anything in His Name, WITHOUT DOUBTING IN THEIR HEARTS, should have whatsoever they asked."

Connect your conscious mind with that divine, superconscious mind by the perfecting of love as you "Think only the most beautiful things possible!" Then let your heart be softened and opened to generate and send out LOVE. As these two centers, the superconscious mind and the Navel center become united in the great power of expanding, out-flowing love there will be no room or power to doubt, which is darkness. And then one will be filled with LIGHT AND COMPREHEND ALL THINGS.

This is the pattern of fulfillment. The pattern by which a mortal can be changed into immortality as he is spiritualized and prepared to "BE BORN OF THE SPIRIT, so that he can have the power to come and go as the wind, and no one will know from whence he came or whither he goeth." (John 3:8)

It is time for man to arise and soar into higher realms of wisdom and of being as he begins to do greater works than he has ever before imagined possible, even though he has always been equipped with the necessary power to function thus, though never before aware of it. And thus this "Chief Cornerstone has been rejected." Arise, oh, man, and you shall outshine the very stars!

CHAPTER XIV.

The Love for God

In Romans, chapter eight and verses thirty-five to thirty-nine, it so beautifully states: "Who shall separate us from the love of Christ? Shall tribulation, or distress, or persecution, or famine, or nakedness, or peril, or sword?

"As it is written, For thy sake we are killed all the day long; we are accounted as sheep for the slaughter?

"*Nay!* BUT IN ALL THESE THINGS WE ARE MORE THAN CONQUERERS THROUGH HIM THAT LOVED US.

"For I am persuaded, that neither death, nor life, nor angels, nor principalities, nor powers, nor things present, nor things to come,

"Nor heights, nor depths, nor any other creature, shall be able to separate us from the Love of God, which is in Christ Jesus our Lord!"

In that thirty-ninth verse, it states, "Nor any other creature," meaning no individual or being save ourselves can ever separate us from this divine, powerful, holy love of God after we have begun to comprehend, accept of it, and appreciate it.

This witness was given to Daniel of old twice. Dan. 9:21-23: "Yes, while I was speaking in prayer, even the man Grabiel, whom I had seen in the vision, at the beginning * * * touched me about the time of the evening oblation.

"And he informed me, and talked with me, and said, O, Daniel, I am now come forth to give thee skill and understanding.

"At the beginning of thy supplications the commandment came forth, and I am come to show thee; *for thou art greatly beloved;* therefore understand the matter and consider the vision."

Then in Daniel, ten, verses four to twelve, is given this information: "And in the four and twentieth day of the first month, as I was by the side of the great river, which is Hiddekel;

"Then I lifted up mine eyes, and looked, and behold a certain man clothed in linen, whose loins were girded with fine gold of Uphaz;

"His body also was like the beryl, and his face as the appearance of lightning, and his eyes as lamps of fire, and his arms and his feet in color to polished brass, and the voice of his words like the voice of a multitude.

"And I, Daniel, alone saw the vision; for the men that were with me saw not the vision; but a great quaking fell upon them so that they fled and hid themselves.

"Therefore I was left alone, and saw this great vision, and there remained no strength in me; for my comeliness was turned in me into corruption, and I retained no strength.

"Yet heard I the voice of his words: and when I heard the voice of his words, then was I in a deep sleep on my face, and my face toward the ground.

"And behold a hand touched me, which set me upon my knees and upon the palms of my hands.

"And he said unto me, *O Daniel, a man greatly beloved, understand* the words that I speak unto thee, and *stand upright;* for unto thee am I now sent. And when he had spoken, I stood trembling.

"Then said he unto me, fear not, Daniel, FOR FROM THE FIRST DAY THAT THOU DIDST SET THY HEART TO UNDERSTAND AND TO CHASTEN THYSELF BEFORE GOD, THY WORDS WERE HEARD, and I am come for thy words."

From the first moment of Daniel's desire to turn all his love and attention to God his words were accepted and heard. And so it is with every individual who abides by that desire and directs his life in accordance with it.

This contact with God is not made through any personal desire to have God verify or approve of the beliefs one has already espoused, but this contact establishes the time when the individual is willing to turn his life over to God. This is the point when one *is prepared to be taught of God!*

And as Daniel was chosen and accepted from the FIRST DAY of his yielding so it is with every human being upon this earth. As one opens up his heart to KNOW AND TO UNDERSTAND TRUTH, he begins to sanctify his life and his love for God, so that nothing henceforth can separate him from that love. It is when one's own love for God becomes as certain and sure as God's love is for him that brings the full flow of Life Eternal into his being and transforms it into the Life Divine and he will be "Born of the Spirit!" And will fulfill all things!

At the beginning of this chapter is stressed that precious, divine love which God has for us, a love that nothing can destroy or influence. Now, for a moment let us reverse that love, not from Christ to us, but from us to Christ and we will have the full understanding of our own advancement into glory.

As one fulfills that First and Great Commandment, or from the first day he sets his heart to fulfill that LOVE it will begin to become his own. It will be established within him. This is how one opens that contact with God. As one continues along this glorious path of OVERCOMING (all his hates and discords and doubts and negation) he not only generates that love and sends it forth, he, in time, WILL BECOME THAT LOVE! "He has interpreted the very wonder of God and becomes that which he has interpreted."

Then is the power of LOVE made manifest right within man. He no longer thinks of this love as God's love for *him*, but rather as *his* love for God. And in this knowledge is the pathway of fulfilling. Such a one could never be lonely, unwanted, friendless or a failure. He will walk in majesty and be clothed in light. And like Daniel, though a slave, rose to the highest position and honors next to the King, though a captive and in bondage in a strange land.

This same condition was also experienced by Joseph, years before, who was sold into slavery by his brothers.

It matters not in the least how hopeless one's condition might be, "if God is with him, none can be against him!"

And he who develops this LOVE so that nothing can separate him from this love he has for God, neither tribulation, nor distress, nor persecution, nor hunger, nor nakedness, nor ragged apparel, nor peril, nor sword, "Will have *proved* that he is determined to serve God at all *H*AZARDS, and will reach the point of FAITH where he will be wrapped in the power and glory of his Maker and will be caught up to dwell with Him."

Then truly, can "neither death nor life, nor angels, nor principalities, nor powers, nor things present, nor things to come, nor heights, nor depths, nor any other creature (with all their guiles and evils) be able to separate," him from that love which he has developed for God, through Jesus Christ. He will have fulfilled that First and Great Commandment and glorified it and HIMSELF. He will have fulfilled *all* and will obtain all the knowledge and the rewards of the greatest prophets who ever existed on this earth.

This is how the great fulfilling is accomplished. And man's perfected love will be glorified and transmuted into Eternal Light and power and Everlasting Life.

This is how one "IS BORN OF THE SPIRIT in which he can henceforth come and go as the wind and no one will know from whence he came or whither he goeth" as an ambassador of the Lord Jesus Christ giving service according to the GREATER WORKS.

All these Promises are for THIS LIFE as one BE-LIEVES and "lays hold" of them. They are for the Great Eternal NOW and not for the *"Afar-off"*—after death. They are the laws used in which one can "change his carnal flesh to flesh divine without descending through the gates of death."

Chapter XV.

The Fullness of the Gospel of Jesus Christ

The word "Gospel" has lost its meaning during the passing centuries. Each Creed and church and religious organization has believed that it alone contains the fulness of the everlasting "Gospel" of Jesus Christ in its doctrines and its orthodoxed beliefs—or its unbeliefs. Often the meager little truths of Christ's Gospel have become so lost or buried in the accumulation of untruths they are difficult to find.

The word "GOSPEL" is from two old Anglo-Saxon words, which meant literally, "God-spel," or "God's Story," or "God's Message." This message or spell is not just in words, but in the power of the vibrating glory which it estblishes in the souls of men. It is the TRUTH contained in a joyous, reverent understanding of adoration that could not possibly be squandered or dissipated in any unseemly display of outside demonstrating, for it is the inside reality of God's own message of majestic power.

Neither did the word "Gospel" mean the books of the New Testament, which were written years after Christ's ministry, by those who had associated with Him. The books were written to preserve the record of His ministry on the earth. The books of the Bible are beautiful and authentic and true but they could not possibly contain the fulness of the "Gospel" for the "Gospel" or "God-spel," in its fulness, was the exalted FEELING of assurance or KNOWING, generated in the soul of each as he followed the dynamic message of Christ's plan of perfection.

"The Spell of God" is the vibrating glory of ecstatic, breathtaking wonder which flows through one's entire being when he is in tune or in contact with God as he travels the Pathway of fulfillment. This is the Path and the power of sanctification. This is the "God-Spell!"

This beautiful information is given by Paul in I. Thes. 1:4-5, as follows: "Knowing, brethren beloved, your election of God.

"For our gospel came not in word only, but also in POWER, and in the Holy Spirit, and in much assurance, as ye know what manner of men we were among you for your sake."

Then we have this glorious information revealed in II. Tim. 1:9. "God; who hath saved us and called us to an holy calling, not according to our works, but according to his own purpose and grace, which was given us in Christ Jesus BEFORE THE WORLD BEGAN."

This testifies of the sacred, eternal calling which rests upon those who were fore-ordained to serve in the fulness of their divine capacities as the light and love of God would be released through them to bless a world and enfold all things and conditions in God's divine LOVE.

The very word "Gospel" means the "fulness of God's LOVE"—the very awe and wonder of His love and the glory of Its outpouring! This great "spell of God's wonder" includes the vibrations of His power which are released through that glory generated within the souls of men as they become enlightened by the unfolding knowledge and understanding of His precepts of Eternal Truth.

This glorious "Gospel" of Jesus Christ therefore is not just a message of words, printed in the scripture or otherwise. It is the penetrating of that Spirit of Almighty God into the center of a man's soul to awaken love and praise and thanksgiving within his heart. It is the FEELING of the glory of TRUTH, not just the HEARING of it. It is the breathtaking "SPELL" of the power of God being released into the human soul of those who permit their hearts to be opened to that love and in turn send it out under divine control and supreme majesty.

"The letter (or written word) killeth. But the Spirit, giveth LIFE!"—"EVEN LIFE MORE ABUNDANT!" Which, in its fulness, is "LIFE ETERNAL!" This "life more abundant" is developed and brought forth as one learns to LIVE pure and holy, with a spirit so contrite and humble it can continually receive more truth, "until it is glorified in TRUTH and KNOWETH ALL THINGS!" And in this development one naturally grows into the powers of "LIFE ETERNAL" so that "he need never die!" This is the Gospel of Jesus Christ. This is the message He came to give. This is the Promise that awaits those who LIVE the laws He gave. This is the "God-spell" that fulfills every Promise. It contains the very fulness of the Gospel of the Kingdom that is not in WORD—but in POWER. It is contained in man's fulfilling Christ's commandments and in the vibrating KNOWLEDGE of the UNBREAKABLE COVENANT which they contain. "BE YE DOERS OF THE WORD, NOT HEARERS ONLY, THUS DECEIVING YOUR OWN SELVES."

"If ye do as I say, then am I bound; but if you do not as I say then you have no promise!" With each and every PROMISE is the *unbreakable* WORD of God. In every PROMISE there is contained the *unbreakable Covenant* of its fulfilling if man will only live up to his part of the COVENANT. Every PROMISE contains this irrevocable Covenant of God contained within its fulfilling. Each Covenant or PROMISE is eternal, unbreakable and everlasting. Each PROMISE or COVENANT is *new* to every individual who takes it upon himself to LIVE by the PROMISE IT' CONTAINS. Each PROMISE stands forever in the eternal, dynamic POWER OF GOD'S eternal COVENANT of fulfilment to all who will only LIVE THE LAWS pertaining to it. "THEN IS GOD BOUND!" AND THE FULFILLING IS SURE!

EVERY PROMISE IS A COVENANT, Unbreakable, eternal!

A Covenant is a sacred, binding contract between two or more. No PROMISE or COVENANT could possibly apply just to one individual. And it is binding upon both parties. In this case, God and *man.* Therefore HIS PROMISES belong to us! They were HIS to give and ours to fulfill! And the rewards of their fulfilling is OURS!

"There is a law irrevocably decreed in heaven, before the foundations of the world, upon which every blessing is predicated; and if we receive *any* blessing (or promise) from God it is by obedience to that law upon which it is predicated." Or put it this way: "There is a COVENANT IRREVOCABLE DECREED IN HEAVEN, (upon which all blessings are predicated) and if we receive any blessing from God it is by OBEDIENCE TO THE COVENANT or LAW or PROMISE upon which it is predicated. Thus stands the eternal word of God. And it cannot fail! Neither can it return unto Him unfulfilled or void!"

In every PROMISE is contained the power of God's eternal COVENANT of fulfilment, if man will only LIVE the laws pertaining to it.

Take any of God's dynamic PROMISES, select your own, and LIVE it! And as you fulfill any one of those glorious PROMISES you will naturally grow into the perfection of LOVE. And no matter which Promise or law you select to live by you will discover that in perfecting yourself in its fulfilling you will have perfected LOVE and then you will discover that every PROMISE leads to the same end—PERFECTION and Eternal Life!

Below I shall list just a few of His special PROMISES: "If your eyes be single to my glory your whole bodies shall be filled with Light and there shall be no darkness in you. And that body which is filled with Light shall comprehend all things * * * and I will unveil my face unto him!"

"Turn unto me in every thought!" is having eyes single to His glory.

"Love God with all your heart, soul, mind and strength and you will have fulfilled all the laws and the Commandments!" And you "WILL RECEIVE EVERY PROMISE EVER GIVEN!"

"He who is thankful in all things SHALL BE MADE GLORIOUS!"

"Cast darkness (negation, doubting, fear and lust) from among you and you shall be ordained of God and all things will be subject unto you, both in heaven and on earth; the life and the Light; the Spirit and the Power * * *" etc.

"The nearer man approaches perfection the clearer are his views and the greater his enjoyments until he overcomes the evils of his life and loses every desire for sin and like the ancients arrives at the point where he is wrapped in the power and glory of his MAKER and *is caught up to dwell with Him!*"

Or take this one: "He that keepeth HIS Commandments RECEIVETH TRUTH AND LIGHT, UNTIL HE IS GLORIFIED IN TRUTH AND KNOWETH ALL THINGS!"

These are just a few of the PROMISES of Almighty God! Yet they each lead to that same dynamic ending of being "BORN OF THE SPIRIT!"

Therefore this glorious "Gospel of Jesus Christ" is not just a message of words, printed in the scripture, or otherwise. It is the penetration of Truth and the Spirit of Almighty God into the center of a man's soul to awaken LOVE and PRAISE and THANKSGIVING within his heart. It is the FEELING of the glory of TRUTH, not just the HEARING OF IT. IT IS THE ACTUAL KNOWING OF TRUTH! It leads to the KNOWING OF GOD, WHICH IS LIFE ETERNAL! And this alone is the fulness of TRUTH—or the PROMISES or of the COVENANT!

"The letter (or written word) killeth. But the Spirit giveth LIFE"—even "LIFE MORE ABUNDANT!", which leads one on to "LIFE ETERNAL!" And this gift of Eternal Life does not include death, or any of life's flaws and failings, for these are overcome by obedience, which most of us learn through such suffering.

As one becomes "A doer of the word, not just a hearer only, not having deceived himself," he will receive the fulness of God's Promises and the Covenants which they contain.

The fulness of the "Gospel of Jesus Christ" is the KNOWING, or EXPERIENCING of His dynamic, everlasting PROMISES as they become one's own. As His PROMISES are accepted, through FAITH, one begins the transformation of himself into that majestic LOVE of all perfection. This is the Kingdom in which "all else is added unto him," every righteous desire is fulfilled and every blessing is bestowed. It is where all knowledge is revealed and all power is granted. This is the FULNESS OF THE GOSPEL OF JESUS CHRIST!" It is that holy, divine contact with God. And it is not in WORDS. It is a vibrating reality of living power.

It is not made manifest through demonstrations or proclamations. It is manifested silently as the cells of the carnal flesh are gradually transformed into flesh divine. It is manifest through perfect love, expressed in every word and thought and act as the "mind and lips lose the power to hurt and wound!" This is the "Gospel of Jesus Christ in its fulness!"

It is not a Kingdom of words or preaching or haranguements. It is a Kingdom of joyous understanding as the doors of one's mortal intelligence opens the gates to his own spiritaul nature. Then such a one is prepared to "COMPREHEND ALL THINGS!" It is the manifestation of God's POWER being brought forth in the fulfilling of His Holy PROMISES. "For my kingdom is not in word but in POWER saith the Lord."

To make it more comprehensible, let us turn to Christ's own words; John 14:15-17, as follows: "If ye love me, keep my commandments!" And His Commandments were entirely of *Love* perfected.

"And I will pray the Father, and he shall give you another Comforter, that he may abide with you for ever.

"Even the Spirit of Truth; whom the world cannot receive, because it seeth him not." (It is because a man has no FAITH that he cannot believe. Those who do not have FAITH can only accept what their five mortal senses bear witness of, therefore they can never receive of this glorious Witness of Truth and Light which is from the unseen, spiritual world).

"Neither can they know him; but ye know him for he dwelleth with you, and shall be in you. * * *

"As the Father hath loved me, so have I loved you: continue in my love."

"If ye keep my commandments, ye shall abide in my love: even as I have kept my Father's commandments, and abide in his love.

"These things have I spoken unto you, that my joy might remain in you, and that your joy might be full." (John 15:9-11).

(I. John 2:3-5): "And hereby we do *know* that we KNOW HIM, if we keep His Commandments.

"He that saith, I know him, and keepeth not his commandments, is a liar, and the truth is not in him.

"BUT WHOSO KEEPETH HIS WORD, IN HIM VERILY IS THE LOVE OF GOD PERFECTED: hereby know we that we are in him." And if the LOVE OF GOD IS PERFECTED IN AN INDIVIDUAL YOU MAY BE SURE HE HAS "FULFILLED ALL THE LAWS," AS the GREAT COVENANT DEMANDS.

I have beheld high potentates of religious orders walk around clothed in the robes of their proud self-righteousness, believing that whatsoever they speak must be acknowledged by God and fulfilled because THEY have spoken it. And their works and their words are a mockery and a lie. And they know nothing of the Truth, "for the TRUTH is not in them." Neither do they know God. They have only *professed* to KNOW HIM "And have blasphemed against Him in the midst of His Holy House."

"No man is justified by the law in the sight of God, it is evident: for, THE JUST SHALL LIVE BY FAITH!

"And the LAW IS NOT OF FAITH!"

"THE PROMISES ARE OF FAITH" And according to Galatians the laws were only given because of the wickedness of the people. But the Patriarchs lived by the PROMISES according to FAITH.

"If ye love me ye will KEEP MY COMMANDMENTS," declared Christ. He also testified: "If ye keep MY Commandments ye need never die!" His laws are revealed in that greatest Sermon ever given on the earth— that sacred, all-inclusive SERMON ON THE MOUNT, which mankind has never really accepted. And even that most precious of all discourses will be completely fulfilled as one fulfills those two greatest of all commandments of LOVE!"

In that Sermon on the Mount is contained the rules beyond all drab, mortal living, or creed-bound preaching. This Sermon, in its fulness is contained in the fifth, sixth and seventh chapters of St. Matthews. And it is the latter part of that most famous of all Sermons that the witness against those who profess and proclaim in vain is recorded as follows: "And many shall say unto me, in that day, Lord, Lord, have we not performed many mighty miracles in thy name . . .?" etc. And He will profess: "Depart from me, ye that work iniquity, I know ye not!" It is not the ones who profess most loudly who are his sheep, but those who LIVE his teachings in a devotion beyond words—as they accept the Covenant and reality of His PROMISES and fulfill them.

Yes, "Write the works of Enoch as a Prophet, Priest and Seer; write of his life of purity and love, and how he changed his carnal flesh to flesh divine without descending through the gates of death." And not only write of his works as you engrave them upon your hearts, but "LIVE THEM, and you will KNOW of their power for you too can EXPERIENCE these same things!" These are the PROMISES! and in them is contained the fulness of God's everlasting Covenant!

These higher instructions are the "Fulness of Christ's everlasting Gospel!" And they contain the fulfilling POWER and the Covenant of their completion as they are accepted and LIVED.

All the little "do's" and the "dont's" and the "wills" and the "wont's," which are only the childish toys of make-believe in the game of pretending, belonging to those who are "NOT WEANED FROM THE MILK OR DRAWN FROM THE BREASTS." These childish things become outgrown as one steps out of the crib that has grown too short and leaves the scant covering behind that is insufficient to take care of his comfort. And one moves into the reality of the "ETERNAL TRUTH AND POWER OF LOVE, MADE PERFECT!"

"For the law made nothing perfect, but the bringing of a better HOPE did, by which WE DRAW NIGH UNTO GOD!" (Heb. 7:19).

The fulness of the Gospel of Jesus Christ is when the Gospel of Jesus Christ, or the glorious, dynamic "God-Spel" of HIS PROMISES AND COVENANTS brings forth "that which IS PERFECT," as promised in I. Cor. 13:9-11.

Chapter XVI.

"All the Laws Fulfilled"

Paul, in his epistles to the Hebrews said: "Therefore, leaving the principles of the doctrines of Christ, let us go on unto perfection; not laying again the foundation of repentance from dead works, and of faith toward God.

"Of the doctrine of baptism, and of laying on of hands, and of resurrection of the dead, and eternal judgment." (Heb. 6:1-4)

The PRINCIPLES of the doctrine of Christ are the building blocks for the children who are being prepared for "THAT WHICH IS PERFECT." But "When that which is PERFECT IS COME *then that that which is in part shall be done away.* When I was a child I spake as a child, I understood as a child, I thought as a child; but when I became a man (A SON OF GOD) I put away childish things."

When one reaches spiritual maturity he is no longer a child, satisfied to sleep in a crib that is too short and with a covering too narrow for comfort. Neither will he longer be entertained with the rattles of sounding brass and the empty clanging of cymbals. Nor will he accept being breast fed, for he will be weaned from the milk and drawn from the breasts. And all the infant toys of childish make-believe will be cast aside, outgrown and forgotten.

This is what Paul was speaking of, when the principles of the doctrine of Christ will have opened up the way for that which is PERFECTION—SONSHIP—MATURITY and FULFILMENT!

The principle of *repentance from dead works* will be lost in oblivion. Repentance means a "right-about-face" from the outward road of conformity or formulas and orthodoxy ond ritualism into that *inward* "Straight and Narrow Path" of true purification that leads to Life Eternal. This is *"Repentance!"* No outside rituals can possibly achieve this inward development and dynamic, glorious accomplishment.

Neither will the ordinance of the "LAYING ON OF HANDS" be sufficient to satisfy the hungering soul of man. His hungering and thirsting will become so deep and so filled with intense desire to KNOW GOD that only *the unveiling of the Face of God* will appease the longing in his soul. And, as he receives the spiritual food, from within, his growth will be beautiful and sure. He will lay claim to the PROMISES, through his FAITH, and thereby the holy Covenants of God will be fulfilled in him.

And the doctrine of the resurrection of the dead and of the eternal judgment will be bypassed as he moves into the PROMISED PERFECTION, or into the fulfilling of the divine, everlasting COVENANTS of God, for "IF YE DO AS I SAY THEN AM I BOUND." And in this beautiful achievement death will have to back down for it will have no claim. Nor will the judgment have any part. The judgment is only for those who will have to "stand before God to be JUDGED." Everyone who yields his spirit up, or who *"gives up the ghost"* goes through death, and in due time will be resurrected. And all who go through DEATH and the RESURRECTION, "WILL HAVE TO STAND BEFORE GOD AND BE JUDGED." These are the ones who did not OVERCOME in this life, or while in the flesh.

For those who OVERCOME there is no death, resurrection or judgment. "Though their sins were as scarlet," at one time, they will become white as snow. "And their sins will never come in remembrance before the Lord!" This is MERCY! This is GLORY! This is the FULNESS OF GOD'S GREAT COVENANT—HIS PROMISE OF LIFE ETERNAL in its fullest perfection. For these will not only have OVERCOME all the weaknesses and bigotry and selfrighteousness and the desire even to sin, they will have OVERCOME THE LAST ENEMY—DEATH!

THIS IS THE EVERLASTING COVENANT! PERFECTION Itself! And as one takes hold of the Promises he lives by them, according to his own perfecting FAITH, as he fulfills all the laws in the dynamic glory of his own perfected LOVE FOR GOD! In this perfection all the principles and the doctrines are set aside in the fulfilling of those TWO GREAT AND DYNAMIC, BREATHTAKING COMMANDMENTS OF LOVE! And the living of these two laws alone can bring one into that Straight and Narrow Path that leads to PERFECTION—even into LIFE ETERNAL!

As one lives that First and Great Commandment, he will automatically grow into the second one, or visa versa. To LOVE GOD perfectly would so transform one's entire being into LOVE there could be no dislikes or hates or evils left in him, no jealousies, no antagonism, no condemnation or self-righteousness or bigotry. There would be only mercy and compassion and tender understanding.

As one learns to LOVE GOD with *all his heart, all his soul, all his mind and all his strength* he will have opened up and brought forth those "Springs of LIVING WATER" right within himself. He will be completely immersed in them. He will be bathed in them. He will be purified and cleansed in them. And he will henceforth be able to partake of the WATERS OF LIFE FREELY. This great, purifying glory of outflowing LOVE is the literal, true baptism of water and the very fulness of its enfolding glory. This is the great perfection that goes beyond the symbolism. It is the purifying reality and essence of all that is.

Those who perfect the gift of LOVE leave the childish things behind, the symbols and the artifacts of immaturity. They evolve into PERFECTION—for "THAT WHICH IS PERFECT IS COME!" And they completely fulfill the divine command to "BE PERFECT EVEN AS THE FATHER IN HEAVEN IS PERFECT!" as given in the Sacred Sermon on the Mount. This divine gift of LOVE brought forth and perfected right within man himself brings about the WORD OF GOD MADE PERFECT and FULFILLED! This contains the glory of His holy, UNBREAKABLE COVENANT: "When ye do as I say then am I bound!" Take hold of any of His Promises and live by them and He is bound by the most sacred, binding Covenant in all existence.

Yes! "There IS a law IRREVOCABLY DECREED IN HEAVEN BEFORE THE FOUNDATIONS OF THE WORLD UPON WHICH EVERY BLESSING IS PREDICATED: And if we receive any blessing from God it is by obedience to that law upon which it is predicated" or PROMISED! And it is SEALED by COVENANT, and even God cannot revoke it! "Live the Laws and you will KNOW!"

In the holy perfecting of LOVE every cell, organ, atom, tissue, and sinew and bone is *renovated and quickened and renewed* by the outflowing, glorifying element of LOVE! And one becomes this LOVE! PURE and PERFECT and DIVINE! This is the PERFECTION that is *promised!* This is the COVENANT of God with man as the LOVE IS MADE PERFECT!

LOVE contains the power to bless and heal and help restore a world as one moves into the GREATER WORKS, ordained of God, "as all things become subject unto him, both in heaven and on earth." In this achievement he becomes a divine instrument in the hands of God.

In this holy accomplishment of perfecting LOVE one is cleansed completely from the *inside*. Only this great, spiritual accomplishment can achieve the physical change so that "the carnal flesh is transformed into flesh divine without descending through the gates of death." And in this fulfillment the resurrection and the judgment will have no part in his existence. This is indeed the fulfillment of Paul's admonition: "to go on unto PERFECTION!" And as LOVE is generated and perfected one knows that Christ is Its Source. It is as man learns to LOVE and to take hold of this glorious vibration right within himself that he becomes cleansed and purified and perfected. Man is the channel through which this LOVE, or the Rivers of Life (or LOVE) flow.

This course contains the full process of *"The purification of the heart."* And as the heart is purified one's whole body gradually becomes cleansed and renewed. This is how one "overcomes the evils of his life and loses every desire for sin." This is how one "casts out the darkness" and the negation as his mind is conditioned and trained to "think only the most beautiful things possible!" And as the writer of those sacred Odes of Solomon testified, he will cast out the darkness and clothe himself in Light and acquire a body free from sorrow or affliction or pain.

This purification alone can prepare one to "Be Born of the Spirit." This great and marvelous accomplishment was Christ's own experience upon the Mount of Transfiguration.

From that day forth Christ had the power to "come and go as the wind and no one knew from whence He came or whither He went," as when he disappeared out of the hands of the mob on the cliff of Capernaum as they were going to hurl him over. Christ displayed this power many times in his life, the most noted one being the night He appeared to His disciples walking on the waters of the Sea of Galilee. And no one could take His life from Him unless He willingly relinquished it. Thus "the LIFE became subject unto Him." This was designated as *"transfiguration."* Or as Christ explained it to Nicodemus as *"Being Born of the Spirit."* Or as it is known today as the law of *"Translation."* It matters not which term is used the meaning is the same. And the dynamic PROMISE of its fulfilling belongs to those who will "purify themselves before Him."

In this great LOVE is contained the complete "purifying of the heart" as one travels that sacred "ROAD TO ZION." Then it is that the soul, or the entire being of man will be *quickened and renewed* or transformed or transfigured or translated or Born of the Spirit. This is the fulfilling of Paul's command to go on unto "PERFECTION." When the great LOVE becomes the living essence, or the River of LIVING WATER that is shed forth through "the belly," then one has fulfilled all things, and henceforth he will be able to "come and go as the wind." This is how one makes that glorious transition from mortality into immortality. *"This is perfection!"* This is the fulness of the Gospel of Jesus Christ, or the fulfillment of it within the soul of man. And this condition contains the effulgent splendor of the completion of every PROMISE in the great *unbreakable, everlasting Covenant of God to man.*

Yes, "Write the works of Enoch as Prophet, Priest and Seer. Write of his works of purity and love and how he changed his carnal flesh to flesh divine without descending through the gates of death."

This is how Enoch accomplished so great a work and how you too may fulfill so glorious an achievement and bring forth THAT WHICH IS PERFECT!

Yes, that First and Great Commandment does fulfill *all the laws and the prophets* insomuch that one receives every PROMISE and COVENANT complete which was ever uttered by any of the prophets, living or dead.

As one fulfills the laws of the prophets the rewards of the prophets will automatically become his own. All the promises the prophets ever uttered will belong to him who will fulfill the laws pertaining to them. Thus one fulfills *all the laws and the prophets* insomuch that all the honors and credits attained by the prophets will belong to him who perfects that fundamental law of LOVE. On this law of LOVE are all the rewards and the honors of fulfilling based.

It is the love for God that qualifies one to become a prophet. It is the fulfilling of the law of the prophets, or of LOVE that exalts one into the status of the prophets, though such a one may never prophesy. His calling may be far different from the prophets, even to the higher honor of the Patriarchs. And then, through the inner perfecting of himself, he may go on unto PERFECTION! This is the ultimate goal! This is the reward of all striving. It is *love made perfect!* It is the complete accomplishment, for though one may have prophesied in part and done all things only in part or in half-way measures, he will now bring forth that which is PERFECT. Then all *the things that were only in part will be done away*, the prophecies that will fail and the erroneous self-righteousness and the inadequate displays of incompleteness will end "WHEN THAT WHICH IS PERFECT IS COME!"

Man can develop that divine gift of LOVE through living the law of LOVE in thought, word and deed. "And when the mind and lips have lost the power to hurt and wound his voice will be heard among the Gods." This is accomplished by *going on to* PERFECTION as he evolves into divinity. There is no seal upon man's possibilities except those which he places upon himself. Man's own individual UNBELIEF is the retarder of his own perfection.

As one moves onward and upward the Spirit of the Lord becomes the glory and the light and the joy of his existence in its tender directing. And this increases through his own expanding comprehension.

In that precious Sermon on the Mount there is the story of human parents giving good gifts to their children, though they themselves are evil, and "How much more will the Heavenly Father give good gifts to those who ask him?" Then in Luke eleven, verse nine, is given this positive information: "Or if your son would ask bread would you give him a stone? Or if he asked for fish would you give him a serpent? Or if he asked for an egg would you give him a scorpion? *Then how much more will your Heavenly Father give the* HOLY SPIRIT TO THOSE WHO ASK HIM!"

This precious, priceless, glorious Gift of the Holy Spirit is therefore offered to everyone who asks for it! SO ASK FOR IT! "It will lead you into ALL TRUTH!" And you cannot possibly be deceived or led astray if you have this Gift! "And God's WORD cannot return unto Him unfulfilled or void!" "Ask and you shall receive!" This is one of the eternal Covenants of God to man: "for *everyone* who asks receives! And he who seeks finds! And unto him who knocks it shall be opened!"

As one travels this glorified road to Zion, or to the complete purification of his heart he is traveling the "Straight and Narrow Path that leads to LIFE ETER-NAL!" And none can travel this road without reaching the full destination of his own complete fulfillment and the fulfillment of *every promise or covenant* ever given by God to man. And the Highway to Zion is the road to the complete purification of the heart; and it is so simple a "fool need not err therein; though the wicked can never cross over."

As one travels this holy Road to Zion, or to the perfecting of LOVE right within himself, he will reach the point of FAITH in which his FAITH will be transformed into KNOWING, FULL AND COMPLETE! And he "WILL COMPREHEND ALL THINGS!" And "ALL

THINGS WILL BECOME SUBJECT UNTO HIM, BOTH IN HEAVEN AND ON EARTH: THE LIFE AND THE LIGHT: THE SPIRIT AND THE POWER, *set forth by the will of the Father through Jesus Christ, His Son.*"

"And this is the confidence that we have in him, that, if we ask anything according to his will, he heareth us.

"And if we know that he heareth us, whatsoever we ask, we know that we have the petitions we desired from him." (I. John 5:14-15).

Then is given this precious scripture that must be engraved deep into the souls of men. It is contained in I. John 2:3-5:

"And hereby we *know* that we KNOW HIM, if we keep his Commandments.

"He that saith, I know Him, and keepeth not His commandments is a lair, and the TRUTH is not in him.

"But whoso keepeth His WORD, in him verily is the LOVE OF GOD PERFECTED!"

Love is developed through expression, through exercised vibrations released from the depths of the heart. It is generated by thought. It is power and holds the keys of fulfillment. Use it constantly. Use it through prayer. "And he who prayeth continually without ceasing shall be given to understand the mysteries of God and the power to reveal things which have never been revealed."

Pray for the earth and the inhabitants thereof. Pray for every living soul and remember: "Of you it is required to forgive all men!" This is a big order! A BEAUTIFUL ORDER!

Pray for your loved ones and dear ones. Pray for your associates and pray for your enemies or those who have criticized you or persecuted you or despitefully used you.

Pray in joy and blessing and send out your love on the glory of your own exercised FAITH in rays of healing LIGHT—"THAT YOU MIGHT BE THE CHILDREN OF YOUR FATHER WHICH IS IN HEAVEN!"

CHAPTER XVII.

The Primal Substance of All Existing Things

O God, I need new words to speak the Truths my soul beheld as I stood upon the threshold of Thy Great Storehouse, which holds the primal element of all creation. To reveal the breathtaking wonder of its living reality, its fragile, delicate texture, the sublime essence of its spiritual power of fulfilling requires more humility and love and tender longing than any tongue can express or pen write. Even "A pen dipped in heaven" as my former prayers requested, seems insufficient to transform such dynamic wonders into concrete form or arrange into words of LIVING LIGHT!

And so I plead, dear Lord, for the outflowing power of Thy perfect LOVE, spiritualized to its highest degree of excellence that I might make these, as yet unspoken, and almost unspeakable TRUTHS stand forth revealed in their true, eternal splendor!

I realize that in order to share the marvel of Thy Revealing, that I might take the very chosen of mankind with me into these sacred realms of everlasting power, where thoughts materialize and are brought forth fullformed, I need Your special help.

I need Your help, Almighty Father, to make it manifest that "THOUGHTS ARE THINGS!" Thoughts are the seeds, the very life force which must be used to lay hold upon this divine, ethereal substance of creation as HOPES themselves are fashioned into tangible form out of the purity of primal matter.

Give me, I pray, the ability and the understanding to reveal the fulness of this everlasting element, this divine substance of creation so that all who will only BELIEVE may reach out into the divine region of the, as yet unformed, to fashion and to fulfill the Promise of their own sacred dreams. Grant me the full power to place this profound, most sacred knowledge into words that can be picked up from these pages and be used to unveil the very glory of Thy eternal, breathtaking wonder of CREATION.

Let me hold forth this sacred, primal substance of all existing things that henceforth man can fulfill the measure of his holy heritage and become Thy son.

The first step is with man's own requesting and his needs as he begins to envision or desire beyond his meager, mortal destitution. "Because thou sayest thou art rich and increased with goods and have need of nothing, and knowest not that thou art poor and wretched and miserable and blind and naked—." And so it is that the mere earthly treasures, that moth and rust can corrupt, lose their glamour and their imagined worth as one moves into the divine realm of pure substance.

Matthew chapter six and verses five and six, states: "And when thou prayest thou shalt not be as the hypocrites are: for they love to pray standing in the synagogues and in the corners of the streets, that they may be seen of men. Verily I say unto you, they have their reward.

"But thou, when thou prayest, enter into thy closet and when thou hast shut the door, pray to the Father which is in secret; and thy Father which seeth in secret shall reward thee openly."

That "Secret Closet" is not one's clothes press, as many assume. It is the "Holy of Holies" in a man's own being, "The Secret Place of the Most High," the very center of one's own soul. Then, closing the mind to all outside distraction, pray to the Father and He will reward you OPENLY, or bring out into the open, tangible world the fulfillment of your requests.

Go into the center and hold forth your heart's desire. And remember, that in that same chapter of Matthew is given these words also: *"The Father knows what you have need of before you ask."*

The Father truly knows what you have need of in order to continue your own growth and progress. And if you have not prepared yourself to receive the fulness of your request He will grant you the necessary opportunities to grow into the things you may desire. And to begin with, the things you *desire* may not be the things you *require* or *have need of*. But as you ask, the Father, knowing what your actual need is, will supply the required condition and provide you with the opportunity for your own development.

The fulness of power cannot possibly be granted to those unprepared or unworthy to receive. However, as one "lays hold of the best gifts" with his mind, according to his own desiring, he will gradually be prepared for the complete fulfillment, or reception of his own requests, full formed.

THE PRIMAL SUBSTANCE OF ALL EXISTING THINGS   175

As one holds mentally, to his own most sacred desires, closing his conscious thinking to all lesser issues and distractions, he will be prepared speedily to receive all that his mind can HOPE for or conceive of. And thus God will reward him openly or bring forth into tangible existence the full measure of his requests. And they will be fulfilled in their fullest, solid, compact reality.

As one closes the door to all the lesser, immaterial wants and holds forth the "Very Best gifts," the deepest yearnings of his own soul, the highest of his aspirations, he literally lays hold of the Primal Element of Creation, which is the divine element of LIGHT! And that element or substance of LIGHT takes form and appears in the OPEN, fulfilled and completely evident as it becomes tangible in visible form—the HOPES of men embodied and made solid.

This primal substance, this glorified element or material of all fulfillment is the very substance of all creation and of all created things. It is divinely glorious! In this LIGHT there can be no darkness, doubts, fears or negation. It is pure perfection, ethereal and divinely exquisite. When generated by FAITH it becomes powerful. And man can generate and use it, "for all that the Father has is yours!" And this is the substance of which worlds were made and brought into form out of the unformed and void. This divine, holy element of all creation, this spiritual substance of LIGHT contains the fulness of all existing things and of all supply and of all forming and power.

And the Father Who knoweth your needs, before you ask, comprehends your individual, personal requirements. Therefore are His Premises made plain so that anyone who will only alert himself into a state of desiring will be prepared to receive the advanced qualification of HOPING.

The Father, knowing before you ask, what you have need of is overwhelming in its truth. I shall try to clarify it this way: a little boy has lost his shoes and therefore shoes are what he has need of. His older brother is going to graduate and he needs a new suit. The father's barn has burned down and his need is for a new barn. The mother's need is for a small storeroom to hold the clutter of provisions and extra odds and ends in order that she can keep the home more orderly. No two needs are quite the same. The little boy could not use the brother's suit or his father's barn or his mother's storeroom. The father could not use his son's clothing. So each, according to his own needs is answered and supplied from the Father's great storehouse, according to his faith, or ability to desire or to ask or to use.

The *higher, spiritual blessings* are for those who have grown into the vision and understanding of them. They are not for the unprepared. And only as the great Promises of Almighty God are comprehended, accepted and desired can the blessings of their fulfillment be brought forth openly or into the open, tangible world of concrete form.

Therefore I adjure you, *"Lay hold of the best gifts!"* And as you lift your minds above mortal, physical desires of worldly possessions you will advance into the higher desires of the Holy PROMISES, or into your own fulfilling—your own perfection—and into the state where "ALL ELSE WILL BE ADDED!" Both the material and spiritual blessings will flow to you.

The very first step to fulfillment often comes as a fleeting flash upon the screen of the mind as a pleasant vision—a wish, to be more exact. And if not taken hold of it dissolves and vanishes away like mist. If held onto it will expand into a dream as the mind develops the ability to take hold of so fragile an essence as a fleeting wish. But as it is entertained, held onto so begins its inception. Then the dream, if not eliminated or destroyed by doubting and unbelief, will evolve or mature into a desire. And as desire matures, if nurtured properly, it develops into a HOPE. And HOPE is the substance of FAITH, which holds within it the power of generated activity that brings it to fruition.

"FAITH IS THE SUBSTANCE," the essence, the divine living energy or element "OF THINGS HOPED FOR" as it generates them into form.

"*Faith* IS *Hope*, motivated into action. *Faith* is the activating life force of the primal substance of all the things that Hope can conceive of. *Faith* is the generator of LIGHT. *Faith* IS *HOPE* in its invigorated, living fulness. FAITH is the life producing energy of the great divine LIGHT of creation and of which all things are originally composed. Light itself is the primal element which FAITH fashions and forms into fulfillment. It belongs to God! It is composed of Spirit and is exquisite beyond description or understanding. And the Father has offered it freely to His children on earth, for "ALL that the Father has is yours!"

As one learns to use this glorious, primal substance or element of Light, by exercising Faith, he moves onward and upward into the realms of ever higher and increasing requirements or needs as he receives the fulfillment of every divine PROMISE, the power of his own OVERCOMING, the glory of his own perfection and becomes a part of God's living Covenant, for every PROMISE of God is sealed with the Heavenly Father's own COVENANT OF FULFILLMENT. And as one advances the requirements expand even to the point where a new heaven will be formed and a new earth—or world.

This realm, this region of "THE NEW PIONEERING," this Kingdom of creating, is not only to be used for temporary requirements or desires or blessings for when it is mastered it is forever and forever a blessing of increasing glory and achievement, reaching beyond earth and time—and on into eternity.

This NEW REALM, this higher spiritual Kingdom, or region, or domain of the primal, creative material can be used NOW as one exercises the FAITH to bring it into form. As one uses this dynamic power of creation he becomes the Master in a joyous, victorious glory of divine accomplishment.

It is as one casts out the darkness and begins to COMMAND the LIGHT that he becomes a singing glory of Praise and Love and gratitude. It is these mastered vibrations of which the Celestial Song of Creation is composed. Thus one can begin to form a new world by altering his surroundings. He can transform every condition into peace and glory as he clothes himself in LIGHT. And as he becomes filled with LIGHT it becomes subject unto him and must obey his command.

And now, this glorious PROMISE of Almighty God must be repeated here: "That which is of God is LIGHT; and he that receiveth LIGHT, and continueth in God, receiveth more LIGHT; and that LIGHT groweth brighter until the perfect day" (or until he himself is perfected).

"And again, verily I say unto you, and I say it that you may chase darkness from among you:

"He that is ordained of God and sent forth, the same is appointed to be the greatest, notwithstanding he is the least and the servant of all.

"*Wherefore he is possessor of all things; for all things are subject unto him, both in heaven and on earth, the life, and the Light, the Spirit and the Power sent forth by the will of the Father through Jesus Christ, his son.*

"BUT NO MAN IS POSSESSOR OF ALL THINGS EXCEPT HE BE PURIFIED FROM ALL SIN.

"AND IF YE ARE PURIFIED AND CLEANSED FROM ALL SIN, YE SHALL ASK WHATSOEVER YOU WILL IN THE NAME OF JESUS AND IT SHALL BE DONE!" (D. & C. 50:24-29).

This power to receive whatsoever one asks is the power to command the LIGHT and to fashion and to form it, through FAITH, into any desired manifestation or condition or substance.

This is how all things become subject unto one. It is accomplished by casting out the darkness of doubting and despair and fear and negation. And this is accomplished through PRAISE and LOVE and GRATITUDE! Then only is one able to take hold of the LIGHT that he might comprehend all things and fulfill all things as he clothes himself in LIGHT. This is how the LIGHT becomes subject unto any individual, as God PROMISED in the beginning.

The LIFE becomes subject unto one as he takes hold of the vibrating force of FAITH and uses it to fulfill and to accomplish all things as he fashions the LIGHT into the ideals, or conditions or objects held forth for forming. Faith is the LIFE force as it is generated into action by the believing mind of man.

The SPIRIT becomes subject unto one as he uses his highest intelligence to fulfill and to comprehend and to manipulate or bring into BIRTH the pure matter or the Great LIGHT of all Creation. One must learn to command and to control the Spirit instead of permitting himself to become a chattering demonstrator, manifesting in some weird, unseemly manner. The Spirit is the glory of pure intelligence which is meant to be held in complete control. As this is understood and accomplished one becomes the Master and these unspeakable POWERS become subject unto him.

Then it is that one is given the full POWER to comprehend all things and to glorify all conditions and all things. This is the fulness of the POWER which also becomes subject unto man as he prepares himself to bring it into subjection for it was and is meant to be subject unto all who cast out the darkness of unbelief and doubting and who purify themselves from all sin.

These forces are of heaven and can be used on this earth, for to him who purifies himself all things become subject, both in heaven and on earth; the LIFE and the LIGHT and the SPIRIT and the POWER. Majesty belongs to him who becomes majestic, through control, awakened understanding and through purification.

From the most ancient records of the world comes this information: "O my son, matter becomes; formerly it was, for matter is the vehicle of becoming. Becoming is the mode of activity of the uncreate and foreseeing God. Having been endowed with the germ of becoming matter is brought into BIRTH, for the creative force (of FAITH) fashions it according to the ideal forms. Matter not yet engendered has no form: it becomes when it is put into operation * * *."

This POWER of transforming that which is without form and void into tangible substance and blessings is contained in the ability to use FAITH which alone can form and fashion the LIGHT into tangible realities. This is accomplished through LOVE and through FAITH generated into action.

"And to know the love of Christ, which passeth knowledge, that we might be filled with the fulness of God." (Eph. 3:19)

"Behold, now are we the sons of God, (as we LIVE his teachings) and it doth not yet appear what we shall be: but we know that when he shall appear we shall be like him, for we shall see him as he is.

"AND EVERY MAN THAT HATH THIS HOPE PURIFIETH HIMSELF, EVEN AS HE IS PURE!" (I. John 3:24).

CHAPTER XVIII.

The Cosmic Power of Light Generated by Faith

The first command and law of creation is: "LET THERE BE LIGHT!" *Light is the primal substance of all existing things.* All things are formed of the element of Light and from it. And Light is generated and put into action by the power of FAITH, which contains the energy of creating or bringing forth into form. FAITH and Light are always united in form and substance in the potency of their energized creating. They belong together. They are one. Where there is no Light FAITH cannot exist. And when there is no Faith LIGHT cannot manifest.

"Ask, believing that you shall receive and you shall have whatsoever you ask."

Or: "If you ask anything and doubt not in your heart you shall have whatsoever you saith."

"Without FAITH it is impossible to please God!" No wonder! Without *faith* there can be no hope, no vision, no *Light* and consequently no power of fulfilment. "And he who is without hope must needs be in despair; and despair cometh because of iniquity," or because he is filled with darkness or doubts or negation. He has lost his contact with God and the powers thereof. And that very contact with God is Light. And Light is manifest in joy and praise and love and thanksgiving and in great inner rejoicing.

Darkness is manifest in hopelessness, in despair, in unbelief and in doubting and in all types and degrees of negation and suffering. The darkness is the powers of destruction and disintegration at work, whether upon one's body or his mind or his surroundings or affairs.

"Cast out the darkness from among you and you shall be ordained of God and sent forth * * * and all things will become subject unto you, both in heaven and on earth: the LIGHT and the LIFE: the SPIRIT and the POWER" to use the LIGHT of Creation to glorify your life and all things that come into it and to receive every blessing you could possibly hope for or desire.

As one learns to cast ou the darkness from his mind and from his feelings and his being he becomes the Master of the Light or the Master of the very powers of Creation. That Celestial Song of Praise and Love and joyous gratitude becomes the divine Creative MELODY OF HIS LIFE. And his life becomes an increasing unfolding of progressive achievements as he "Clothes himself in Light" which contains the power and intelligence to "Comprehend all things!" Thus flows from such a one the power, as he lets his Light shine forth, not in an ego-crazed desire to pound and club others with his beliefs and opinions, but with the healing benediction of his own selfless love. Then truly he automatically becomes "the least and the servant of all."

As one sends forth this Light in a blessing of true, compassionate *love* he will be able to help glorify the world—and heaven—with the very powers that will be vested in him.

THESE ARE THE PROMISES! And *they are yours!*

"Cast out the darkness! Cast out your fears by *love*, for *perfect love casts out all fear!"* Cast out your worries which are but the darkness manifesting in every negation or every negative idea of doubt. Cast out your desperate, moody feeling or moments of despair and hopelessness by praise and love and gratitude and the LIGHT will flow into your being to fill the void left by the elimination of the darkness. This is how one OVERCOMES THE DARKNESS!

This is how one becomes the Master of the Light insomuch that it truly becomes subject unto him. This is how one brings into subjection all things: "For *all things* become subject unto him; both in heaven and on earth; the LIGHT and the LIFE; the SPIRIT and the POWER!" And in that *power* is contained the understanding to use the Creative Light or the divine Substance of Creation for forming the things and the conditions of perfection and everlasting joy as one becomes the master of his LIFE and receives the power to exalt it into everlasting glory, without descending through the gates of death.

And the SPIRIT will become subject unto him as he learns not to dissipate or squander the breathtaking wonder of Its God-given revealing. It is in the glory and the majesty of this divine self-control that the SPIRIT is brought into subjection or into Its highest service of perfected excellence. It is never mastered by any desecration of unseemly display. Only majesty can bring it into subjection. And only when the little, egoself ceases to demand all credits and rewards and glory. It is only as the Holy Spirit, or divine Messenger of God is placed on the throne that the Spirit can be glorified and then glorify one's actions with its perfect power of unified companionship.

As one gives forth that divine, all-powerful FIAT: *"Let there be Light"* he is not thinking of himself at all. He could not possibly be. In the glory of God's great Light and Power of Creating, and of bringing forth, the self is forgotten and cast aside.

The *Light*, plus its energizing glory of Faith, is put into action as man begins to become filled with Light— the Light of comprehension, devoid of doubts and darkness.

This LIGHT is sent out from the great *Central Sun*, the very throne of God, and is held forth for man to use, "For all that the Father has is yours!" And "It is the good pleasure of God to give you the Kingdom" of glory and expansion and joy and comprehension and everlasting Power.

From this great Central Source of Light the tiny, infinitesimal rays of Cosmic, universal LIGHT are rayed out to bring life and intelligence and the powers of creation in continual streams of everlasting out-flowing.

Many of these cosmic rays, as they hit the atmosphere of the earth are transformed into atoms. In this transformation the Light Ray is curled upon itself, holding within its nucleus the everlasting wonder of God and the very fulness of His creative power. Every atom is a living, minute cell of intelligence and dynamic glory. And each atom is a marvel of divine, perfect creation. This is the unspeakable power and wonder of God's own glory, for it is true that the very power and intelligence of God "Is in the midst of all things!" Yes! This Light or power is contained within the nucleus of every atom, every man and every inspired idea.

And the great truth of existence is contained in this unfailing power of fulfilling: "As you cast out the darkness from among you you shall be ordained of God and sent forth" to serve in a capacity as you have never before imagined for the very element of creation will become yours to use and to create with. And you will be able to transform those cosmic rays of Light into atoms to form the perfection of your requests. This is the exact opposite of the work of the present day scientists as they use it in reverse, splitting the atoms apart. They do not yet know the supreme or higher power of bringing atoms into being by using and transforming the Light.

And it becomes a simple procedure to use this Light even as the glorious writer of the "Odes of Solomon" declared: "I cast out darkness and clothed myself in LIGHT, and acquired a body free from sorrow or affliction or pain."

Then again is given this wondrous information: "If your eyes be single to my glory your whole bodies shall be filled with LIGHT and there shall be no darkness in you. And that body which is filled with LIGHT shall comprehend all things!"

Any individual on this earth has the power and the right to cast out their own negatious thoughts and feelings of darkness; their doubts and their fears and their evils as they hold out that Almighty *fiat:* "LET THERE BE LIGHT!" As Light is generated, or used one becomes more and more cognizant of its power and the glory of its creative purpose.

As one holds forth a desire, true and well-formed, he can, with his mind shape the mold or pattern which THE LIGHT WILL FILL, first with the spiritual design of his enlightened thinking, then with its condensed reality as those cosmic rays of living Light are transformed into tangible atoms and molded into the shape of man's requests or desires. This is the gift of creation being used to bring forth the "ALL ELSE THAT WILL BE ADDED," when one finds that Kingdom of Heaven, which he is instructed to seek for FIRST and above all else. And it is true: "That all that the Father has is yours"—to use, to enjoy and to develop and to increase and enhance.

Learn to overcome the darkness and the LIGHT *will become subject unto you.* It will bring you joy and happiness and peace and POWER and the fulness of understanding insomuch that "you will comprehend all things and all things will become subject unto you, both in heaven and on earth, the LIGHT and the LIFE and the SPIRIT and the POWER" with which to form the most glorious, gracious gifts possible to imagine or desire as you use the *power* to create the fulness of your own envisioning.

LIGHT and FAITH are the primal substance, the creative material or the foundation element of all existing things. They are also the very substance or essence of the things or material HOPED FOR. This Faith-engendered Light is the fact or *evidence* or the very proof of things unseen, waiting but the touch of man's imagining to transform it into tangible existence as it awaits its own opportunity of *"becoming."*

Learn to take hold of the LIGHT mentally, at first. The LIGHT eliminates the darkness, dispels the gloom and banishes the despairs for within it is joy and understanding and the power of all creative fulfilling. And "Joy is of the Saints and none can put it on but they alone!" *Joy* IS *Light* and limitless happiness and power brought into complete subjection as it is brought to obey your commands. Within it is the keys of LIFE—even of LIFE EVERLASTING AS THE GENERATIVE ENERGY OF FAITH molds or fashions it into form.

At first this holy substance of Creation, this divine essence of Spiritual Faith-engendered LIGHT, is so sacred it is almost intangible. It is exquisitely divine and is dfficult to comprehend and to take hold of. It is so spiritually perfect and glorious it is almost impossible to fathom it even in thought. One must look upon it with his higher, mental vision as desires or HOPES become generated and stirred into the pattern of their forming by that unspeakable element of FAITH. And only the power of FAITH itself can give one the ability to behold the true power and glory of the divine, creative essence of all perfecting—the very substance of all creation.

FAITH is the energy that manipulates the LIGHT. FAITH is an integral ingredient of LIGHT. FAITH contains the determining factor of action. The LIGHT is activated and set in motion by the substance of FAITH. FAITH contains the divine element of fashioning as the LIGHT is generated into formation for until it is activated or moved upon it is without form or void. This holy substance of all fulfilling is brought into physical existence through unwavering desires held forth in the mind of men —or Gods. FAITH is the living embodiment of HOPE as it generates the LIGHT into materialization. Therefore as you fashion your dreams into desires and your desires into HOPE be sure it is the most, pure, ardent

THE COSMIC POWER OF LIGHT GENERATED BY FAITH 189

request possible for your soul to conceive. *Then never doubt it!* BELIEVE IN IT! This is your own claim as you stake out a portion of the divine, spiritual substance or Kingdom for your very own.

Believe in the possibility of your HOPE taking form! Thank God for it! Cherish it! Love is as you would love a little child and be as protective of it as you shield it from the destructive forces of doubting. Rejoice in it continually! *"For we are saved* by HOPE; for what a man seeth, why doth he yet Hope for; but if we Hope for that we see not, then do we with patience wait for it." (Romans 8:24-25).

FAITH and LIGHT are so intermingled it is difficult to separate them. One is an integral part of the other. Without Light there can be no Faith. And without Faith there can be no Light made manifest to fulfill the glory of the Promises Hope envisions in the human heart. Light and Faith are twin powers, walking hand in hand as they stand poised upon the spiritual borders of *here* and *there*. And these stupendous powers are but awaiting the touch of man's mental command to swing into action and do his bidding as they fulfill his holy requests or decrees. The glory of the Creative element of Light, and Faith, the soul and life of its substance are man's to use. And they are powerful beyond man's, as yet unawakened imagining. "For all that the Father has is yours!"

"The Spirit of Revelation is in connection with these blessings. A person may profit by noticing the first intimation of the Spirit of Revelation; for instance, when you feel pure intelligence flowing into you, it may give you sudden strokes of ideas, so that by noticing it, you may find it fulfilled the same day or soon; (i.e.)*those things that were presented unto your minds by the Spirit of God will come to pass:* and thus by learning the Spirit of God and understanding it, you may grow into the principle of revelation, until you become perfect in Christ Jesus." (Joseph Smith, the American Prophet). It is through this divine gift of REVELATION that one's mind is conditioned and opened to behold and to desire the BEST GIFTS, and to bring them into manifestation. (See next chapter for Spirit of Revelation).

"We consider that God created man with a mind capable of instruction, and a faculty which may be enlarged in proportion to the heed and diligence given to the Light communicated from heaven to the intellect; and that the nearer man approaches perfection the clearer are his views, and the greater his enjoyments, till he has overcome the evils of his life and lost every desire for sin; and like the ancients, arrives at the point of faith where he is wrapped in the power and glory of his Maker and is caught up to dwell with Him. But we consider that this is a station at which no man ever arrived in a moment; he must have been instructed in the laws and the government of that Kingdom by proper degrees, until his mind is capable in some measure of comprehending the propriety, justice, equality and consistency of the same."

Since this perfection and the power to fulfill must be attained gradually one must use the glorious power of PATIENCE. It is when "Patience has had her perfect work that one becomes perfect and entire, wanting nothing." *This developing of patience* is as much a part of one's spiritual growth as is food and time for the forming and maturing of the physical body. One must be conditioned mentally, spiritually and physically in order to

"BE BORN OF THE SPIRIT" that all things might become subject unto him, both in heaven and on earth. This gift of translation is as great a change as the chick's emergence from the egg, the child from the womb. It cannot be rushed or hurried. It is a condition into which one grows or evolves through the joy of fulfilling the laws pertaining to such divine developing and power.

As PATIENCE is developed one out-grows the tendency to be a wavering wave of the sea. Patience is the element on which HOPE is established and FAITH is fulfilled. As one develops *patience* he cannot be driven and tossed at random in an uncontrolled, haphazard way by his own negative emotions and doubting. He becomes firm and steady, like a rock—THE ROCK OF REVELATION, promised to Peter.

One learns to hold his course by keeping his eye on his goal. As one aims for a target he must never aim for the outer circles of that target. He must always aim for the bull's eye, the point of his deepest desire. This is how the image of his Hope is implanted upon the celestial substance of all-forming—the element of creation and of fulfilling. As one holds his attention upon his own greatest hope or desire he will of necessity bring it forth. This Path belongs to man and the powers thereof. And the glory of its fulfilling is sealed by THE HOLY SPIRIT OF PROMISE which is the divine, *Holy Covenant of Almighty God!* IT CANNOT FAIL!

When one uses this power of Creation to bring into outer manifestation the substance and reality of his needs and desires he is PLEASING GOD, indeed!

My blessed mother, in her mortal life, could forgive anyone any sin or transgression but one. That one, unforgivable sin, in my mother's mind, was EXTRAVAGANCE! She did not realize that the GREAT extravagance was in not using God's abundant source of all-supply fully, but in permitting it to go to waste. This is EXTRAVAGANCE! There are those who limit God and His great source of supply by holding warped, mediocre, skimped little ideas of His boundless plentitude. They believe that all want and poverty and suffering is their own alloted service to God. And they mock Him in their destitution of misery and lack, denying His proclamation that man was to have dominion over the earth and all things pertaining to it.

The "illions" of cosmic rays that bombard this earth every hour of every day cannot be measured or numbered. They are boundless and limitless. And they are the source of all substance whether mineral, vegetable, animal or pure perfection in man himself and in his surroundings. And those with mortal thinking qualifications only do not realize that the very cosmic rays, and the promised atoms of their forming are but awaiting the glorious PROMISE to come forth and fulfill—or take form.

It is for man to learn to use their potency for man was given dominion over the earth and the sky and the elements thereof.

Christ gave the full understanding of the law of creation when he rejected the temptation to turn the stones into bread to appease his hunger. The stones were already formed into tangible substance. They did not need to be brought forth into material manifestation. The same substance of which the stones were made was there to be used. It only required self-restraint and a higher understanding to use the law in its highest demonstration of perfection to produce the needed requirement. Christ may not have fully comprehended the law at that time, but His soul must have comprehended the higher accomplishment. In refraining from misusing that holy law Christ's needs were ministered unto by the very Angels of Heaven. And he was then taught the fulness of the law and the glory of it. He was instructed in the use of the divine law of creation and the sacredness thereof.

So it was that when He turned the water to wine He did not misuse the law. He used the water, blessed it, and added to it from the original element the pure ingredients of perfect wine.

The alchemists of old failed in this one thing. Their greatest desire was for wealth and they misused the law by transforming one element into another. They transformed lead into gold, which is quite possible, but inferior. It is but a mediocre achievement. It is only accepted by those who are willing to sell their great inheritance and their birthright of creatorship for a mess of pottage.

Had the alchemists learned to fully master themselves and their desires they could have literally clothed themselves in LIGHT and the full intelligence of power as they would have created from the Universal Substance the fulness of their desires in a purity of divine *bringing forth* according to the Holy Order of God. If they had refrained from using the law amiss their works would have lived forever. They however failed in that they accepted the temptation for appeasment instead of for the fulness. Their greed for wealth and prestige was their downfall.

Chapter XIX.

True Prayer is Faith in Action

The eternal, all-powerful PROMISE of God to all men is: "Ask and you shall receive; Seek and you shall find; Knock and it shall be opened unto you, for EVERYONE who asks receives; and he who seeks shall find" the realm of the great Universal, Primal Element of all forming, for the doors to that realm will be opened unto him. This is the realm or Kingdom of God which is PROMISED to those who seek for it FIRST and above all else.

And I hear your query, "Then why hasn't its powers been made manifest?"

And I am glad you asked, and I shall answer you.

Remember, "He who asketh in Spirit asketh according to the *will of God,* and he shall have whatsoever he asketh."

Mumbling a prayer is not asking in Spirit. Making a wish is not asking in Spirit. To ask in Spirit is to form a definitely, clearcut picture of your desire, so clear there can be no smeared, smudged, weak, questionable pattern formed. Then this desire must be held in the mind until it is perfect and becomes established on that Spirit element of all forming. As it is thus held, without wavering or doubting it will finally find its true lodgment within the heart. This is its full, manifest conception. This is the law of its coming forth and the power of its fulfilling. Then it is that the very pattern and Hope will draw to it the Pure LIGHT Rays of glory in increased, dynamic power. And thus the desire becomes established in the realm of Eternal Light as one begins to use the element of Creation to fulfill his needs and desires. As this is accomplished the PROMISED *"All Else"* will soon be added. This is *"The asking in Spirit"* that is required for man's completion of his part of the Covenant or deal. This is the type of asking that fulfills the pledge or COVENANT of Almighty God: *"For everyone who asks receives!"* The asking must be deep and sincere and the request held to without doubting or until patience has perfected its work.

This "asking" is not just a lip service or a momentary request. This "asking" is the shaping of the pattern or design so that it takes hold of the primal element of Spirit or pure LIGHT and molds it into form as those holy rays of Divine Light are advanced into atoms of their destined forming. And everyone on this earth can use the law. "For everyone who asks receives!" Yes, "God gives to all men liberally and upbraideth not! *And it shall be given him!* But let him ask in FAITH, nothing wavering for he that wavereth is like a wave of the sea driven by the wind and tossed; and let not that man think that he shall receive anything of the Lord." One must hold the request forth without doubting and without wavering or changing and with exceeding great joy in the assurance that he will receive it. "For when ye pray, BELIEVE THAT YOU RECEIVE and you shall have whatsoever you ask."

This great primal substance of all Creating, this divine, holy element of Light can be used NOW! It can be used by anyone! It only takes the exerted energy of FAITH to mold it into form. And FAITH is but the activated power of holding steadfastly to the LIGHT as darkness and doubting are eliminated. This is the forming or patterning or the ASKING that is required. And this dynamic power of Creation is but awaiting man's acceptance of it. And this is how one *"asks according to the will of God!"*

"And it is God's will to give you the Kingdom" of all HOPE and of all fulfilling for you were created to have dominion over the earth and the elements thereof and over the fish of the sea and the fowls of the air and over your own desires as you pattern them into the power and glory of their fashioned fulfilling. And in that forming is held the glorious Song of Creation. The Song which none but the righteous can learn—the Song of Praise and Love and Gratitude and Everlasting Joy as one steps out of the old shrouds of mortal miseries and wants and suffering and fears and darkness into the higher Realms of Light and Power and Life—Even Life Everlasting, which holds the PROMISE of all-fulfilling and perfecting.

Truly "NOTHING IS IMPOSSIBLE!" No desire is too great if unselfish and pure. No request can be ignored or slighted if FAITH is generated by casting out slothfulness and the darkness of doubting. "FOR EVERYONE WHO ASKS RECEIVES!" And each receives according to the use he makes of the element of LIGHT and the energy of FAITH, which belong to him and are eternally his to command.

"All that the Father has is yours!" It is yours NOW! It has always been yours. It will always be yours unless you relinquish your claim to it by loving the darkness rather than the LIGHT! "Cast out the darkness from

among you!" Cast out your fears and negation and doubting and you will be filled with LIGHT and will be able "TO COMPREHEND ALL THINGS!" "AND ALL THINGS WILL BECOME SUBJECT UNTO YOU!"

You cannot possibly aim too high. As you take hold of the responsibility of your own perfecting and accept of the divine, holy gifts of your Divine Sire, The Almighty God of all Creation, you will indeed be pleasing Him greatly!

This glorious LIGHT can be generated by man himself for man is so constructed that he can become a dynamo of Spiritual Power as he places himself in tune with those higher vibrations or realms of LIGHT. Man is a magnetic force which can attract to himself a double portion of Cosmic Light to do his bidding and to take form according to his command. And man can generate Light a hundred fold as he sends it forth in love and blessing to encircle the earth. And in so doing It will return unto him increased a thousand fold to clothe him in the glory and power of LIGHT and thus will he become filled with LIGHT until "he comprehends all things and has all POWER."

This is the heritage of man as he lays claim to it.

* * *

The Holy Spirit of Promise is the Spirit of Revelation, for the Spirit of Revelation is the Holy Spirit of Promise in its fullness. It is the LIGHT of TRUTH and KNOWLEDGE and of fore-knowing as one grows into it by his attentive, humble awareness and his own dynamic love as it is generated from within. This Holy Spirit of Promise, this divine Spirit of Witness of Revealing is increased by a desire to obey Its disclosing and give heed to Its instruction.

It is also "Given to abide in you; the record of heaven; the Comforter; the peaceable things of immortal glory; the Truth of all things; that which quickeneth all things, which maketh alive all things; that which knoweth all things, and hath all power." The foregoing PROMISES are held in their completeness within that Holy Spirit of Promise. It is the Witness of them, the Revealer of them and the unsealer of them.

It is the divine blessings which are given to abide in man that are true and lasting when developed. They are based on the most sacred, "Holy Covenant of Almighty God and are enfolded in the Holy Spirit of Promise which the Father sheds forth upon all who are Just and True."

The Holy Spirit of Promise is a very sacred, special gift bestowed upon man when he is worthy to receive It. It is forever his as he becomes JUST AND TRUE. And when one feels this enlightening glory of HOPE whispering, if only for a moment, that these great, dynamic *truths* can be fulfilled in him, he is receiving the divine Witness of that Holy Spirit of Promise. If he understood and fully accepted that Witness and would hold to It, without doubting, the Promises would soon be his in their completeness and power.

It is because man permits the doubts to enter and seal off the Testimony of that Most Holy Witness that it takes so long for some to fulfill the Promises which are whispered into their soul during those high, inspired moments of contact. And there are those who shut out forever the holy, fulfilling powers of God through their own encouraging unbelief.

As one learns to hold that contact, without doubting, the Promises, whatever they are, will become his own and he will become a divine instrument of glory. And all may be so chosen and precious if they will only choose to take hold of the LIGHT-bearing WITNESS to their souls of the Truth of God's Promises.

The Promises are true and faithful. They cannot fail! Only man can fail as he reaches out to take hold of the darkness and literally wraps himself in it. And makes of it his shroud.

As one accepts the Witness of that Holy Spirit of Promise It will open the way before him, revealing the Path of his own appointed destiny and will help him to fulfill it in honor. The Spirit of Promise is the divine Witness of God and of the TRUTH OF HIS WORDS! This precious, sacred gift of revealing is for those who are *"Just and True"*—true to Its revealing and just in their actions and their thinking insomuch that they condemn not the weaknesses and failings in others in a blind, selfrighteous, superior arrogance.

Neither can the Holy Spirit of Promise operate in man's self-appointed unbelief. It cannot fulfill when man seals his mind to Its breathtaking encouragements of Truth. It is the very Voice of God whispered through the Holy Spirit and It is appointed to lead into ALL-TRUTH for the TRUTH of all things is contained within It. It contains the power of revealing and of PROMISE and of quickening and of renewing. It PROMISES all things and has the *power* of all fulfilling. And It is given to abide in man! It is the Messenger of God, the divine Witness of Him and of His LIGHT!

This Holy Spirit of Promise is LOVE personified and is the joy and glory of all accomplishment. In It is contained the Peaceable things of immortal glory. It can only abide where peace is and It is the Messenger of Peace, the Witness of God and of His Son Jesus Christ. It will fulfill every Promise ever given if man himself only believes in Its PROMISES and holds to them without doubting.

We could almost say that the Holy Spirit of Promise is the LOVE of God which is shed forth through the hearts of the children of men! It is precious beyond all ordinary comprehension. It is one's contact with God. It contains the power of all revealing and of all fulfilling. It is the fulfilling glory of FAITH. *"It promises* all things and fulfills all things!" And it is given to abide in those of pure hearts. And all men were created to receive this most precious gift in Its fulness if so be they will prepare themselves by casting out the darkness through their own believing. To such will be the eternal honor and everlasting companionship of that Holy Spirit of Promise. Within It is contained the humility and pureness of divine accomplishment for only in humility can one ever be "JUST or TRUE!" And only in humility can one learn to manipulate the divine Light of Creation for in humility alone can the power to BELIEVE be accomplished.

This divine, Holy Spirit of Revelation or Promise will continue to lead one into "ALL TRUTH" as It reveals all things, even the deep and hidden mysteries of God. And It Promises to fulfill those divine Promises to the individual who will accept of Its revealing. It is as one follows the gentle, peaceful, powerful leading of that Holy Spirit of Promise that he is prepared to "COMPREHEND ALL THINGS * * * EVEN UNTIL HE BECOMES PERFECT IN CHRIST JESUS." This is the condition Promised by Almighty God to those who believe.

This is the "Spirit which the Father sheds forth upon all who are JUST AND TRUE!" It is the Spirit of Revelation! It is indeed the Holy Spirit, for within It is contained the power of each man's fulfillment.

"Yes, he that repenteth (which means to turn and travel that inward path of purification) and exerciseth FAITH and bringeth forth good works, *and prayeth continually without ceasing* unto such is given to know the mysteries of God. Yea, unto such is shall be given to reveal things which have never been revealed; yea, and it shall be given unto such to bring thousands of souls unto repentance." And those who keep the higher laws "Shall receive WISDOM and GREAT TREASURES OF KNOWLEDGE, EVEN HIDDEN TREASURES!"

All the dynamic possibilities of the future, including Man's individual powers and calling and perfection, his hopes and fulfillings are still waiting in the formless LIGHT, the divine, primal element or substance of all forming and of all Creation. And it is the Holy Spirit of Promise that casts the vision or manifests the reflection of that which can be, or reveals that which holds the germ or pattern of "BECOMING," even as God Promised to YOU individually before the world was.

But it is YOU yourself who must take hold of the vision, the desire, the HOPE as the Holy Spirit of Promise reveals the Truth or pattern of its forming.

Every living soul can learn to generate LIGHT! This is man's heritage, the ability to generate LIGHT! Man cannot create LIGHT. LIGHT already exists. Man can draw It to himself increased a thousand fold as he generates It or gathers It into Its full potential power. As one generates the LIGHT, or increases Its flow to himself, through his belief in the PROMISES held out to him by the Holy Spirit of Promise, the LIGHT itself becomes subject unto him. And thus he overcomes the darkness. Then only can one become a Creator.

LIGHT is indeed the spiritual element of forming. It is the energy of creation and lies dormant until generated into action by man's own thinking processes or awakened envisioning of pure desires as he accepts the Witness of the Holy Spirit of Promise which holds the keys of all fulfilling, revealing those things which were meant to "BECOME"—the glory and perfection of man himself.

CHAPTER XX.

The Treasure House of God

"And whatsoever you desire when you pray, BELIEVE THAT YOU RECEIVE IT AND YOU SHALL HAVE IT!" So promised the Lord Jesus Christ, Who is the ruler of this divine Kingdom of new Creations. "And if you ask anything of the Lord, and DOUBT NOT IN YOUR HEART, YOU SHALL HAVE WHATSOEVER YOU ASK."

The real, true power of prayer, *that invitation to ask*, does not necessarily need to be in words. The deepest, truest prayers are the yearning desires held forth in a human heart as they evolve into HOPE, which, when held forth without *wavering* or changing or doubting will be clothed in the spiritual essence of that primal substance and fashioned into reality according to the pattern held forth in the mind of man.

Hope IS *Faith*, the element or substance of all fulfillment as it is generated, by thought, into the condition of its full materialization, or until the Father rewards you openly.

Think upon your heart's desire! "Lay hold of it" with all your mind, which should be conditioned to vibrate only LOVE. LOVE that desire as you nourish it always in your heart! Thank God for it continually and it will become your own.

Do more! Live as though you have it! This brings forth its accomplishment more speedily! Rejoice in it! Let the tenderness of your heart embrace it in thanksgiving and singing appreciation. This purifies the very essence of its materialization and keeps it unsullied from the darkness of doubts, which have the power to destroy it utterly, like noxious weeds in a garden. Doubts are death to the spiritual growth of anything. And all existing things were created spiritually first. And that spiritual creation is held in the thought or the plan of their forming. Doubts are like the hoar-frost, blighting the tender sprouts—and they perish—unfulfilled. Doubts are also the noxious weeds.

And this is the PROMISE, or the COVENANT of God: "If you chase darkness (which is doubting and unbelief and negation) from among you (or out of your life) YOU SHALL BE ORDAINED OF GOD, and all things will be subject unto you, both in heaven and on earth: the Life and the Light; the Spirit and the power, sent forth by the will of the Father through Jesus Christ His Son."

Hold to the vibration of enthusiasm. This is the fundamental key as the element of "HOPE" is generated into the form of your own planning. Remember "doubting is of the devil and is the sister of sadness!" And "despair cometh because of iniquity!" And enthusiasm is the creative vibration set in operation by the HOPES of man.

HOPE is the perfection of the vision and the desire as it matures and becomes established. This is why "He that is without HOPE must needs be in despair, and despair cometh because of iniquity," or because one has walled himself out into an exiled condition of darkness.

Without HOPE life is a blank. It is a purposeless, meaningless experience of grubby mortal existence. It is, at best, only an ugly shadow when compared to a life with vibrant HOPE holding forth the PROMISE of its divine accomplishments. And anyone who Permits himself to be thus cheated, drifting through life in the dark void of unbelief is already "DAMNED" for his progress is stopped.

With an understanding of HOPE the vision becomes the dream, and the dream can take form in the awakening desire. And when desire is developed into a HOPE, FAITH becomes the fulfilling factor of achieving all that one can possibly envision, dream of, imagine, desire or HOPE for!

In the perfecting of a HOPE the primal substance takes form as FAITH swings into action. HOPE is the body, the form, the pattern and FAITH is the Spirit, or the element which makes alive.

"Faith is the very substance and the required life energy or force as It begins to manipulate the element of things "waiting to become." Faith generates the LIGHT, transforming it into atoms as they are drawn, through thought, into the pattern of their fulfilment.

Then the words of St. James must be remembered always: One must ask, or hope or desire, "Without wavering; for he that wavereth (changes his desires, or weakens in the strength of his hope) is like a wave of the sea, driven by the wind and tossed. And let not that man think that he shall receive anything of the Lord." He has failed to lay claim to the eternal elements that were but awaiting the fulfilling of his own command.

In that most ancient temple of Egypt is engraved this dynamic truth: "O my son, matter becomes; formerly it was, for matter is the vehicle of becoming. Becoming is the mode of activity of the uncreate and foreseeing God.

Having been endowed with the germ of becoming, matter is brought into Birth, for the creative force of thought fashions it according to the ideal forms. Matter not yet engendered has no form; it *becomes* when it is put into operation by the mind of man." This is a perfect analysis of the primal element and how it is acted upon by desire or HOPE.

The more one uses the gift or element or substance of FAITH, which is the power of creation, the more proficient he becomes until, "all things are added unto him," or until "All things become subject unto him." And then it is that his every need and every righteous desire is fulfilled. This is the PROMISE given under Covenant to those who will but seek that glorious Kingdom of God. And such will no longer need to "labor for the things that perish," or be satisfied with the treasures that can be stolen or corrupted by moth and rust devouring them.

It was this law of FAITH in action which Christ used in producing wine, feeding the five-thousand and in every miracle He ever wrought.

This is the substance and the law upon which it works that must be comprehended and accepted in order that one can receive the reward of fulfilment. It requires time, at first, but as one becomes more proficient the time required is diminished until the divine requests are answered speedily and at length only the spoken word, or thought is needed for the immediate accomplishment. Yes! "Before they ask I will answer!"

This is the divine law of fulfilment which Almighty God has established for man's use. It is man's privilege to bring forth or create with as he learns to use this unspeakable power in humble, joyous understanding. And he who masters it will be using it henceforth and forever, even to the end of eternity. As one progresses the requirements for his needs expand according to his own growth and enlarged visioning until he comprehends fully that the worlds themselves were formed of the LIGHT, generated by FAITH.

As one uses the divine, holy law of creation, he passes from dull, mediocre mortality as he "changes his carnel flesh to flesh divine without descending through the gates of death."

And so my assignment is to share these great truths of creation with all those whom God has sanctified and ordained unto the power of receiving. No others will be able to lay hold upon these glorious realms of light and everlasting power or be able to fulfill the glory of the PROMISE contained in them through the eternal Covenant of our loving, Heavenly Father.

And so I stood upon the threshold of the unformed and gazed in reverent awe into the realm of primal matter, into that region composed of the very elements of God in all the wonder of their primal glory as they are "Waiting to become" all that anyone could ever dream of or desire. This kingdom of primal matter, pure and undefiled is exquisite beyond thought or all imagining. It is as vast as all existence and as boundless as space. It is pure perfection, unmarred and unsullied in its uncreated state of glorious, spiritual "awaiting" for an existence in tangible form according to the patterns held forth to shape it into concrete reality.

This primal substance contains the essence of all things as yet unformed, which God established in the far eons of beginnings and the breathtaking glory of all endings. And since there is no beginning and will be no end it is established forever and forever, awaiting man's desire to fashion it into reality. It is the realm of fulfilling as all HOPES take form in the primal substance of things that are to come.

It is yours to use! It always has been! Its essence and power is limitless and perfect beyond the dreams of man, for only qualified HOPE, which is FAITH in action can fashion it into birth.

This realm contains the element of all materials, the fragile essence of a humming bird's song, the elusive magic of a sunbeam flickering through a tiny crack, the whisper of a breeze, the vanishing colors of a sunset, the dewy moisture of the dawn, the sighing of a fleeting wish, the fulfillment of every HOPE deep hidden in the soul of man.

It also contains the concrete elements of which cities were formed upon the lands God has before-time imagined into being. Or as the ancient philosopher, Plotinus stated: "My thoughts took form as though they fell from my broodings."

And within this realm of eternity is also contained the very substance of man's own soul's perfection as he evolves into the glory of his own waiting heritage.

This realm contains the substance of all exciting things —and of all things as yet unformed that will ever come into existence. "FAITH is the substance of things hoped for." It is also composed of the power, when activated upon by burning desire, to mold it into any form possible to imagine, including man's own perfection. It is as fragile and as delicate as the breath of angels, yet more powerful than the greatest lightning bolt. It consists of a material so ethereal, so heavenly and so divinely celestial it can never be looked upon by mortal eyes. Yet this very element contains within itself the very *"evidence of things unseen"* as they hold forth the patterns of their own becoming. This glorified element or substance is generated into form by thought as it is acted upon by man himself in the expanding vision of his own creating.

This great realm of primal element is established on the threshold of eternity, yet every individual is surrounded by it, enfolded in it. It belongs to every living soul who will only believe and purify himself that he might handle it with touch unsullied and undefiled, lest he destroy himself with its misuse.

Truly, "All that the Father has is yours!" And it is so! This supreme, primal substance of all created forms or creative ideas is awaiting but the touch of man's own high thoughts as he takes hold of it and molds it into form according to the righteous desires held within his soul.

Yes, "Seek first the Kingdom of God and its righteousness and all else will be added unto you!" Such is the COVENANT! Today it may be but a request for the fulfilling of your daily needs; tomorrow the vision of your own fulfilling as your own view expands; the next day may come the desire to OVERCOME MORTALITY AND DEATH, and so, quite naturally is one's self fulfilled and glorified as he lays claim to this heritage so exquisitely divine. This is how one "evolves from the man kingdom into the God Kingdom," or the method of "changing his carnel flesh to flesh divine without descending through the gates of death."

All that is required is that man accepts the boundless gift of all fulfilling. With it goes the responsibility of self-purification as one naturally "overcomes the evils of his life and loses every desire for sin, and like the ancients, arrives at the point of FAITH where he is wrapped in the power and glory of his Maker and is caught up to dwell with Him." And this Promise too was given under COVENANT! It is irrevocable!

To comprehend fully the wonders of this realm of full-forming one will naturally evolve as FAITH ITSELF is transposed from the UNSEEN condition into the *experience* of full KNOWING. And no one can actually KNOW anything until he himself *experiences it*. This involves the experience of stepping out and beyond the mortal realm of shadows and sorrows into that which is forever perfect.

As one begins to use the endless, eternal, potential power of creation he begins to experience his own degree of FAITH as he grows into perfection, and then he will henceforth have access to this realm of all-fulfilling. LIGHT is this realm, the very fulness of it as it is fashioned into form, according to the plan or pattern held forth by the mind of man, as it is generated by FAITH.

FAITH, the wonder word! "The glory of existence." It is a word so simple its meaning has been lost in the dim ages of man's forgetting. Yet it is so powerful its substantial reality has been uncomprehended. However, as one begins to "lay hold of this *best gift*," this patent energy of FAITH, he can become the master, for its purpose and nature is to obey! AND LIGHT IS ITS SUBSTANCE!

The sublime substance of Creation is molded into

form by the vibrations of thought, as FAITH is activated by believing.

Vibrations are generated by thoughts, either noble or degenerate and when put into action they go forth to fulfill and bring forth their own results. Evil vibrations can take hold of the creative material and in their darkness congeal it into man's vicissitudes and ills and sorrows. Man himself is the creator of that which befalls him. Wrinkles, old age, sickness, poverty and DEATH are of negative thought vibrations and become congealed into form and made manifest when man clings to the evils and the darkness. Encouraged DOUBTS are destroyers of perfection as they are released to mar and desecrate the glorious materialization of one's HOPES and dreams.

If one is pure and noble "All things will work together for his good" and will be fashioned unto him for glory and honor.

Faith and love generate the highest vibrations possible and transform or solidify that supreme, HOLY element of LIGHT into the highest perfection of one's HOPES or dreams or desires as they take form in the tangible world of mortal reality.

Thoughts are the generator of vibrations or of FAITH when used with love and understanding. Wishes and dreams and HOPES, when holy and pure, are held within the solidifying power of FAITH as it vibrates with the energy released to fashion and to form and to bring forth. And "NOTHING IS IMPOSSIBLE" to him who learns to use it aright. Wishes and dreams and desires and HOPES are formed into realities as they reach the point of their own fulfilling. Faith takes hold and vibrates them into their own patterns of released perfection according to the firmness of the plan held forth in LIGHT!

The veil has been rent, that dismal veil of unbelief, that has shut man out from experiencing or KNOWING the GREAT TRUTH! Man has been tricked and cheated down the centuries. He has accepted mortality and the evils and vicissitudes and suffering and the fulness of its trials and heartbreaks. He has accepted misery and darkness and anguish as he has reached out his very arms to embrace death. And he has been mocked. He has been duped and pummeled by mortality and the evils thereof as he has plodded his blind, weary way along that long desolate trail of increasing problems and remorse to the grave—unfulfilled and unfulfilling.

"For we are saved by HOPE; but HOPE that is seen is not HOPE; for what a man seeth, why doth he yet HOPE for?" (Rom. 8:24).

Each living soul is now invited to step into this new spiritual realm of understanding and unspeakable glory to stake out his own claim in the realms of eternal Light. But in doing so he must be sure that his desires injure no one and carries with them none of the clutterings of his own evils. Thus in reaching into this higher realm of divine fulfilling he automatically "OVERCOMES the evils of his life!" They are left behind.

This higher realm is only for the PURE IN HEART! And the heart itself becomes purified as one lays hold of these "best gifts" and develops the attribute to BELIEVE —and doubt not!

I. Peter 1:6-7: "Wherein rejoice, though now for a season, if need be, ye are in heaviness through manifold temptations:

THE TREASURE HOUSE OF GOD 213

"For the trial of your faith, being MUCH MORE PRECIOUS THAN GOLD THAT PERISHETH, though it be tried with fire, might be found unto praise and honor and glory at the appearing of Jesus Christ, "Whom not having seen, ye love * * *." All perfection, all glory, all achievement must first come through belief and not through seeing. It is FAITH that turns into KNOWLEDGE and knowledge turns into POWER—even the power of creating.

And LIGHT is the basic element of all TRUTH and all existing things. Light is the pure radiance of a great idea springing forth in the mind of man. Light is Intelligence in action. "It was not created nor made, neither indeed can be." And man himself was that LIGHT or idea or intelligence in the beginning. He was the spirit of Truth, the intelligence, the Light of glory which was co-existent with God.

Man was brought forth into being by the reaching desires he developed within himself. Each man is the sum total of his own thoughts. He is a nothing, a knave, a cheat, a sex-pervert, a criminal or a monster or just an ordinary mortal according to his own selected level of thought. Or he is already evolving into divinity and can ultimately reach it according to the use he makes of the ideas or thoughts or the Light he is willing to accept and nurtures in the temple of his heart.

Man can become so filled with LIGHT, as he casts out the darkness, that he will "COMPREHEND ALL THINGS." And only the doubting and negation and darkness, which one encourages within himself, can keep him from his highest destiny.

* * *

When the Light becomes subject unto one, by overcoming the darkness, the Cosmic Rays can be used to form atoms with which to create material things and to fulfill one's needs.

This method of transforming the Cosmic, divine Light into atoms or tangible material substance has been fully revealed.

Now there is a higher, even more glorious purpose or reason for one to overcome the darkness that he might have the Light and consequently the Life become subject unto him. When one "transforms his carnal flesh into flesh divine" or is "Born of the Spirit" he becomes completely spiritualized. This can only be accomplished by fulfilling that First and Great Commandment. Only as one loves with all his heart can it be softened and melted in-so-much that "The Love of God can be shed forth through his heart, which is indeed the *Fruit of the Tree of Life.*" And only in righteousness can one partake of this glorious gift of Life Eternal!

And as one lets that love pour out through his own heart into the cells and atoms of his body he is beginning to transfigure his body. This is the LOVING with all the soul, which is the body and the spirit united. It is in this great LOVE that the very atoms of the flesh will be changed into flesh divine, or the carnal flesh be transformed into flesh divine without descending through the gates of death.

The atoms, which were originally composed of the Cosmic Rays of Light, as those rays curled upon themselves, locking the glory and the power of God within the very center or nucleus of their beings are transmuted back into the Light, glorified, perfected and forever indestructible. This is the power known of old as "ascension," "transfiguration," or "translation," for it is the glorification of one's own being as it is transformed or spiritualized.

This is the goal for which the hungering souls of men are forever yearning and which is awaiting those who will only perfect their faith and fulfill the laws pertaining to it. And this work is given unto man by the Most Holy Covenant of Almighty God. It is true and faithful! It is irrevocable! It is everlasting! It cannot fail!

This is the purpose of FAITH and of Creation and is Perfection. This is how the Light and the Life become subject unto one as he becomes the Master of the Light and the Life and the Spirit and the Power as he overcomes the evils of his life and reaches the point of FAITH where he is literally wrapped in the power and glory of his Maker and is caught up to dwell with Him.

This is how all things truly become subject unto one, "Both in heaven and on earth!"

The things of earth become subject unto one as he uses the Light Rays to form earthly, tangible substance or matter. The things of heaven become subject unto him as he uses the Power to transform the tangible atoms back into the great Cosmic Light of all perfection. By this method one can literally clothe himself in the great Celestial Light of all glory. Or as the writer of the Odes of Solomon testified: "I clothed myself in Light and acquired a body free from sorrow or affliction or pain!"

This is the purpose and the meaning of Life. And it is sealed by that most Holy Spirit of Promise upon all those who cast out the darkness of doubting and exercise the great and mighty Faith that contains the power to manipulate the Light and to fulfill all things. So be it, Amen!

Chapter XXI.

The Magic Switch or Button

These chapters on FAITH contain the information I have waited so very long to share. This privilege of comprehending and revealing the dynamic wonder of FAITH was what I so intensely desired when I began my search so long ago. I would never have put so much effort into anything that involved just myself, but it was the years of the great depression and suffering and want and poverty was filling the land. The very misery I beheld filled me with the almost overwhelming desire to KNOW what FAITH IS and how it works, so that mankind could be lifted from the dregs of poverty and want and fear into the peace and plenty which I felt God had planned for His children.

The intensity of my desire to comprehend FAITH FULLY increased as I continued with my search. I spent almost every spare moment of my life in prayer. I carried the prayer with me. I slept with it. I lived with it. It was silent and those who associated with me were unaware of the burning request I held within my heart. I had to KNOW what FAITH IS and how it could be used to conquer the ills and the distresses and the wants of life and supply all the needs for those who desired to use its fabulous powers.

I realized from the beginning that FAITH was not just a word. It was a power that could be used by turning on a switch. And I had believed from childhood that scientists would harness FAITH, LIKE ELECTRICITY, at some future date. Then we would be able to turn a switch and use the breathtaking potentiality of its divine power to accomplish the needed things of life. It would be, I thought, like turning on the giant turbines with their full force of action. Or, at least, it would be like turning on the electric button in one's home to release the limitless energy needed for the appliances one possessed as they were used to fulfill the individual assignments required in order to employ fully the purpose of their fashioning. But mostly that switch would be used to turn on the light of understanding that one would not need to abide in darkness. FAITH is the generator of LIGHT!

AND IT IS SO! For LIGHT generated by FAITH contains all power.

FAITH is the greatest power in existence. It can, when used with knowledge and skill remove mountains, raise the dead and perform all the necessary tasks that go beyond the physical manipulating of man's frail, physical hands.

FAITH is truly a power that can be used just by turning on the magic switch or button. And each man has the full equipment with which to operate that switch and use the unspeakable power to its fullest extent. FAITH is the generative force of LIGHT Itself.

The method is so very easy and oh, so simple. There are no great complicated, intricate pieces of machinery to learn about or master. Man himself is the instrument and within him is the magic switch. It IS as simple as turning on the electric button to light one's own living room. And it is a very part of man himself. That divine switch is an intricate part of man's own being. It is Intelligence in action. This power and this switch is within his reach always and everywhere. Man totes it with him as he carries himself around upon his individual assignments of daily living. But few have ever learned to use it, or even dream of its existence and its priceless value.

It is true that "perfect love casts out all fear!" This fact has been proved beyond all question or controversy. And it can be proved anew by anyone upon this earth at any time. All one has to do is to perfect the gift of LOVE and he will KNOW for himself.

And as "Perfect love casts out all fear" so can FAITH banish all darkness and conquer every evil and fulfill all things. FAITH can achieve all things! It can not only feed a multitude it can perform all the miracles of perfect living and divine accomplishment.

FAITH, shall we say, is but an attitude of mind. FAITH is composed of the highest vibrations released from a human being when FAITH is fully clothed in LIGHT. Faith endowed Light is a singing glory of perfect assurance and fulfilment. FAITH in action is LIGHT held forth on its highest level of anticipation as doubts are banished and the evil of darkness is dispelled. FAITH carries with it that quality of expectancy, like an open vessel knowing it will be filled as it is dipped into the flowing stream of supply.

FAITH is power! Dynamic! Limitless! Creative Power! FAITH is the exerted energy of *thought* and *feeling* as it generates *LIGHT*. It goes beyond thought, or rather carries thought with it into the true realm of divine reality. The higher realm or sphere or domain is that in which the material of dreams is fashioned and spun from the very element of LIGHT into the perfect fabric of fulfilment as it becomes embodied in tangible, material form. FAITH is the living soul of LIGHT where all the creative substance of existence lies "waiting to become" as it is called forth from that realm of primal purity. FAITH and LIGHT compose the realm or region of all that can be. It is where the vibrations of thought form and fashions this divine primal substance into the desires held forth within the soul of man.

Thought builds bridges of the LIGHT across the deepest chasms and FAITH generates the LIGHT into atoms and substance and fulfilment. Thought can scale the highest mountains in existence, whether material, mental or spiritual as FAITH IS generated into action. Thought constructs skyscrapers from the element of LIGHT, to caress the very clouds. And with its powers in action men are transported across space to walk upon the moon while all the world stands by to view the breathtaking wonder of it. LIGHT generated by FAITH is the very material which can construct highways to the stars in the not too far future. And those very stars themselves were created and formed from the substance of LIGHT, activated by FAITH as thoughts formed the pattern of fulfilling.

"WITHOUT FAITH IT IS IMPOSSIBLE TO PLEASE GOD!"

FAITH is not only the *substance*, or material, or essence of THINGS HOPED FOR—FAITH IS THINGS HOPED FOR as it generates the LIGHT or the Idea into tangible formation. FAITH manipulates the idea, the dream, the desire, the very HOPE itself for it is the embodiment of the *Faith engendered Light.*

One of the greatest attributes that God has shared with man is the ability to dream, to hope and to aspire. And man, in this sphere of action, is the creator of his dreams. Man was brought forth with this divine attribute of God established within his very soul so that he could "bring forth" or "create" that for which he truly yearns. "For all that the Father has is yours!" Man was created with a mind with which to dream, to hope, to fashion and so to fulfill that for which his hungering soul yearns.

This realm of HOPE is beyond the mere threshold of fleeting aspirations. And even wishing is merely the immature pastime of make-believe. It is the child's inadequate state of momentarily pretending. But it is the fleeting caress of a fragile wish that can enfold the illusive pattern of a dream, when taken hold of. And a dream, when nourished, matures into a desire. And desires evolve into HOPES—and HOPES which are the idea or the Light of Spiritual forming beginning to evolve into reality. And so the sperm becomes the embryonic idea beginning its own term of maturing and of growth and fulfilment.

HOPE is a living, vibrant condition of exercised desire as it lays hold upon the element of LIGHT, permitting FAITH to generate and fashion it according to one's highest vision.

Man has the full equipment and the ability and the power, if he will so use it, to bring any HOPE forth into visible reality as it takes shape in tangible, touchable, substantial existence or material form.

It does take time to fashion and to form these mental pictures into their visible realities just as it requires time for the infant to mature within the mother's womb.

But LIGHT IS GLORY and FAITH is ecstasy in its

joy of released power. FAITH fulfills all things! Light envisions them. Together they are the singing power of creation vibrating in a human heart as they fill the pattern or mold held forth for their completion. This is how all things were formed. This is how the primal substance or material of all creating fulfills any given assignment of bringing forth from the universal substance that which will satisfy every good desire. The LIGHT reveals all things and FAITH generates the power to fulfill them.

When FAITH is completed the idea is no longer an intangible hope or a dream or just a righteous desire or an unfulfilled yearning smothered and silenced without recognition or the generated energy to bring it forth. This primal substance of Light engendered by FAITH is God's own special, creative energy and its sublime element of fulfilling and of glorious creating, endowed with the everlasting power to "BECOME!" FAITH holds within its embrace all the fashionings and the creations of the future—worlds without end—realm beyond realm—glory beyond glory! For FAITH alone has the power to solidify LIGHT.

And so it is that a FAITH inspired idea, which is LIGHT, cannot fail. It is forever real and powerful and true! Man may fail to make use of so great a substance and its ineffable power. But the realms of Light will always be, awaiting FAITH'S sacred touch to generate it into *becoming* a reality in tangible existence.

FAITH engendered Light is the glory and the substance and the material of "THINGS HOPED FOR." It embraces the reality of all existence. Within it is the very life essence and spiritual power of all tangible things and manifestations and accomplishments. It is boundless! It is the very glory of existence! It is the creative element of all that is or will be! The LIGHT, when engendered by FAITH is eternal and unfailing and powerful beyond man's finite mind to appreciate.

Yet anyone in existence can dip his fingers into this sublime element of creation and take hold of it and use it to fashion and to form and to bring forth into reality the living, breathtaking wonder of his dreams. He can mold it with his thoughts for it can be controlled by man's own thinking and visioning or deep desiring. Man has the power to fashion and form his dreams and desires and hopes into their tangible, earthly counterparts, if it is for material blessings he is reaching. Or he can take that spiritual perfection of himself and bring it forth into its true, everlasting glory as he is transformed, or "Born of the Spirit!" It is for man to say what he will bring forth.

And it is when one's dreams are dark and hopeless and filled with doubting and despair that he brings forth the elements of God into the fulfilling of his own destruction as he plods his weary, desolate way to the grave.

This primal element of Light when engendered with Faith was intended to be used in its true glory of divine forming for it is the sacred element supreme. And though it is an almost unspeakable, indescribable power or substance it belongs to all alike, without price or bickering or greedy monopolies.

The switch that manipulates this most beautiful power of all creation is just a simple little lever. It is waiting but the touch of thought to put it into operation. It has been beyond all previously conceived ideas simply because man has not used his mind to investigate its inexpressible powers and true reality. It has lain dormant like the Promises of Jesus Christ simply because none have been willing to LIVE the laws in order to PROVE THEM and thereby use their power.

This tiny switch or magic button is located within the mind of man and can be used by him at all times if so be he becomes willing to exert himself to the point of testing. It is always available and at hand.

This miraculous switch, when used, has the full power to turn one's mind from darkness and doubting into the exalted realm of hope and joyous anticipation as LIGHT is generated and brought forth to light up one's understanding and banish the darkness of despair. To turn that magic switch one has but to take hold of his own thinking apparatus as he controls the caliber of his thoughts. This right and this power belongs to all men. And the power of its operating is but the awakening of desire and the exerted power to believe strongly enough to put it to the test.

As this God-given ability to choose one's thoughts is used, one will have gained access to the very doors of the KINGDOM which will be opened to all who will only "KNOCK!" "For unto all who knock, it shall be opened!" This is one of the great PROMISES of God, sealed by the most sacred Covenant of the Almighty!

As that switch is mastered and used all darkness can be instantly banished. It can be dissolved as thoroughly and completely as the conquering of the darkness in a room when the light is turned on. It works exactly the same and is as absolutely consistent in its perfection. LIGHT conquers and eliminates the darkness even as "Love casts out all fear!" And FAITH manipulates the magic switch.

This great primal substance of Light fills one's mind

with understanding and knowledge, revealing the things that were not apparent before. It is the glory and the reality of illuminated thought as the evils of life stand forth as beautiful opportunities for one's own progress. And thus are they transformed into blessings: "For all things work together for good to those who love God!" So it is that the darkness is dissolved and the evils of doubting are conquered by the glory of the Light. And it is the privilege and within the power of every man to lay hold of the very element of creation and to fashion it into the glorified desires of his heart.

It is as the light reveals the ideas of truth and power to the mind that one begins to create and to bring forth his high hopes and worthy ambitions and holy desires into their dynamic, glamorous fruition and fulfilment as FAITH materializes them into reality. Thus FAITH itself evolves and becomes KNOWLEDGE, AND KNOWLEDGE IS POWER.

This is how the darkness within oneself is OVERCOME FIRST. And the mud becomes fertile soil and the terrifying shadows of the darkness are revealed as treasures of beauty and joy. And all mankind can begin to stand up in the sunlight of the great reality and sublime purification.

Those of you who read, and who can take hold of these great truths were ordained and prepared for this work before ever the world was formed. And "Your NAMES were written in that sacred, holy *Lamb's Book of Life* before the foundations of the earth were laid."

And as FAITH is used to activate the LIGHT man himself emerges from the caterpillar state of his mortal existence as surely as a butterfly takes wings to soar above the drab, dull earth.

Man again becomes divine as he learns to open up those hidden realms of Light right within himself, or as "he fills himself with light." Man has the power to switch on the full comprehensible, revealing glory of TRUTH and LIGHT and FAITH and can actually become them.

LIGHT has within it the very qualities of its own perfection as it is accepted for LIGHT enfolds and contains the highest ideas possible to conceive. And FAITH, in its purest essence is just the substance or energy or hope, though yet invisible and unformed. But as it is generated and exercised FAITH turns the LIGHT into KNOWLEDGE or the substantial reality of complete KNOWING.

Any individual on this earth can manipulate that magic switch as he turns his own thinking apparatus away from the darkness of his doubting and failures and dismaying negations into the realm of dynamic, singing ecstasy of hopeful desiring. This IS *Light* as it becomes activated by FAITH to fulfill the measure of itself and of man's dreams, glorified. This is how one fulfills the command to "EXERCISE GREAT AND MIGHTY FAITH!"

Chapter XXII.

"Ye Are Gods!"

"Nothing is impossible to him who believes!"
And the magic switch that transforms one from a dull, unbelieving being, with all the drab, ugly tendencies of grubby mortality into a person of radiance and dynamic personality, is accomplished by the mere touching of that magic button of everlasting power as one learns to turn on that LIGHT and then holds himself within its glow.

This divine, magic switch is operated by one's own desire as he fills the realms in which he dwells with the full light of understanding and locks out the darkness of unbelief, doubting and their fostered off-spring of despairs and griefs and sorrows and suffering. This magic switch is invisible, as yet, but so are all the great things that are waiting to come forth from that invisible realm into the world of tangible reality.

As one begins to use that magic switch within his mind, determined to exclude the darkness and the doubting and the negation from his life, he takes hold of this limitless power of FORMING. Just as one begins to manipulate this switch, in his testing, he will soon learn the full measure of its power and he will become the master thereof—"AND IT WILL BECOME SUBJECT UNTO HIM!" With the manipulating of this magic switch or button the very caliber of one's thoughts are transformed from the realm of gloom and failure into the region of LIGHT in which FAITH can be taken hold of as it fashions into the breathtaking reality the very glory of one's dreams.

In the manipulating of this switch the caliber of one's thoughts can be changed and exalted from the realms of desolating despairs and dismal conjectures of anguish into the glorified reality of HOPE prepared for fulfilment as it is brought forth in solid manifestation by one's own exerted efforts of pure desiring.

It takes practice, at first, to learn to manipulate that switch, because in the beginning it seems one has to search for it and locate it in the darkness of his own established unbelief. Next he must have within his mind the pattern of his most cherished dream or hope as he holds forth his secret yearnings to be fashioned and formed and brought forth into the open. And as he does so they will be produced or be brought forth into the realm of material existence.

In this work one need not be too concerned about the whole, vast sea of the divine, holy, primal substance. One needs only hold his attention upon the container of his own desires, the pattern of his divine request. This is how one *"lays hold of the best gifts,"* which are always best to him according to his own desiring.

This bringing forth is God's own fulfilling, as the pattern or desire is filled full. It is the fulfilling of that ancient law which proclaims aloud to all the world and to all creation: "There is a law irrevocable decreed in heaven, before the foundations of the world upon which all blessings are predicated. And if we obtain any blessing (or desire) from God it is upon obedience to that law upon which it is predicated."

And now, to explain that law more clearly it will be necessary to continue with the unfolding of that most sacred plan of the Almighty, to bring forth your own innermost desires.

"Faith is the substance of things hoped for, the evidence of things unseen." FAITH truly is the energizing life force or activating element of things ardently hoped for. Within the seed or the plan or the pattern or idea is the reality of its forming. The very idea itself is formed of the LIGHT of creation. And within it is the very *evidence*, the spiritual design of that which can be—or which will be. It is like the child in the womb which has not yet been born into this outside, tangible world. Nevertheless it does exist and is most real, though unseen. And though HOPE or the desire has not been activated upon by FAITH it still exists in its unseen form—waiting its own fulfilment. It is a reality else it could not have been thought or taken form in the realms of desiring. And this realm is composed of the great spiritual essence or substance of all forming. The very thought or idea or desire, when activated upon by FAITH is then fashioned from the element of Eternal LIGHT.

FAITH is the evidence or the spiritual life force of forming that generates the element of spirit into the establishment of the hope held, without wavering in a human heart. FAITH and LIGHT are the supreme element of all creation, the glory of all that is or can ever be. Within the element of Light (the idea) and Faith is contained the dynamic energy of creation, or of "becoming" fashioned into the very essence of its own PROMISED PERFECTION. Any doubts or negation, when encouraged or indulged in, can mar or completely destroy the vision, the hope, the dream utterly. And even neglect will let it die still-born in the womb of eternity, unglorified, unquickened and unfulfilled.

Hope itself is pure LIGHT and contains the very *evidence* of its PROMISE. Without the spiritual glory and reality of LIGHT no beautiful desires could ever be formed and brought into existence. Life itself would be hell, with no meaning or purpose. The glorious fact that *hopes* can be formed in human minds is the *evidence* of their, as yet unseen possibility. To have a dream or hope is the very proof that it does exist in the realms of the, as yet unseen, intangible substance of all forming. It is already established in mental or spiritual form when the dream or hope is envisioned. "And *without this divine gift of vision the* people will perish." And the vision also will perish without the strength of a human mind to form and contain it.

To have a dream or a hope or an idea is the very evidence that it can be brought forth from the, as yet unformed substance, waiting to BECOME. It is established in mental or spiritual form when the dream or the hope is envisioned. Yes, "Without vision the people perish." There is no progress, no creating, no hope, no glory, only a dull, dead, stupid existence of unprogressiveness.

"ALL EXISTING THINGS WERE FORMED SPIRITUALLY FIRST!" Or to express it in other words: "All existing things were formed mentally first." And the meaning is the same. This spiritual forming is the mental plan or pattern being established in that realm of primal substance in order that it might fulfill its period of gestation. And when it is completely established the divine element of spiritual glory and LIGHT take tangible form in physical existence as the atoms are formed from LIGHT to fill full the pattern of their design. Thus man is the creator of his own hopes and ambitions and the fulfiller of them as he obeys the laws of their coming forth.

"And they were called Gods, unto whom the Word of God came, and the scriptures cannot be broken." (John 10:34). And the Word of God is HIS PROMISES, His Holy Covenants expressed in Words, or thoughts, or as inspired ideas of glory penetrating into the minds of those prepared to receive them.

And if "they were called Gods unto whom His Words" or PROMISES or inspired Truths came, then they could fulfill those Words and thus become Creators. *Gods are Creators*—Creators of their God-given dreams or visions or divinely revealed ideas. And any humble individual who can open his heart to believe and to take hold of the PROMISES, or to receive inspiration or newly revealed Truths from God is moving or evolving into divinity. He is becoming a god or a creator as he uses the elements of LIGHT and FAITH to fashion and to form and to fulfill the PROMISES his soul beholds. This is the power of Creatorship when used with full understanding and in perfect love.

The Patriarchs of old had the gift and the power to lay their hands upon the heads of their children or descendants and reval, in blessing, their individual destinies or missions of PROMISE. But the blessing had to be taken hold of by the one receiving it, for it was only fulfilled as he believed it, desired it and lived for it, holding the pattern or desire in his mind always. This alone brought forth the fulfilling.

It is possible for any man to receive such a blessing. All he has to do is to take hold of his own deep and holy desires and live for them. Within his own soul is engraved the pattern of his own individual calling and perfection. It is his own hopes or vision that reveals the pattern which the sublime essence of creation is destined to fulfill in holiness and truth. It will take time and patience. But it is only waiting to "BECOME" as the individual begins to lay hold of it—*the best gift*, his own anointment completed.

"Mind is the arbiter of life; it is the creator and the shaper of conditions, and the recipient of its own results."

"Mind is the infallible weaver of destiny."

"Dream lofty dreams, and as you dream, so shall you become. Your vision is the promise of what you shall one day be; your ideal is the prophecy of what you shall at last unveil."

"He who has conquered doubt has conquered failure."

"A man is made or unmade by himself; in the armory of thought he forges the weapons by which he destroys himself; he also fashions the tools with which he builds for himself heavenly mansions of joy and strength and peace. By the right choice and true application of thought, man can ascend to the Divine Perfection; by the abuse and wrong application of thought, he descends below the level of the beast. Between these two extremes are all the grades of character, and man is their maker and master."

(The five quotations above are all from James Allen's little book "AS A MAN THINKETH.")

And it is true: "They are recognized as Gods unto whom the Word of God comes. And the scriptures cannot be broken." Live the Promises of God for they are His Word. "And *His Word will become flesh!*" Your own flesh!

And as you become *"just and true"* you will receive His Holy Spirit of PROMISE, for the Father bestows it upon all such. It will be your eternal, unfailing guide as you open up your souls to receive it. This Holy Spirit of Promise is the Spirit of Revelation and will lead you into all Truth and fulfilment as you become a God or a Creator of Truth and Perfection and beauty within yourself.

"Dream! Dream nobly! Dream manfully and your dreams will be your prophets!" (Heber J. Grant).

"For as many as are led by the Spirit of God they are the sons of God—the spirit itself beareth witness with our spirit, that we are the children of God; and if children, then heirs; heirs of God, joint-heirs with Christ." (Romans 8:14, 16-17).

"Let this same mind be in you, which was also in Christ Jesus:

"Who, being in the form of God, thought it not robbery to be equal with God." (Phil. 2:5-6).

It is only as FAITH IS EXERCISED to manipulate the LIGHT that one becomes a true creator as he fulfills, *knowingly* and with complete understanding, the designs FAITH holds forth for such divine fulfilling.

This is why it is "Impossible to please God without FAITH!" For God Himself gave man the ability to fashion and to form and to bring forth from the universal substance the fulfilment of his glorified hopes. In this creating the element of LIGHT or Spirit is transformed into the very atoms of fulfilling as they take shape in the material world.

HOPE is composed of the divine element of LIGHT as it is generated into the activity of its own forming by the divine power of FAITH.

It is the element of the divine, primal substance of Creation, as it is stamped with the image or pattern of one's own desiring or thought pictures or hopes that produces and brings forth. And it is also with this divine power that the world, or the inhabitants thereof, create their own miseries and ills. And each man is the designer of his own calamities and his own downfall, as well as the creator of his own glories. And in this truth is contained the knowledge which Christ endeavored to reveal: "Any man who looks on a woman to lust after her has committed adultery with her already in his heart." The pattern has been formed and established. And that pattern is real.

But man can change himself from a creature of evil and corruption and destruction and become a divine instrument worthy of his own perfection if so be he chooses to accept the responsibility of his own thinking processes. As one changes his thinking habits he also changes himself.

Man not only has free access to the divine element of creation, he has the power and the ability to decree what it is he will bring forth. This is the power of true creatorship or god-hood.

"Whatsoever you desire when you pray, believe that you receive it and you shall have whatsoever you ask!"

"If you do as I say then am I bound; but if you do not as I say then YOU HAVE NO PROMISE." To PROVE anything one has to LIVE the laws pertaining to its fulfilling. Nothing can be proved or disproved by denying.

You are a God—a divine Creator—a fashioner of the Primal element of Faith-engendered LIGHT as you receive HIS WORD and so fulfill HIS PROMISES.

And "NOTHING IS IMPOSSIBLE TO HIM WHO BELIEVES!"

And it is possible to "Deck oneself in majesty and excellence and to array oneself in glory and beauty" as God demanded of Job. To accomplish this it is quite necessary that one become completely spiritualized as Christ explained to Nicodemus in St. JOHN 3:3-12.

When Christ spoke to Nicodemus about the need to be born of the water and of the spirit before it would be possible to see the "Kingdom of God" He was speaking of the *Waters of Life* which were to flow forth through the very heart centers of the children of men. And these holy waters are LOVE perfected.

When He was speaking of being "Born of the Spirit" He was explaining not only the possibility but the necessity of "being born again" or of having the carnal flesh changed or perfected or spiritualized. Then only is it possible to "see the Kingdom of God." No earthly ordinance can possibly achieve this divine, holy accomplishment except being "Born of the Spirit" with the power to travel with the speed of Light giving service wheresoever it is required.

And then Christ demanded of Nicodemus an explanation of his dead and lifeless works of futility in these words: "Art thou a master in Israel, and knowest not these things?" In other words He was asking, "How dare you go forth professing to be a teacher without knowing these things?" And remember, to KNOW anything one must experience it. Nicodemus was professing to be a master or teacher in Israel and had never even heard of this required power and so consequently had never believed in it.

Then Christ testified: "Verily, Verily, I say unto thee, *we* speak what *we* do KNOW, and testify that *we* have seen; and you receive not our witness.

"If I have told you earthly things and ye believe not how shall ye believe if I told you of heavenly things?"

This law of being "Born of the Spirit" is truly an *earthly* achievement. It must be accomplished here on this earth as one *hungers and thirsts after righteousness* and so changes his carnal flesh to flesh divine without descending through the gates of death. And only from this earth plain can this divine accomplishment be achieved. And if one cannot believe in this *earthly* wonder and fulfill it how can he possibly be prepared to be told or see or believe the heavenly things?

The fulfilling of this divine Law of Spiritual Power will indeed clothe one in majesty and excellence and array him in glory and beauty and everlasting life.

CHAPTER XXIII.

"All That the Father Has Is Yours"

"ALL THAT THE FATHER HAS IS YOURS!"
"That which is of God is light; and he that receiveth light, and continueth in God, receiveth more light; and that light groweth brighter until the perfect day.

"And again, verily I say unto you, and I say it that you may chase darkness from among you:

"He that is ordained of God and sent forth the same is appointed to be the greatest, notwithstanding he is the least and the servant of all.

"Wherefore, he is possessor of all things; for all things are subject unto him, both in heaven and on earth, the life and the light, the spirit and the power, sent forth by the will of the Father through Jesus Christ, His Son.

"BUT NO MAN IS POSSESSOR OF ALL THINGS EXCEPT HE BE PURIFIED AND CLEANSED FROM ALL SIN.

"AND IF YOU ARE PURIFIED AND CLEANSED FROM ALL SIN, YE SHALL ASK WHATSOEVER YOU WILL IN THE NAME OF JESUS AND IT SHALL BE DONE!" (Doc. & Cov. 50:24-29 or as it is given on page 328 of "Ye Are Gods.")

The foregoing scripture has been mentioned before in this work. But now its very fulness must be completely unveiled. It must be held in mind always that that which is of God is Light! It is always light and there is no darkness in it. *Not ever!* And as one holds to the light he will continue to receive more and more light, which is joy and confidence and understanding until *"there is no darkness in him."* Such is promised that his light will increase until the PERFECT DAY. This perfect day is when the individual himself has OVERCOME the darkness, the negation, the doubting and fears within himself by learning to turn on that magic switch as his mind shuts out the darkness and turns on the light. And this LIGHT is intelligence. And it is perfected in the individual who learns to hold his mind single to the glory of God, or who mentally thinks only the most beautiful things possible. Such will become glorified in light and *"Will comprehend all things!"* Then it will be that he will be ordained of God and sent forth to become the servant of all, in the glory of the "greater works" as he is "BORN OF THE SPIRIT!" This is the ordination of God. And this is the PROMISE and the COVENANT OF ALMIGHTY GOD. This is the ordination and the fulfilling that no man can bestow upon another. Only God can bestow it when man has fulfilled his part of the Covenant.

And he who thus OVERCOMES the darkness is "possessor of all things; for all things will become subject unto him; both in heaven and on earth, the life and the light, the spirit and the POWER—." As ALL THINGS become subject unto one, both in HEAVEN and ON EARTH he has gained full access into the realms of divine wonder where the understanding and the power to take hold of that holy, spiritual substance, the primal matter, is henceforth his own to use as he brings into earthly form the full accomplishment or fulfillment of his yearning HOPES and desires.

The very purification mentioned, "the cleansing from all sin" is but the OVERCOMING of one's own doubts and fears and negations. These are "the evils of one's life." And the OVERCOMING is achieved by the using of that switch as the individual becomes the master of his thoughts instead of being mastered and enslaved by them.

Thus as one masters these realms of darkness by learning to use that divine switch to turn on the LIGHT he becomes filled with Light. And eventually he will become that LIGHT. "He becomes glorious," according to the PROMISE, or COVENANT. And the very realms of heaven become his to explore and to use, as all things in heaven, the elements the glory and the power become subject to him. This subjection is but the ability to take hold of the elements of Light and the Primal substance or divine material and mold it into form, useable and dynamic in its power of fulfilling. These are the things of heaven that become subject unto one as he begins to make use of them—"WHEN THE DARKNESS IS CAST OUT!"

"The things of earth" that become subject unto one are the material things which he has developed the power to bring forth and to fashion from that primal element. Thus they take on earthly form. These gifts belong also to the one who "overcomes the evils of his life," as he brings forth the desires of his own envisioning holding steadfastly to his Hope until it materializes and takes tangible form. This is the law and the PROMISE.

Thus all things do become subject unto him, both in heaven and on earth as he uses that divine gift of creating to bring forth onto the earth plane the fashioning of his own righteous desires. The Primal matter becomes his to manipulate and to create with. This is the matured reality of which a child's molding clay is but the toy. "And all things are possible to him who believes!"

The command of God to man is: "to ask, to seek and to knock." And the assured PROMISE or COVENANT OF GOD is eternal, unfailing and everlasting. The fulfilling of this divine invitation to search is sealed with the divine Covenant of God upon it. And God is literally bound to fulfill the PROMISE to all who will only accept the challenge or the invitation to "ask, to seek or to knock. For *everyone* who asks receives! And he who seeks finds! And unto him who knocks it shall be opened."

The very asking is the establishing of the request. It is the desire or the spiritual pattern being stamped upon that sacred element "waiting to become!" The desire must be fulfilled if one does not "WAVER" or DOUBT and who refuses to cease to ask before his request is fully established. This is the law of fulfilling. It cannot fail! Man can fail and has failed down the centuries because he ceases to ask before his desire is completely established on that Primal, Spiritual element of Creation, the substance of "things HOPED for."

That divine substance, that holy, spiritual element is waiting for man himself to take hold of it MENTALLY as he fashions it into the pattern of his HOPE. And this procedure is FAITH in action and man was ordained to use this breathtaking element of creation and glory and power.

In this way the very things of heaven and of earth do become subject unto the individual who will cast out the darkness of doubting and unbelief, which is the impurity of sin that must be OVERCOME. And only by the intelligent use of that divine switch, as one lights up the realms of his own thinking, can this be accomplished.

Yes, "All that the Father has is yours!" To use! To glorify and to be glorified by!

Next, the privilege to *prove* one's FAITH or ability to use this primal substance of creation comes in the suggestion of praise as one gives thanks continually for his own hope or desire. This thanksgiving releases the power to *believe* within the heart of man. And this brings forth his request more speedily and more perfectly than any other method in existence. This very attitude of praising and the vibrations of gratitude opens up those higher realms of light, and thus the very Light itself becomes subject unto the individual. This light, which can become subject unto man is his forever as he learns to cast out the darkness of his own thinking and feeling habits.

The released praise and thanks for the things one *desires* clothes the desire in form and helps to bring forth the true spiritual essence as the request is held to "WITHOUT WAVERING or DOUBTING." And in this manner do they take form in the tangible world.

The vibrating praise issuing out of one's own soul and the LOVE and gratitude, when sincere and constant, establishes that vibration of expectancy and assurance, and most of all that exuberant, inner enthusiasm which is the sacred, divine attitude carrying its own laws of accomplishment. It is this singing vibration of glory that carries the power to fully and completely "cast out the darkness" and conquer it forever.

Thus the Light does become subject unto one. He can use it at all times, clothe himself in it and "Cast the darkness out of his life!" The Light is also the intelligence and the understanding that is promised in which an individual will be given the power to "COMPREHEND ALL THINGS."

The "Life also will become subject unto him," for he will "BE BORN OF THE SPIRIT" and after that "no one will be able to take his life from him," except he permits it.

"The Spirit becomes subject unto him," when he has learned the dynamic, majestic control as he holds his being in a hallowed majesty of divine awareness. In this control only can one possibly take hold of that glorious spiritual element of primal matter and mold it into form and bring it forth as tangible substance.

"The Power becomes also subject unto him," when he has learned to cast out the darkness, so that the fulness of the gift of creation will be subject unto him as he uses it for the fulfillment of his needs and to glorify and benefit a world. These are the PROMISES! And God has sealed them upon man by the most sacred divine COVENANT possible to give.

"And this is the confidence that we have in him, that, if we ask anything according to His will (or His law) He heareth us;

"And if we know that he hear us, whatsoever we ask, we know that we have the petitions that we desired of him." (I. John 5:14-15).

This information is indeed perfect. And we ask according to the will of God always when we ask without doubting. When we ask Him in confidence we are asking according to His Will and as we ask in this manner we can absolutely KNOW that our request has been heard for our desire is established upon that divine, spiritualized element of primal matter. This is how our asking becomes powerful, for it is established in FAITH and by FAITH. And in this manner "we KNOW that we have the petitions that we have desired of Him."

The very vibrations of assurance opens wide the door to the substance of FAITH as the HOPE is established in confidence. And the more one uses this method and this substance the more proficient he becomes and the more speedily will his requests come into materialization, until *"he shall receive whatsoever he asks,"* or needs, or desires or HOPES for *"even before he asks."*

This is the power of "asking according to the will of God." One need not approach God in a begging, pleading, wailing supplicating attitude of hopelessness and despair. Remember, "despair cometh because of iniquity." This dismal attitude of groveling, cringing dismay establishes the very darkness of doubting and unbelief. And "IS NOT ACCORDING TO THE WILL OF GOD!" And as a rule, any request released under desolating, anguished moaning IS not answered because the only pattern held forth for fulfilling is the doubting, desolation of failure and anguished self-pity. And there is no FAITH in it. Nor can it reach into the realms of FAITH and fulfilment. There is no power with which to establish the pattern or HOPE to plant or impress the desire upon that sacred element of primal matter except man's own power to accept and to BELIEVE.

When Job began to bemoan the day of his birth in a lamentation of self-pity, God spoke to him out of the whirlwind commanding: "Gird up now thy loins like a man (not a cry baby); for I will demand of thee, and answer thou me—."

"Asking according to the will of God is to ask in confidence!" Ask, without doubting as you hold forth your desire for fulfilling. And know this: You could not possibly hold a righteous desire forth in your heart unless it was from God in the beginning. Pure, holy desiring is always of God, and is God's will. There has been no command or instruction in all existence, or even a shadow of a suggestion that forbids any individual from desiring, and hoping and asking and seeking for ANYTHING he could possibly imagine or HOPE FOR. "Ask! Seek! and FIND!" These are the eternal admonitions of God. "And if you are without HOPE you will of very necessity be in despair. And despair cometh because of iniquity." And to be "iniquitous" is laying hold upon the very depths of darkness and failure. And it is contrary to the Will of God and all the PROMISES and Covenants and instructions of God to accept such a condition.

Show me an individual who has become so lost in negation he cannot lift his mind or heart or soul to contemplate "THE BEST GIFTS" and "ASK FOR THE BEST GIFTS" and I will show you a person who is damned into the frustrated condition of *everlasting failure!*

As one casts out the darkness by laying hold of the creative power of Light and the substance of HOPE, or *dreams* and who can lift his soul to desire, the very doors of glory will open to fulfill his requests. He will truly "be thankful in all things and will become glorious!"

"For *everyone* who asks receives!" And "he who seeks finds and unto him who knocks" those doors to all fulfilling will be opened. "For all that the Father has is yours!"

Now, in returning to Job chapter thirty-eight, verses one to ten, we are given a very breathtaking picture of the forces of creation in action. When the Lord answered Job out of the whirlwind He said, "Who is this that darkeneth counsel by words without knowledge? (meaning Job's three false comforters—and the world is full of such).

"Gird up now thy loins like a man: for I will demand of thee, and answer thou me.

"Where wast thou when I laid the foundations of the earth? Declare if thou hast understanding.

"Who hath laid the measure thereof, if thou knowest? Or who hath stretched the line upon it?

"Whereupon are the foundations thereof fastened? Or who laid the corner stone thereof;

"When the morning stars sang together, and *all the sons of God shouted for joy?*

"Or who shut up the sea with doors when it break forth, as if it had issued out of the womb?

"When I made the cloud the garment thereof; and thick darkness a swaddlingband for it.

"And brake up for it my decreed place, and set bars and doors."

Then in Job chapter forty and verse ten is given this Command: "DECK THYSELF NOW WITH MAJESTY AND EXCELLENCE: AND ARRAY THYSELF WITH GLORY AND BEAUTY!"

Yes, man is commanded to "deck himself with majesty and excellence" as he stands before God, arrayed in glory and beauty, fulfilling his own divine nature. Man was not meant to grovel or crawl or belittle himself in the death shrouds of the defilement of doubting and unbelief. And in that realm of God's "DECREED PLACE" mentioned, God fashioned the region of His own glorified substance of Primal matter, the material or element of all HOPES and desires, as yet unformed, to wait for man's own transforming.

On that GREATEST OF ALL DAYS—the day when the "FOUNDATIONS OF THE EARTH WERE LAID," God's daughters sang together in the joy and wonder of a NEW WORLD being created for their future abode. And *ALL the sons of God shouted for joy* at their great anticipation of the future existence which was to be theirs.

It was to Job that God hurled out the magic mystery of the unfathomable powers of creation with the foundations of a world being laid without anything to attach those foundations to or anything to hold the great cornerstone of its tangible, earthly form. The powers of creation were used by God Himself as He brought forth from the primal substance of LIGHT the decreed designs of His own divine planning. He revealed a glimpse of the magnificent splendor of a world formed from the creative wonder of His own imagining.

It is as though God was familiar with each grain of sand and loved each one tenderly. And as though He brought forth with His own hand the fashioning of the sea and the clouds for its garments. The very dew drops seem to be held in loving tenderness in the joy of His creating. The monsters of the deep are His and of His own bringing forth. The spectacular glory of creation is for a moment revealed as the doors are opened to permit a brief, penetrating glance into the mysteries of God's great planning and the breathtaking wonder of the fulfilling as all things were formed, taking shape from the glory of His thoughts.

"And all that the Father has is yours!" All the elements and all the powers of creation are man's to use, as FAITH IS EXERCISED AND DEVELOPED AND EMPLOYED. Such is the PROMISE! And such is the COVENANT of its fulfilling.

The first inspired glimpse of an idea, the very thought of some seeming remote possibility, the material of a wish, the glorious wonder of a HOPE is fashioned from that holy element of LIGHT. The LIGHT of inspiration is the element of that primal substance taking form. It may be only a vague sketch of a blue-print, a revealing flash of that which can be. But it holds within it the Spirit of Revelation. And it is within man's power to bring it forth.

CHAPTER XXIV.

The Day the Foundations of the Earth Were Laid

When God commanded Job to gird up his loins like a man and recall the day when the foundations of the earth were laid, "When ALL the sons of God shouted for joy," He was demanding that Job remember his own great anticipation that had vibrated across the universe on that prodigious occasion. He was also demanding that Job recall the ecstatic rejoicing in the hearts of those who were to inherit this new world as their abode. God was awakening Job to the recollection of his own reactions upon that glorious day of long ago.

And as Job was there on that momentous occasion so were the rest of us.

"Then the word of the Lord came unto me (Jeremiah) saying,

"Before I formed thee in the belly I knew thee; and before thou came forth out of the womb I sanctified thee, and I ordained thee a prophet unto the nations." (Jer. 1:4-5).

In Phillipians 4:3, is given an admonition by Paul for the Saints to be mindful of those who had labored with him, "Whose names are in the Book of Life."

This sacred "Lamb's Book of Life, written from the foundations of the world," is mentioned many times in the Bible.

In Revelations, 3:5, it was revealed that there are those *whose names will be taken out of that Book of Life*, if they fail to fulfill the Promises which belonged to them, before time began.

Then is given the information that there are many whose names were not written in that sacred record, "The Lamb's Book of Life!"

The names that *were* written upon that most sacred scroll were not placed there because some capricious god had a hobby of writing down names—then later, along the unfolding of the centuries we were brought forth just to fill those names. THOSE WERE OUR NAMES! And they were engraved upon that hallowed record *because we had earned the right to have them there.* In exercising our free agency in the ages of the past some had proved more valiant, more obedient and more desirous of fulfilling the laws of their own progress. Some had proved themselves more trustworthy and more loving and gracious. Or as the Writer of the Odes of Solomon stated: "Love is of the elect and who can put it on except those who possessed it from the beginning?"

And there were those who were indifferent and slothful and negligent and even some who developed jealousies and dishonesty. And as it was said of Lucifer, "He was a liar from the beginning." These, of course, did not have their names written in that sacred record. These did not have the qualifications necessary to have their names written upon that scroll of honor and eternal Promise, simply because they had not earned it. And there were many of them.

In Revelations, chapter twelve and verse ten it states clearly that Satan or the Devil was "the accuser of his brethren" even before the foundations of the world, "That he accused them before the throne of God day and night." For even then he had developed the desire to rule over his brethren. He desired that man's gift of free-agency be withdrawn and he be given the power of dictatorship over all the children of God. Because of this there was of necessity an election, as all were given a right to voice their opinion. And in that election "CHRIST WAS CHOSEN BEFORE THE FOUNDATIONS OF THE WORLD." And because of this "there was War in heaven" —a war of ideologies. (Rev. 12:7-9). The Book of Revelations also declares plainly that Christ was CHOSEN before the foundations of the world. And if He was *chosen* there had to be others to *choose* from.

And there were many who made no choice at all, or took no part in the great issue. These were not cast out with Lucifer and his rebellious hosts, but neither did they have their names written in that Holy Book of Life because they had not earned the right to be so greatly honored. These inferior ones were assigned to inferior races, such as the Syrophenician woman, whom Christ designated as "dogs." (Mark 7:26).

In Ephesians one and four, is given this scripture: "According as *he hath chosen us in him before the foundations of the world,* that we should be holy and without blame before him in love." In verses five and eleven it speaks of having been "predestinated." This is inaccurately translated. From the original it states plainly that were "fore-ordained." "Fore-ordained" means that we had a choice and still do. We were fore-ordained or chosen because of merits we had accumulated *before* we came to earth. "Predestinated" suggests that no choice had been or is given. Man has always been given a choice. This gift of free-agency is God's eternal gift to man. Only when the powers of darkness take over is man robbed of this right. "Satan's plan, from the beginning, has been to rule by undisputed dictatorship.

In the Odes of Solomon, that sacred writer has left us this record in the 8th Ode, 7-8 and 14-16: "For the right hand of the Lord is with you; and He is your helper:

8. "And PEACE was prepared for you before ever your war was."

14. "Love me with affection, ye who love:

15. "For I do not turn away my face from them that are mine.

16. "For I know them and before they came into being I took knowledge of them and on their faces I set my seal."

In the eighth chapter of Romans, starting with verse twenty-four, we are given the following information: "For we are saved by HOPE: but *hope that is seen is not hope:* for what a man seeth, why doth he yet hope for?

"Likewise the Spirit also helpeth our infirmities; for we know not what we should pray for as we ought; but the spirit itself maketh intercession for us with groanings which cannot be uttered.

"And he that searcheth the hearts knoweth what is in the mind of the Spirit, because he maketh intercession for the Saints according to the will of God.

"And we knoweth that all things work together for good to them that love God, to them who are called according to his purpose.

"For WHOM HE DID FOREKNOW, HE ALSO DID FOREORDAIN TO BE CONFORMED TO THE IMAGE OF HIS SON, THAT HE MIGHT BE THE FIRSTBORN AMONG MANY BRETHREN.

"Moreover WHOM HE DID FOREORDAIN, THEM he also called and whom he called, them he also justified; and whom he justified them he also glorified."

With only these few references mentioned I must go on because there is not time or space here to make a longer discourse upon this great, eternal wonder of our preexistence, for we too existed before the world was. This is not reincarnation. This is a statement of eternal fact and a brief reminder of our primeval, spiritual existence before the world was formed.

There is no living soul upon this earth who has not had the experience of meeting a seeming stranger and recognized in him or her, an old friend, though unrembered as far as earth memory is concerned. And there are those who, even among the members of their own families, have found themselves to be strangers. And there are neighbors, living side by side for years, who find no congenial contacts and who feel no warmth for each other. Whence came these ties of love and friendship—and the lack of them?

With this brief mention or reminder of that long ago, I must go on to hold forth, for a moment, the wonder of that DAY when the foundations of the earth were laid and ALL THE SONS of God shouted for joy!

"Then the Lord answered Job out of the whirlwind (after he, Job, had cursed the day he had been born with a violence of misery and self-pity so intense it almost held within it the powers to destory his soul).

Then it was that God's rebuke came forth full and without soft-pedaling: "Gird up now thy loins like a man; for I will demand of thee, and answer thou me.

"Where wast thou when I laid the foundations of the earth? Declare if thou hast understanding (or think you know so much).

"Who hath laid the measure thereof, if thou knowest? Or who hath stretched the line upon it?

"Where upon are the foundations thereof fastened? Or who laid the corner stone thereof;

"When the morning stars (daughters) sang together, and ALL THE SONS OF GOD shouted for joy!"

The command for Job, and all mankind for that matter, to live up to the divine expectations of that glorious DAY are summed up thus by God: *"Deck thyself with majesty and excellence, and array thyself with glory and beauty!"*

Or, as the writer of the Odes of Solomon expressed it: "I put off darkness and clothed myself in light, and my soul acquired a body free from sorrow or affliction or pain."

No man was meant to sit in the dump-yard and ashes of his troubles and intensify the suffering of his boils by holding his full attention upon them and his earthly affliction. This only establishes them more permanently.

On that DAY, so long ago, when the foundations of the earth were laid we were celebrating the most momentous experience of our existence. Nothing so great and so breathtakingly glorious had ever taken place before in the eons of our development and progression. A NEW WORLD was to be created for our future abode in which we could be given physical bodies and learn to handle tangible, physical materials. There was also the promised opportunity to thoroughly prove ourselves. That DAY held the reward for the past and also a promise and a challenge for the future. It contained all the things we had been preparing ourselves for from the beginning.

And as we gathered to take part in the breathtaking wonder of that celebration and the miracle of that greatest of all Days, we were celebrating all its PROMISES for it held all that we had ever been conditioned to hope for. It was a reward for the past. It was also a PROMISE for the future and a challenge to each of us. It contained all the things we had been preparing ourselves for from the cradle of our Spiritual inception as our individual personalities began to evolve toward our own leanings.

It is most assuredly true, "THAT WE WERE ALL CREATED EQUAL IN THE BEGINNING!" But since that beginning some had progressed far beyond others by their own efforts and interests and desiring and the exerted use of intelligence. We were no longer equal only in the fact that we could still make a choice in selecting our goals and in the development of our talents and gauge the speed at which we wished to travel. In that alone we were still equal. We come to earth with the developed degree of our own talents and intelligence that we ourselves expanded.

And as we gathered to take part in that most dynamic of all celebrations and to participate in the PROMISES

OF ALL THAT IT HELD, our very souls rejoiced in a released gratitude of exultation that echoed across the universe in an elation so great it could help to hold the foundations of the earth firm as they rested upon our own exuberant, triumphant, delighted jubilation.

We were a very part of God's own plan. We were there to receive the fulfillment of past PROMISES as God Himself rejoiced and our own joy was full. And in that exotic celebrating God stood forth to speak His Words of PEACE and LOVE and DEDICATION and FUTURE PROMISES. And He sent His Words out in their primal, vibrating splendor of unspeakable beauty. And those Words were clothed in Light so perfect it held the perfection of all the Celestial music of Creation as His divine PROMISES rolled forth across the universe to embrace eternity. And each PROMISE was clothed in the wonder and the breathtaking power of God's own divine COVENANTS as they were contained in each pledge released.

His PROMISES were sent out on the wings of vibrating Light, across the heavens in an harmonious melody of everlasting grandeur. And every symphony since that time, that has been brought forth by the masters, is but a fragment of the whole carillon, pealed out on the bells of glory and echoed on the chiming cymbals of God's own WORDS sent out on the wings of LOVE ETERNAL AND EVERLASTING as they were carried on the vibrational glory of His Light. There are no words to describe it! I cannot possibly reveal it! I can only ask that you open your own hearts and souls to recall that breathtaking experience. It is your own as you remember and as you "Gird up the loins of your minds" to recall, and "Deck yourselves with majesty and excellence, and array yourselves with glory and with beauty!" Even as upon that DAY OF LONG AGO.

HIS WORDS flowed out to encircle and to enfold us and to vibrate out across the universe—and then to come echoing back to find their resting place within the hearts of each of us. They were God's PROMISES TO US. And each PROMISE was enfolded in an holy COVENANT as they engraved themselves within the archived hearts of our throbbing souls. They belonged to us henceforth and forever! God Himself gave them to us on that great DAY OF DEDICATION SO LONG AGO. And the yearning for their fulfillment has been but the lonely longing cradled in the depths of our own beings since time itself began. All those inner longings, the loneliness, the desperate, unshed tears are but the whispered echo of that which our own souls are waiting to express as those PROMISES are fulfilled in us and brought forth in the completion of their glory.

And as those PROMISES, SENT OUT ON THE WINGS OF LIGHT, CAME ECHOING BACK TO US WE EACH RECEIVED AN INDIVIDUAL PORTION, or a *special anointing* according to that for which we had prepared ourselves. To those who were most worthy the greater were the Promises vouchsafed unto them and the responsibility for their fulfilling for: "TO WHOM MUCH IS GIVEN MUCH IS REQUIRED."

Nonetheless any PROMISE when taken hold of, as one lays claim to it as the "BEST GIFT" he personally can desire, will lead into the fullness of all the PROMISES—the divine perfection—the complete restoration of all that we ever did have plus the added rewards of all that we have attained to in the deep and intense schooling of this life.

Why have we not claimed the PROMISES before? Because they were hid up in the depths of our own souls "from the foundations of the world because of the blindness of our eyes, and the hardness of our hearts, and because of the gross wickedness of our unbelief." As we took upon us the privilege of mortality the things of the Spirit were more or less submerged and laid aside until such time as we would awaken and lay claim to them again and thus regain our lost estate.

This PROMISE was also given: "That when we would rend that veil of unbelief, which caused us to remain in our awful state of wickedness and hardness of heart, every PROMISE God gave upon that sacred, holy DAY would be brought forth in us—and be fulfilled. That is the reason that at last, those PROMISES can be unveiled to those who are in tune as they stir up the ancient HOPES and the glorified wonder of that long ago. And with that unveiling the power and reality of God's Everlasting Covenant will stand forth revealed and fulfilled. And it is to those who had their names engraved upon that sacred scroll, "the Lamb's Book of Life" who will be best prepared to comprehend the possibility of their own fulfilling as they become *righteous* in the truest sense of the word. And this "righteousness" can only be attained by those who perfect the divine and holy gift of LOVE.

God sent those PROMISES forth on the wings of celestial music. It was a symphony, glorious beyond man's power to express. No one person could gather it all back again unless he himself had fulfilled all things. But down the centuries there have been those talented ones, in tune with the divine, who, for a moment or long enough to reach out into the archives of eternity have brought back portions of that melody to us. And in hearing it we can partially recall the wonder of that DAY of DAYS!

Often in hearing the rendition of some inspired selection by those great masters, Handel, Mozart, Beethoven and any of those who have brought forth the haunting melodies for our souls to respond to with such infinite, inner longing or an exalted feeling of satisfaction are but giving a reminder of those ancient, forgotten memories.

And the prophets and the seers of the past, under the power of divine attunement have revealed those PROMISES—and as the years went by they were dropped and hidden between the crowded passages of scripture gathering through the dust of the ages. The PROMISES, when revealed were so hidden in the verbiage of many words crowded around them no eyes could look upon their glory. And no heart opened to recognize the wonder of their revealing until this present day.

And at this wondrous time God commanded that I gather those divine and eternal PROMISES back into one—and they have been placed by His command, in that sacred volume *"Beyond Mortal Boundaries."*

This is the day of their unveiling. This is the day of their fulfilling. This is the time to complete the miracle and the wonder of that "DAY when the foundations of the earth were laid." This is the day when all those glorified PROMISES of Almighty God are unveiled as they stand forth revealed. This is the day when that veil of unbelief is to be rent. For the time is NOW!

This is the day when God has opened wide His Treasure House of PROMISES, and revealed the holy Covenant contained in each—and the glory of their fulfilment. Man is now invited by the Most High Father of All Creation to open up his heart and lay claim to all that the Father promised before the world began.

Yes, *"Deck thyself, now with majesty and excellence; and array thyself with glory and beauty!"*

Reach your hands in and take hold of any of those most holy PROMISES, for they are yours! They were given unto you when the foundations of the earth were laid! Lay claim to them! The Treasure House of God is opened to you! Take hold of the jewels of PROMISE and bring them forth into reality as you implant your most sacred desires upon that divine element of Primal Matter, to bring into outward form the very glory and fulfilling of all that God can give—or you can possibly desire, for it is given unto you by an unbreakable Covenant as you fulfill or HOPE.

"Nothing is impossible to him who believes!" And "All that the Father has is yours!"

Then we are informed, by the very power and *Word* of God that, "God's Words cannot return unto Him unfulfilled or void!" This is true. In the volume *"Beyond Mortal Boundaries"* is given the information that only man himself can return those PROMISES or WORDS to God. God sent them out as they were echoed forth like glory upon that DAY, so long ago. But it is not for God to gather them up again. It is for us to whom they were given to return them back to HIM.

And so His Promises or Words or Covenants cannot return unto Him unfulfilled or void. It is up to us to lay hold upon them and return them to God—FULFILLED.

We are required to FULFILL THOSE PROMISES before they can ever be returned unto God as they become the everlasting Covenant of all fulfilling. We, as participants in His Holy Covenanting, are the members of that second party under which His pledge was given.

As we lay claim to those PROMISES only can they be fulfilled. And as we ourselves become the embodiment of His Words and Promises do we have right to lay claim to the Covenants they embrace as we thus return them unto Him—OURSELVES FULFILLED. This is how we can return unto Him glorified. Thus we too become the WORD, the actual living Word of God, as it becomes our flesh.

In the thirteenth Ode of Solomon, verses eleven and twelve, it states: "For the dwelling place of His Word is man; and its truth is LOVE!"

The eternal archives of those PROMISES of Almighty God are in the hearts of the children of men. The Dwelling Place of His Word or Promises to God FULFILLED as the everlasting Covenants of God are claimed. The very power to fulfill those divine Promises is held out in that divine element of Primal matter as FAITH is generated to bring it forth full fashioned and complete. As we take hold of the information contained in this record we can use God's Power to bring forth. We can lay hold of that Primal Substance, the element of *things Hoped for* and transform it into tangible, visible elements. Thus we inherit the full realization of all that God ever PROMISED—and MORE!

Dip your hands into the Treasure House of all that is possible to fulfill, according to your own power to envision. And hold firmly to your requests. Yes! "Lay hold of the best gifts" and they will become your own.

This is the very purpose for which the foundations of the earth were laid—that in the receiving of physical bodies we could thereby learn to handle material, earthly elements. Or, as the plan was, that we could learn to transform the spiritual substance of HOPE or DESIRE into earthly tangibility. This is the purpose and the meaning of mortality.

I. Cor. 2:5-10, is revealed some of the great truths of that pre-mortal time, as follows: "That your faith should not stand in the wisdom of men, but in the power of God.

"Howbeit we speak wisdom among them that are perfect: yet not the wisdom of this world, nor of the princes of this world, that come to nought.

"But we speak the wisdom of God in a mystery, even the hidden wisdom, *which God ordained before the world unto our glory.*

"Which none of the princes of this world knew: for had they known it, they would not have crucified the Lord of glory.

"But as it is written, Eye hath not seen, nor ear heard, neither hath it entered into the heart of man, the things which God hath prepared for them THAT LOVE HIM.

"But God hath revealed them unto us by His Spirit; for the Spirit searcheth all things, yes, the deep things of God."

And as one's soul searches that which is given to abide in him will be returned as a memory, beautiful and eternal, *"for it is given to abide in you the record of heaven * * *."*

"And he who is thankful in all things shall be made

glorious, and the things of this earth shall be added unto him an hundred-fold, yea, more!"

The very vibrations of gratitude and appreciation places one in tune with the divine. And thanksgiving is the law of bringing forth from the universal substance of Primal matter, as FAITH swings into action to fulfill the needs, increase the supply or to create the magnificent glory of one's HOPES.

God never intended anyone to go through life in want and poverty and desolation, existing in shacks or hovels, clothed in the shabby rags of mortal misery or feeding on the crumbs of charity.

Without access to these divine powers of the Almighty even the rich man is living in a forlorn, forsaken condition of incomprehensible destitution, for God said: "Because thou sayest, I am rich and increased with goods and have need of nothing; and knowest not that thou art poor and wretched and miserable and blind and naked."

Just being clothed in mortality without contacting the true powers of creation is a desolating condition of inner anguish.

"Man is that he might have joy!" So declared God upon that *Holy Day*. Man was created to rejoice! As one advances in purity his understanding increases until he evolves into an exuberant glory of fulfilment and "ALL THINGS WORK TOGETHER FOR HIS GOOD!"

Christ Himself verified this to me when I had prayed so earnestly and constantly for the healing of my child that she would not have to live a life so marred with illness it would not be worth the living.

On that night, when I thought my child was dead, and in the tears of utter heartbreak I released her to God,

I learned the power of prayer. Christ stood there and my child was brought back to life and healed. Then it was that Christ showed me the unspeakable wonder of His blessings, which my mind had never been conditioned to comprehend. He stood with his arms laden with the treasures of life and of eternity. They were PROMISED for this life—for the NOW—for the glory and the wonder of perfect, everyday living. And they were also for all eternity. I saw the gifts, though I could never explain how. I beheld them with my eyes. I gazed upon them with wondering incomprehension, unable to grasp the truth at that time for I had been trained to believe that only desolate suffering could claim any rewards.

But in Christ's arms was the gift of perfect health, of poise and majesty and peace and plenty and joy and happiness and power to rule one's life and control all conditions in a glory of sublime dominion. Man's true and full heritage is to "HAVE DOMINION OVER THE EARTH AND EVERY CONDITION UPON IT—AND OVER HIS OWN LIFE!" There was not only the power to reach into eternity and help glorify the world beyond and use the essence of its glory fully and completely.

And Christ, the Beloved Savior, spoke these words in the vibrations of His eternal, glorious LOVE and understanding compassion and divine comfort: "These are the blessings I am so anxious and eager to bestow upon the children of men as soon as they are prepared to receive them!" And I who had been taught that only misery had any rewards, was at that time unable to receive the full import and glory of His message.

And now, in deepest humility, I bow my head and say, "Thank You Blessed Savior, Thou Son of the living God, for opening the way that mankind might be *prepared* to receive these everlasting blessings in their fulness as the eternal PROMISES and their divine COVENANTS are unfolded and fulfilled unto those who BELIEVE.

At last I have been given the privilege of sharing these wonders of creation and of fulfilling as His Dynamic TRUTHS and the power of their completion are unveiled.

And so it was that God blessed my "unbelief" as I struggled for many months to open my soul to understanding. And then, at last, the glory and the knowledge of those almost "unspeakable blessings" have been placed in my hands that I might share them with you. And this *sharing* is the greatest blessing of all, for it is time that these things be made known.

And God bless you forever! And may He give you the LOVE and the unselfishness to understand and to use the limitless powers of this divine, holy gift of Creation, through the exercising of your own FAITH, for it is the power of all fulfilling! And it is yours!

At the close of this work I pray that the writer and the writings be forgotten—that the words of expression will be dissolved and disappear and only the revealed TRUTHS stand forth with the great power of Almighty God alone supporting them. Let the glory of these indestructible realities, these eternal principles of PROMISE never again be *"hid up"* and forgotten. Let TRUTH alone stand forth in all its dynamic power of witnessing. Let these everlasting blessings of glory be proclaimed and established and made known.

Chapter XXV.

The Promises of God

II. Peter 1:3-4: *"According as His divine power hath given unto us all things that pertain to Life and Godliness, through the knowledge of Him that hath called us to glory and virtue.*

"Whereby are given unto us exceeding great and precious PROMISES, *that by these ye might be partakers of the* DIVINE NATURE, *Having escaped corruption that is in the world through lust."*

Return with me in memory to that great Day of PROMISE, for in it is contained all that the hungering soul of man can possibly yearn for.

Step with me across the millenniums to live again the anticipated joy released that Day to vibrate out through space as the PROMISES pealed forth to return again to find entrance within our own hearts. Then you will know why *expectation* is always so much greater than realization. We expect each day of Promise, each anticipated holiday to be as great as was that most glorious Day of Days. Then in disappointment we discover that nothing is as great as we had secretly calculated or planned. Nor will it be until we ourselves take hold of those everlasting PROMISES and bring them forth from the archived treasure house of our own hearts.

And the foundations of the earth were formed out of the "substance of things hoped for," and they were established upon the joy of our own anticipated fulfilling. And so they stood firm, resting on the spiritual glory of our own divine expectancy as it was called forth to uphold the foundations of the new world—the world called EARTH, for so was it named.

And then God spoke and His speaking was a symphony of dedication and of eternal blessing, poured out in PROMISES so great our ears were over-awed with the grandeur of their proclaiming. Only a few were able to grasp fully the lighted wonder of those PROMISES of eternal, everlasting beauty as they were sent out under the binding COVENANT of Almighty God, to endure forever! These PROMISES were to stand for all eternity, to await our full acceptance of them as we bring them forth full formed, in time, to lay as tribute at the Father's throne—His WORDS returned unto Him fulfilled—our very selves—glorified.

Christ alone understood fully the WORDS that were released, and gathering them into His heart, HE BECAME THE WORD upon that Holy Day!

Others of us gathered portions of those eternal PROMISES and then buried them so deeply within ourselves they have been almost forgotten in an echo that is but a haunting memory, unclaimed and unfulfilled.

But on that momentous day, as that Symphony of everlasting glory rolled forth across the universe, "ALL THE MORNING STARS SANG TOGETHER" as they picked up the rhythm and melody of that dynamic symphony of splendor and sang in unison with its great releasing.

"AND ALL THE SONS OF GOD SHOUTED FOR JOY!"

As the Father's WORDS were proclaimed and sent out on that divine harmony of heavenly, eternal radiance of splendor the WORDS rang forth to return from space, to find their own place of lodgement in our own singing hearts.

I cannot give all the Words or all the PROMISES to you as they rang forth upon that stupendous Day of DAYS, so long ago. I can only chant the echo of time as I hold them forth for you, who are at last prepared to receive the fulness of their glory as you open your own hearts to their releasing. The awakening desire, which their memory brings forth in you NOW was the ordained purpose of creation.

And God spoke and the sound thereof was as the rushing of many waters leaping in a jeweled cascade of singing exultation. The vibrations were such as no created thing or being had ever before felt or heard or experienced or imagined. It was the triumphant reward of all that we had ever hoped for, or that the eons of existence had ever PROMISED. It was the fulfilling of an epoch. It contained all the accumulated desires and hopes and rewards for the ages of our past labors and preparing, the essence of our true natures and being and our futures of co-existence as children of our Almighty Sire, the only True and Living God! Glorious! Eternal!

"And in the beginning God created the heavens and the earth.

"And the earth was without form, and void; and the darkness was upon the face of the deep, And the Spirit of God moved upon the face of the waters.

"And God said, Let there be Light; and there was Light." And with the Light came the dawning of new understanding as each of us took part in that which was to be.

And in time we helped to fashion the flowers for the Earth, the grasses that were to clothe her and the shrubs and the trees that were to adorn and beautify her. We placed a portion of ourselves and our own creative arts into the fashioning as God held forth the symphony for the rhythmed building of a world so new with promise, so shining with hope, so gloriously real and all the unfolding of the ages of its forming were ours to share in and to wait upon.

And God's words continued to echo and to re-echo and rebound within our hearts in that inspiring symphony of PROMISE held forth.

AND GOD SPOKE:

"Your life on earth will be the time of your fulfilling and of your perfecting, if so you are willing to lay claim to its promised blessings.

"As you go forth clothed in your earthly garments of flesh and bone and skin, you shall have dominion over the earth and over the elements thereof. You shall have dominion over all conditions and circumstances—and life, if so be you live up to your holy heritage. The birds of the air will be in subjection to you, and the animals, and the fish of the sea shall be at your command as you learn to bring your own physical beings into subjection, obeying the laws of your own progressions, for they are yours.

"The physical, mortal bodies you will receive, or be clothed in, will be precious beyond your present comprehension. They will be sacred, holy temples and if you live up to the great and wonderful PROMISES of this Day you will be able to exalt the physical forms into the fulness of their destined, spiritual glory. And you will be *born of the Spirit.* This Birth of the Spirit will be the glorious reward of all righteousness. It will contain the full recompense for your stepping down into the physical plane that thereby you can exalt your mortal bodies into the highest excellence of spirit substance, perfect, eternal, flawless and with a fulness of joy your everlasting reward. And you yourselves will be crowned with glory and honor and be filled with Light insomuch you shall comprehend all things. *And all things will become subject unto you, both in heaven and on earth; the LIFE and the LIGHT; the SPIRIT and the POWER*, that you might have dominion over all the realms beneath and above you forever as you become endowed with eternal glory.

"There is no PROMISE that is not yours as you lay claim to it, for *all that I have is yours!* The PROMISES that I now speak to you, and seal upon you, by eternal COVENANT are mine to give and yours to receive! And any and every righteous desire of your hearts shall be *added* unto you as you fulfill the laws of their coming forth.

"No one will ever be damned for BELIEVING too much or HOPING too much! Damnation is the condition that stops one from progressing and it comes because of believing too little, hoping too little and so experiencing nothing of PROMISE or of TRUTH. It is in small, skimped desiring and thinking that one fails as he shrivels into a condition of unbelief and wickedness.

"Think the most beautiful things possible and you

will become as beautiful as your thoughts. Think the most powerful things possible and as you send out your vibrations of LOVE AND FAITH you will become POWERFUL!

"Nothing will be impossible to him who believes or who will BE and LIVE according to the PROMISE he sets his heart upon. The desiring or hoping is the exercising of FAITH as it is generated in energy to contact the powers of heaven and to fulfill the requests. The divine powers of creation and of fulfilling are yours! I give them unto you this day. They will always be waiting for you to take hold of and use. It is up to you to exercise the energy necessary to contact or use them. This is the exercising of FAITH as you lay hold of the gifts you desire for your sojourn on Earth.

"As you keep your hearts pure, or as you purify them after the things of the flesh have been proven to be false and unsatisfying you can lift your minds and your hearts above all fleshly desires as you turn your thoughts to the spiritual things, which are yours. All that is necessary is that you desire them and turn to me with all your hearts. And trust not in the arm of flesh.

"As you *learn to hold your minds upon the Peaceable Things of Immortal Glory you will become glorious* for you will become a living symphony or prayer of unfanatical devotion. In time this symphony or rhythm of joyous adoration will be established within you as you bring it forth, a living power right within yourselves. It will become a song of inner praise and gratitude and will increase in your hearts until they are purified and *you will be cleansed from all sin. And he who prayeth continually, without ceasing shall have his mind opened to comprehend my mysteries. And unto him will be given power to comprehend all things and he will be given power to reveal things which have never been revealed and bring thousands of souls unto repentance* or unto a knowledge of my powers centered in their own souls.

"*The nearer you approach perfection the clearer will be your views and the greater will be your enjoyments, until you OVERCOME the evils of your life,* the darkness, the doubting, the self-righteousness and mortal negations, and *you will arrive at the point of Faith* where you will automatically *be wrapped in my power and my glory* and will *Be Born of the Spirit* and exalted. And I will call you back into my presence with your mortal bodies completely glorified without descending through the gates of death. And you will have the privilege to go on and do the Greater Works, according to your own desiring. This "POINT OF FAITH," which one reaches in this journey of OVERCOMING AND OF PERFECTION is when your own FAITH has been used and developed and when it turns into KNOWLEDGE—THAT YOU MIGHT SEE AND KNOW FOR YOURSELVES! This is my special PROMISE to you who prepare yourselves to receive. Hold to this PROMISE, you who desire it, for I seal it upon you NOW —and it will stand forever as you lay claim to it.

"*All that I have is yours! Ask and you shall receive! Seek and you shall find! Knock and it shall be opened unto you! For everyone who asks shall receive* regardless of his past mistakes, or his situation or condition! And you who seek for knowledge and understanding or for a recollection of these days of preparation, or to KNOW ME shall find whatsoever you seek. Knock and it shall be opened unto you! For unto him who knocks, the doors to the realm of primal, creative substance shall be opened wide.

"*Nothing will be impossible to him who believes!*

"And he who turns the strength of his searching toward these spiritual realms, from whence he came, shall have the hosts of heaven beside him to assist him in the fulfilling of his own great destiny and in the perfecting of himself as his understanding expands.

"As you seek to KNOW you shall increase in knowledge until you are filled with Light and are glorified in TRUTH and become PERFECT in the Lord, Jesus Christ, for unto you it will be given to comprehend all things and to receive all power.

"Accept the new world and its new conditions with the same gratitude you feel this day and you will become glorious, for *he who is thankful in all things takes on the vibrant glory of his own released vibrations.* And the things of the Earth will be *added* unto him an hundredfold, yea, more! And the things of the Spirit will be multiplied in everlasting glory.

"*Joy is of the Saints and none can put it on but they alone!*

"*Love is of the elect and none can receive it fully except you who have been developing it within you, from the beginning.*

"My commandments are but the laws of your own progressing and your own fulfilling. They do not pertain to me. They are yours! And they are for your own glory! And *I give no Commandment or PROMISE save I have already prepared the way for you to fulfill it.* The fulfilling unfolds with the DESIRE TO LIVE the command.

The DESIRE to accept and to fulfill is the law of their germination and of their production and growth and completion.

"The way to fulfill every PROMISE is this day given unto you. It is your own! Open your minds to behold the PROMISES and your hearts to desire them and they will begin to mature for their seed is this day implanted within your own hearts. And as you believe, and doubt not, they will grow and produce all that My WORDS contain. I seal this power to fulfill upon you through my own unbreakable WORD as you accept and desire.

"*Without vision the people perish,* because they will go beneath the level of mere mortality into the unimaginative condition of the animals, rejecting the PROMISES as they seal their souls and minds against belief, hardening their hearts into a condition that even I will not be able to melt or soften, and thus they may relinquish their claim upon the PROMISES forever. This you must know, it is in a softened heart that the seed of PROMISE takes root and begins its growth and maturity and perfection. A hard heart is barren and cannot possibly produce anything of virtue and goodness.

"All PROMISES are yours, and all the powers of their fulfilment. But unto each of you is given the choice of your goals, and the desire to accept, or reject, or to fulfill and so to receive all that the PROMISES CONTAIN— and MORE!

"It is forever true, *nothing will be impossible to him who believes,* for my WORDS are his. They are his strength and his power if he will only accept and fulfill.

"For you who desire to return into my Presence and reclaim your heavenly rights with unspeakable powers and glory added unto you forever, I PROMISE that you shall put darkness under your feet as you bring forth the Light. And *if your eyes be single to MY glory your whole bodies shall be filled with Light* and every physical atom and tissue and fibre of your mortal beings shall take on Light and be exalted into a glorified, spiritual condition of everlasting power and wonder. And there shall be no darkness in you, neither sickness nor decay. *And that body which is filled with Light shall comprehend all things* for Light is the Spirit of intelligence and comprehension and LIFE. And *I will unveil my face unto you* for you shall have the privilege and the power to return into my presence, forever glorified.

"This PROMISE to return into my Presence glorified, is the Great and Last PROMISE. IT IS RESERVED FOR THOSE WHO OVERCOME ALL THINGS, who cast out all light-mindedness and their excess of laughter far from them. Hilarity is not joy. It is but the pastime of those without thought. And it will be used as an implement of Lucifer. He will use it to detain the sons of Earth that their minds be not *"single"* but occupied with the nonsense of display and in an occupation of witty self-importance or self-indulgence as they seek for notice and acclaim.

"LIVE the laws and you will KNOW for you will experience the wonder and the glory of their fulfilling right within yourselves.

"And the Two Greatest of all laws, when LIVED, will fulfill all the other laws. They will fulfill every PROMISE OF THIS DAY and all the days that are past and the PROMISES THAT ARE TO COME! They will glorify you who take hold of them, for *all that I have is yours!*

"LOVE ME WITH ALL YOUR HEARTS and your

hearts will be softened and opened so that you will be prepared to bring forth every righteous desire of your hearts, every PROMISE ever uttered, or thought; every glory ever imagined for as you LOVE with your heart it will be prepared to receive all things, even all the riches of Earth and eternity. And I will be with you in tenderness forever. For your own opened, softened heart is the only offering that can be given in order that you yourselves might receive the fulness of my glory and my PROMISES.

"Love me with all your souls and the atoms and the fibres and the tissues of your beings will receive the gift of Eternal LIFE as you become quickened and renewed. And *you will rise up with wings as eagles*—and *be able to come and go as the wind, and no one will know from whence you came or whither you go, for you will be glorified in the service and the power of the Greater Works.* You will become so completely spiritualized no evil or sickness or pain or suffering will be able to touch you. And you will truly *Be Born of the Spirit* as you are called back into My Presence, without descending through the gates of death—and without the Judgment, for you will have OVERCOME ALL THINGS.

"LOVE ME WITH ALL YOUR MINDS *and your minds will become single to My Glory and you will take upon you that same glory as you become filled with Light and comprehend all things!*

"LOVE ME WITH ALL YOUR STRENGTH and all the powers of your being, both physical and spiritual will be united and unified and perfected.

"AND I WILL BE YOUR GOD! AND YOU SHALL BE MY PEOPLE! And as you live by the PROMISES *you will evolve from the man kingdom back into the God*

Kingdom for you will become exalted and glorified. Your first step will be to live according to the laws of the Patriarchs, which was according to the PROMISES and through their FAITH. LIVE ACCORDING TO THE PROMISES AND YOUR FAITH WILL BE PERFECTED INTO KNOWLEDGE. AND YOU WILL HAVE THE PRIVILEGE OF SEEING AND KNOWING FOR YOURSELVES.

"Hereby is my LOVE for you glorified as you return it unto Me. And thus is my LOVE increased and *your* LOVE is exalted into perfection.

"I seal upon you My PROMISES that you might OVERCOME mortality and all that it contains and thus exalt yourselves and your physical bodies and your associates and your new world into a state of everlasting glory.

"I seal my eternal PROMISES upon you with My Everlasting, Irrevocable Covenant, which cannot be broken! It shall stand forever, for it is MINE—and I give it unto you!

"And my LOVE is upon you as you fulfill My WORDS and bring them forth within yourselves.

"The PROMISES I give unto you are clothed in the Holy Spirit and they are composed of it. And thus are they sealed by the Holy Spirit of Promise, which I shall shed forth upon all who are just and true.

"This Holy Spirit of Promise is the Spirit of Hope which shall abide in the hearts of the children of men as they accept of it. And he who is without hope must needs be in despair and despair cometh because of iniquity. Those who open up their hearts shall receive the Holy Spirit of Promise which is HOPE in all its rapturous glory! And their hopes shall grow and increase and materialize as they cast out all doubting for doubting is the darkness. And it is the darkness of doubting that the righteous will OVERCOME as they become clothed in LIGHT.

"Thus as you are true to the song or the radiant vibrations of the sacred, Holy Spirit of Promise it will become perfected within you and you will become perfect and will be clothed in Light. And so it will be that ALL PROMISES will be fulfilled unto you.

"This Holy Spirit of Promise is the Witness and the Covenant to my WORDS. And this Holy Spirit of Promise will become sealed upon those of you who are just and true. In such the deep despair of hopelessness can never find lodgment for you will be cleansed from all iniquity and the great sin of unbelief.

"This is the Seal and the Covenant of My PROMISES which this day I place upon my *words* and upon those of you who accept them, without doubting. This Holy Spirit of Promise I hereby bestow upon you who desire it and who believe in My Words and lay claim to the glory of their fulfilling for *you will be just and true* to ME and to YOURSELVES and to *the things which are waiting to become—which your eyes have never yet beheld.*

"This you must also understand, for it is given to abide in you the record of heaven, the Peaceable things of immortal glory, the COMFORTER, the Truth of all things; that which quickeneth all things, and maketh alive all things; that which KNOWETH all things, and hath all power, according to My wisdom, mercy, truth, justice and judgment.

"The Record of Heaven, which is given to abide in you will be when you, through faith and love open your memories to all your past experiences and to these PROMISES which I give unto you this day. As you believe in them and lay claim to them their powers will be forever your own, and the knowledge contained therein.

"It is also given to abide in you the Peaceable things of Immortal glory if so be you will use it for it is established deep within the centers of your souls and can be contacted and rejoiced in under every circumstance and condition and within it is the power to heal every adverse situation, eliminate every disturbance and glorify every happening. For all things will work together for your good if you will love and obey My counsel for in it is contained the keys of your own glorification and perfecting.

"The Holy Comforter is also given to abide in you and will give comfort to any and all who will only open up their hearts to receeive of its tender, priceless benediction. Those who love the darkness rather than the light and who rejoice in their sorrows to such an extent they cannot let them go cannot be helped. These will never know the glory of the Power and Perfection of the Comforter's priceless, tender healing joy.

"The Truth of all things is also given to abide in you so that you need never be deceived or led out onto that broad open way that leads to destruction.

"And hereby I proclaim that it is given to abide in you that which quickeneth all things and maketh alive all things; or the power to change your carnal flesh to flesh divine, without descending through the gates of death, for that which maketh alive all things is yours to bring forth and to use.

"It is also given to abide in you the power to KNOW or COMPREHEND ALL THINGS—and THAT WHICH HATH ALL POWER, according to My Wisdom, Mercy, Truth, Justice and Judgment.

"In bringing forth and using these inborn powers is FAITH MADE PERFECT. This contains the glory and the power of all fulfilling as *you become filled with Light.* Thus *You shall be given the power to comprehend all things!* AND ALL THINGS WILL BECOME SUBJECT UNTO YOU, BOTH IN HEAVEN AND ON EARTH, THE LIGHT AND THE LIFE, THE SPIRIT AND THE POWER, SENT FORTH BY ME THROUGH JESUS CHRIST, MY SON.

"These unspeakable powers and blessings I give to abide in you and they shall be yours as you open your souls to bring their powers forth. Nothing will be impossible to you who believe and who will cast out the darkness of doubting and the blighting desolation of pride-filled self-righteousness.

"These are My WORDS and My COVENANT. And My Words cannot be broken or returned unto Me unfulfilled or void.

"Any PROMISE which I have uttered this Day shall be yours as you lay claim to it. And any PROMISE, when perfected and fulfilled in you, will have the power to bring you back into My Presence—glorified! Thus every PROMISE contains the law of your own perfection and the fulfilling of all glory for EARTH *is the school for Gods.* All the training you will receive will be but the opportunity and the preparation for your own graduation. No test or hardship should be resented or ignored. You can each receive the highest degree, with honor, or you can fail to take advantage of so great a privilege. The choice is your own as to the use you will make of your life on earth.

"In the fulfilling of the FIRST and SECOND GREAT COMMANDMENTS of LOVE one will have *fulfilled* ALL THE LAWS AND THE PROPHETS, or all the PROMISES GIVEN TO YOU THIS DAY, which will be reaffirmed by the PROPHETS in the days ahead. In the fulfilling of this great LOVE, in bringing it forth within yourselves I will be BOUND. All of My Holy Covenants are predicated upon the perfecting of this great LOVE, as you, through your own efforts bring it forth within yourselves. Thus will you have the power to evolve back into the God Kingdom, fulfilled and glorified for you will have become divine. This is the law of perfection which has been irrevocably decreed in heaven before the foundations of the earth! And it is everlasting and irrevocable! Live it and you will KNOW!

"All PROMISES have been Mine to give and yours to receive. And the law of LOVE, which I offer to you now is the law of all fulfilling.

"And I lie not!

"This work is of Me. If any seek to destroy it they shall themselves be destroyed or delayed, perhaps for eons in their own progress.

"Behold, I Am God, the Creator of heaven and of earth! I AM THAT I AM! And My Promises are yours as you become these PROMISES AND RETURN THEM UNTO ME FULFILLED—YOURSELVES GLORIFIED!

"AND THIS IS MY WORK AND MY GLORY, TO BRING TO PASS THE IMMORTALITY AND THE ETERNAL LIFE OF MAN!

"And this is your work and your glory, as you take advantage of every golden opportunity for advancement, whether it be a great sorrow or a great joy or just the trying of your patience in a monotony of seeming unprogressiveness as you assimilate your opportunities and turn all things and all conditions into glory and honor. Thus every occasion can become an occasion of utter triumph. And You who are thankful in all things shall be made glorious and shall have the power to transmute all conditions into glory. SO HAVE I SPOKEN AND I LIE NOT! And so is My blessing sealed upon you!

Chapter XXVI.

The Glorified Road to Zion

Those precious Promises of God penetrated our beings and became embedded in our spirits at that time. They became a part of the actual fibres of our existence according to our individual degree of advancement and progress. Each received according to his own capacity to receive and retain. (And that capacity may still be enlarged and expanded with effort and sincere desire). Existence is eternal progress or retrogression. Nothing stands still or remains static. It continually grows more beautiful and perfect or shrivels up, decays and dies. And so it is with man himself.

These great and glorious Promises of God were thereafter to become a part of the living essence of our souls, glorifying our lives as we fulfilled them.

It is the cry of these Premises or this WORD OF GOD from within, pleading for fulfilment, which causes such hungry, desolate yearnings in human hearts.

Each has felt at sometime or other in his life moments or days or mayhap years of lonely melancholy or of inner anguish and unfulfilment as his soul cried for—HE KNOWS NOT WHAT.

Those divine, glorious Promises of our Almighty Father of glory were the WORD. They were His WORD!

And each individual who reaches into the depths of his own being and brings them forth as a part of his own living existence *becomes* the WORD. This is how the WORD BECOMES FLESH! Our flesh! This is how Christ became the WORD. It is how each individual can become that WORD as all things become subject unto him. In this fulfilling we are truly co-heirs with Christ. Yes, joint-heirs with Him. And this great and holy status can be earned according to the power of the Promises as we take hold of them. This state of achievement must be earned. One must grow into it by effort and desire.

And since God's WORD cannot be returned unto Him unfulfilled or void it can only be returned unto Him as we ourselves fulfill it. And as we take hold of His Promises we become those Promises or His WORD made perfect and fulfilled. And only then and in this manner can we ourselves return back into His Presence.

"We are to purify ourselves, even as He is pure. We are to sanctify ourselves" and in so doing we glorify God and become exalted in an effulgent splendor of eternal radiance and power.

The Devil doctrine, which lulls mankind into carnal security, is that we need do nothing, that Christ did all. And the fallacy of the doctrine of "THE GREAT RAPTURE," in which Christ is expected to come and lift us up glorified into the highest exaltation is a lie! It is a soothing syrup of narcotic deadliness. And he who partakes of it is being cheated. It is the sounding brass music, the tinkling of chiming cymbals to keep mankind lulled into a state of quiescent childishness. It has lulled mankind into a state af stupid passivity in that infant crib that has grown too short, and with a covering that is too infantile for comfort. It is for those who are neither weaned from the milk nor drawn from the breasts, as Isaiah declared.

"The Great Rapture" comes only when man himself has matured into manhood and is weaned from the milk and drawn from the breasts and stands up in his own divine right—A SON OF THE LIVING GOD!

This WORD being made the actual flesh is when those divine, glorious Promises are brought forth as a living part of every cell and tissue of man's body. This is the WORD MADE PERFECT. And God's WORDS must be LIVED in order to be fulfilled.

Self-righteousness brings not the inner fulfilling or the glory of His WORD made flesh. Only the devoted LIVING of His WORD or Promises, through FAITH, can possibly perfect an individual. "LIVE MY WORDS AND YOU WILL KNOW!" "You must be doers of the WORD, not hearers only, thus deceiving your own selves."

In the twelfth Ode of Solomon, verses seven to twelve, is given the following information: "For as it (the Word) is, so is its end; for it is LIGHT and the dawning of thought.

"And by it the worlds talk one to the other; and in it the WORD there were those who were silent;

"And from it came love and concord; and they spake one to the other whatever was theirs; and THEY WERE PENETRATED BY THE WORD.

"And they knew Him who made them, because they were in concord; for the mouth of the Most High spake to them; and His explanations ran by means of it;

"For THE DWELLING PLACE OF THE WORD IS MAN and its truth is LOVE.

"Blessed are they who by means thereof have understood everything, and have known the Lord in His Truth.

"Hallelujah!"

And part of the scriptures, according to Christ, which cannot be returned unto God unfulfilled and void is: "They were called Gods unto whom the WORD of God came." (Psalms 82:6 and John 10:34-36). It is those who bring that WORD of God forth and make it a LIVING part of their existence who are called Gods, for they are on the path toward divinity—into Godhood.

"To be carnally minded is death. To be spiritually minded is life everlasting." Carnal means physical or things pertaining to the earth life. The scriptures explain that at the time of man's fall "he became carnal, sensual and Devilish." To be carnally minded is to have one's thoughts centered entirely upon the things of the world. To be "sensually minded" is to have one's mind taken over by lusts and physical desires such as gluttony, sexuality and any type of degenerate dissipations. In this day when the teachers of darkness are stressing sex as the real meaning of life realize not that they are creating a cess-pool of sensuality that only the cleansing of the earth by great catastrophes, such as the destruction of Sodom and Gomorah, can possibly atone for. Uncontrolled indulgences of any sort is dissipation that thwarts one's progress. And if it is true, as the wicked would have the gullible and weak souls believe, that sex is the meaning of life then truly life has no meaning.

"Enoch changed his carnel flesh to flesh divine without descending through the gates of death!" "To be carnally minded is death!" And it is as true now as it was in the days of Enoch. "To be spiritually minded is life everlasting." It is through the mind that one "lays hold of the best gifts" or Promises and makes them a part of his life, through FAITH, even as the Patriarchs of old. And such advance beyond all the carnal laws of the earth as they transform themselves into a higher status of existence. Such are called Gods because they have accepted the invitation of divinity in seeking to fulfill His Promises. The complete fulfilling takes time even as a small child is numbered among mankind, though he has not yet reached the status of manhood.

In this overcoming of the flesh, through transposing the cells and atoms of the body into flesh divine by imbuing them with the glory of vibrating, selfless love is how the change takes place. This is how death is overcome! It is conquered by one taking hold of the Promises as love is perfected in every tissue and atom of the physical body. Death is banished from man's being as he takes hold of those Promises and perfects them through LIVING them. One must use his mind to cast out the darkness of doubting. As one begins to perfect the gift of Love the Premises become easy to take hold of and to fulfill. They become glorious and one automatically evolves into a higher realm. And it is assuredly true that he who fulfills those first two great commandments of LOVE IS NO LONGER UNDER THE LAW. He has advanced into the realm of the Patriarch, through FAITH, as he begins his own complete acceptance of the Promises. Then is he truly advancing into Divinity.

As one exerts himself to undertake this journey of fulfilling he finds that he is traveling a highway of Lighted glory along that STRAIGHT AND NARROW PATH into the realms of Everlasting Life. And anyone can travel this highway of magnificent wonder who desires to change his carnal flesh to flesh divine by relinquishing his physical, mortal cravings for credits and rewards and for prestige and pride or for his lusts and animal appetites.

The Promises are brought forth and become flesh as one lays hold of them through the exercise of FAITH, or by his own controlled thinking processes and lives by them. This is how *one lays hold of the best gifts;* the gifts of Eternal Life, in which death is conquered; the gifts of knowledge and of peace and of power and of physical renewing and of perfection and endless glory. This is the Pathway back into the Presence of God. It is the Pathway to the Purification of the Heart. It is the road to Zion—or to God.

And IT IS YOURS!

The laws were given because of wickedness. And as wickedness has increased the laws have increased. And because of the great wickedness of these last days there are laws being made just to justify the wickedness and the laws that protect the wicked. And in such cases all may know that wicked men have made the laws.

Before any laws were given the ancient Patriarchs lived by the PROMISES, which had been given by God in the beginning. These *Promises were lived through* FAITH. Faith in the Promises is all that is required to lay hold of any Promise, or all of them. "And the Way is so perfect and so easy a fool need not err therein."

The potential life power in a seed is a living thing of intelligence, though invisible. Any living seed will sprout and grow under the right conditions and environment. This is the eternal, everlasting law and is unchangeable. No one needs to worry or be concerned as to where it is or how it is, not any more than the farmer has to know where every seed was dropped. The seed is there. And it will grow and fulfill the perfectly designed destiny if it is only permitted to do so. And FAITH itself is one with the Promises. One cannot exist without the other.

Lovely Faith is a seed at first. Yet it is so powerful in its potentiality it can Promise all things—and it can fulfill all things. Faith is the power that can raise the dead and move mountains. Faith is the living power of that seed which automatically grows into a tree and can fulfill any and every Promise ever given by God or conceived by man.

Faith is nourished and brought forth in its full potential of limitless power right within the being of man. It abides dormant and still along with all the holy Promises ever given to man. As one lays hold of the "Best Gifts" or any divine gift, for that matter, the slumbering seed awakens. It is quickened into its first degree of expansion and growth. It is awakened to begin its reaching and its fulfilling. And as it is protected, by man's own thinking processes, from doubts and fears it must grow. It has no other choice. It has the power to fulfill its own divine potential. It becomes a tree in which the concrete blocks of mortal or mental constructions are broken and crumbled and cast aside.

Faith is power! And when Faith becomes directed by the understanding and controlled thoughts of men it can calm the ocean for waves obey it. It can quell the storm, quench raging flames, move mountains of difficulties and achieve anything, even the seeming impossibilities. It can move mountains literally, raise the dead, and fulfill any righteous desire or divine Promise of Almighty God! In fact, those released Promises of long ago are its feed and its purpose and the power and plan of its existence. It is divine energy in action, released from within man to fulfill all things—ANYTHING when used. It is glorious! And without it it is impossible to please God. It contains the boundless energy of all creation for even the worlds were framed through Faith. It is the building energy of Gods, for it is Theirs to use. And They have used it always. And men begin to evolve toward Godhead when they begin to exercise the right to use it.

Faith is indeed power when put into action as doubts and fears are cast out and overcome by its understanding glance. And when used FAITH advances from the unseen energy into knowledge. It is transformed from the invisible realm of vibration into the tangible world of complete and full knowledge. It becomes an established reality of full power, for knowledge is POWER! It transforms the Light of an idea or dream into solid substance.

The more Faith is brought forth into the powerful action of fulfilling the more pleased God is. And the more dynamic an individual becomes who learns to wield so great an instrument of glory. Faith is the very power of God in action. It is also the power of man in action as he uses it for it is his to use. It is breathtaking to comprehend that man can be the wielder of a power so great. It is always awaiting his command to arise and hold forth his pure desires.

THE GLORIFIED ROAD TO ZION   289

Lay hold of them, THE BEST GIFTS, the most dynamic Promises, for they are yours as they await your awakening to lay claim to them. Arise from your infant crib, cast aside your scant covering which man has long since outgrown, and stand forth a child of your Divine Sire as you begin your own development into Divinity.

Love alone opens up the heart, the soul and the mind to bring forth the Promises in a complete power of fulfilling as they become flesh. As one loves with all his heart, and soul (which includes the spirit and the body) and with his mind, the LOVE he generates through his being transforms the physical cells into cells divine and death cannot touch him, neither old age nor sickness nor suffering.

And the law and the power thereof belong to all who will only LIVE the Promises, through FAITH. To believe is the first requisite of fulfilling. One must BE and LIVE according to his own deepest desiring. And as this great transition is accomplished the lower levels of mortality are left behind, outgrown and overcome like the infant crib and the skimpy covering.

This is how one advances into the realms of the Patriarchs. And from the status of the ancient ones one continues to go on to ever higher degrees of exaltation and advancement and wondrous glory without relinquishing the flesh to death. This is how one's body is changed and exalted as he takes it with him and is "born of the Spirit with the powers to come and go as the wind," even as Christ explained to Nicodemus. And through their beings flew the GREAT RIVERS OF LIVING WATER, OR THE ETERNAL FOUNTAINS OF LIFE as they go forth to bless and heal and to glorify a world. This is the Greater Works Christ promised.

This very perfecting of the physical body is the completion of that divine, holy "ROAD TO ZION," the pathway of the purification of the heart. And "Blessed indeed are the pure in heart for they shall see God!" This complete fulfilling is accomplished only by LIVING the glorious Truths contained in the PROMISES.

The great Promises given by God upon that eventful day when the "Foundations of the earth were laid" are just as much a part of our existence now as they were in that long ago. And there are again the true Patriarchs, who are inspired by God, having the authority and the spiritual power to lay their hands upon the heads of individuals to unveil a glimpse of his or her own individual pattern of life. But there are also those who need no such intermediary or go-between to bring forth those holy Promises from within themselves. Any who begin to take hold of the Promises are on their way to becoming Patriarchs, or ones advancing beyond all mortal laws. One begins to emerge into the status of the divine as he fulfills the promise of his own potential covenants of Promise. These are the ones of Promise brought forth out of the ages to fill a special place in this day and time.

A Patriarch may give a blessing of Promise and encouragement and revelation and it is but the pattern, the design, the plan, or the architectural dream of the reality. One's life contains the material from which the edifice, the pattern, the divine plan is to be formed. And it is the individual himself who must make use of his life, which is the material of the forming as he lives according to his own highest hopes and worthy ambitions and righteous desiring.

This is how the Promises are fulfilled. And how all Promised Blessings are attained. This is how one lays hold of the best gifts. This is how one works with God to perfect the pattern of his own individual life, as he travels that divine Road to Zion—the road of the purification of his own heart and life as he changes his carnal flesh to flesh divine.

Not one of the great Promises of God can be taken hold of and LIVED without the life and heart and soul of that individual being purified. And as Isaiah declared: "The road is so simple a fool need not err therein; though the wicked can never cross over it."

This is the work about which God spake in Prophecy through His holy, anointed ones, in "WHICH ALL MEN WOULD BE LEFT WITHOUT EXCUSE!"

No one can possibly fail to reach the highest goal of fulfillment as all Promises are completed and glorified in him who walks the radiant path of their fulfilling—"THE STRAIGHT AND NARROW PATH" of joyous, ecstatic wonder, the Road to Zion—The Road of Eternal Life.

This is the path Enoch trod and Moses and Elijah and the many, many others of olden times. And this Path is now opened wide and the Way made so plain even a fool need not err therein.

It is your own Path as you follow it into the true Promised Land where death is overcome and Eternal Life awaits the triumphant Overcomers with songs of joyous, unspeakable welcome. This is *the Great Rapture* so many erroneously expect Christ to fulfill and bring to pass for them.

They truly err greatly in such a belief as they let their own appointed time of fulfilling slip away before their journey ever began. Such will find themselves waiting in desolating disappointment.

Christ does not travel this path for any individual or group of individuals. Each must travel it for Christ, for "When he appears we are to be like Him!" *"We are to purify ourselves even as He* is pure!" And it is up to every individual to sanctify his own life. This is the only way man can truly glorify God as he fulfills His WORDS or PROMISES and returns them unto Him completed—himself—glorified!

Christ truly did the works of OVERCOMING as He traveled the Road in its most difficult aspects, alone and without precedent. He left the perfect pattern for all who desired to travel the divine Road of Overcoming, that Straight and Narrow Way which leads to Life Eternal. And the command was: "you are to do the works which I did."

This is man's road to travel. It is yours! It belongs to you NOW! Not in the afar-off! This road is the street paved in transparent gold, spoken of in the scriptures. This Road is being paved now with the glorious, radiant vibrations of the marching feet of those who are beginning to travel it in the power and the purity and the divine wonder of their own OVERCOMING. This is the "Road to Zion!" This is "The Pathway in which a fool need not err therein," as Isaiah foretold.

"And the Spirit and the Bride say COME! And he that is athirst let him say, COME! And let all who will, say, COME! AND PARTAKE OF THE WATERS OF LIFE FREELY!"

This is the gift of Eternal Life which God has Promised, which is being held out to you now, freely and without price!

Yes! The time is NOW! And may your hearts rejoice in the glory of your journey as you leave all pride and selfishness and self-righteousness behind. For as you journey along this road you become, like John the Baptist, the greatest that is within you to become. Then it is that you discover that you are clothed in the hallowed, radiant robes of pure humility, as you feel yourselves to be the least, for you will realize that as you travel this Highway of Truth you are walking with God. Then you will know, as Enoch of old was informed, "THAT HE PLEASED GOD!" This is FAITH made perfect!

And as "The first requisite to knowledge is the ability to believe" so is the fulfilling of the Promises based upon this ability. And the first step toward having the ability to believe is to have the desire to believe. It is within that *desiring* that one opens up his mind to "ask, to seek and to knock!" And with that desiring can come the petition, "Dear God, help Thou my unbelief!" This is an eternal invitation to use when only the desire stands alone. The very sincerity that can be generated in such asking can produce profound results.

With the ability developed to begin to BE and LIVE according to one's deepest desiring comes the germination of that precious seed of FAITH. And Faith itself grows with use. It expands to the need or the call for assistance as the seed responds to sunlight, water and the richness of good soil.

Doubting itself is a killer so deadly poisonous that even FAITH cannot stand up against it unless one takes upon himself the responsibility of eliminating the weeds of doubt that would destroy his priceless crop. Faith must grow if given the opportunity for it is the seed of production. And Faith grows with use and exercise until eventually it becomes a tree in which the messengers of heaven find lodgment. And as FAITH grows and matures it evolves into knowledge. Its invisible essence takes on a tangible body of everlasting beauty and power. It has clothed the wish, the desire, the dream with substance as it holds them forth full formed.

Faith was destined in its essence and formation to evolve into knowledge. And Knowledge IS POWER! It is the fulfilment, the accomplishment, the realization of wishes or ideas or hopes brought into form.

When I was still young enough to be enthralled with fairy tales and fairy godmothers and wishful thinking I used to wonder about those privileged ones who would be granted just ONE WISH. And in my contemplating of such a breathtaking opportunity I decided that if ever I was given the chance to make such an entreaty I would wish that "EVERYTHING I EVER WOULD WISH FOR WOULD COME TRUE!"

I did not then realize that if that one wish were fulfilled I would be granted the very fulness of the gift of Faith, for through Faith alone can all else be added or accomplished. Faith is the master key to all achievement. It is truly the magic switch. Through Faith one can receive the fulfillment of every divine Promise and the powers of them. He will have received the fulness of the WORDS: "Whatsoever you ask for when you pray believe that you receive and you shall have whatsoever you ask."

Faith can perfect the gift of love. Faith can overcome

death! Faith can renew the body, bring to pass that state of glory in which "all else is added" in an overflowing abundance in which there is not room enough to receive the great out-flowing. Faith is the golden key that unlocks the doors of that magic Kingdom of Promise—The Kingdom of heaven. It is truly power unspeakable! But faith without works is dead. One must Be and Live according to his requesting—without doubting, for Faith can only be used when doubts are banished.

"Even the Devils believe!" But they have no power to take hold of the Light or to fulfill the Promises because of their own encouraged hates and darkness.

There have been many miracles wrought by Faith when the human intellect has been transcended by dynamic emergencies, when the habitual thinking processes have been stilled and placed in abeyance.

When I was a small child in Pocatello, Idaho, I used to play with little Josie Norton. We were both four years old and when all the other children of the neighborhood and our own brothers and sisters were in school we always played together. I have never forgotten Josie Norton. He was a gracious, kind little boy with red hair and freckles.

Then the Nortons moved away and so did we. And several years later I heard that a load of lumber had tipped over on Josie, and his older brother, in the excitement of that moment, lifted the whole load from his little brother's body. The very shock of the occasion put in suspension the process of thought in which doubts are generated.

And then there was the man named PETER, who walked on water until his mortal mind took over with its faulty reasoning and its doubting, and he began to sink.

And the question remains, "Wherefore didst thou doubt?"

Faith cannot function with the negative vibrations of doubts.

"And if your eyes be single to my glory your whole bodies shall be filled with Light and there shall be no darkness in you." Darkness is the doubting and the fears and the source of all the failures to achieve, or even to believe. When the darkness is overcome the doubting is eliminated. "With eyes single to the glory of God," all darkness or doubting is forever conquered and one becomes filled with Light, that divine substance of creation. And whenever LIGHT exists FAITH, its generator, is also present, waiting to swing into action. Faith, remember, is the generator of Light. And Light is the substance from which all desires are formed and all Promises fulfilled and Faith itself is the substance of things hoped for.

"Perfect LOVE casts out all fear!" Perfect desiring casts out all doubting. When doubting and fear are conquered one has "OVERCOME THE WORLD" and "ALL ELSE WILL BE ADDED."

And now, another mystery about FAITH I am instructed to share. That "Magic Switch" which holds the key controlling the mystic power of FAITH also has the divine power to OVERCOME darkness and doubting. It is the switch that can banish the darkness and turn on the breathtaking, effulgent, powerful glory of LIGHT in which no darkness can possibly exist. And that magic lever, that dynamic switch controls the great LIGHT, which is the power and the substance of creation. It is put into action as FAITH takes control. FAITH IS THE SWITCH, THE LEVER, THE RELEASING POWER OF ENERGY, directed by intelligent desire to use the fabulous, limitless element of LIGHT.

As one takes hold of that manipulating button of FAITH, which controls or turns on the voltaic current of power he can truly turn on the LIGHT. And in that process he can lift himself out of the deep caverns of darkness and doubting and despair into the realms of lighted glory. He can lift himself from a craven creature of negation and failure into one clothed in LIGHT and joy and power.

The primal command of "LET THERE BE LIGHT," when spoken with deep desire, becomes authoritative, and must be obeyed. As it is uttered with BELIEF, the LIGHT is made apparent. First the darkness of doubting and unbelief is banished. The doorway to despair is closed and sealed. Next the Light of understanding and comprehension is permitted to permeate one's mind. And third, the joy of the Power of God is released into one's life.

There can be no joy or true happiness or achievement brought forth from the regions of doubting and despair. "And despair comes because of iniquity," or as one joins forces with the desolating anguish of "THE LOST," those who are lost in the darkness of unbelief, where *hopes* and *desires* are squelched and smothered and only failure reigns with the desolation of agonized distress and darkness. And "Woe be to those who go forth to foster their darkness and unbelief upon others!" These are the ones who have completely rejected the Witness of that Holy Spirit of Promise and have become UNTRUE and UNJUST and are left to wallow mayhap forever in the darkness of their own selection.

"The Road to Zion" is truly the inner Pathway of purification "in which a fool need not err therein." It is the Path which is LIGHTED and revealed by that divine, Holy Spirit of Promise. And as one lays hold of those PROMISES, through FAITH he will no longer be a "fool" but will be directed into ALL-TRUTH and will eventually comprehend all things. He will become wise and gracious and wonderful. He will indeed "deck himself in majesty and excellence and array himself in glory and beauty," even as God commanded Job.

Such will complete the purification of their own hearts, in righteousness and TRUTH and will assuredly be admitted into the Presence of God—AND THIS IS LIFE ETERNAL! In other words: "They will have reached the point of FAITH where they will be wrapped in the power and glory of their Maker and will be caught up to dwell with Him!"

This is the Road for which Christ left the map. And the guide to it is that divine Holy Spirit of Promise, for it is only as one believes in the PROMISES and holds to them, through FAITH, that he can possibly fulfill all things.

So be it! Amen!

CHAPTER XXVII.

The Three Gifts of a Wise Man

Since the "Road to Zion" is the road of the purification of the heart, or of the navel or center of one's heart and soul and all that this marvel entails, this stupendous Path must now be mapped in such a way that henceforth it will be so easy to travel "even a fool need not err therein," as Isaiah promised. And its breathtaking purpose must be made plain in the wonder and glory of exquisite desirability.

Since it is only "The pure in heart who shall see God" then the plan for the purification of the heart must be unveiled. And the Promise of heaven goes with this sacred purification that "They shall have Eternal Life!" This is the everlasting pledge of God to all men that those who travel this Path need never die. They shall not taste of death and the decaying discomforts of aging and the pain and anguish and suffering that leads to dying.

Isaiah reveals in his 40th chapter, beginning with verse 31, the following: "They that wait upon the Lord shall renew their strength; they shall mount up with wings as eagles; they shall run and not be weary; and they shall walk and not faint." To *mount up with wings as eagles* is the promise of being "Born of the Spirit."

And in the fulness of this revelation it reads thus: "They shall receive treasures of knowledge, even hidden treasures. They shall receive health in the navel and marrow in the bones and strength in the loins and in the sinews, and I, the Lord, give unto them a promise that the destroying angel (death) shall pass them by and not slay them." And all such will truly be prepared to "Be Born of the Spirit insomuch that they will be able to come and go as the wind" in a service so great even Christ acknowledged that it would be a greater work than that which He accomplished, because He was going to His Father and would not be permitted to remain on this earth in such a service. It is called "THE GREATER WORKS!"

The first step upon this Straight and Narrow Path of purification is begun when one opens his mind and heart and soul in a desire to fulfill and LIVE by those Two First and Great Commandments of LOVE! To actually LIVE them is much more than just accepting them as Christ's sayings. It means to make them a living part of one's life.

This Road to Zion or to the purification of the heart is the Pathway of all-fulfilling. It is indeed "The Straight and Narrow Path that leads to Life Eternal!" It is the road of OVERCOMING. It contains the joy and the glory of all existence and the divine purpose of it. In traveling this road one takes upon himself to truly LIVE Christ's Words and not just hear them, that he might KNOW and EXPERIENCE the truths of them for himself.

This Royal Road to Zion, or to the purification of the heart, is the Road the Three Wise Men traveled in their journey as they followed *the Star*. This road is every man's to follow who so desires or chooses to travel it. It is not an instantaneous journey, nor a short one. It is a long journey as one travels it "from AFAR" even as the Magi of old. It must be traveled from one's first glimpse of it or from his first awakened desire for the purification of his heart even to the fulness. But so many think they are already upon the Path who have never set one foot upon the sacred, Holy Way.

"There is a way, and ways and THE WAY,
And the High man travels the High Way
And the low man travels the low;
And in between, on the misty flats,
The rest drift to and fro.

But for every man that goeth
There's a high way and a low—
And every man decideth
The way his soul shall go!"

Even the greatest sinners deceive themselves as they seek to justify their wickedness. And those who assume they are righteous and have no faults or failings are often farther from the path than the wicked. But as the slothful, indolent, wicked or the self-righteous travel this sacred Path, in their wish to behold the KING, they begin their own purification. The sinner becomes repentant. The self-righteous begin dropping one by one their bigotries, their self-acclaim, their distorted, erroneous beliefs and cluttering precepts and their pride. And the slothful, lazy individual becomes awakened. On this Holy Path the weaknesses the negative attitudes and all personal ideas of self-importance drop away. And the gifts he bears within himself become ever more real and exquisitely beautiful. The hidden glory of those fabulous jewels begin to become apparent and desirable to the bearer. The very gifts themselves begin to make manifest the increasing purity of the individual who carries them. They become sacred, hallowed gifts, fit for a King—A GOD!

Of those in this day who desire to travel the sacred High Way it is also required that they follow the Star of Promise in an increasing wonder of anticipation and devotion. These holy ones, for so they become, who continue upon the Path, must keep their eyes upon that Star always, never upon the deserts being crossed nor the deep, rocky canyons, nor the rugged passes of high, desolating peaks. It is quite necessary to keep one's vision focused above the vicissitudes of earth in order to overcome them. They do not need to be denied, but in the glory of the journey they must not be given the power to detain, overwhelm or retard one's progress. And with this attitude "All things work together for the traveler's good." This is indeed a sacred road, full of joy and power and increasing satisfaction. It is how one becomes a Wise Man, a Magi, a Priest in the hands of God.

And as one travels this Path he becomes the bearer of the three priceless, sacred jewels of all existence—his own gifts for the King of glory.

As one travels this Royal Road of purification the three divine, exquisite jewels are the jewels he bears within himself. And they become ever more effulgent and beautiful as one guards them humbly and in true devotion. They become divine, polished gems of everlasting glory, fit for the God of Heaven.

The first jewel is of the mind. It is the sacred gem of FAITH. And Faith is the first requisite required in undertaking this journey of purification. This jewel of Faith is the key of power. It is dynamic in its scope and assignment of fulfilling. This is the first gift made apparent or visible as it is brought forth in the journey to behold the King.

But in this jewel of Faith lies a temptation to detain the unwise. This jewel of Faith is the first gem one becomes aware of, as a rule, as he takes his journey to Zion. This is the journey of the wise. But all can become wise who become aware of this one trap and avoid it, by deep humility and deeper desire to fulfill.

The jewel of Faith is so desirable and so blinding in its power there are literally thousands who have become so entranced by its brilliance they have sought to hold it to themselves, seeking to display it for their own satisfaction and credit and self-glory. These are the ones spoken of in I. Cor. 13:1-3: which is as follows: "Though I speak with the tongues of men (or many nations), and with the tongue of angels, and have not charity (Pure, Christ-like Love), I am become as sounding brass or a tinkling cymbal." And often such become only a great noise of proud self-acclaim.

"And though I have the gift of prophecy, and understand all mysteries, and have not the pure Christ-like love, *I am nothing.*

"And though I bestow all my goods to feed the poor, and though I give my body to be burned, and have not charity (or the divine Christ-like love) it profit me nothing."

Yes, Faith is the jewel of power, but it can be so coveted by lower mortals they can be blinded by its power and beauty as they seek to hold it to themselves as their very own.

And so it is that some may forget the purpose of their journey to bestow their gifts upon the King of Glory.

This jewel of Faith can never be worn in self-display without destroying the wearer. Yes. "Enter ye in at the Straight Gate, for wide is the gate and broad is the way that leadeth to destruction, and many there be who go in thereat.

"Because straight is the gate and narrow the way, which leadeth to life, and few there be that find it." (Matt. 7:13-14).

And also from that divine Sermon on the Mount must be quoted this warning to those who seek to glorify themselves with the breathtaking power of Faith, which can so easily be used amiss. "Not everyone that saith unto me, Lord, Lord, shall enter into the Kingdom of Heaven; but he that doeth the will of my Father which is in heaven.

"*Many* shall say to me in that day, Lord have we not prophesied in thy name; and in thy name have cast out devils; and in thy name done many wonderful works?

"And then will I profess unto them, *I never knew you; depart from me, ye that work iniquity.*" (Matt. 7:21-23).

"By their fruits ye shall know them," not by their words or much speaking. And the list of the "Fruits of the Spirit" are named and identified and cannot possibly be mistaken. (Matt.7:15-20).

The signs and the works of Faith, being used amiss, as it is worn by individuals seeking acclaim and credits and rewards, is so deceptive and so adored by the self-seeking that God is forgotten and one's own imagined power is worshipped. These unwise ones do not realize that the jewel of Faith can never be worn on self-display, without stopping the progress of such so that their journey to Zion has been turned into the broad open way which leads to destruction. Instead of purifying themselves they are increasing their impurities of soul and mind. They become but an empty shell of vanity—*a nothing*. "For if I have all the powers on earth and have not charity I am NOTHING."

Faith is one of man's sacred gifts to be held in trust as it is guarded and glorified in humility and a constant awareness of thanksgiving. This very awareness is the continued consciousness that the jewel is being held and glorified for a gift to the King of Heaven. It is to be perfected that it might be bestowed even as a divine offering of the WISE to be released in thanksgiving and everlasting gratitude when one reaches his journey's end. Or one may use it in silent reverence without self-acclaim as he meets those on his journey to whom God signifies that his gift of Faith may be shared for a moment, to bless or heal. But always it must be used for the glory of God, for it is of God.

The second jewel is exquisite beyond thought. It is the divine gem of LOVE held deep within the heart. It is the glorified treasure of "Charity" that alone can completely exalt the gift of Faith and give it true meaning. LOVE can never be worn on self-display. It is the fulfilling glory of Faith itself. Only LOVE can magnify and enhance Faith and make it perfect. LOVE contains all the divine purity of rare, exquisite, highly wrought beauty and perfection! It is eternal! It never fails! LOVE is the jewel of jewels! It is the gem of glory and fulfillment and when brought forth humbly from a human heart one becomes divine. It works with Faith to complete and fulfill and glorify as both jewels are perfected—FAITH and LOVE united in celestial LIGHT!

What is LOVE like? May I tell you? It is described beautifully by Paul in I. Cor. 13:4-11, thus: "Charity (or the perfect Christ-like Love) suffereth long and is kind. It envieth not; It vaunteth not itself, is not puffed up.

"Doth not behave itself unseemly, seeketh not her own, is not easily provoked, thinketh no evil.

"Rejoiceth not in iniquity, but rejoiceth in Truth;

"Beareth all things, believeth all things (the great Promises of God without doubting), hopeth all things, endureth all things.

"LOVE never faileth; but whether there be prophesies, they shall fail; whether there be tongues they shall cease, whether there be knowledge it shall vanish away.

"For we know in part, and we prophesy in part.

"But *when that which is perfect is come,* then that which is in part shall be done away.

"When I was a child, I spake as a child (and many times only babbled), I understood as a child, I thought as a child, but when I became a man, I put away childish things," the sounding brass and the clanging cymbals or rattles, as I outgrew the milk and the infant crib with its inadequate covering. And only in this discarding could I become a man—"A SON OF GOD."

The third precious jewel is of the soul. It is the very glory of heaven. It is LIGHT! It is the Light of understanding in which all the darkness is cast out and banished! It is the jewel of wisdom. It is the gem of infinite fulfilment and eternal glory. Light is not only the divine substance of all created things it is the *purifier,* the precious jewel of rapture and full OVERCOMING! It is the joy and the eternal glory to all who perfect it within themselves. It is the STAR which becomes forever enthroned within the soul of man. It is his glory! And so it is that one perfects his gifts for God—himself made perfect and clothed in LIGHT and radiance and limitless power.

And so it is that one is admitted into the Presence of God to bestow his gifts of pure, holy FAITH and LOVE and the fulness of Glory as the LIGHT is brought forth perfected and radiant. The Light of the *Star* becomes a very part of man himself as he follows its Light or Guiding. This divine gift of Light is the holy gift of the soul made perfect in the fulness of one's journey to Zion—the journey to God. And then it is that one can kneel in His Presence and bestow the gifts he has developed and polished and glorified in his journey to the complete purification. And henceforth and forever he is a SON OF GOD, no longer an infant entertained by the clanging noise of shouting self-acclaimers or by the showy display put on in childish make-believe. He has reached the Kingdom of Heaven as his heart becomes purified and then will "all else be added"—all the jewels of PROMISE and whatever else he can wish for or desire.

And Faith, when united by the Light of the Star, or with the divine gift of understanding, along with the great LOVE one becomes a divine generator of the pure radiance of Divinity.

These three jewels must be perfected right within each one as he travels that divine Highway to Zion, the Straight and Narrow Way into the very presence of God. "And the Path is so plain a fool need not err therein, though the wicked can never cross over it."

And so it is that when accompanied by LOVE and

the great LIGHT of understanding the wonder of FAITH becomes glorious and powerful and can accomplish all things, for they will become subject unto him.

And as one offers his three gifts or priceless jewels to the King they become forever his own with all that goes with them, for they are a part of man—MADE PERFECT. "Be ye therefore perfect even as your Father in Heaven is perfect!" And it is so!

And now I must share with you some of the words to Daniel as they were delivered by an angel centuries ago.

Daniel 12:9-10: "And I, heard, but I understand not; and then said I, O my Lord, what shall be the end of these things?

"And he said, "Go thy way Daniel; for the words are closed up and sealed till the time of the end." (WHICH IS NOW!)

"And many shall be purified, and made white, and tried, but the wicked shall do wickedly; and none of the wicked shall understand, but the wise shall understand." Remember, it is the wicked who can never travel over the road of purification to Zion.

Then in verses three and four of that twelfth chapter of Daniel we are given this glorious information: "And they that be wise shall shine as the brightness of the firmament, and they that turn many to righteousness as the stars forever and ever.

"But thou, O Daniel, shut up the words, and seal the book, even to the time of the end; when many shall run to and fro, and knowledge shall be increased." Yes— when great free-ways shall span the continents to make that running to and fro possible. And there are the ship lanes and the sky-ways. And as for the increase of knowledge, both the atom and the universe are being explored, and the hidden secrets of all time and eternity are being revealed for knowledge has increased and is constantly being increased. And the time is NOW!

And the wise are beginning to travel that Holy Road to Zion as they themselves take on the brightness of the firmament and will eventually shine with the STARS— their own Star, forever and ever as they become purified and made white and tried, but the wicked shall do wickedly; and none of the wicked shall understand or be able to behold what is taking place for it will not at first be visible to mortal eyes. But the wise, the purified, they will understand.

"Perfect Love casts out all fear!" "Perfect Faith casts out all doubting!" And it may be said that, the casting out of all doubting will perfect Faith. With the jewels of LOVE and FAITH made manifest the holy gift of LIGHT will be fully revealed and perfected in all its radiant brilliance of pure creative power. It is pure intelligence! It is the exquisite substance of all perfection and of creation! It is eternal splendor! It is the effulgent glory of the firmament brought forth in man. He becomes clothed in It as "he clothes himself in Light!" (Odes of Solomon 21:2-3).

Anyone can take a swift, weak, negative glance at these great Truths and Eternal Premises and harden his heart against them, deny them, or use his strength to fight against them. But such only hurts himself. None can possibly hurt these Truths. They are eternal and indestructible. These who are slothful, expecting others to do their fulfilling for them, or the rebellious can only reject them and those who do so are rejecting the Sacred Road to the purification of their own hearts. Only a softened, believing heart can be purified. To seal one's heart against Truth and Purity and Everlasting Glory is such a tragic mistake for one's denial but places him upon that Broad Open Way that leads to destruction in which the "Many go!"

The Broad Open Way has been traveler by the multitudes and the Priesthoods and the Clergies and the laymen as they have "Trusted in the arm of flesh" to guide them, blindly following the blind along that road that leads to destruction—or DEATH. And there are those who follow no leaders but "trust in their own understandings" while they have never sought to KNOW GOD! "This is Life Eternal to KNOW THEE, *The only true and living God and Jesus Christ, Whom You have sent!*" These rejecting ones have been satisfied just to *"know about God"* but who have never sought to actually KNOW HIM!

The invitation has always been: "Seek me diligently and you shall KNOW ME!" Or, "Seek me early and you shall FIND ME!" This very seeking, as one goes directly to God instead of to men, refusing to trust "in the arm of flesh," places him upon that ROYAL ROAD TO ZION, which leads into the very Presence of God!

The millions down the ages who have been satisfied to LIVE and die as mere mortals, trusting in some chosen leader or in some dogmatic doctrines "know nothing at all about ZION, THE CITY OF GOD," the abode of the OVERCOMERS! The Glory of Glories! They have neither believed in the Promises nor sought to fulfil them. These have been the ones who have accepted the doctrines, the formulas or rituals of the conformists and often the radical dissenters, but have never accepted God's Words as being true and eternal and unfailing—when LIVED!

To look at the generations of the past and the millions living on the earth today and say, "This is an illusion and a lie! It is nonsense! None I have ever known have proved these things!" Then know this, you can be a chosen emissary of God sent to do that proving, for this way is a "Straight and Narrow Way and few there be who find it!" And you may think you are alone upon the road because it is so uncrowded. And then you will find at the end of your journey that the greatest, the most noble, the bravest and the most holy ones who have ever trod upon this earth have traveled this Way and some are traveling it now! And you will, in time meet them and recognize them and rejoice in them.

Remember that upon that broad open way the multitudes travel. They may have honored God with their lips, and with their tongues confessed him, while their hearts (or lives) have been far from Him, while their fear (LOVE) toward Him has been taught by the precepts of men. These have not only accepted that Broad Open Way that leads to destruction, they have embraced it, even worshipped it.

Only those who who will look at the great Truths and Promises of God and *believe in them,* can possibly travel this sacred, holy Highway, this Magic Street paved with transparent gold. And those who travel this divine Path add the contribution of their own vibrations of glory to that Sacred Way of Eternal Life, making that "Straight and Narrow Path" ever more gloriously desirable.

This work maps that "Way to Eternal Life so plainly that indeed even a fool need not err therein." As one travels this Path the Promises become realities! The Truths become proven facts of dynamic power! Each Promise becomes a signpost, a stepping stone, a measurement of progress along that sacred, glorious, exquisite Path of OVERCOMING—the Road to Zion!

The desire to KNOW GOD for oneself is a great and holy desire. And as this desire grows within one he grows into the power of its fulfilling. The desire increases as one travels that "Straight and Narrow Path which leads to Life Eternal!" And "This is Life Eternal to KNOW THEE, *the only true and living God and Jesus Christ whom You have sent!*"

Nothing short of this should ever satisfy anyone. This is the purpose for which we came to earth that we might OVERCOME the things of earth and return into God's Presence, "Without descending through the gates of death," even as Enoch of old and the many others who sought diligently to KNOW HIM!

Those who place the desire to "Be Born of the Spirit," which is actually to know God for themselves, above everything else, are prepared and conditioned to be "Born of the Spirit" which includes all other gifts and Promises. As one takes hold of "THIS BEST GIFT," refusing to be sidetracked or put-off, he becomes *"Filled with desire!"* This desire becomes the very aim and purpose of his life as he LIVES it! Thinks it! Loves it! Breathes it! And holds to it "without wavering or doubting!" And this *"laying hold"* of a divine gift, or Promise can only be done by one taking hold of it mentally and believing in it until his very soul holds forth the pattern for its fulfilling as FAITH generates the Light of understanding into the full forming of his request!

As one becomes *filled with the desire* to "Be Born of the Spirit," his soul takes up the rhythm of his request and holds that perfect pattern of his own hope glorified. AND IT WILL BE FULFILLED! This I Promise, in the name of God, for it is God's own Promise given before the world began, and verified anew to you! No power in existence can withhold this fulfilling for in such desiring one becomes that desire, alive, powerful and radiant with LIGHT. And then is God bound for He must fulfill His part of the Holy Covenant. And it is His joy to grant such a requesting. And it is every man's glory to receive it!

Yes, "Let the same mind be in you which was also in Christ Jesus, who being in the form of God thought it not robbery to be equal with God!" This becomes a reality, not a blasphemy as the weak and groveling and wicked maintain.

Train your hearts and minds and souls to become "FILLED WITH DESIRE." The desire to "Be Born of the Spirit" and you will receive all that your soul requests —AND MORE!

This is the Path! This is the accomplishment! This is the threshold that opens up the doors to the GREATER WORKS—and *unveils the face of God!* This contains the full glorification of God by man, (by yourself made perfect). It contains also the glorification of man by God, according to God's own divine desire and power of fulfilling.

And as one holds his eyes and attention upon that Path, or upon his request to *know God* it becomes ever more apparent and desirable. This is the Path! And in this sacred journey those pledges of Almighty God, those hallowed Promises, those Eternal Covenants become one's own! They become one's own individual covenants to God, for a covenant must be made between two or more in order to become a covenant. As man takes up these Promises or Covenants, and returns them to God, they are literally fulfilled and the Word of God is perfected, "For if you do as I say (or live according to the Covenant I make to you), then am I bound!" "And my WORDS cannot return unto me unfulfilled or void!" In this acceptance and believing the Covenants are made binding to both parties. In this manner are they proven and fulfilled. These Covenants or Promises are man himself glorified!

This Path is open now to every man! It is his to travel or to reject. In rejecting these Truths one is but judging himself to be unworthy or unprepared for such infinite joys and bounteous glories!

Never before has such an opportunity been given with such love and such plainness. This is the Promise Isaiah gave concerning that divine Road of purification, which leads to Zion. "It is the Straight and Narrow Way" of singing glory and peace that takes one back into the very Presence of God, glorified and purified and perfected and powerful in understanding and in LOVE!

Chapter XXVIII

The Message and Seal of Jesus Christ

"I, Jesus Christ, the Son of the Living God, have spoken to you throughout the pages of these books. They contain my words, and I lie not!

"My sheep hear my voice and they know me, and a stranger they will not follow!

"No one on the earth need ever be deceived by false doctrine for the truth is so plan there can be no mistaking it. Neither can the Truth longer be hidden. The time has come for the unveiling of the hidden mysteries of God to come forth that all men might be left without excuse.

"This sacred Road to Zion, this road to the Purification of the heart, is so plain and so preciously revealed even a fool need not err therein, though the wicked can never cross over it, as Isaiah proclaimed centuries ago. This Holy Road to Zion or to the Purification of the Heart is my own Straight and Narrow Path that leads to Life Eternal. And I Am that Way.

"This must be remembered: Everything that teaches a man to LOVE and to serve God and to Pray is of God! Let any man deny this and he is denying the TRUTH and the power of God.

"Prayer is the gateway into my Kingdom. And Prayer is a condition in which the PRAY-ER enters into my Presence and converses with me, or talks to me as one man talks to another. However, true PRAYER is not a vain repetition of words or phrases or sentences which are recited daily, without thought or feeling as a stupid, monotonous ritual, without life or vitality, performed merely from habit. When one enters my presence and talks to me, not reciting a monologued recitation, he could not possibly utter the same prayer twice, not any more than he could hold the same conversation with his neighbor each time they came into contact.

"Prayer is usually at an appointed time, which is good and acceptable for thus our meeting can be by appointment. But true prayer is the surging gratitude, the joy, the happiness, the yearnings of pure desire speaking at all times, in moments of free thought, as one carries in his heart the joy and the glory of his deepest requests. This is not done by appointment, or at any specified time. This is a spontaneous privilege and carries with it powers beyond the present understanding of man to fathom.

"Prayer is a privilege of sacred communication, offered to mankind. It is divine and should never be wasted. Use it well! Talk with me and let me talk to you. LEARN TO LISTEN! Learn to love those moments we may have together as our hearts commune, and soon that time of association will be increased until you will be walking with me at all times. So learn to love those moments when your desires become my desires and my love becomes your love! Never think of prayer as a duty or an obligation or a burden. Know only that it is a privilege and a blessing beyond knowledge—and thank God for it.

"Anyone who lives his life without prayer has been like a person confined to the darkness of a dungeon, without sunlight or hope or perspective or true purpose. Let your prayers be offered from your hearts, not just your minds or lips. Let them be a song of praise and love and gratitude and in such joy your every request will be heard and will be implanted upon that divine substance of BECOMING! In such joy your every petition and desire can be ANSWERED. This will be when you have prepared yourself to receive the fulness of your requests.

"Or, as I gave to my servant Ammon over two thousand years ago: 'He who prayeth continually, without ceasing, shall be given to understand the mysteries of Godliness. And unto such shall be given to reveal things which have never been revealed, and to bring thousands of souls unto repentance, or to an understanding of the joys of my kingdom.' This praying continually is not a fanatical, tortured offering of wailing, weeping lamentation. It is a singing glory of peace and assurance as one learns to rejoice with me. This is prayer, the offering of the self in a surrender of fulfillment as mortality is gradually released and one is so filled with the Spirit every cell and fibre of his being becomes imbued with Spirit—and he is thus prepared to 'Be Born of the Spirit!'

"To be 'Born of the Spirit' is the great step of full OVERCOMING. It is the OVERCOMING OF THE WORLD and all that pertains to it, for this the step that takes one beyond mortality, without descending through the gates of death. And always it is an experience of divine, controlled majesty. These blessed OVERCOMERS take their bodies with them, completely spiritualized, glorified, perfected and exalted, with DEATH OVERCOME! These are the works which I did. These are the works which you may do also.

"No one can come to the holy altar of prayer, within his own heart, and be slighted, ignored or unheard.

"Always give the Lord's Prayer, which is My Prayer! Give it with meaning and with LOVE. Then speak your own words, *giving thanks* first, then make your requests known. And thus shall we rejoice together. And thus shall you walk with me, for your errors and mistakes of the past shall be cleansed and released, and finally they will be blotted out and forgotten. And in this divine process even the tendency to err or blunder or sin will be eliminated. And your heart will be purified and your Road to Zion will be completed in the great glory of 'Being Born of the Spirit,' which holds the power of releasing all mortal ties of the physical flesh as the cells of the body are glorified and spiritualized and lifted beyond decay and illness and death. And in this glorious achievement of being 'Born of the Spirit' you will be lifted back into my Presence.

"Yes, Come unto me all you who labor (under the burdens and vicissitudes of mortality) and I will give you rest—WHICH REST IS THE FULNESS OF MY GLORY! Take my yoke upon you, for my yoke is easy, FOR IT IS LOVE, and my burden is LIGHT—even the great LIGHT of knowledge and fulfilment and power.

"There is no Promise too great for you to receive if you can only open up your hearts to believe. *Nothing is impossible to him who believes!* All negation and doubting will be banished as you become clothed in Light. And this great, divine Light of eternal power and understanding is MY BURDEN. And it is also yours as you take it upon you to fulfill my words and my PROMISE.

"And as you become clothed in LIGHT the keys of knowledge and understanding will be yours and *you will reach the point where you will comprehend all things!*

"Throw off your swaddling clothes of fleshy mortality and mortal thinking. THINK AS GOD THINKS and your minds and lives will lose the power to hurt and wound. Array yourselves in the glory of the PROMISES for I have not left you Comfortless. Every Promise ever given is alive and everlasting. Each Promise is a ray or beam of divine Light streaming down from the heavens above. The very Promises are the rays of my glory pouring down Light and understanding and the perfect plans and the pattern of your own fulfilling and everlasting glory. But it is required that you take hold of these and clothe yourself in their Light.

"Yes, Lay hold of the best gifts, the best PROMISES, the divine HOPES and you will grow into them for they shall be yours! Deny them, ignore them, reject them, doubt them and you will continue to dwell in the outer darkness of your own unbeliefs, your despairs and miseries, which lead to death.

"Defile yourselves by the feeling of pride or self-righteousness and there is no progress or hope or way to escape opened to you out of the dismal darkness of your own unprogressing, for you alone can seal this condition upon yourself. Only in great LOVE and pure HUMILITY can one journey this sacred, divine ROAD TO ZION, or to the complete purification of the heart. And the heart is only purified when all doubting is OVERCOME and LOVE is established in every cell and atom and fibre of the soul.

"I opened the door to life, yet few have followed.

"Now I hold that door open for you to enter and as you do so you will realize that you are truly the door to everything—to LIFE ITSELF FOR THIS IS THE DOOR THROUGH WHICH ONE IS BORN OF THE SPIRIT as he himself completes the perfecting of his own soul, and his flesh takes on the divine qualities of the Spirit. Then it is possible to enter the realm of Spirit, taking his body with him. And henceforth he will be able to come and go as the wind and no one will know from whence he came or whither he goeth as he is directed forth to do the *greater works,* even as I explained to Nicodemus.

"This Promise I leave upon you now, and I SEAL it by the power of my Redemption, that as you accept this most glorious gift, or Holy Spirit, and offend it not, but only BELIEVE IT, all things shall be unfolded unto your understandings. Its mission is to lead into *all* TRUTH—and to assist you in fulfilling all things. For the PROMISES are yours if you can accept them and doubt not in your hearts.

"Behold, I am Alpha and Omega, the first and the last * * *.

"I am he that liveth, and was dead; and, behold I am alive for evermore! I am Jesus Christ, the Son of the Living God, and I hold forth my words and my Promises before you this day that you might partake of the blessings thereof.

"This is my SEAL and it will stand forever! So be it! For I have spoken! Amen!"

Chapter XXIX

The Holy Spirit of Promise

II. Peter 1:3-4: "According as His divine power hath given unto us all things that pertain unto LIFE and GODLINESS, through the knowledge of Him that hath called us to glory and virtue.

"Whereby are given unto us exceedingly great and precious PROMISES, *that by these ye might be partakers of the* DIVINE NATURE, having ESCAPED CORRUPTION, *that is in the world through lust.*"

I am now instructed to reveal the marvel and the beauty of the Holy Spirit of Promise. It is glorious beyond mere mortal knowledge because mortals have never before been given a view of Its divine, stupendous powers.

Every seed has within it the germ of its own producing. The seed only needs the conditions of its own developing in order to fulfill its own perfect pattern or destiny.

And every Promise ever given by God is sealed with the Holy Spirit of Promise insomuch that the very laws of fulfilling are already perfected within it. However man contains the conditions and the materials or elements necessary for its germination and production as It fulfills all things contained within the PROMISES of Almighty God.

The Patriarchs of old did not live under the laws, as explained in the book *Beyond Mortal Boundaries* and

321

verified in Paul's Epistle to the Galatians. Those ancient, holy men of God lived by the PROMISES, THROUGH THEIR FAITH. This was a far higher order of existence than mere mortal living, under the law. This was the type of living associated with the Divine. This was the type of living that went beyond grubby, everyday existence. And the ancient ones had the authority and the calling to receive from God the plan and the pattern of their own special missions on earth, and to reveal to others the fulness of God's plans for them also.

It was when wickedness and an insatiable desire to excel and rise above others in wealth and dominion and self-importance that the laws were given. This very desire to surpass all others, or to be *first* contains but the demonstrating anguish of a lack of LOVE both for one's brother or neighbor. And it was because of lack of LOVE and of greed and selfishness that the laws were given. And that is why the laws still remain. They have continued to increase and are increasing as evils have multiplied. At the present time there are so many laws there are cases locked within the courts that take months to consider and more months to evaluate and judge, while true justice is forgotten.

These ancient Patriarchs, who *lived* by the PROMISES, believed in their vision or Hope which they held and nourished in their hearts. They kept the hope or the vision of the Promises before them continually. Each Promise was their own individual message from God and they accepted it as such. And as they *lived true* to it it would be fulfilled unto them.

Then God gave these words to be held forth forever for those who would only open their hearts to receive and their minds to comprehend: *"God will shed forth His Holy Spirit of Promise upon all who are just and true."* This sounds so simple and so easy but few can measure up to it. It is for all men, but only those who open up their souls to accept it can possibly receive the benediction and the glory of Its fulfilling.

This is the Covenant of the Holy Spirit of Promise: "You who will open up your hearts shall receive the HOLY SPIRIT OF PROMISE, which is HOPE expressed in all its rapturous perfection and glory."

This Holy Spirit of Promise is the SEAL or the COVENANT of Almighty God enfolding every Promise uttered or thought. It is there always. And It belongs to all who will only fulfill the laws of its bestowal. All have felt It momentarily at some time or other in their lives. It has enfolded them in Its ecstatic glory when they have reached beyond their ordinary level of achievement. It is God's most holy witness of approval. But only those who are JUST and TRUE can receive It as a permanent gift. Yet every PROMISE of God carries with it the everlasting Power of its divine completion. The Father truly sheds It forth, but only the *just* and *true* can receive or use it.

The Just are righteous men who do not prey upon others to "out-smart" them, disqualify them, belittle them, rob or accuse them or who mis-judge or injure any living soul. And this must be known, it is almost impossible for a jealous person to be JUST or TRUE. Those who are unjust or untrue are in no way qualified to lay hold of so sacred a gift as the fulfilling of all righteousness— the glory of their own perfection as they are prepared to "Be Born of the Spirit!"

And the TRUE are those who are *true* to the PROMISES of God as they are held forth without doubting. It is the elimination of doubting that makes one TRUE to God and to His PROMISES.

There are many indeed who have gazed with longing hearts upon these dynamic PROMISES of Almighty God as they have been opened to their view, and who have desired them greatly that they might appear before men in the robes of their own proud self-righteousness. But these were not TRUE, neither could they remain TRUE to the Promises they desired. They relinquished their requests expecting God to do the fulfilling for them. And they neglected to take into consideration the fact that "Patience must have its perfect work, that one might become perfect and entire, lacking nothing." In patience does the perfection of each and every PROMISE find the needed condition of its own unfolding, even as a seed, planted in the field needs time to grow.

I have met those, oh so many of them, who have rejoiced in these revealed Promises of Almighty God, and who have desired them greatly as the Holy Spirit of Promise unveiled their glory. I have seen that Holy Spirit of Promise enfold them as with a mantle of living Light as It sought for their help in the fulfilling. And all the Promises were there for their own selection. And the Holy Spirit of Promise was there bearing witness of God's unfailing, everlasting Covenant. All that was lacking was the FAITH and the PATIENCE of the individual to be TRUE, or to lay hold of, or to hold onto the Promise, with patience.

It is an everlasting truth that only those who are JUST, which includes the humility to use the gifts of God only for the glory of God and for the benefit of man, and not for any personal show of pride or self-aggrandizement who can receive that most Holy Gift. Thus is one's quality of justice measured.

And only those who can remain TRUE to that vision of glory which the Holy Spirit of Promise, unfolds to their minds can be qualified to receive the fulness of the Promises.

This is how the Father sheds forth the Holy Spirit of Promise upon those who are JUST and TRUE for only they can receive it in its overwhelming fulness of eternal, fulfilling glory.

Those who are given the WITNESS of the Holy Spirit of Promise under the divine COVENANT of Almighty God, and who betray that testimony later, returning again to their old ways of unbelief and doubting are likened to "dogs that return to their vomit," or to "swine that return to their wallow." To such the vomit is a stench though they may not realize it. And the "wallow" is the prolonged desolation of the darkness, which may be forever. For such there is no Promise for only as they are JUST and TRUE to the Witness or Holy Spirit can they advance into the fulness of the Promises. And, "If you do as I say, then am I bound! But if you do not as I say (or bear witness to you) then you have no PROMISE." These unfortunate ones realize not that they have themselves rejected His PROMISES and His Holy Spirit in their refusal to even attempt to PROVE HIS WORD THUS DISCARDING HIS PLEDGED COVENANT.

Every Promise of God can be PROVED just by the living of them. And every soul can have that Holy Spirit of Promise as a constant Companion, bearing eternal Witness to him that the PROMISES can and will be fulfilled if he is only *just* and *true*.

Those who reject the Witness of that Holy Spirit of Promise have sinned against the Holy Ghost, and unless they speedily repent they cannot be forgiven in this world or in the world to come for they have sealed themselves into the darkness of unbelief and mediocrity. Thus they remain mere, grubby mortals.

And again, you who open up your hearts shall receive the Holy Spirit of Promise, which is HOPE expressed in all its rapturous glory!

In other words, those, who through their FAITH and LOVE, have felt or do feel the rapturous glory of Hope singing in their souls are receiving the assurance and the wonder of the Holy Spirit of Promise as It bears Witness to them that the HOPE within them can and will be fulfilled if only they are *true* to it and doubt it not. This is God's Witness unto those who are worthy of the Promises. This is also the Witness Enoch received before his translation, "THAT HE PLEASED GOD!" This is the Witness that will come to those who cast out the darkness of doubting and who are TRUE to their Hopes or desires. To such the HOPE will be established unto them through that Holy Spirit of Promise, which cannot fail! Only when man himself fails to hold to the Promise of his heart can failure possibly come. It is man himself who fails.

The Holy Spirit of Promise is God's Promise going forth in an eternal Covenant of Truth within the souls of men, if they will but accept it and lay hold of it. That Holy Spirit of Promise that holds forth the vision of God's great and unfailing Words, as it sings in your heart, is the Witness of God, our Eternal Father, that *you please*

Him, even as Enoch of old. As you accept this Witness and hold to it all the things that Enoch accomplished shall be yours also. If you lose this contact or Witness even for a moment pray until it is again your own. Never cease to pray and it will never leave you.

The Holy Spirit of Promise is also FAITH ADVANCING INTO PERFECTION as one becomes TRUE to so holy a WITNESS. This Witness is of God. It is God's Holy Covenant bearing testimony to one's own soul that "HE PLEASES GOD!" The fulfilling will come according to one's belief and his HOPES, for all PROMISES are released under the eternal, *forever* glory of God's own Word. And they belong to those who lay claim to them, through FAITH, *as doubting is overcome.*

Know that, if even for a moment, your hopes soar high and a song of glorious assurance sings in your soul, then be sure that the Holy Spirit of Promise is bearing Witness to you that *you please God*. And as you hold to that vibrant, glorious assurance it will become the divine, fulfilling reality in your life, exalting you above the sordid conditions of earth. This is the first step beyond ordinary mortal living. Then FAITH IS PERFECTED AS THE DARKNESS OF DOUBTING IS OVERCOME. Then it is that the Holy Spirit of Promise, and all that it contains become your own—a constant power of fulfilling as you are TRUE to its enfolding glory of eternal, triumphant victory, even to the OVERCOMING of *mortality* and *death*. And you will be BORN OF THE SPIRIT!

The Holy Spirit of Promise is sensitive beyond man's understanding. It must be accepted, appreciated and reverenced in order that it can become a permanent Witness of divine fulfilling. This is TRUTH! Then the fulfilling is accomplished. Such will be able to perfect their Faith and become glorified even as Enoch of old, Moses, Elijah, John the Beloved, the glorious Virgin Mary and many I could name, if permitted to do so, who fulfilled the Promises and by so doing became glorified—even as you can—for the same PROMISES ARE YOURS!

Behold, I am the Holy Spirit of Promise—the Comforter, the Holy Ghost or the Holy Helper. And my mission is to give Comfort in time of trouble or sorrow, to reveal Truth and to bear Witness of Its everlasting Powers. It is also my assignment to be a constant Companion of instruction and protection to those who are prepared and willing to receive me.

And now, I shall speak to you from the Lost Books of the Bible, for through Hermas, the Bishop of Philippi, I imparted the following as recorded in II. Hermas, Command IX.

1. "Again He said unto me, (Hermas), remove from thee all doubting—

4. "Wherefore purify thy heart from all vices of this present world; and observe the commands I have before delivered unto thee from God: and thou shalt receive whatsoever good things thou shalt ask, and nothing shall be wanting unto thee of all thy petitions; if thou shalt ask of the Lord without doubting.

5. "But they that are not such shall obtain none of those things which they ask. For they that are full of faith ask all things with confidence, and receive from the Lord, because they ask without doubting.

6. "Wherefore purify thy heart from doubting, and put on faith, and trust in God, and thou shalt receive all that

thou shalt ask. But if thou shouldst chance to ask somewhat and not (immediately) receive it, yet do not therefore doubt, because thou hast not immediately received the petition of thy soul.

7. "For it may be thou shall not presently (or immediaetely) receive it for thy trial, or else for some sin which thou knowest not. But do not thou leave off to ask, and then *thou shalt receive*. Else if thou shalt cease to ask, thou must complain of thyself and not of God, that He has not given unto thee what thou didst desire.

8. "Consider therefore this doubting, how cruel and pernicious it is; and how it utterly roots out many from the faith * * *. For this doubting is the daughter of the devil, and deals very wickedly with the servants of God.

9. "Despise it therefore, and thou shalt rule over it on every occasion. Put on a firm and powerful faith: for faith Promises all things and perfects all things."

It is in the continuing of prayer that the darkness is banished. Though sometimes it may seem that there is no answer forthcoming, let it be here known that anyone who continues to pray, regardless of the seeming lack of help or attention, that he is purifying himself. By his own continued praying no matter how halting or imperfect it may be, he is cleansing himself, and strengthening himself and is preparing himself for the very fulness of all that is.

No one can pray and not receive a blessing or go unheeded or unbenefited. As one continues to pray, though he may at first even be asking amiss, he will grow into the glory of true requesting and will soon be asking according to the will of God. And true prayer is an inner song of praise and adoration. And as one continues to pray he is being purified and prepared to receive, even the impossible. Prayer cannot fail! And anyone who turns his heart to prayer will find me there beside him, and if he is *just* and *true* to his desire the divine Promise of God's fulfilling will enfold him and he will begin to take on the Light of purification—and to KNOW and to RECEIVE.

Hermas also revealed this information, as recorded in II. Hermas X:18-20: as follows: "Remove therefore sadness from thyself, and afflict not the Holy Spirit which dwelleth in thee, lest he entreat God, and depart from thee. For the Spirit of the Lord which is given to dwell in the flesh, endureth no such sadness.

19. "Wherefore clothe thyself with cheerfulness, which has always favor with the Lord, and thou shalt rejoice in it. For every cheerful man does well; and relishes those things that are good, and despises sadness.
20. "But the sad man does always wickedly."

Such was one of my special messages in the past, and it is still true and alive with power—for it is forever.

My message to you now is to take upon you the Light of Jesus Christ, in the joy of perfect LOVE, free from self-righteousness, which is one of the greatest evils, and from doubting which is the darkness. "Accept of me, the Holy Spirit of Promise, your Holy Helper, as a living Companion and I will never fail you!"

James I:5-8: "If any of you lack wisdom (or anything else in existence, for that matter), let him ask of God, that giveth to all men liberally, and upbraideth not (for past errors or mistakes); and it shall be given him.

"But let him ask in faith, nothing *wavering*. For he that WAVERETH is like a WAVE of the sea driven with the wind and tossed.

"For let not that man think that he shall receive any thing of the Lord.

"A double minded man is unstable in all his ways."

Blessed children of the Most High, it must be understood that it is quite necessary to TAKE HOLD of the PROMISE you desire most, or THE BEST GIFT, according to your vision or desiring, though it is the highest, most seemingly impossible, the most blinding in its glory, hold onto it *without wavering.* Do not lose faith in your ability to receive it or in God's power to grant it. Do not modify your request to some lesser desire, or close your eyes to the blinding glory of the deepest desire in your soul. Rather take hold of the highest, most holy, most exquisite desire possible to imagine and DO NOT WAVER, or *change or modify it!* Do not move around it gradually in your requesting. Lay hold of the PROMISE, whatever it be, and never let go! Never relinquish your hold! Never change! Never WAVER! This is FAITH PUT INTO ACTION!

And to those who have prepared themselves to accept it, the TRUTH of Christ's Words to Nicodemus concerning the glory and power of BEING BORN OF THE SPIRIT becomes the greatest desire possible to implant in a human heart—your own heart! Nevertheless it is your own when you open your hearts to receive.

For some time it takes years to prepare themselves to lay hold of so glorious a gift because of their lack of FAITH and therefore their WAVERING! This most divine, holy gift belongs to you as you lay claim to it, even as it belonged to Enoch, who changed his carnal flesh to flesh divine without descending through the gates of death. This supreme, most holy gift holds the keys of

OVERCOMING *mortality* and the joy of all fulfilling. This gift alone fulfills the PROMISE quoted before: "The nearer man approaches perfection the clearer are his views and the greater are his enjoyments, until he overcomes the evils of his life and loses every desire for sin, and like the ancients, arrives at the point of FAITH where he is wrapped in the power and glory of his Maker and is caught up to dwell with Him!"

Ask and it shall be given unto you! Seek and you shall find truth and honor and power and fulfilment! Knock and it shall be opened unto you, even the realm of the primal matter of all forming and fulfilling. And blessed is he who hungers and thirsts after righteousness and knowledge for he shall be filled with the power of God and in that wonder he will know humility and will become the LOVE—and be clothed in glory.

Whenever FAITH sings in your heart, when hope vibrates in its pulsating ecstasy of joy, then know that I, the Holy Spirit of Promise am bearing WITNESS to your soul, that GOD IS PLEASED WITH YOU!

Such is my Witness and my message to you, as God has decreed. And through the divine, holy LOVE of the Father I send it forth to you.

So be it—Amen!

THE 33rd ODE OF SOLOMON
From the Lost Books of the Bible

1. "Again Grace ran and forsook corruption, and came down through Him to bring it to nought;

2. "And He destroyed perdition from before Him, and devastated all its order;

3. "And He stood on a lofty summit and uttered His voice from one end of earth to the other;

4. "And drew to Him all those who *obeyed* Him; and there did not appear as it were an evil person who gathered, for those who obeyed Him not did not hear His voice.

---

5. "But there stood a perfect virgin who was proclaiming and calling and saying,

6. "O ye sons of men return ye, and ye daughters of men, come ye:

7. "And forsake the ways of that corruption (DEATH) and draw near unto me, and I will abide with you, and will bring you forth from perdition,

8. "And make you wise in the ways of truth; that you be not destroyed nor perish;

9. "Hear me and be redeemed. For the grace of God I am telling among you; and by this means you shall be redeemed and become blessed."

Behold, I am Annalee Skarin, a daughter of the living God. And I have been ordained and commissioned to be a humble scribe.

By some of those who are very near and dear I am known as Nansela, the grace and the love of God. So be it! Amen!

CHRONOLOGICAL DISPLACEMENT IN BIBLICAL AND RELATED LITERATURES

SOCIETY OF BIBLICAL LITERATURE

DISSERTATION SERIES
David L. Petersen, Old Testament Editor
Pheme Perkins, New Testament Editor

Number 139

CHRONOLOGICAL DISPLACEMENT
IN BIBLICAL AND RELATED
LITERATURES

by
David A. Glatt

David A. Glatt

CHRONOLOGICAL DISPLACEMENT IN BIBLICAL AND RELATED LITERATURES

Scholars Press
Atlanta, Georgia

CHRONOLOGICAL DISPLACEMENT IN BIBLICAL AND RELATED LITERATURES

David A. Glatt

Ph.D., 1991
University of Pennsylvania

Advisor:
Jeffrey H. Tigay

© 1993
The Society of Biblical Literature

Composition by Kelby Bowers,
COMPublishing, Cincinnati, Ohio

The Hebrew font used to print this work is available from Linguist's Software, Inc., PO Box 580, Edmonds, WA 98020–0580 tel (206) 775–1130

Library of Congress Cataloging in Publication Data
Glatt, David A., 1961-
    Chronological displacement in biblical and related literatures/ David A. Glatt.
       p. cm.—(Dissertation series/ Society of Biblical Literature; no. 139)
       Originally presented as the author's thesis (Ph.D.)—Univ. of Pennsylvania, 1991.
       Includes bibliographical references and index.
       ISBN 1-55540-817-6.—ISBN 1-55540-818-4 (pbk.)
       1. Bible. O. T.—Chronology.   2. Semitic literature—Chronology.
I. Title. II. Series: Dissertation series (Society of Biblical Literature); no. 139.
BS637.2.G534 1992
221.6'7—dc20   92-43672
                                                           CIP

Printed in the United States of America
on acid-free paper

DEDICATED TO

my parents

Rabbi and Mrs. Melvin J. Glatt

in appreciation for their constant
love, support, and encouragement.

כאשר ישא איש את בנו בכל הדרך
אשר הלכתם עד באכם עד המקום הזה
(Deuteronomy 1:31)

כאיש אשר אמו תנחמנו כן אנכי
אנחמכם ובירושלם תנחמו
(Isaiah 66:13)

TABLE OF CONTENTS

Abbreviations ix
Preface xii

Introduction 1

1. Mesopotamian Material 10

Introduction 10
Sargon II's Prisms and Related Texts 12
Esarhaddon's Restoration of Babylon 16
Assurbanipal's Conquest of Babylon 19
Nabonidus's Rebuilding of the Ehulhul 26
The Creation of Barren Women in *Atraḫasis* 39
Excursus: Naram-Sin and the Fall of Akkad 43
Summary of Chapter One 52

2. Biblical Material 55

Introduction 55
2 Samuel 5–6 and 1 Chronicles 13–15 57
1 Kings 2:1–9 and 1 Chronicles 22:5–16 61
1 Kings 22:49–50 and 2 Chronicles 20:35–37 64
2 Kings 22–23 and 2 Chronicles 34 68
Summary of Chapter Two 73

3. Post-Biblical Material 75

Introduction 75
Genesis 35–41 and Jubilees 34–41 79
Joshua 8:30–35; Tôseftā´ Sôṭāh 8; and
    Josephus, *Antiquities* 5:68–70 83

Judges 17–21; Sēder ʿÔlām ch. 12; and
  Josephus, *Antiquities* 5:132–179 89
1 Kings 14:1–18 and LXX 3 Reigns 12:24g–n 100
1 Kings 20–22 and LXX 3 Reigns 20–22 109
Ezra 1–6; 1 Esdras 2–7; and Josephus, *Antiquities* 11:1–113 113
Esther 2:21–23 and Addition A to Esther 142
Summary of Chapter Three 145

4. Chronological Displacements Inferred from Internal Evidence ... 149

Introduction 149
Genesis 35:27–29 150
Exodus 18 152
Judges 17–21 157
1 Kings 11 162
Ezra 2:1–4:5 167
1 Chronicles 11:4–9 174
2 Chronicles 20:1–30 179
2 Chronicles 25:25–27 181
Summary of Chapter Four 184

Concluding Remarks 188

Appendix 191

Bibliography 195

Index 219

ABBREVIATIONS

AB	Anchor Bible
ABL	R.F. Harper, *Assyrian and Babylonian Letters*
AfO	*Archiv für Orientforschung*
AJSL	*American Journal of Semitic Languages and Literatures*
ANET	J.B. Pritchard (ed.), *Ancient Near Eastern Texts Relating to the Old Testament*. 3rd ed.
ARAB	D.D. Luckenbill, *Ancient Record of Assyria and Babylonia*
AS	Assyriological Studies
B.	Babylonian (Talmud)
BA	*Biblical Archaeologist*
BHS	K. Elliger and W. Rudolph (eds.), *Biblia Hebraica Stuttgartensia*
BKAT	Biblischer Kommentar: Altes Testament
BWANT	Beiträge zur Wissenschaft vom Alten und Neuen Testament
CAD	E. Reiner (ed.), *The Assyrian Dictionary of the Oriental Institute of the University of Chicago*
CAH	I.E.S. Edwards, et al. (eds.), *Cambridge Ancient History*
CBQ	*Catholic Biblical Quarterly*
E.M.	*'Enṣiqlôpediyāh Miqrā'ît*
FRLANT	Forschungen zur Religion und Literatur des Alten und Neuen Testaments
HAT	Handbuch zum Alten Testament
HKAT	Handkommentar zum Alten Testament
HSM	Harvard Semitic Monographs

HTR	*Harvard Theological Review*
IB	G.A. Buttrick (ed.), *Interpreter's Bible*
ICC	International Critical Commentary
IDB	G.A. Buttrick (ed.), *Interpreter's Dictionary of the Bible*
IEJ	*Israel Exploration Journal*
JAOS	*Journal of the American Oriental Society*
JBL	*Journal of Biblical Literature*
JCS	*Journal of Cuneiform Studies*
JJS	*Journal of Jewish Studies*
JNES	*Journal of Near Eastern Studies*
JNWSL	*Journal of Northwest Semitic Languages*
JSOT	*Journal for the Study of the Old Testament*
JTS	*Journal of Theological Studies*
KAT	Kommentar zum Alten Testament
KHAT	Kurzer Hand—Commentar zum Alten Testament
LXX	Septuagint
LXX^B	Septuagint, Codex Vaticanus
MGWJ	*Monatsschrift für Geschichte und Wissenschaft des Judentums*
MT	Masoretic Text
NJV	New Jewish Version (*Tanakh*. Philadelphia: The Jewish Publication Society, 1985).
OLZ	*Orientalische Literaturzeitung*
OTL	Old Testament Library
P.	Palestinian ([Jerusalem] Talmud)
PAAJR	*Proceedings of the American Academy for Jewish Research*
PAPS	*Proceedings of the American Philosophical Society*
PBS	Publications of the Babylonian Section (University Museum, University of Pennsylvania)

RA	*Revue d'Assyriologie*
RLA	E. Ebeling and B. Meissner (eds.), *Reallexicon der Assyriologie*
RSV	Revised Standard Version
SBL	Society of Biblical Literature
SH	*Scripta Hierosolymitana*
S.O.	*Sēder ʿŌlām*
VAB	Vorderasiatische Bibliothek
VT	*Vetus Testamentum*
WO	*Die Welt des Orients*
ZA	*Zeitschrift für Assyriologie*
ZAW	*Zeitschrift für die Alttestamentliche Wissenschaft*

PREFACE

This study was originally submitted as a Ph.D. dissertation at the University of Pennsylvania in 1991. In presenting it to the general public, I wish to acknowledge the exceptional and unstinting support of my thesis advisor, Prof. Jeffrey Tigay. His accessibility and encouragement saw me through a task that originally loomed larger than life. Many other outstanding teachers also contributed to my scholarly development, a process which took me through Bar-Ilan University in Ramat-Gan, Israel, as an undergraduate student, the Jewish Theological Seminary of America as a masters student, and the University of Pennsylvania as a doctoral student. Among these teachers, I have in mind particularly Prof. Uriel Simon, Prof. Yehudah Elitzur, Dr. Aaron Demsky, Dr. Shmuel Vargon, Prof. Yochanan Muffs, Prof. David Weiss Halivni, Prof. Barry Eichler, Prof. Erle Leichty, Prof. Judah Goldin, and Dr. Randall Garr.

I was privileged all through my years in graduate school to be the beneficiary of many prestigious and generous fellowships, including a grant from the Gustav Wurzweiler Foundation, the Ellis and Lane fellowships in Oriental Studies at the University of Pennsylvania, and the Mellon and Dissertation fellowships of the School of Arts and Sciences, University of Pennsylvania. Special recognition is due to the Memorial Foundation for Jewish Culture, whose support I enjoyed as a doctoral fellow for four consecutive years. Finally, I express my appreciation to the Israel Academy of Sciences and Humanities, whose Wolfson fellowship has supported my work during the period of this book's publication.

My thanks to Dr. Edward Breuer for his technical assistance in preparing this book for publication. Last but not least, it gives me great pleasure to acknowledge the boundless love of my family members, particularly my parents, to whom this book is dedicated.

INTRODUCTION

Statement of Purpose

Any study of a particular literary phenomenon in Biblical historiography ought to take its lead from what we can refer to as "Sternberg's law." In his influential study *The Poetics of Biblical Narrative*, Sternberg states:

> Functionally speaking, it [Biblical narrative] is regulated by a set of three principles: ideological, historiographic and aesthetic. How they cooperate is a tricky question...but that they do operate is beyond question. For at some points—or from some viewpoints—we find each laid bare, as it were, asserting its claims and exerting its peculiar influence on narrative selection and arrangement.[1]

In essence, Sternberg is saying that Biblical narrative by nature reflects a three-way inner tension between the desires to promote certain beliefs, to produce a work of history, and to be artistically pleasing. Furthermore, each of these desires on occasion might overtake and overshadow the other competing purposes. The phenomenon which I shall be studying, namely chronological displacement, is a case in point. I shall be using the term chronological displacement to refer to a situation in which an author or editor intentionally transfers an episode from its original chronological context (of which he knew through general historical awareness or from another written source) into a different setting. Now, since chronology is the supreme linchpin of historical writing and analy-

---

[1] Sternberg, *Poetics*, 41.

sis,[2] it would be completely reasonable to conclude that any intentional deviation from a straight chronological order of presentation indicates a conscious preference either for an ideological concern or for an artistic purpose.[3] Indeed, many of my examples of chronological displacement will highlight precisely these two alternatives, which I will be labeling the "ideological" and "thematic" motivations, respectively. Yet, it is also possible that an author or editor strayed from a strict chronological presentation precisely in order to achieve a more effective historical composition. The general primacy of strict chronological sequence in historiography notwithstanding, the lines of demarcation between a thematic arrangement as a purely artistic means or as an historiographic tool may, on occasion, be somewhat blurred. In other words, by substituting thematic continuity for chronological sequence, an author or editor could have been aiming for historical clarity no less than for aesthetic or didactic effect. In addition, it is conceivable that an author or editor could have reversed the "original" order of a previous written source because he truly believed that the order reflected by that source was chronologically inaccurate or at least problematic.

In sum, Sternberg's assertion that the nature of the cooperation between the ideological, historiographic, and aesthetic principles is "a tricky question" is undoubtedly correct to the point of being an understatement. Our task in accounting for the phenomenon of chronological displacement will be to attempt, where possible, to sort out and weigh the three competing variables which enter into the analysis of Biblical historiography and to determine their relative application to each particular case. However, before spelling out my methodological procedures, I shall take up previous treatments of the phenomenon in order to more precisely sketch the concerns of, and need for, the present study.

History of Research

Already in late antiquity, the rabbis of the Midrash and Talmud were sensitive to what they perceived to be anomalies in the Bible's sequential patterns of formulation and arrangement (i.e., what moderns would call the Bible's "editorial" practices). The classical expression

---

[2] See J. Vansina, *Oral Tradition as History*, 173.
[3] Cf. Sternberg, *Expositional Modes*, 33–34.

which is used to describe such cases is *'ên mûqdām ûmĕ'ûḥār battôrāh*, literally, "there is no earlier or later in the Torah [i.e., the Bible]."[4] Although this expression appears to carry distinct chronological overtones, in reality *'ên mûqdām ûmĕ'ûḥār* takes on a somewhat broader connotation so as to include various types of perceived sequential disorders in the Biblical text.[5] We shall cite a few Rabbinic sources in which chronologically related considerations are given explicit formulation.

1) In commenting on the literary position of Numbers 9 vis-a-vis Numbers 1, the *Sifrê Numbers* states:

> For at the beginning of the book [of Numbers] it says: "The Lord spoke to Moses in the wilderness of Sinai in the Tent of Meeting on the first [day] of the *second* month [in the second year following the exodus]" (Num. 1:1) and here [Num. 9:1] it says: ["The Lord spoke to Moses in the wilderness of Sinai in the second year following the exodus] in the *first* month," to teach that there is no earlier or later in the Torah.[6]

Thus, the *Sifrê* raises the question of why Num. 9, which records a communication that occurred in the month preceding the communication of Num. 1, nevertheless appears in a later literary context.

2) Another example of explicit chronological argumentation is found in the *Midrāš Haggādôl* to Genesis which records the question posed by a sectarian to Rabbi Abbahu concerning the superscriptions of Psalms 3 and 57. The sectarian queried:

---

[4] For treatments of the rabbinic material, see Bacher, *'erkê midrāš*, Vol. 1, 114–15; Berlin and Zevin (eds.), *'Enṣiqlôpediyāh Talmûdît*, Vol. 1, 302–03; Heschel, *Theology of Ancient Judaism* (Hebrew), Vol. 1, 199–202; E.Z. Melammed, *Bible Commentators* (Hebrew), Vol. 1, 18–21.

[5] For example, many of the verses cited by the *Mĕkiltā'*, Shirta 7 (Horovitz-Rabin ed., 139) and *Kôhelet Rabbāh* 1:31 (Soncino English ed., 37–38) as illustrating the principle of *'ên mûqdām ûmĕ'ûḥār* were chosen because they were thought to represent the true opening statements of a given book, chapter, or prophet, despite their present position *within* the particular book, chapter, or prophetic collection (e.g., Exod. 15:9; Jer. 2:2; Ecc. 1:12). Although pedantically speaking, one could refer to such instances as "chronological displacement," since the very words thought to have been spoken first are set within the text following other material, the issue is really one of editorial and literary style. None of the verses quoted in the above sources (with the exception of Isa. 6:1) offers a specific date or context which would encourage one to understand them as actually having preceded (in time) the material which appears before them.

[6] *Sifrê Numbers* 64 (Horovitz ed., 61). Emphases are my own.

It says "A psalm of David when he fled from his son Absalom" (Ps. 3:1) and it says "Of David. A miktam, when he fled from Saul into a cave" (Ps. 57:1). Which of these [incidents] was prior? Was the incident with Absalom prior or was the incident with Saul prior?[7]

Obviously, since Saul was long dead by the time of Absalom's revolt (see 1 Sam. 24; 26; 2 Sam. 1; 15), the question concerning the arrangement of the psalms is why Ps. 57 was not placed before Ps. 3. Rabbi Abbahu goes on to explain the placement of Ps. 3 in midrashic fashion, but the theoretical premise of the question is clear for all to see.[8]

3) Still another example is found in *Mišnat Rabbi Eliezer* 2:33 which sets down the exegetical principle of *mûqdām ûmĕ'ûḥār šehū' bapparšiyôt*, literally, "earlier and later which is [found] in whole sections." The illustrative text cited is the covenant between the pieces in Gen. 15.

And He [God] said to him [Abram], "Bring me a three-year-old heifer..." [Gen. 15:9]. When was this section written? After the battle of the kings [Gen. 14]. But this incident [of Gen. 15] occurred five years before Abraham left Haran, as it is written, "At the end of four hundred and thirty years ... all the ranks of the Lord departed from the land of Egypt" [Exod. 12:41].[9]

The midrashic scheme enunciated here reflects an attempt to reconcile various chronological data in Genesis and Exodus, including the discrepancy between the 430 years of Israelite sojourn in Egypt mentioned in Exod. 12:40–41 and the 400-year period mentioned in Gen. 15:13.[10] In so doing, it winds up dating the covenant between the pieces thirty years prior to Isaac's birth, thus to Abraham's 70th year (see Gen. 21:5), five years prior to his journey from Haran to Canaan (see Gen. 12:4). Thus, the question arises why an earlier event (Gen. 15) is nevertheless recorded as occurring in a later literary context.

The above examples have been cited to show how the classical rabbis were attuned to issues relating to the presence of non-chronological

---

[7] Margulies ed., Introduction, 38–39.
[8] Ibid. Cf. also *Midrāš Tĕhillîm* 3:2 (Buber ed., 33–34).
[9] Enelow ed., 40–41.
[10] See Rashi to Gen. 15:13 (Rosenbaum and Silbermann *Pentateuch*, Vol. 1, 61); Heinemann, "210 Years."

arrangement in the Bible. However, none of these examples completely suits the focus of our study. In Numbers 1 and 9, the relevant dates are stated explicitly. Although the placement of an event from the second month before an event from the first month raises a legitimate question, such a situation is still a far cry from cases in which a text obscures the original chronological setting of an event by presenting it as if it occurred in a different time frame. The present study concentrates specifically on cases of the latter variety. The case of Ps. 3 and 57 is not relevant for the same reason as well as for the fact that principles governing the arrangement of poetic material cannot readily be brought to bear on historical narrative material with which the present study is concerned. The case from Gen. 15 must also be excluded from consideration since its force derives from midrashic assumptions, specifically that the chronological data of Exod. 12:40–41, Gen. 15:13, and related texts can and ought to be harmonized with each other.

There remains one celebrated case of possible chronological displacement mentioned by the rabbis, namely Exod. 18, which I shall take up in detail later in the book (see below, pp. 152–57).

The medieval Jewish commentators[11] continued in the Rabbinic tradition by applying the principle of *ʾên mûqdām ûmĕʾûḥār battôrāh* to various kinds of disorder beyond the chronological displacement of entire pericopes[12] and by allowing for midrashic considerations to enter into the identification of cases covered by the principle.[13] In addition to cases already noted by the rabbis (e.g., Num. 9), Rashi points to chronological displacement in the following verses: (1) Gen. 6:3, (2) Gen. 35:29, (3) Josh. 8:30, (4) Jud. 17, (5) 2 Sam. 21:19, (6) 2 Ki. 13:12–13, (7) Ezek. 29:17, (8) Ps. 72:20.

Of the above cases, examples 1, 3, and 8 are based on midrashic computations or suppositions. Example 7 has to do with the order of

---

[11] For an inventory of cases of *ʾên mûqdām ûmĕʾûḥār* cited by the medieval Jewish commentators, see Melammed, *Bible Commentators* (Hebrew), Vol. 1, 433–35; Vol. 2, 539–44; 835–38.

[12] E.g., Ibn Ezra who uses the principle to account for disorders in the sequence of particular narrative details. Thus, in commenting on Exod. 4:19, which logically belongs before v. 18, Ibn Ezra invokes *ʾên mûqdām ûmĕʾûḥār* in order to give the opening word of v. 19 (*wayōʾmer*) a pluperfect meaning.

[13] E.g., Rashi on Gen. 6:3. Rashi takes the verse as referring to a 120-year grace period granted to mankind before the flood. Thus, the verse would belong sequentially before Gen. 5:32 whose time frame is only 100 years before the flood (cf. Gen. 7:6).

dated prophecies (as opposed to historical narrative). This leaves examples 2 and 4–6, which fall within the parameters of the present study's concerns. Indeed, we shall be returning to examples 2 and 4 later in the book (see below, pp. 150–52; 89–100; 157–62).

Ibn Ezra, in a well known comment to Num. 16,[14] argues that Korah's rebellion ought to be dated to the period of the encampment at Mt. Sinai. Consequently, Num. 16 appears to be displaced in its present literary setting in which the location of the Israelite camp has already shifted from Sinai to the wilderness of Paran (see Num. 10:12; 12:16). Although Ibn Ezra's reasoning is not entirely compelling (cf. the comments of Ramban ad loc.), the fact that he broaches the issue at all points to the ever-growing creative spirit of the medieval commentators which induced them to search for previously unnoticed examples of chronological displacement.

In modern study, the phenomenon of chronological displacement has received surprisingly little attention. To be sure, the term is invoked on occasion, but not always in a manner which overlaps with the focus of our study. For example, Sternberg uses the term in conjunction with the literary technique which he refers to as an "expositional gap," i.e., the withholding of pertinent background information from the first possible point in the narrative where that information can be supplied to a later point in the narrative.[15] An example from the Bible which Sternberg cites in another work is Num. 31:16 which reads: "They [the Midianite women] are the very ones who, at the bidding of Balaam, induced the Israelites to trespass against the Lord in the matter of Peor." Here, we hear for the very first time that Israel's licentiousness at Peor, which was already related in Num. 25, was brought about through the instigation of Balaam. In Sternberg's view, this constitutes a variance between the order of occurrence (earlier) and the order of narration (later), in other words a chronological "disordering."[16] However, this type of example, along with numerous other cases of "flashbacking" and "flashforwarding" cited by Sternberg, clearly is not part of the phenomenon under investigation here. For in such cases, the text does not intimate that an event which actually occurred in time frame A occurred in time frame B or

---

[14] Ibn Ezra to Num. 16:1.
[15] Sternberg, *Expositional Modes*, 240–41.
[16] Sternberg, *Poetics*, 315. For the term "disordering," which Sternberg appears to use synonymously with "discontinuity" and "displacement," see ibid., 309.

vice-versa, but rather that an event which already occurred in time frame A or has yet to occur in time frame C can help shed light on time frame B.

Halpern, in his recent work *The First Historians*, moves much closer to the type of chronological displacement investigated in our study. Referring to the Deuteronomistic History, Halpern writes: "Chronological displacement appears to be common. Thus 2 Kings 19:9 probably makes Tirhaqa a king a decade too early. And 2 Kings 19:36f. suffixes Sennacherib's murder to his 701 campaign: Sennacherib died in 681 B.C.E."[17] The only problem with Halpern's formulation is that it does not distinguish between displacement and misplacement. In other words, it is rather difficult to ascertain whether, in his view, the chronological inconsistencies with extra-Biblical sources result from the Deuteronomistic Historian's *intentional* manipulation or simply from his ignorance. The present study concentrates only on cases in which there is strong evidence for intentional displacement rather than unwitting misplacement.

In closing this section, I wish to recapitulate the criteria and limitations noted to this point for examples of chronological displacement which will be investigated in the present study:

a) The material with which I am concerned is only that which can be broadly classified as historical narrative, as opposed to prophecy, poetry, and the like.

b) The displacement must be recognizable through historical-philological (as opposed to midrashic) methodology.

c) The displacement must reflect a primary concern of transferring the chronological locus of a given event from one time frame to another, as opposed to merely noting or alluding to an admittedly earlier or later event in a non-sequential manner.

d) The displacement must derive from the author/editor's intentional reversal of a setting for the event known to him either through general historical awareness or through a previous written source to which he had access.

---

[17] Halpern, *The First Historians*, 208.

Methodology and Structure

The present study does not venture into completely untrodden territory. There have been significant contributions, particularly by Tadmor and Cogan, to the understanding of chronological displacement. Tadmor's seminal studies on the inscriptions of Sargon II and Nabonidus, published in 1958 and 1965, respectively,[18] will be referred to repeatedly in Chapter 1, below, which deals with cases of chronological displacement in the Mesopotamian royal inscriptions. Likewise, Cogan's recent study, which uses Assurbanipal's inscription from Babylon to illustrate patterns of chronological displacement in the Biblical book of Chronicles, has served as a guiding paradigm for the present study. Cogan's presentation appears as a chapter in J. Tigay's *Empirical Models for Biblical Criticism*.[19] The essays in this collection are based on the theory that empirically documented attestations of a particular literary phenomenon help support scholarly conjectures regarding the presence of the same phenomenon in material where empirical documentation is currently unavailable. With regard to chronological displacement, an empirical attestation of the phenomenon exists wherever one text diverges from the chronological framework of an extant earlier text, or external data, of which the author/editor was demonstrably aware. A non-empirical example of the phenomenon occurs wherever the case for displacement within a given text can be supported solely by hints and allusions emanating from the very same text.

At this point, it ought to be candidly admitted that the categories "empirical" and "non-empirical" are employed in the present study in relative terms. Thus, not all "empirical" demonstrations of displacement can display equal clarity with regard to the precise dates of and relationship between the sundry texts which offer opposing chronological frameworks for the same event(s). The resolution of these issues might require some deductive reasoning on the part of the modern scholar, even when the variant texts are known to have originated in close proximity to one another and certainly when they are separated from one another in time and space (e.g., the examples drawn from post-Biblical

---

[18] Tadmor, "The Campaigns of Sargon II;" "The Inscriptions of Nabunaid."
[19] Cogan, "The Chronicler's Use of Chronology."

material, see below, chapter three). Indeed, there are those who would dismiss the whole notion of "empirical models" in connection with the modern exegesis of ancient texts. Such skepticism has been expressed most bluntly by E. Greenstein who claims that any scholarly conclusion, even regarding a text which evidences an organic connection with and/or development from another extant text, is ultimately the product of one's starting assumptions and is thus rendered subjective.[20] However, without quibbling over the philosophical connotations of the term "empirical," which by Greenstein's understanding could not be applied to the so-called "hard sciences" either, the validity of the "empirical models" theory lies in the fact that it offers the scholar a unique control over textual interpretations which would otherwise lack any kind of external validation. In other words, although, strictly speaking, Greenstein is correct in stating that subjectivity enters into any human intellectual endeavor, the degree of objectivity is nonetheless greater when the scholar has identifiably separate and comparable pieces of evidence at his/her disposal than when evidence of this nature is lacking.

Having expressed the preceding qualifications, it is the contention of the present study that patterns emerging from empirically recognized examples of chronological displacement can point the way to the elucidation of similar patterns which appear to be present in the examples that lack an empirical basis. For this reason, the major part of the book (chapters 1–3) will set forth empirical examples of chronological displacement found in Mesopotamian, Biblical, and post-Biblical material, respectively. The presentation of each example will offer an analysis of the setting for the displacement, i.e., the background information necessary to identify and evaluate the displacement. From there, I will offer the most likely motivation or reason for the displacement. Finally, I will suggest the methods or specific literary techniques through which the author or editor anchored the displaced material in its new chronological context. In the last chapter of the book (chapter 4), I will delve into non-empirical examples of chronological displacement which can be illuminated through the results obtained from chapters 1–3. Summations and concluding remarks will follow each chapter and the book as a whole.

---

[20] Greenstein, *Essays*, 55–59.

CHAPTER I

MESOPOTAMIAN MATERIAL

Introduction

The phenomenon of chronological displacement in Biblical texts can best be appreciated by surveying the occurrences of this literary practice in other literatures of the ancient Near East. From the many and variegated genres of this vast corpus, Mesopotamian historiographical texts, and in particular the royal inscriptions, provide the most useful data for comparative purposes.[1] This determination is based on two major considerations, which are crucial to the thesis being developed:

1) The Mesopotamian royal inscriptions often record the same event in more than one version. While this phenomenon exists in the Bible as well (e.g., Samuel-Kings vs. Chronicles), the unique advantage of the Mesopotamian material is that each of the variant versions was produced not long after the events described therein, and all the versions stem from the same milieu, namely the royal court. Moreover, it is often possible to trace the particular sequence in which the variant versions were composed. The proximity of the variant accounts to the time of the events which they describe and to each other, as well as their demonstrably linear relationship, provide us with a more objective basis than we have in the case of the Biblical material for identifying and tracing the phenomenon of chronological displacement.

2) Although, according to Finkelstein, "All genres of Mesopotamian literature that purport to deal with past events, with the exception of omens and chronicles, are motivated by purposes other than the desire to

---

[1] For a convenient categorization of the various types of Mesopotamian historiographical texts, see Grayson, "Assyria and Babylonia," 140–94.

know what really happened...,"[2] it is also true that Mesopotamian historiography presents history within certain bounds of causal credibility. Details may not be totally accurate or consistent from our modern standpoint, but neither is historical integrity completely set aside in the face of ideological presuppositions. For example, a recent study comparing the various versions of Sennacherib's first campaign against Babylonia demonstrates that the slightly later versions revised the narrative according to new contemporary conditions.[3] In the earliest versions, the Babylonian king, Merodach-Baladan, is said to have fled to Guzumani, where searches for him proved fruitless. The clause referring to a fruitless search is used in royal inscriptions as a motif for someone who is regarded as lost and gone forever. However, by the time the later versions of the same campaign were composed, Merodach-Baladan was once again a force with whom to be reckoned. The revised accounts, therefore, simply say that at the time of the first campaign, Merodach-Baladan gave up the fight and fled, thereby saving his life. The reascendence of Merodach-Baladan in the south also induced the revised accounts of Sennacherib's first campaign to limit the scope of power given to Merodach-Baladan's successor, who was handpicked by Sennacherib at the time of the first campaign. According to the earlier versions, the Assyrian sponsored Bel-ibni was given control over both Sumer (south) and Akkad (north). However, the later versions describe Bel-ibni as being chosen only to rule over Akkad. Now, while it can be said that in both instances, the later versions conceal some of the truth in order to put the best face on Assyrian-Babylonian relations (from the Assyrian perspective), neither can the later versions be accused of relating information which is outright false. Thus, these examples point to an important similarity between Mesopotamian historiography and the so-called "historical narrative" books of the Bible,[4] namely the fusion of ideological concerns with historical sensitivity.[5]

---

[2] Finkelstein, "Mesopotamian Historiography," 469.
[3] Liverani, "Critique of Variants," 252–57.
[4] The genre "historical narrative" is used to refer to the "Former Prophets" corpus (Joshua–Kings), Ezra-Nehemiah, and Chronicles. See Ackroyd, "The Historical Literature," 297.
[5] For a strong case for the historical orientation of the "Former Prophets" corpus, see Halpern, First Historians. For scholarly formulations on the historical orientation of Ezra-Nehemiah and Chronicles, see Bickerman, From Ezra to the Last of the Maccabees, 20–31, Japhet, The Ideology of the Book of Chronicles (Hebrew), 426–31.

Chronological Displacement

Although our primary emphasis in this chapter will be on Mesopotamian historiographic texts, we do not rule out sources which are conventionally classified as "literary texts."[6] Even though such texts date from long after the events which they describe, and thus do not share the advantage of the royal inscriptions, the presence of opposing chronological time frames in literary texts can still be used cautiously for demonstrating the workings of chronological displacement.

Sargon II's Prisms and Related Texts

Setting

Our first examples of variant chronological reckonings in Mesopotamian royal inscriptions come from texts belonging to the reign of Sargon II of Assyria (721–705).[7] Any historical reconstruction of Sargon II's reign has to take into account the fact that certain texts, in particular the Nineveh prisms, exhibit a pattern of dating Sargon II's campaigns one *palû* ("year of reign") earlier than the *palû* number listed for these same campaigns in the Khorsabad annals. Three such divergencies are noted by Tadmor in his important study of the chronological framework of Sargon II's reign:[8]

1) The prism fragment VA 8424 assigns Sargon II's preliminary expedition to Urartu and his major campaign there in the following year to the sixth and seventh *palûs*, respectively.[9] However, in the annals, the same events are assigned to the seventh and eighth *palûs*, respectively.[10]

2) The prism fragment Sm 2021 briefly tells of Sargon II's major campaign to Urartu in the context of the seventh *palû*, and of the subsequent campaign to Karalla in the eighth *palû*.[11] However, the annals record the same events as having occurred in the eighth and ninth *palûs*, respectively.[12]

---

[6] Cf. the classification "Myths, Epics, and Legends" in *ANET*, v–vii.
[7] On Sargon, see Roux, *Ancient Iraq*, 287–92.
[8] Tadmor, "The Campaigns of Sargon," 22–24.
[9] The cuneiform text was published by Weidner in *AfO* 14 (1941), p. 43. The relevant lines are col. B, 12–24 and col. C, 2–12.
[10] Lie, *Annals*, 16, 22 (lines 101, 127).
[11] Revised publication in Tadmor, "The Campaigns of Sargon," 24.
[12] Lie, *Annals*, 22, 28 (lines 127, 165).

3) A fragmentary text (A 16947) published by Tadmor[13] appears to refer to the conquest of Carchemish in the context of the fourth *palû*,[14] and begins to tell of "Ullu[sunu, the Mannean]," in the account of the fifth *palû*.[15] However, according to the annals, these events are to be dated to the fifth and sixth *palûs*, respectively.[16]

Now, theoretically, one could side with Weidner in postulating that the prism scribes used the the term *palû* to cover two or even three calendar years.[17] This explanation would remove the conflict between the variant texts insofar as actual chronology. However, as Tadmor notes, not only is the evidence for such a supposition exceedingly tenuous, but Weidner's explanation still does not alleviate the lack of congruence between the variant texts insofar as the numbering system itself.[18] In the ensuing discussion, therefore, we shall proceed under the assumption that in all of the relevant texts, *palû* refers to a successive and distinct year of reign, just as it does from the annals of Tiglath-Pileser I (1114–1076) and onwards.[19] Our immediate objective, then, is to determine whether the annals are postdating the events in question, or whether the texts conflicting with the annals are antedating these events.

Luckily, to this end we can enlist the testimony of the eponym canon taken together with the Babylonian Chronicle. These sources are particularly helpful since, regarding our problem, they are "unbiased," that is to say, they have no prior interest in altering the chronology of Sargon II's reign. The eponym canon lists the names of the Assyrian officials who served a yearly term as *limmu* ("eponym"), along with a notation of the pre-eminent event of each *limmu*'s term. The absolute dates from the tenth through the seventh centuries are well established by the fortuitous mention of a total solar eclipse during the *limmu* of Bur-

---

[13] "The Campaigns of Sargon," 22–23.

[14] Due to the fragmentary state of the text, Carchemish isn't mentioned explicitly. However, the placement of A16947, lines 1–14 immediately before the mention of a new campaign against Ullusunu the Mannean (see next note) makes it likely that the fragment is indeed referring to Carchemish and its king Pisiris. Note that both texts (A16947, lines 8–10 and Annals, line 73) refer to the king and his family being taken prisoner.

[15] The preserved text reads: *ina 5 palûya Ullu*, "In my fifth *palû*, Ullu..." The restoration *Ullu[sunu Manna]* "Ullusunu, the Mannean," follows from the annals text concerning the sixth *palû* (see next note).

[16] Lie, *Annals*, 10–14 (lines 72–90).

[17] Weidner, *AfO* 14 (1941), 52–53.

[18] Tadmor, "The Campaigns of Sargon," 24–25 with n. 26.

[19] Ibid., 27–30. Idem, "Observations on Assyrian Historiography," 209–10.

Sagale.[20] Astronomical calculations prove that this event occurred on June 15, 763. The dates for all the other *limmus*, who are listed in succession both before and after Bur-Sagale, flow accordingly.[21]

As for the events which concern us in Sargon II's reign, the campaigns against the Manneans, Urartu, and Ellipi, are listed in the eponym list in the slots for 716, 714, and 713, respectively.[22] The question, then, is whether these dates correspond to the sixth, eighth, and ninth years of Sargon II (as per the annals), or to his fifth, seventh, and eighth years (as per A 16947, VA 8424, and Sm 2021). This is where the Babylonian Chronicle comes into the picture. The eponym list makes mention of the accession of Sargon II's predecessor, Shalmaneser V, in the slot for 726.[23] According to the Babylonian Chronicle, Shalmaneser V took over on the twenty-fifth day of Tebet and ruled for nearly five years until Sargon II took over on the twelfth day of Tebet.[24] Putting the evidence together, Shalmaneser V's reign would have commenced in January, 726 and Sargon II's in December, 722–January, 721. According to standard practice, Sargon II's first full year would be counted from Nisan (April) of 721. Thus, assuming that campaigns were generally embarked upon in the summer season (i.e., following Nisan),[25] the reckoning of the annals concerning the various campaigns in question proves to be the accurate one, with 716, 714, and 713 equaling Sargon II's sixth, eighth, and ninth years, respectively. One further verification of this conclusion comes from the eponym list's entry for the slot of 709, which reads *šarru-kīn qātā bēl iṣṣabat*, "Sargon took (the god) Bel's hand."[26] The identical formula appears in the Babylonian Chronicle and is dated explicitly to Sargon II's thirteenth year.[27] Thus, 721 (beginning with Nisan) is seen to be Sargon II's first full year, and the argument that the three texts cited above are antedating events is proven.

---

[20] This *limmu* appears in the eponym canon in Ungnad, "Eponymen," *RLA*, Vol. 2, 422.
[21] Ibid., 414.
[22] Ibid., 433 (list Cb4).
[23] Ibid., 432 (list Cb3).
[24] Grayson, *Chronicles*, 73 (Chronicle 1, col. i, lines 27–31).
[25] Cf. the Biblical expression *lĕʿēt ṣēʾt hammĕlākîm* ("the season when kings go out to battle," 2 Sam. 11:1).
[26] Ungnad, "Eponymen," list Cb4. *RLA*, Vol. 2, 433. The reference is to the king's role in the *akītu* New Year festival.
[27] Grayson, *Chronicles*, 75 (Chronicle 1, col. ii, line 1′).

Motivation

In Tadmor's opinion,[28] the explanation for this phenomenon goes back to the tumultuous circumstances of Sargon II's first year and a quarter in office (i.e., Tebet/January 721–Nisan/April 720). During this period, Sargon II, who was a usurper to the throne, was faced with massive internal unrest.[29] Therefore, it is highly unlikely that he was able to undertake any military campaigns until his second year. This conclusion is implicitly confirmed by the text known as the Assur Charter,[30] which makes no mention of any military activity on Sargon II's part prior to his second year. The reality of Sargon II's military inactivity during his *rēš šarrūti* ("accession year," i.e., the period between actual accession and the following Nisan)[31] and his first full year was a source of embarrassment for the king. One "solution," reflected by the prism texts and A 16947, was simply to antedate all of Sargon II's campaigns by one *palû*. Even though there are no extant prisms which cover the events of Sargon II's first two years, Tadmor presumes that were such texts to come to light, they would undoubtedly record the campaigns of Sargon II's second year as taking place in his first *palû*.[32]

Tadmor's explanation is convincing primarily in light of the tradition found in Assyrian royal inscriptions of assigning a campaign to the king's *rēš šarrūti* or first year. In a separate study, Tadmor lists many examples of texts in which an inordinate number of campaigns or extraordinarily difficult campaigns are attached, either explicitly or implicitly, precisely to the king's *rēš šarrūti* and/or first year. The examples span a long period of time, from Shalmaneser I (1274–1245) down to

---

[28] "The Campaigns of Sargon," 30–31.
[29] For a statement of the turmoil that accompanied Sargon's first year, see Dalley, "Yahweh in Hamath," 26–27.
[30] K 1349, published by Winckler in *Sammlung von Keilschrifttexten*, Vol. 2, 1. English translation in Luckenbill, *ARAB*, Vol. 2, 69–71.
[31] See Tadmor, "The Campaigns of Sargon," 27.
[32] Another "solution" which Tadmor theorizes (ibid., 31) was taken up by the annals themselves was to artificially fill in the *rēš šarrūti* and first *palû* slots with campaigns which, in reality, either preceded the reign of Sargon (i.e., the initial conquest of Samaria under Shalmaneser), or which occurred only in his second year (i.e., the war with Elam and Tu'munu). I have not included these cases in the discussion due to the extremely fragmentary state of the first section of the annals.

Assurnasirpal II (883–859).³³ Evidently, a successful military campaign was regarded as one of the legitimizing stamps of a new reign and thus could not be dispensed with, even if reality showed otherwise. Thus, the motivating factor for the antedating to which we have pointed would be distinctly ideological with strong political overtones. It should be kept in mind, though, that the ideological motivation goes beyond mere secular political propaganda. This is because the Assyrian kings viewed their military campaigns as serving the interests of the gods.³⁴ Thus, the purpose of antedating a military campaign would be not only to boost the king's prowess, but also to demonstrate that he was resolute in fighting for the honor of the national gods.

Method

It was precisely the ubiquitous overlap of *palû* with "military campaign" that enabled the scribes to effect their antedating. Although strictly speaking, *palû* referred to a "year of reign" as noted above (p. 12), it could easily have been associated in the popular conception with a campaign number, since each and every *palû* of the king was connected with a particular campaign. Thus, by dating what was in fact Sargon II's fifth campaign to his fifth *palû* and what was in fact his sixth campaign to his sixth *palû* etc., the scribes were taking advantage of the popular conception without admitting outright that the fifth campaign did not occur until Sargon II's sixth year, and the sixth campaign did not occur until his seventh year, etc. In a nutshell, then, the method identified here is the (mis)use of a term, the technical meaning of which was coalesced with its popular connotation.

Esarhaddon's Restoration of Babylon

Setting

Esarhaddon was the third of the Sargonid kings. After a brief power struggle with his brothers, he took over the throne from his father

---

³³ Tadmor, "History and Ideology," 14–19. See also Borger, *Einleitung*, 82, with examples from Tukulti–Ninurta I.
³⁴ See Speiser, "Ancient Mesopotamia," 66–67.

Sennacherib, who was assassinated in 681.³⁵ Perhaps in an effort to undo his father's sacrilegious sacking of the holy city of Babylon,³⁶ Esarhaddon put the restoration of this city at the top of his agenda. The text which tells of Esarhaddon's reconstruction of Babylon and its famous esagila temple is a building inscription which can conveniently be referred to as Esarhaddon's Babylon inscription.³⁷ The text appears in no less than eight recensions, composed over a number of years during Esarhaddon's reign.³⁸ Although the various recensions differ in certain details and in the space given to particular activities relating to the construction,³⁹ they all bear the colophon "the accession year (*šanat rēš šarrūti*) of Esarhaddon, king of Assyria."⁴⁰ As we have noted above (p. 15), the term *rēš šarrūti* refers to the period between the king's actual accession to the throne and the following Nisan (the first month of the year). Thus, the implication of the colophon in the Babylon inscription is that all of the protracted and arduous building projects which the inscription records occurred within the king's first fraction of a year in power. In addition to the logical improbability of such a compressed chronological framework particularly in light of the civil strife which marked Esarhaddon's rise to power, scholars have often challenged the Babylon inscription's dating based on the clear-cut evidence of Esarhaddon's own Nineveh inscription. In this latter source, Esarhaddon states that on the eighth (or the twenty-second) day of Adar (the last month of the year), he joyfully sat on his father's throne, i.e., he took over the kingship.⁴¹ Thus, according to this testimony, Esarhaddon's *rēš šarrūti* lasted less than a month. Corroborative evidence for the Nineveh inscription's date comes from the Babylonian Chronicle, which states that Esarhaddon ascended the throne on the eighteenth or twenty-eighth (reading unclear) day of Adar.⁴² Since Esarhaddon obviously couldn't have engaged in such massive building projects as described in the Babylon inscription in the space of a mere twelve or two days, the inescapable conclusion is that

---

35 For a general survey of Esarhaddon's reign, see Roux, *Ancient Iraq*, 299–304.
36 See Brinkman, *Political History of Post-Kassite Babylonia*, 245.
37 For the text, see Borger, *Inschriften Asarhaddons*, 10–29 (Sec. 11).
38 Ibid.
39 See in particular Cogan, "Omens and Ideology."
40 Ibid., 85.
41 Borger, *Inschriften Asarhaddons*, 45 (episode 2, col. i, line 87–col. ii, line 2).
42 Grayson, *Chronicles*, 82 (Chronicle 1, col. iii, line 38).

the Babylon inscription is intentionally antedating these projects to the *rēš šarrūti*.[43]

Motivation

Just as it was important to assign a military campaign to the king's *rēš šarrūti* in order to depict him as a worthy militarist and servant of the gods (above, p. 16), so was the early and expeditious care for a major temple regarded as a desirable activity for a new king.[44] Once again, an ideological explanation is strengthened by the recurrence in a number of Assyrian royal inscriptions of a particular theme, in this case the temple-building activities of a king in his *rēš šarrūti*. In addition to the Esarhaddon example, Tadmor cites similar cases from the annals of Tiglath-Pileser I (1114–1076), and Esarhaddon's son, Assurbanipal (668–627).[45] To be sure, these latter examples do not carry the same empirical force as Esarhaddon's Babylon inscription, in that their dating cannot be as starkly challenged by conflicting sources. Nevertheless, they express the same concern for depicting the king as attending to matters of cultic renewal at the earliest possible date.

Method

Short of attributing conscious "pseudo-dating"[46] to the royal scribes, it can be suggested by way of conjecture that they rationalized their dating procedure by viewing the entire building project in terms of its inception. Thus, even if just one brick was laid, or less so, even if only the *intention* to rebuild Babylon was voiced during the *rēš šarrūti* , the entire process could be viewed symbolically as having been accomplished forthwith. Needless to say, the fact that there was literary precedent in the Assyrian royal inscriptions for dating major building projects to the

---

[43] See Cogan, "Omens and Ideology," 85–86 who adds further internal considerations; idem, "The Chronicler's Use of Chronology," 200–01; Tadmor, "History and Ideology," 22.

[44] Cogan, "Omens and Ideology," 87; "The Chronicler's Use of Chronology," 201; Tadmor, "History and Ideology," 21.

[45] Tadmor, "History and Ideology," 22–23. A further example from the inscriptions of the Babylonian king Nabonidus will be taken up in greater detail below (pp. 26f.).

[46] See Cogan, "The Chronicler's Use of Chronology," 201.

rēš šarrūti paved the way for Esarhaddon's scribes to do the same, even if it was just a statement of ideals rather than literal fact.

Assurbanipal's Conquest of Babylon

By way of introduction to the historical narrative format found in the annals of Assurbanipal (668–627),[47] it is important to recognize that the sequential framework is no longer arranged in a year-by-year fashion according to eponym officials (*limmu*) or years of reign (*palû*). The guiding organizational term is *girru* ("campaign"), which is no longer intended to represent successive regnal years, but simply refers to a particular country or geographic area to which the king led his forces on a particular occasion.[48] In fact, the overall arrangement of Assurbanipal's annals is geographical, with the various *girrus* consistently listed in each edition in the order west-north-east-south (e.g., Egypt-Tyre-Elam-Arabia), no matter what the actual dates of these battles may have been.[49] At the same time, some chronological format was maintained in that the individual campaigns to each particular region were narrated in their historical order of occurrence, even as they were concentrated together. The numbering of the *girrus* could thus fluctuate greatly from one edition of the annals to the next. For example, if at the time of the publication of an edition (X), the king had undertaken a total of six campaigns, including two to the west, one to the north, two to the east, and one to the south, but had subsequently undertaken an additional campaign to the east, the next edition (Y) would not simply tack on this new campaign at the end as *girru* number seven. Rather, following the geographical arrangement, the new campaign would be inserted as the last of the eastern expeditions, hence in slot number six, while the southern campaign, which originally appeared as *girru* six, would now become *girru* seven.[50] Also, a later edition (Y) might omit a particular campaign mentioned in an earlier edition (X), with the result that the numbers as-

---

[47] For a general survey of Assurbanipal's reign, see Roux, *Ancient Iraq*, 304–11.
[48] For this and the following points, see Gerardi, "Assurbanipal's Elamite Campaigns," 233–34.
[49] See Grayson, "Chronology of Ashurbanipal," 245, appendix F.
[50] E.g., Edition A of Assurbanipal's annals, composed after the close of the fifth Elamite campaign, raises the number of the Arabian campaign from *girru* eight to *girru* nine.

signed to the campaigns from the point of omission and onwards would decrease by one in edition Y as compared to edition X.[51] Assurbanipal's annals are preserved in eight major editions, dating from his fourth year (665) to his twenty-sixth year (643). The editions in their presumed order of composition are those designated as E, HT (Harran Tablet), B, D, K, C, F, A.[52] Some of the editions (B, D, F, A) are dated in their colophons by eponym. The dates of composition for the editions in which the colophons are not preserved are inferred primarily from external evidence relating to the last-mentioned events in each edition, the assumption being that the respective editions were composed shortly after their last-mentioned events.[53] The later editions thus represent a more updated recording of events. In the following section, we shall trace the potential effect of unfolding events on the chronological presentation embedded within a particular geographical vignette, namely Assurbanipal's third Elamite campaign. Our discussion is indebted to Gerardi's lucid presentation and interpretation of the data in her recent dissertation.[54]

Setting

Assurbanipal's crushing of Elam in 653,[55] during which he replaced that country's rebellious king Te-Umman with Ummanigash, turned out to be very short lived. This was primarily due to the machinations of Assurbanipal's brother Shamashshumukin who, from his throne in Babylon, began in 652 to stir up opposition to Assyrian domination.[56]

---

[51] E.g., Edition F of Assurbanipal's annals, which omits the first campaign to Egypt.
[52] See Cogan and Tadmor, "Gyges and Ashurbanipal," 85, for a list of the editions and their places of publication. See Grayson, "Chronology of Ashurbanipal," 245, appendix E, for their dates of composition. An expanded discussion of the various editions, including their dates of composition, can be found in Gerardi, "Assurbanipal's Elamite Campaigns," 49–72.
[53] Cf. Gerardi, "Assurbanipal's Elamite Campaigns," 34, 52–53.
[54] Ibid., 165–72.
[55] This campaign is dated, among other things, by the mention in Assurbanipal's inscriptions of a lunar eclipse. See Grayson, "Chronology of Ashurbanipal," 236.
[56] The date 652, corresponding to the sixteenth year of Shamashshumukin, is derived from the Babylonian Chronicles 16: 9–16 and 15:6 (see Grayson, *Chronicles*, 129–32). Echoes of this unrest are reflected in Assurbanipal's letter to the people of Babylon, which dates to 652 (*ABL* 301, apud Gerardi, "Assurbanipal's Elamite Campaigns," 175).

The new anti-Assyrian movement quickly spilled over from Babylonia into neighboring Elam, forcing Assurbanipal to embark on yet another campaign to the southeastern domains of his empire. Of course, in order to root out the trouble at its source, Assurbanipal had to direct his military might against Babylon as well as against Elam, no matter what the risk might be in repeating the offences of his grandfather Sennacherib toward Mesopotamian religious sensitivities.[57] It is most probably to offset any notion of overstepping religious bounds that Assurbanipal justifies his move against Shamashshumukin by relating how the latter had brought the orderly offering of sacrifices in Babylon to a halt (edition A, col. iii, lines 112–117).[58] Through this action, Shamashshumukin is described as "plotting evil"—*ikpud limuttu* (line 117). Further legitimization for Assurbanipal's cause comes in the form of a dream oracle from the moon god Sin, stating that those who plot evil against Assurbanipal (a clear reference to Shamashshumukin) will be punished with various forms of death and destruction, such as the "swift thrust of the iron dagger, conflagration of fire, famine, and the outbreak of plague" (ibid, lines 118–126).[59]

It is at this point, however, that edition A shows signs of chronological displacement. Immediately following the prophecy, edition A launches into an account of Assurbanipal's sixth *girru*, during which he is said to have first defeated Shamashshumukin (col. iii, lines 128–135)[60] before settling scores with Tammaritu of Elam. The latter had just recently seized the throne from Ummanigash, but had continued the alliance with Shamashshumukin (col. iii, line 136–col. iv, line 41).[61] After relating Tammaritu's exile to Nineveh, edition A's narrative curiously reverts back to a detailed account of the gruesome end of Shamashshumukin and his supporters, closing with a notice of how Assurbanipal purified and renewed the neglected Babylonian shrines (col. iv, lines 41–96).[62] Now, the fact that the destruction of Babylon is related twice, being interrupted by the description of Elam's surrender,

---

[57] See above, n. 36.
[58] Streck, *Assurbanipal*, Vol. 2, 30, 32; Luckenbill, *ARAB*, Vol. 2, 301–02.
[59] Ibid. Cf. van Seters, *In Search of History*, 66 with n. 39. Cf. the familiar Biblical expression *ḥereb deber wĕrāʿāb* ("sword, pestilence, famine") Jer. 21:7; 24:10; 29:17; Ezek. 6:11; 14:21.
[60] Streck, *Assurbanipal*, Vol. 2, 32; Luckenbill, *ARAB*, Vol. 2, 302.
[61] Streck, *Assurbanipal*, Vol. 2, 32–36; Luckenbill, *ARAB*, Vol. 2, 302–03.
[62] Streck, *Assurbanipal*, Vol. 2, 36–40; Luckenbill, *ARAB*, Vol. 2, 303–05.

would imply that the conquests of Babylon and Elam occurred simultaneously. Yet, a careful scrutiny of other sources (including the Babylonian Chronicles and earlier editions of the annals) shows that even though the siege of Babylon and the Elamite campaign were conducted simultaneously, Tammaritu's exile definitely preceded the final defeat of Babylon. In other words, col. iii, lines 128–135 of edition A relate the conquest of Babylon in too early a context. The evidence runs as follows:

1) The Babylonian Chronicles 1:col. iv, lines 30–38;[63] 14:lines 34–39;[64] and 16:lines 1–8,[65] all date Shamashshumukin's accession to within one year following that of Assurbanipal. The latter occasion is firmly set by the chronicles and the eponym chronology in Kislev (December) of 669.

2) The Babylonian Chronicles 16:lines 9–16 [66] and 15:line 6 [67] date the beginning of hostilities between Assyria and Babylonia in the wake of Shamashshumukin's rebellion to Shamashshumukin's sixteenth year, i.e., 652. Chronicle 15:line 19 [68] dates the beginning of the Assyrian siege on Babylonia to Shamashshumukin's eighteenth year, i.e., 650.

3) Edition B of the annals, which is dated by eponym to 649,[69] already contains the full account of Elamite involvement in Shamashshumukin's rebellion, culminating with Tammaritu's exile to Nineveh.[70] Thus, the latter event has a *terminus ad quem* of 649. The final fall of Babylon, though, is *not* related in edition B.

4) A variety of sources indicate that Shamashshumukin was still holding out on the throne of Babylon at least through the summer of 648 (thus implying that the final fall of the city could not have occurred before then):

a. The Ptolemaic Canon assigns twenty years to Shamashshumukin. That would bring his final year to 648.[71]

---

[63] Grayson, *Chronicles*, 86.
[64] Ibid., 127.
[65] Ibid., 131.
[66] Grayson, *Chronicles*, 131–32.
[67] Ibid., 129.
[68] Ibid., 130.
[69] The eponym of Ahilayya. See Ungnad, "Eponymen," *RLA*, Vol. 2, 428.
[70] Piepkorn, *Historical Prism Inscriptions*, 76–81.
[71] Grayson, "Chronology of Ashurbanipal," 239, appendix B.

b. The Babylonian Chronicle 16 (the "Akitu Chronicle") notes the cancellation of the *akītu* ("new year") festivities in Babylon for the seventeenth through the twentieth years of Shamashshumukin[72] (651–648), undoubtedly due to the ongoing siege. Following that, there was no further interruption of the *akītu* festival until the accession year of Nabopolassar (625).

c. The last known tablet dating to the reign of Shamashshumukin is from the 30th of Ab of his twentieth year, i.e., July-August, 648.[73]

In sum, although Assurbanipal's engagements of the Babylonians and their Elamite allies overlapped to a great extent, there can be no doubt that col. iii, lines 128–135 of edition A preempts the final defeat of Babylon to an earlier point in the narration than historically warranted. We now turn to questioning why such a literary structure was employed.

Motivation

In her discussion of this passage,[74] Gerardi stresses that the narrator wished to keep the focus on Shamashshumukin, since he was the prime instigator behind Assurbanipal's move on Elam. The background information concerning Shamashshumukin and his rebellious activities is related already at the end of the fifth *girru*. By commencing the narration of the sixth *girru* with a brief notice of Shamashshumukin's defeat, the scribe is reminding us immediately that the main target of the campaign was Shamashshumukin, even though this required putting the cart before the horse from a chronological standpoint. A further impetus for placing the opening notice in its present position is to have it follow immediately upon the heels of the prophecy guaranteeing punishment to "those who plot evil," which, as we saw above, refers above all to Shamashshumukin. Indeed, from a literary point of view, the brief notice of defeat serves as an immediate fulfillment of the oracle. This is probably why a couple of the same punishments referred to in the oracle, namely *lipit Irra* ("outbreak of plague," line 126) and *ḫušaḫḫu* ("hunger," line 125), are repeated exactly or in parallel form in the following lines describing

---

[72] Grayson, *Chronicles*, 132.
[73] Gerardi, "Assurbanipal's Elamite Campaigns," 175.
[74] Ibid., 165–71.

Shamashshumukin's defeat (*lipit Irra*, line 134; *sunqu bubūti*, "famine and hunger," line 135). Thus, the presence of lines 128–135 in their current position sets the theme for the entire campaign, as well as intimating that for Shamashshumukin, the battle in effect was finished before it even started. His fate had been sealed by the word of Sin, the moon god, who had manifested himself through the oracle to Assurbanipal.

In sum, the motivation for the chronological displacement found in lines 128–135 can be attributed to both literary and ideological considerations. From a literary point of view, the scribe wished to identify Shamashshumukin as the main target of Assurbanipal's sixth *girru*, with the simultaneous Elamite campaign functioning as an important but ultimately secondary military objective. Nevertheless, one can object that in order to achieve this purpose alone, the scribe could have simply described the laying of the siege on Babylon (as opposed to its final defeat) before getting into the Elamite hostilities, thus preserving a truer chronological sequence. Therefore, it is necessary to supplement the literary explanation with the ideological motivation, namely the scribe's desire to express an immediate, albeit idealized, fulfillment of the prophecy against Shamashshumukin, who is thus portrayed as doomed from the outset of the campaign.

Methods

The use of a theme setting or expositional type of paragraph at the beginning of a narrative section is a perfectly valid way of directing attention to the narrative's main subject, even if the contents of this opening statement anticipate the outcome of the plot to some degree. However, lines 128–135 go beyond mere exposition. By spelling out the immediate efficacy of the oracle, the scribe was left in the somewhat awkward position of having to relate the defeat of Babylon twice, both in its idealized, literary position, and in its sequential position at the end of the campaign. This problem was overcome through the use of the loose chronological catch phrase *ina ūmēšu* ("at that time"), in order to link the separated portions of the narration relating to Shamashshumukin. The very first mention of Shamashshumukin, set at the end of the fifth *girru*, opens with this formula (col. iii, line 70).[75] This correctly connects the beginning of the rebellious movement with the events of 652.[76] The formula is repeated in introducing the oracle (col. iii, line 118),[77] so as to convey the message that Assurbanipal's concerns were allayed immediately, i.e., at the same time that the rebellion broke out. The most resourceful use of the formula, though, comes in the final section recapitulating and detailing Shamashshumukin's defeat (col. iv, line 41).[78] This section, as we have seen, follows the narration of Assurbanipal's dealings with Elam. However, by restating the formula *ina ūmēšu*, the scribe keeps the precise time frame of the final defeat of Babylon very much in doubt. Is it to be understood as following the events on the Elamite front (as implied by the *ina ūmēšu* of col. iv, line 41) or as preceding them (as implied by the *ina ūmēšu* of col. iii, line 118 leading directly into lines 128–135)? Actually, this ambiguity is intentional. The scribe's technique implies an artificial linking of the time frames of the oracle and the final victory (in both of its renditions), with the Elam events bracketed off in between and understood to have occurred simultaneously with the smooth quelling of the Babylonian uprising.[79]

The use of a vague linking phrase such as *ina ūmēšu* to cover over chronological inexactitude is attested elsewhere in the Assyrian royal inscriptions,[80] and is thought to have Hebrew manifestations in the Bible.[81] However, our example is particularly useful, since we have empirical chronological evidence at our disposal to back up the proposed loose interpretation of *ina ūmēšu*. Thus, this example can serve as a paradigm for the other Assyrian and Biblical examples, in which the case for chronological displacement through the use of *ina ūmēšu* and similar formulae is likely, but not empirically provable.

---

[75] Streck, *Assurbanipal*, Vol. 2, 28; Luckenbill, *ARAB*, Vol. 2, 300.
[76] See above, p. 20 and n. 56.
[77] Streck, *Assurbanipal*, Vol. 2, 32; Luckenbill, *ARAB*, Vol. 2, 302.
[78] Streck, *Assurbanipal*, Vol. 2, 36; Luckenbill, *ARAB*, Vol. 2, 303.
[79] Gerardi, "Assurbanipal's Elamite Campaigns," 165–71.
[80] Tadmor, "History and Ideology," 14–15; van Seters, *In Search of History*, 61.
[81] Talmon, "Synchroneity and Simultaneity," 11; Long, *1 Kings*, 24–25.

Nabonidus's Rebuilding of the Ehulhul

Setting

One of the most poignant examples of non-chronological presentation in the Mesopotamian royal inscriptions has to do with the restoration of the temple of Sin (the Ehulhul) in Harran by the last of the Neo-Babylonian kings, the enigmatic Nabonidus (556–539).[82] The relative proliferation of sources relating to the issue, and the various possibilities of interpretation regarding these sources' dates, meanings, purposes, and relations to one another, all make for a particularly complex but interesting analysis. At the outset, we shall briefly summarize the sources which relate directly to the rebuilding of the Ehulhul, taking particular note of these sources' probable dates of composition, the variant dates or time frames to which they assign the Ehulhul project, and their historical reliability.

1) *Harran Stele* (also known as H2A).[83] Sin appears in a dream to Nabonidus, instructing him to rebuild the Ehulhul, since "the lands, all of them, to thy hands are verily committed" (col. i, lines 11–14). Nevertheless, Nabonidus, citing the impiety of the priests and people of Babylonia, removes himself to distant Teima, where he resides for ten years (col. i, lines 14–27). Finally, on a propitious date, with the encouragement of diviners, Nabonidus makes his way back to his country, and builds the Ehulhul (col. ii, line 11–col. iii, line 33). This text clearly places the Ehulhul project after Nabonidus's return from Teima. Now the Nabonidus Chronicle (col. ii, line 23) [84] has the Teima sojourn lasting at least through the king's eleventh year (the text breaks off after that point). However, Beaulieu has assembled more evidence which shows that Nabonidus's ten-year sojourn in Teima is to be dated from his fourth to his thirteenth years.[85] Consequently, the Harran stele would most likely have been composed in the fourteenth or even in the fifteenth year, allowing enough time for the Ehulhul project to have been com-

---

[82] For a general survey of Nabonidus's reign, see Roux, *Ancient Iraq*, 352–58.
[83] Gadd, "Harran Inscriptions," 56–65; ANET, 562–63.
[84] Grayson, *Chronicles*, 108.
[85] Beaulieu, *The Reign of Nabonidus*, 149–69.

pleted.[86] On the basis of a comparison with the Sippar cylinder (see below), some scholars have claimed that the Harran stele displaces the Ehulhul restoration to a much later chronological point than when it actually occurred. We shall examine this argument in detail below.

2) *Sippar Cylinder* (also known as Nabonidus text 1).[87] Marduk and Sin appear to Nabonidus in his *rēš šarrūti* ("accession year"), with Marduk instructing Nabonidus to rebuild the Ehulhul (col. i, lines 16–22). When Nabonidus objects that the Umman-Mandas'[88] presence in Harran will prevent him from taking on the task, Marduk prophesies that when three years have passed, Cyrus will completely destroy the Umman-Manda (col. i, lines 23–33). Following this prophecy is a description of how Nabonidus carried out Marduk's order without delay (col. i, line 35–col. ii, line 25). The rest of the text relates Nabonidus's restoration of the Ebabbar of Shamash in Sippar (col. ii, line 47–col. iii, line 21) and the Eulmash of Anunitum in Sippar (col. iii, lines 22–42).

Internal evidence for the date of the text's composition is equivocal. On the one hand, the presence of external enemies might presuppose a time earlier than that of the Harran stele, by which time security had been achieved.[89] On the other hand, the inclusion of Marduk as a main actor might reflect a later revision of a version dominated by the god Sin such as the Harran stele, in deference to Babylonian sentiments.[90] Neither is the chronological framework of the text of great help. Although Nabonidus is said to have experienced the theophany in his *rēš šarrūti*, none of the projects described in the text is dated satisfactorily. Indeed, the Sippar cylinder is remarkably evasive concerning the precise dates of the various temple restorations. Nevertheless, the general implication is that the Ehulhul project was completed early in Nabonidus's reign, either immediately in the *rēš šarrūti* despite the danger of external enemies, or in the "third year," once the danger had been lifted. Of course, this stands in stark contrast to the Harran stele. One or the other

---

[86] Ibid., 32.
[87] Langdon and Zehnpfund, VAB 4, 218–29.
[88] The term *Umman-Manda* is applied generically to a number of "barbarian" peoples who swept over Mesopotamia. For example, in the *Cuthean Legend of Naram-Sin* (see below, p. 44), the term refers to the Gutians. Here, it refers to the Medes. See Gadd, "The Dynasty of Agade," 454; Speiser, "Some Factors in the Collapse of Akkad," 100 with n. 36; Gurney, "The Sultantepe Tablets," 97.
[89] See Moran, "Notes on the New Nabonidus Inscriptions," 134.
[90] Ibid., 132.

of these texts must be indulging in chronological displacement. To be sure, our analysis of Esarhaddon's Babylon inscription (above, pp. 16–18) makes us somewhat more suspicious of a text such as the Sippar cylinder, which loosely connects a major building project with the king's *rēš šarrūti*. Nevertheless, so long as the evidence in favor of the Harran stele isn't crystal-clear, we must proceed along the assumption that either of the variant time frames could be correct.

3) *Adad-guppi Inscription* (also known as H1B).[91] In this inscription, which was set up side by side with the Harran stele, Adad-guppi, the mother of Nabonidus, tells of all her efforts on behalf of the gods, especially Sin (col. i, lines 1–16). She prays to Sin, asking him to allow Nabonidus to rebuild the Ehulhul (col. i, line 44–col. ii, line 4). Sin appears to her in a dream and responds in the affirmative (col. ii, lines 5–11). Adad-guppi then states, "The word of Sin, king of the gods, which he spoke to me I honored, and I myself saw (it fulfilled); Nabu-na'id, (my) only son, offspring of my womb, perfected the forgotten rites of Sin, Ningal, Nusku, and Sadarnunna, he built Ehulhul anew and perfected its structure" (col. ii, lines 11–16). Finally, Adad-guppi gives thanks for having reached the age of 104, corresponding to the ninth year of Nabonidus (col. ii, lines 26–34). A postscript informs us that Adad-guppi died in that same year (col. iii, lines 5–7). Interestingly, the precise date of Adad-guppi's death during the ninth year of Nabonidus (on the fifth day of Nisan) can be established independently from the Nabonidus Chronicle (col. ii, line 13).[92] Ostensibly, then, the body of H1B would appear to have been composed entering Nabonidus's ninth year, by which time the restoration of the Ehulhul would have been completed. However, as Tadmor has noted, the very fact that the Adad-guppi inscription and the Harran stele were erected as a pair next to the same building indicates that they were composed at the same time.[93] As we have seen above (p. 26), the Harran stele was composed following Nabonidus's return from his ten-year sojourn in Teima, i.e., after

---

[91] Gadd, "Harran Inscription," 46–53; *ANET*, 560–62. The text fills in the more fragmentary H1A = Nabonidus text 9 (Langdon and Zehnpfund, *VAB* 4, 288–95), which was reworked by B. Landsberger in *Halil Edhem Hatira Kitabi* I (Ankara: 1947), 115f.

[92] Grayson, *Chronicles*, 107.

[93] Tadmor, "The Inscriptions of Nabunaid," 356, who also notes the close stylistic similarity between the two inscriptions.

Nabonidus's thirteenth year. Thus, to the extent that the Adad-guppi inscription might preserve an accurate date for the completion of the Ehulhul, it can hardly be taken as an eye-witness account, since its supposed author had already been dead for at least four years prior to its composition. This fact in itself mitigates against the historical worth of the inscription, in addition to which no other text supports the contention of H1B that Nabonidus interrupted his Teima sojourn to attend his mother's funeral. In a similar vein, Beaulieu notes that the inscription has obvious connections with the so-called *narû* literature, i.e., the genre of fictional autobiographies[94] (e.g., its closing with a *mannu attā* = "whosoever you are" formula—col. iii, lines 43–44).[95] As such, in Beaulieu's words, "Adad-guppi's statement that she witnessed the rebuilding of the Ehulhul would then be an apocryphal declaration of piety,"[96] not to be taken at face value.[97] We thus find ourselves on shaky ground in trying to determine the actual date of the Ehulhul restoration from this inscription.

4) *Nabonidus Verse Account*.[98] This text represents a pro-Cyrus propaganda piece. It details Nabonidus's personal and cultic excesses, and closes with a triumphant recounting of how Cyrus undid Nabonidus's works and restored Babylon to a state of liberty. It thus dates to some time after Nabonidus had been deposed. Among the accusations made against Nabonidus was his favoritism toward and misrepresentation of

---

[94] For a survey of the genre, see Longman, *Fictional Akkadian Autobiography*. The best known example is the *Cuthean Legend of Naram-Sin* (see below, p. 44).

[95] Beaulieu, *The Reign of Nabonidus*, 209. The *mannu attā* formula is directed to future rulers who might uncover the inscription, charging them to take note of its contents and not to damage it. The reading *mannu* in our text follows the restoration of Moran, "Notes on the New Nabonidus Inscriptions," 130. Interestingly, the formula is used in the Harran stele (col. iii, line 35) and the Sippar cylinder (col. iii, line 43) as well.

[96] Beaulieu, *The Reign of Nabonidus*, 209. Beaulieu compares this with the inscriptions of Belshazzar's regency, in which Nabonidus is depicted as personally leading excavations and restorations of temples, even though he was hundreds of miles away in Teima.

[97] Tadmor ("The Inscriptions of Nabunaid," 357, n. 36) makes a case for *āmur* forming a hendiadys with *atta'idma*, both meaning "I honored attentively" (the word of Sin), rather than "I saw it fulfilled." However, apart from the fact that *amāru* is not attested elsewhere in this way (Beaulieu, *The Reign of Nabonidus*, 209), the text immediately notes Nabonidus' completion of the Ehulhul.

[98] Smith, *Babylonian Historical Texts*, 83–91; Landsberger and Bauer, "Zu neuveröffentlichen Geschichtsquellen," 88–94; *ANET*, 312–15.

the moon god. To this end, Nabonidus resolved to build the Ehulhul while neglecting the observance of the regular festivals, including the *akītu* New Year's festival (col. ii, lines 4–11). The text goes on to relate that after Nabonidus had finished building his abomination (sic), "when the third year was about to begin," he set out on a military campaign to Teima, where he took up residence (col. ii, lines 16–27). Thus, the Verse Account clearly places the Ehulhul building early in Nabonidus's reign, prior to the Teima sojourn. However, there are grounds for taking the evidence of the Verse Account with a grain of salt. In its desire to vilify Nabonidus, the poem might be heedlessly interspersing earlier and later events. For example, we can infer from the Nabonidus Chronicle (col. ii, lines 5–6)[99] that the cancellation of the *akītu* went into effect only while Nabonidus was already in Teima.[100] This inference raises the possibility that the Verse Account purposely suggested an early date for the Ehulhul restoration in an attempt to denigrate Nabonidus, since the poet viewed the Ehulhul project as a liability.[101] Moreover, as was the case with the Adad-guppi inscription, the very genre of the Verse Account is not one which inspires great historical trust.

Thus far, out of the four texts we have seen, only the Harran stele dates the Ehulhul project as late as after Nabonidus's return from his ten-year stay in Teima. This brings us to Nabonidus's eleventh year at the very earliest, and more probably, to his fourteenth year (above, p. 26). The other three texts all indicate earlier dates, with the Sippar cylinder making a connection between the Ehulhul project and Nabonidus's theophanic experience in his *rēš šarrūti*, the Verse Account boxing the event into Nabonidus's first three years, and the Adad-guppi inscription limiting the event to within Nabonidus's first nine years. However, both of the two latter sources are historically suspect. Thus, we are left with the variant time frames reflected by the Harran stele and the Sippar cylinder. In seeking to determine which of these preserves the more original sequence of events, we must now consider additional circumstantial

---

[99] Grayson, *Chronicles*, 106.
[100] The Chronicle notes the cancellation of the *akītu* only during the years of Nabonidus's prolonged absence. See Tadmor, "The Inscriptions of Nabunaid," 355.
[101] Interestingly enough, by linking the completion of the Ehulhul with the cancellation of the *akītu*, the Verse Account itself might be silently acknowledging a later date for the Ehulhul's restoration, since the *akītu* ritual was in fact suspended until Nabonidus's return from Teima. See Beaulieu, *The Reign of Nabonidus*, 208.

evidence from other written sources which could sway our judgement one way or the other.

1) *Nabonidus text 8*.[102] This text contains a political-cultic history of Babylonia beginning from Sennacherib's attack on Babylon (col. i, lines 1–17).[103] It goes on to relate the decline of Assyria, which opened the way for barbaric hordes (the "Manda" people)[104] to destroy many more Mesopotamian cultic centers (col. i, line 18–col. ii, line 31). Following the preliminary attempts of Neriglissar (560–556) to restore Uruk and Sippar (col. iii, line 1–col. iv, line 33), Nabonidus came to power and received favorable dream messages from Nebuchadnezzar and the goddess Gula (col. v, line 1–col. vii, line 22). These dreams encouraged Nabonidus to continue on the course of temple restoration (col. viii, lines 26–20), including the Ehulhul in Harran, which had been lying in ruins for fifty-four years (col. x, lines 1–31).

Text 8 appears to reflect a very early stage of Nabonidus's reign. It represents an overt expression of Nabonidus's quest for legitimacy, especially in its description of Labashi-Marduk, whom Nabonidus had ousted from power, as "a minor (who) had not (yet) learned how to behave" who had "sat down on the royal throne against the intentions of the gods" (col. iv, lines 37–41). The subsequent appearance of Nebuchadnezzar in a dream serves to justify Nabonidus's ascendance. Such apologetics are typical of a king who has just recently attained power.[105] Furthermore, the campaign to Hume, during which 2850 prisoners were taken (col. ix, lines 31–41), is dated in the Nabonidus Chronicle to the king's first year (col. i, line 7).[106] None of the important activities of the second year, such as the restoration of the Ebabbar in Sippar or the consecration of Nabonidus's daughter as an entu priestess (see below on Lambert inscription) are mentioned in this text, which implies a *terminus ad quem* in the first year for the text's composition.[107] Even the fifty-four years mentioned as having passed since the destruction of Harran fit nicely starting from Nabonidus's first year in 556, and

---

[102] Langdon and Zehnpfund, VAB 4, 270–89; ANET, 309–11.
[103] See above, n. 36.
[104] See above, n. 88.
[105] Beaulieu, *The Reign of Nabonidus*, 22.
[106] Grayson, *Chronicles*, 105.
[107] Beaulieu, *The Reign of Nabonidus*, 22.

dating back to 610, shortly after the destruction of Nineveh.[108] Since the text appears to faithfully record events limited to Nabonidus's first year, the critical question is whether the passage concerning the Ehulhul necessarily refers to its actual rebuilding, or merely to the initiation of the rebuilding.

The key lines here read: *ītekpuš itti ilāni adannu salimu 54 šanāti enumu sin itūru ašrussu, inanna ana ašrišu itūramma, sin bēl agî iḫsusu šubatsu,* "when the gods were to be reconciled (that is) 54 years approached, when Sin would return to his place. Now, Sin, the crown-bearer, did return to his place and remembered his lofty residence" (col. x, lines 15–26).[109] Tadmor holds that the expression of a god "returning to his place" is just a figurative description of the god becoming reconciled with his temple, following the period of anger during which the temple had been abandoned.[110] Tadmor's suggestion seems reasonable if only because an actual building effort on Nabonidus's part would have merited a much fuller and more elaborate recounting in the text. As such, the text cannot be used as concrete evidence that the Ehulhul had already been restored during Nabonidus's first year, although the project was definitely on Nabonidus's mind from the very beginning, and might have even gotten under way on a very modest scale.

2) *Lambert Text.*[111] This text tells of some events up until the beginning of Nabonidus's third year (col. iv, line 57), including Nabonidus's dedication of his daughter Ennigaldi-Nanna as a high priestess to Nanna in Ur, and the restoration of the Ebabbar, Sin's temple in Sippar. However, it makes no mention of the Ehulhul. The twin conclusions emerging from this evidence are that the text was probably written sometime during Nabonidus's third year, and that up until that time, work on the Ehulhul had probably not yet progressed very far, if indeed it had commenced at all. It ought to be noted that none of the

---

[108] Ibid., 107.
[109] Langdon and Zehnpfund, *VAB* 4, 284; *CAD*, Vol. 4, 69. For an English translation of the entire text, see *ANET*, 311.
[110] The evidence derives mainly from ritual psalms, in which the expression is used in conjunction with divine anger. See Tadmor, "The Inscriptions of Nabunaid," 355–56 with n. 29.
[111] Lambert, "A New Source for the Reign of Nabonidus," 1–8.

other building inscriptions which can be dated to early in Nabonidus's reign mention the Ehulhul either.[112]

3) *Nabonidus Chronicle*.[113] The text contains a year-by-year cataloging of Nabonidus's major achievements and pertinent events. Although some sections are now broken off, the preserved parts cover most of the reign, from the beginning through the eleventh year, and the final year (the eighteenth), during which Cyrus defeated the scattered Babylonian forces and entered Babylon unopposed. The *terminus a quo* for the chronicle's composition is, therefore, the year after Nabonidus's downfall. The Ehulhul is not mentioned explicitly, but relevant to the issue is the dating of Cyrus's victory over the Medes to Nabonidus's sixth year (col. ii, lines 1–4),[114] and the recording of Nabonidus's residence in Teima between his seventh and eleventh years (col. ii, lines 5–23). The sixth year date is significant, for it further heightens the impression that the Sippar cylinder, in which deliverance from the Umman-Manda (Medes) is predicted for the "third year" (above, p. 27) is chronologically suspect.[115] As for the Teima notices, the evidence of the Chronicle shows that the time frame for the Ehulhul project indicated by the Harran stele (namely, after the Teima sojourn) cannot be earlier than Nabonidus's eleventh year (see above, p. 26).

It is clear that the circumstantial evidence provided by the above texts does not break the deadlock between the Sippar cylinder and the Harran stele, since the evidence which could support the time frame of the former is indecisive (Nabonidus text 8), while the evidence which could support the time frame of the latter is largely based on silence (Lambert and Beaulieu texts, Nabonidus Chronicle). As such, the priority one gives to the time frame of either the Harran stele or the Sippar

---

[112] Beaulieu, *The Reign of Nabonidus*, 42, texts 2–11.

[113] Smith, *Babylonian Historical Texts*, 110–118; *ANET*, 305–07; Grayson, *Chronicles*, 104–111.

[114] Actually, the date is broken. However, the information appears in the context immediately preceding year seven.

[115] Cf. Smith, *Babylonian Historical Texts*, 44, n. 1, who attempts a harmonization of the sources by explaining that the third year only marked the beginning of Cyrus's attack, which lasted until its climactic conclusion in the sixth year. However, Smith's proposal was made without the benefit of all the other evidence which is available today. Röllig ("Erwägungen zu neuen Stelen König Nabonids," 257–58) argues unconvincingly that the sixth year originally referred to the sixth year of Cyrus, corresponding to the third year of Nabonidus. Cf. Tadmor, "The Inscriptions of Nabunaid," 357, n. 34.

cylinder boils down to adjudicating the internal merits and drawbacks of each source. Is it more likely that the Harran text is postdating an earlier event, or that the Sippar text is antedating a later event?

The major proponent of the first approach is Moran.[116] Although Moran feels compelled to admit that the Sippar text, as we now have it, gives the impression of being a theological reworking of the Harran version in order to minimize Sin's importance, he nevertheless postulates that both the Harran stele and the Sippar cylinder go back to a common prototype, of which the Sippar version, once purged of its references to Marduk, would reflect the more original exemplar. In practice, this means that Moran holds the account of the Teima sojourn in the Harran stele to be a secondary interpolation, which resulted in the chronological displacement of the Ehulhul project until the latter years of Nabonidus's reign. This displacement was necessary in order for the new text to conform to the Assyrian literary model of putting descriptions of building projects at the end of a royal inscription.[117] Moran adduces the following arguments for his position:

1) Typologically, the Harran text is strange, in that "after Sin's message in the dream, we are told nothing either of Nabonidus's reaction to the experience or even of his attempts to obey the divine command."[118]

2) The passage describing Nabonidus's reaction to the divine command in the Sippar cylinder—*amat bēlu rabû Marduk u Sîn nannari šamê u erṣetim ša qibīssunu la innennû. ana qibītišunu ṣērti aplaḫ akkud nakutti aršēma dulluḫū panūya*, "The word of the great lord, Marduk, and Sin, the light of heaven and earth, whose utterance cannot be altered. I feared their exalted command, [my heart] pounded, I became afraid, and my face was anguished" (col. i, lines 34–37)[119]—doesn't appear to be reflected in the Harran stele until after the Teima pericope, where the similar formula *amat ilūtišu rabīti attaṣarma*, "The word of his great godhead I observed" (col. iii, line 17) seems just to hang on loosely. From that point on, however, the Harran stele follows the Sippar cylinder al-

---

[116] "Notes on the New Nabonidus Inscriptions," 130–34. Moran's position is followed by Röllig, "Erwägungen zu neuen Stelen König Nabonids," 257–58, and van Seters, *In Search of History*, 62–64.
[117] Moran, "Notes on the New Nabonidus Inscriptions," 131–35.
[118] Ibid., 132.
[119] See *CAD*, Vol. 11/1, 198.

most verbatim in describing the swift building of the Ehulhul (Harran col. iii, lines 18–28 // Sippar col. i, lines 38–45; col. ii, lines 18–25).[120]

3) The Sippar cylinder, in Moran's words, "clearly reflects an early text when it has Nabonidus object to Marduk the presence of the Ummanmanda at Harran; this fits perfectly the situation at the accession of Nabonidus and has the ring of being genuine. Its *Vorlage*, therefore antedates the composition of H [Harran stele]."[121]

Now, each of these points can be challenged in turn. First, we *do* have Nabonidus's reaction to the initial divine command in the Harran stele, namely that the wickedness of the population prevented him from carrying out the plans. Secondly, the formula used in Harran col. iii, line 17 is not particularly similar to Sippar col. i, lines 34–37, and it reads satisfactorily in its own context as referring back to the various divinations and oracles which Nabonidus received on his way back from Teima. The passages describing the actual building of the Ehulhul are indeed closely parallel, but this fact in and of itself does not prove the priority of one text over the other. Finally, the Sippar cylinder's "ring of being genuine" appears to be no stronger than its ring of being apologetic. After all, the text was addressed to a Babylonian audience, and Nabonidus could hardly afford to repeat the accusation of Babylonian impiety found in the Harran stele. Blaming any potential or actual delay on the Umman-Manda was a perfect solution to absolve the Babylonians of any wrongdoing. In short, we have no more reason to suppose that the Harran stele added the Teima material than that the Sippar cylinder removed it.

This, then, leads to an examination of the second approach, namely that the Sippar cylinder is the text which, in fact, displays chronological displacement. Despite Moran's contention that the Harran stele reversed the chronological order of events, putting the account of the Ehulhul construction after the Teima period merely for stylistic reasons, Tadmor argues, "It is rather unlikely that an inscription intended for display would offer deliberately a late date for the restoration of the very temple in which it was set up. There are parallels for the editorial practice of antedating later events to the *rēš šarrūti* of a king, but I know of no parallel for the opposite."[122] In concurring with Tadmor, we note that the whole

---

[120] Moran, "Notes on the New Nabonidus Inscriptions," 133–34.
[121] Ibid., 134.
[122] Tadmor, "The Inscriptions of Nabunaid," 357.

tone of the Sippar cylinder, especially its distinctive evasiveness with regard to firm dates (see above, p. 27), renders it the more likely locus for chronological displacement. In addition, the composition of the Sippar text, unlike that of the Harran stele, was most likely separated by a good many years from the period during which it attempts to place the Ehulhul restoration. We have already mentioned the prominence given to Marduk, which even Moran acknowledges as a later development. Alongside that observation are a couple of technical insights by Beaulieu. As outlined above, the Sippar cylinder reviews the construction not only of the Ehulhul in Harran, but of the Ebabbar and Eulmash temples in Sippar. Now, besides the absence of the Ehulhul construction from building inscriptions which can be assigned to Nabonidus's early years, the Eulmash is similarly not mentioned in these texts. The Ebabbar, of course, is mentioned as early as the Lambert text in a context relating to year two (see above, p. 32). However, the Ebabbar's *ziggurat*, which the Sippar cylinder includes in its building description (col.iii, lines 4–5), was evidently erected at a later point in the reign, and was celebrated in a separate inscription most likely dating to year ten.[123] Although this still does not leave us with an absolute date for the composition of the Sippar cylinder, the balance of evidence presently at our disposal bears out the chronological framework of the Harran stele, namely that the Ehulhul restoration took place only after Nabonidus's return from Teima. Thus, the Sippar cylinder would *ipso facto* also date to after the Teima period, and would reflect a desire to push up the Ehulhul building to Nabonidus's early years.

Motivation

The somewhat contorted chronology of the Sippar cylinder offers us a classic case of the clash between the historiosophic ideals attached to the portrayal of a king's reign and the trend toward registering historical events within their authentic sequential framework. Sophisticated chronological muddling, such as we find in the Sippar cylinder, repre-

---

[123] Beaulieu, *The Reign of Nabonidus*, 34. The other inscription is Beaulieu's text 11 (*Oxford Editions of Cuneiform Texts* I, 32–37). Beaulieu bases its dating on the archival text Nabonidus 428 which reads: "Silver disbursed for 5 talents of bitumen for work to be done on the Ziggurat. Abu, day 10, tenth year of Nabonidus" (Beaulieu, 13, 31).

sents the best form of compromise between the two objectives. This technique was capitalized on especially in relating an event which, if reported in its strict, unadulterated chronological sequence, could be a source of embarrassment to the king. Thus, it comes as no surprise that the Sippar cylinder in particular, which was addressed to the subjects of Nabonidus most likely to criticize him for his patronage of the Harran cult, was composed in pseudo-chronological fashion. In Beaulieu's words:

> It is known that the rebuilding of the Ehulhul was one of the earliest projects of Nabonidus, since it is already mentioned in inscription 1 [= Nabonidus text 8],[124] but that for reasons which escape us, he was unable to carry it out until late in his reign. Being aware that this long delay could undermine his credibility among his Babylonian subjects, especially as this particular project had been publicized by him already in his first regnal year, Nabonidus would have given a somewhat distorted account of the rebuilding of the Ehulhul in inscription 15 [= Sippar cylinder] which was intended for Babylonia, while inscription 13 [= Harran stele], intended for Harran, fully acknowledges that the rebuilding of the Ehulhul took place after the return from Teima.[125]

Thus, the Sippar cylinder intends to project the most important of Nabonidus's cultic enterprises back to the early part of his reign, while accounting for the fact, in a manner palatable to the Babylonians, that this project couldn't be carried out immediately in one swoop. Nabonidus's reputation as a champion of Sin is upheld, without offending potential detractors. In sum, the motivation behind the Sippar cylinder's displacement can be labeled as ideological, reflecting a blend of political savvy and cultic apologetics. The motivations for the displacements in the Adad-guppi inscription and the Nabonidus Verse Account are similarly ideological, although their foci are diametrically opposed to each other. The Adad-guppi inscription, by antedating the Ehulhul project, celebrates Nabonidus's achievements as a cultic benefactor, while

---

[124] Beaulieu should be qualified here. The Ehulhul was not necessarily one of the earliest projects that Nabonidus actually started, but just one of the earliest that he had in mind.
[125] Beaulieu, *The Reign of Nabonidus*, 207.

Methods

The ingenuity of the Sippar cylinder's presentation is that it overcomes the tension between history and ideology through subtle camouflaging rather than by overt distortion. Primarily, it succeeds in blending together the initiation of the Ehulhul project through Marduk's theophany in the *rēš šarrūti*, and the completion of the project, by not specifying when the implementation of Marduk's command actually occurred. To be sure, the text invites us to understand that the construction took place no later than the third year following the theophany (*ina šalulti šatti ina kašādu* [col. i, line 28]), when the Medan threat was to have been removed. This inference is suggested by the close conjunction of Nabonidus's declaration of trust in the gods' words and his undelayed acting upon those words (col. i, lines 34–38). However, the literary continuity present in these lines covers over an unspecified chronological gap. For unless we are to suppose that Nabonidus moved ahead with the project in his *rēš šarrūti* despite the continued Umman-Manda occupation (an inherently unlikely scenario), the period which elapses over the course of lines 34–38 is abundantly obscure. Even the formula *ina šalulti šatti* may be a means for non-specification, since it functions elsewhere to indicate a cycle of time in literary-epic contexts (cf. Nabonidus Verse Account col. ii, line 17), rather than as a literal chronological indicator in historical chronicling.[126] Yet a further way in which the text points to an early date for the Ehulhul building without expressing it openly is by juxtaposing the Ehulhul project with the Ebabbar work, which can confidently be dated to Nabonidus's second year (see above, p. 32 on the Lambert text). In sum, the literary seaming of chronologically separated events, the use of typological formulae, and the omission of precise dates, all aid the Sippar scribe in creating an impression without imposing a rigid chronological framework.

---

[126] Tadmor, "The Inscriptions of Nabunaid," 353–54; Cf. Cogan, "The Chronicler's Use of Chronology," 207–08. For a position contrary to Cogan, see Halpern, "A Historiographic Commentary," 130.

It is important to note that the ability of the Sippar scribe to manipulate chronology in a tactful and relatively inconspicuous manner sets this text apart from a composition such as Esarhaddon's Babylon inscription (above, p. 17), in which the scales are tipped disproportionately in favor of ideological punctiliousness as opposed to historical credibility. The Sippar scribe may adopt some key phrases culled from the literary-epic sphere, but he does not completely overlook historical realities in shaping his presentation of Nabonidus's efforts on behalf of the cult. He acknowledges that Nabonidus was faced with overwhelming impediments in carrying out the Ehulhul project. The background suggested for the initial delay, namely the hostility of the Umman-Manda, is essentially reliable, as is the reason offered by the Harran stele, namely internal opposition on the part of the Babylonians. The Sippar cylinder does not so much clash with the Harran stele on this point as complement it, in accomodating the early history of Nabonidus's reign to Babylonian sensitivities. All together, the Sippar cylinder reflects a sophisticated attempt at constructing ideologically conditioned narrative, while maintaining a modicum of historical verisimilitude.

The methods employed in the Adad-guppi inscription and the Nabonidus Verse Account are not nearly as subtle. Like Esarhaddon's Babylon inscription, these texts appear to view the entire building project in question in terms of its early inception. In other words, they explicitly place the entire Ehulhul construction in a patently artificial early time frame, thereby completely sacrificing historical accuracy for polemical purposes.[127]

The Creation of Barren Women in Atraḫasis

Setting

Unlike our previous examples, the present discussion draws from "literary" as opposed to historical sources. Both the Akkadian text

---

[127] In a short appendix, Beaulieu cites new evidence which might indicate that the rebuilding of the Ehulhul got under way during Belshazzar's regency, i.e., during the years that Nabonidus was in Teima. However, Beaulieu acknowledges that the evidence is too fragmentary for establishing new conclusions (*The Reign of Nabonidus*, 240–41).

Atraḫasis[128] and the related Sumerian text *Enki and Ninmaḫ*[129] are myths of origin, which serve to explain the world order known to their authors. Since these myths deal with events which precede the dawn of history and are thus not subject to verification, it would be inappropriate to weigh the account of one myth against the other for the purpose of establishing an original historical sequence of things. Nevertheless, in the event that the two myths narrate the same event as occurring in different time frames, it behooves us to question why the later myth would alter the sequence of its parent text, assuming that such a relationship of literary dependence can be reasonably established.

The links between *Atraḫasis* and *Enki and Ninmaḫ* are indeed readily apparent. According to both texts, the purpose of man's creation was for him to serve the needs of the gods, who felt that they had been working too hard.[130] The creation process itself is similar in both accounts. At Enki's direction, man is fashioned from clay, either by Enki's mother Nammu who is attended by the birth goddesses (including Ninmah)[131] or by the birth goddess Nintu herself.[132] There are some differences between the two accounts as well. For example, only the Sumerian version envisions an actual delivery (birth) as part of the original creation process.[133] The motif of mixing clay with the blood of a slaughtered god is definitely present in the Akkadian version,[134] but might not be part of the Sumerian account.[135] Still, the two myths are closely enough related for one to suppose that they follow the same line of tradition, especially when one compares them to a widely divergent Sumerian tradition, according to which Enlil created man single-handedly with a pickaxe.[136]

The relationship between *Atraḫasis* and *Enki and Ninmaḫ* highlights the need to account for a fundamental sequence difference between

---

[128] For the text, see Lambert and Millard, *Atraḫasis*.

[129] For the text, see Benito, "Enki and Ninmaḫ." Cf. the recent treatment and translation by Jacobsen, *The Harps that Once*, 151–66.

[130] Lambert and Millard, *Atraḫasis*, 54–57; Benito, "Enki and Ninmaḫ," 23–24, 36, referring to man's task of "carrying baskets," i.e., labor.

[131] Benito, "Enki and Ninmaḫ," 24, 37.

[132] Lambert and Millard, *Atraḫasis*, 56–59.

[133] Jacobsen, *The Harps that Once*, 156–57.

[134] Lambert and Millard, *Atraḫasis*, 56–59.

[135] Benito, "Enki and Ninmaḫ," 12, n. 6.

[136] The latter tradition is represented by the *Myth of the Pickaxe* (see Kramer, *Sumerian Mythology*, 51–53 with references). For the contrast between the two traditions, see Lambert, "The Creation of Man in Sumero-Babylonian Myth," 101–02.

them. In *Enki and Ninmaḫ*, Ninmah's power as a creator and controller of the fates is contrasted with that of Enki. In response to Enki's challenge, Ninmah fashions six types of abnormal people. These types include someone with an arm problem, someone with constantly blinking eyes, a cripple, a man with uncontrollable semen emission, a barren woman, and someone with no sex organs. Nevertheless, Enki is able to provide viable tasks for all of these people.[137] When the roles are reversed, however, Ninmah is unable to change the fate of an old and sick person created by Enki.[138]

The presentation of *Atraḫasis* differs drastically in regard to the theme of disabled people. The theme is completely absent in the account of the original creation process. *Atraḫasis*'s scope, however, extends beyond the original creation. It also narrates the story of the flood, which was decreed by the gods to wipe out the human race because humans had become too numerous and noisy for the gods to tolerate. It is only after the flood that Enki summons Nintu, instructing her to create various categories of women who for one reason or another will not be able to have children. Included in this group are barren women, women whose newborn babies will be carried off by demons, and women who will be designated for special cultic roles which forbid them to have children.[139] The text is rather broken at this point, so it is impossible to know what other types of handicaps, if any, were mentioned. Nevertheless, the presupposition that the phenomenon of barrenness postdates the flood represents a clear difference from the account of *Enki and Ninmaḫ*, in which a barren woman was included among the abnormal types fashioned at the very outset of the creation process. However, the question remains as to which version can be said to have displaced the time frame of the barren woman's creation, i.e., which version is primary and which is dependent?

In my judgement, the evidence is stronger for viewing *Enki and Ninmaḫ* as the primary version from which *Atraḫasis* diverged. Although *Enki and Ninmaḫ* is a comparatively late Sumerian piece (Old Babylonian period),[140] *Atraḫasis* appears to derive from an even later point in the

---

[137] Benito, "*Enki and Ninmaḫ*," 25–28, 38–40. Cf. the slightly different enumeration of Jacobsen, *The Harps that Once*, 159–61.
[138] Benito, "*Enki and Ninmaḫ*," 28–30, 40–41. Jacobsen, *The Harps that Once*, 162, takes Enki's creation to be a premature fetus.
[139] Lambert and Millard, *Atraḫasis*, 100–03.
[140] Å. Sjöberg, oral communication, based on the grammar.

same period.[141] In arguing for the primacy of *Atraḫasis*, Frymer-Kensky observes that *Enki and Ninmaḫ* exhibits a couple of seeming "Akkadianisms."[142] However, the direction of language borrowings at this comparatively late period (O.B.) is quite fluid, so Frymer-Kensky's observation is not decisive. Furthermore, the barren woman in *Enki and Ninmaḫ* is only one of a heterogeneous group of odd types, as opposed to *Atraḫasis* in which she appears only in the company of other women with child-bearing limitations. It is more likely that *Atraḫasis* plucked the barren woman from the more extended inventory of *Enki and Ninmaḫ* than that the latter's list developed out of *Atraḫasis*'s limited register. As such, it behooves us to explain why *Atraḫasis* displaced the barren woman's creation to a later point in time.

Motivation

It is obvious that the creation of barren women in the two myths not only occupies different time frames, but also serves very different functions. In *Enki and Ninmaḫ*, as we have seen, the creation of a barren woman is part of a competition of sorts between *Enki and Ninmaḫ*, which serves to highlight the superior skill of Enki. By contrast, the creation of barren women in *Atraḫasis* has nothing at all to do with any divine rivalry. Rather, it represents a post-diluvian compromise between the gods' need for man's toil on the one hand and their aversion to man's noisy proliferation on the other hand. Man will be given a second chance, but his numbers will be limited by natural and other causes.[143] The differing conceptions of how and why barrenness came to be leads us to identify the motivation for *Atraḫasis*'s displacement of the phenomenon's origins as etiological. Simply put, the author(s) of *Atraḫasis*, when faced with the original setting of the phenomenon (as recorded in *Enki and Ninmaḫ*), felt that it could be utilized more appropriately for explicating the nature of man's reproductive limitations. Since according to *Atraḫasis* the issue of man's overpopulation only came to a head with the flood, the safe-

---

[141] The best known edition of *Atraḫasis* dates from the reign of Ammiṣaduqa, who reigned in the second half of the seventeenth century (Lambert and Millard, *Atraḫasis*, 5).
[142] "The Atrahasis Epic," 155.
[143] Frymer-Kensky, "The Atrahasis Epic," 149–50.

guards against the problem (including barrenness) had to be viewed as taking effect only after the flood.

Methods

Although, as mentioned above, the lines in the vicinity of the passage in question in *Atraḫasis* are damaged, it is rather doubtful that the creation of other types of abnormal people was also mentioned at this point, given the narrow focus and purpose of the *Atraḫasis* narrative in adopting the barrenness phenomenon. If this is so, then the displacement wrought by the *Atraḫasis* account would have been extremely selective, i.e., transposing the creation of just one out of the six types of abnormal people listed in the Sumerian myth. It is also noteworthy that in *Atraḫasis*, barren women are grouped together with women who were not mentioned at all in the Sumerian myth as having been created early on, i.e., those women who lose their children and those who serve as cultic functionaries. This perfectly logical combination of the barren woman with her childless peers (who were never said to have been part of the original creation process) makes the displacement of the barren woman's creation less conspicuous.

EXCURSUS: Naram-Sin and the Fall of Akkad

The justification for our taking up this celebrated case derives not only from the goodly amount of attention it has received from Assyriologists, but more importantly from the desire to demonstrate how tantalizingly complicated and inconclusive an investigation of an apparent chronological displacement can be. Although the inconclusiveness of this case prevents me from including it in the roll call of empirical examples, I offer it as an excursus in the hope that a reader will discover light where previous scholars have found confusion. Like our previous example, this one also is based primarily on "literary" sources, as opposed to annals, chronicles, and similar sources contemporary with the events in question. There are approximately ten known literary texts relating to

Naram-Sin (2291–2255)[144] of the Old Akkadian dynasty.[145] Two of these sources, the *Cuthean Legend of Naram-Sin* and the *Curse of Agade*, along with a late chronicle known as the *Weidner Chronicle*, offer opposing schemes regarding when the Akkad dynasty came to an end. First, we offer a brief resume of these sources.

1) The *Cuthean Legend of Naram-Sin* was first partially published in 1901.[146] A somewhat fuller edition was published by Güterbock in 1934,[147] but the fullest edition (to date) was not known until Gurney's publication of the Sultantepe tablets in 1955.[148] Although the text reads as a first person account of Naram-Sin himself, Güterbock already noted the text's affinities with the so-called *narû* literature, or Akkadian fictional autobiographies (usually of a king).[149] This genre incorporates legendary features and motifs and lacks chronological precision.[150] For example, Naram-Sin introduces himself as the son of Sargon, even though in reality he was Sargon's grandson (line 2). He proceeds to tell of the misfortunes that befell his empire at the hands of a coalition of quasi-supernatural forces over the course of "three years" in succession (lines 31–87).[151] At the New Year festival of the "fourth year," Naram-Sin obtained an apparently favorable oracle (lines 104–119), which he then followed up on by capturing twelve prisoners (lines 120–123) but leaving their punishment to the gods (lines 124–146). The text closes with a *mannu attā* ("whosoever you are") formula (line 147), which is characteristic of such literary pieces.[152]

The text's literary genre not only precludes treating it as a first-hand account, but makes pinpointing the date of its composition and its rela-

---

[144] These dates are taken from *CAH* (3rd ed.), Vol. 1, pt. 2, 999. Jacobsen, *Sumerian King List*, Table II (following p. 208), is representative of the "high chronology," while Hallo and Simpson, *The Ancient Near East*, 60 and Roux, *Ancient Iraq*, 150, give slightly lower dates than the ones adopted here.
[145] See Cooper, *The Curse of Agade*, 16.
[146] *Cuneiform Texts from Babylonian Tablets in the British Museum* XIII (London: Trustees of the British Museum, 1901), plate 44.
[147] Güterbock, "Die historische Tradition," 69–73.
[148] Gurney, "The Sultantepe Tablets," 98–109.
[149] Güterbock, "Die historische Tradition," 73–76.
[150] On the *narû* literature, see Longman, *Fictional Akkadian Autobiography* and cf. above, p. 29 on the Adad-guppi inscription.
[151] The motif of quasi-supernatural forces had a long presence in ancient Near Eastern literature, cf. Ezekiel 38–39. On the literary use of a three-year cycle, see above, n. 126.
[152] On the *mannu attā* formula, see above, n. 95.

Mesopotamian Material 45

tion to the actual course of history exceedingly difficult. Nevertheless, neither the text's legendary nature nor the likelihood that it originated many generations later than Naram-Sin precludes the possibility that its account may have some basis in authentic historical recollection, especially when relevant external evidence can be brought to bear (see below, p. 49). For now, we shall just take note of the overall import of the text, namely that Naram-Sin suffered severe but not fatal setbacks by invading hordes.

2) The *Curse of Agade* is a long Sumerian poem, parts of which were known already in the early years of Assyriological research. Güterbock put together the known portions as of 1934,[153] but the fullest current edition was published by Cooper in 1983.[154] The poem narrates the initial misfortunes which befell the capital city, Agade (Akkad), during the reign of Naram-Sin when Inanna and then the other gods removed their favor from the city (lines 54–84). At first, Naram-Sin was very contrite about this turn of events (lines 85–90), but after seven years of pious acceptance, he took out his frustrations by ravaging the Ekur temple of Enlil in Nippur (lines 91–144). In order to avenge the Ekur's desecration, Enlil then brought on the Gutians who wrought massive destruction on the entire Akkad empire (lines 145–208). In the end, however, Enlil went along with a plan devised by the other gods which singled out Agade for total and permanent destruction, while presumably sparing the rest of the countryside from further damage (lines 209–269). At that point, Agade was in fact completely and forever destroyed (lines 270–281). Thus, the *Curse of Agade* differs from the *Cuthean Legend* in two respects: a) It specifically identifies the Gutians as the invaders of Akkad. b) It portrays a fate of far greater finality for Naram-Sin's empire than the *Cuthean Legend*.

As for the text's date of composition, we are on firmer ground than was the case with the *Cuthean Legend*, since there are three known exemplars of the *Curse of Agade* dating from the Ur III period.[155] Thus the latest possible date for the *Curse of Agade* is circa 2000, a relatively short period of 150 years after the actual destruction of Akkad (see below, p. 48). This is important to note, since it makes it more difficult for us to

---

[153] Güterbock, "Die historische Tradition," 25–34.
[154] Cooper, *The Curse of Agade*. See also Falkenstein, "Fluch über Akkade," 50–75 and Kramer in *ANET*, 646–51.
[155] Cooper, *The Curse of Agade*, 11–12.

dismiss the *Curse of Agade* out of hand as a source that was unaware of the historical realities.

3) The *Weidner Chronicle* was first published in part in 1926.[156] It was treated more extensively by Güterbock in 1934 [157] and published most recently by Grayson.[158] It covers intermittently the reigns of Mesopotamian rulers from the Early Dynastic Period (beginning circa. 2700) through Shulgi of the Ur III Dynasty (2095–2048)[159] in terms of how attentive these rulers were in providing fish for the Esagil temple of Marduk in Babylon. The text's distinctive Babylonian perspective earmarks it for the period of the First Dynasty of Babylon (2000 at the earliest[160]), when Babylon was first achieving prominence.[161] Like the *Curse of Agade*, the *Weidner Chronicle* attributes the Gutian takeover of Naram-Sin's kingship to the latter's cultic sins, though the object of Naram-Sin's aggression is said to be Babylon rather than Nippur (Chronicle, lines 53–55).

This summary shows that the chronological tension between the *Cuthean Legend* on the one hand, and the *Curse of Agade* and the *Weidner Chronicle* on the other hand, boils down to one crucial question, namely when did the Akkad dynasty come to an end? The *Curse of Agade* and the *Weidner Chronicle* locate the end of the dynasty with Naram-Sin, while the *Cuthean Legend* allows for Naram-Sin's recovery from the blows he absorbed. Now, theoretically, one could claim that the Cuthean Legend reflects an earlier stage of Naram-Sin's rule, and therefore the reprieve that it grants Naram-Sin was short-lived and does not conflict with the accounts of his ultimate defeat as represented by the other two sources. One could even strengthen this claim by noting that in the *Cuthean Legend*, the Gutians are listed among the victims of the invading hordes (lines 56–57), whereas in the other two sources, they have gotten strong enough to rise to the status of invaders. Nevertheless, it is hard to avoid the impression that each of the literary works intends to leave its readers with a more or less complete conception of Naram-Sin's reign and his life-and-death struggles with external enemies. If such

---

[156] A. Boissier, *Babyloniaca* 9, 23–26 with plate II.
[157] Güterbock, "Die historische Tradition," 47–55, texts A, B, and C.
[158] Grayson, *Chronicles*, 145–51.
[159] For the dates, see *CAH* (3rd ed.), Vol. 1, pt. 2, 998.
[160] See Hallo and Simpson, *The Ancient Near East*, 98.
[161] See Finkelstein, "Mesopotamian Historiography," 467, n. 24; Grayson, *Chronicles*, 43–45.

Mesopotamian Material 47

is the case, we can only begin to tackle the question of which, if any, of the conflicting chronological schemes represents a more authentic view (and consequently, which scheme[s] represents chronological displacement) by appealing to the circumstantial evidence of other sources, which are both more historically oriented and closer in time to Naram-Sin than any of the literary works we have cited to this point. This evidence breaks down into three categories:

1) The royal inscriptions of Naram-Sin, including monuments in remote parts of the Akkad empire, generally give a picture of successful expansion.[162] The one exception is a text published by Grayson and Sollberger in 1976, which tells of a general uprising against Naram-Sin.[163] Naram-Sin was successful in putting down the rebellion, although not without the Gutians inflicting a defeat on him before stopping short of entering Agade. That the Gutian threat continued unabated after Naram-Sin's death is evident from an inscription of Naram-Sin's son, Sharkalisharri, indicating that he also fought the Gutians.[164] In addition, a letter dating from the time of Sharkalisharri describes the pressured conditions occasioned by the growing Gutian domination.[165]

2) The omen traditions concerning Naram-Sin are all favorable, and the omens concerning the destruction of the Akkad dynasty are not connected to a particular king.[166] In general, the omens, which aimed to provide specific guidance for royal decision making, tend to preserve reliable historical information.[167]

3) The Sumerian king list has the Akkad dynasty continuing past Naram-Sin not only with Sharkalisharri, who ruled for twenty-five years, but beyond him with four shadow figures who vied for the throne over the subsequent three years, followed by Dudu, who ruled for twenty-one

---

[162] Finkelstein, "Mesopotamian Historiography," 467–68.
[163] "L'insurrection générale contre Narām-Suen," RA 70 (1976), 103–28.
[164] Gadd, "The Dynasty of Agade," 455. For a full list of the inscriptions of Naram-Sin and Sharkalisharri, see Gelb, Old Akkadian Writing, 198–204 and Hirsch, "Die Inschriften," 17–30.
[165] Smith, "Notes on the Gutian Period," 295–97.
[166] Finkelstein, "Mesopotamian Historiography," 467–68. There is one possible exception in which the destruction of Akkad might be connected with Sharkalisharri. Gadd, "The Dynasty of Agade," 457, quoting Nougayrol in École Pratique des Hautes Études Annuaire (1944–45), 9, no. 21, translates, "The omen of Sharkalisharri—ruin of Akkad; the enemy will fall upon thy peace." However, according to Finkelstein, "Mesopotamian Historiography," 468, n. 29, the reading is unclear.
[167] Finkelstein, ibid., 462–64.

years and then Shu-Durul, who ruled for fifteen years.168 Jacobsen has made a convincing case that all of the Akkad kings following Naram-Sin ruled in Agade simultaneously with the Gutian rulers who governed the former domains of the Akkad empire.169 Still, the fact remains that the Akkad dynasty survived some sixty-five years beyond Naram-Sin, which makes circa. 2150 a likely date for the destruction of Agade.

When put together, the above evidence seems to indicate that Naram-Sin's reign came to a reasonably peaceful close after weathering one major threat, although Gutian domination over Akkad would accelerate shortly thereafter. On this basis, the accounts of the *Curse of Agade* and the *Weidner Chronicle*, which throw the final and conclusive Gutian attack on Akkad back to the reign of Naram-Sin, can certainly be excluded from an historical reconstruction. The same conclusion emerges from other considerations as well. For example, there is a well known text (CBS 13972+) dealing with the reigns of Sargon of Akkad and his son Rimush.170 The text dates from the Old Babylonian period, but was copied from texts appearing on the shoulder blades of statues from the Ekur at Nippur. Had the Ekur really been destroyed anytime before the Old Babyonian period (as the *Curse of Agade* claims), these statues would not have survived.171 In fact, certain cultic texts may indicate that sacrifices were offered to the statues of Sargon and Naram-Sin himself at Nippur during the Ur III period, which would make it quite impossible to suppose that Naram-Sin was responsible for destroying the Ekur.172 The *Weidner Chronicle*'s credibility suffers a further setback in light of the fact that Babylon and its Esagil are not even known to have been in existence until slightly after the time of Naram-Sin.173

The question remains, though, concerning the portrayal of the *Cuthean Legend*. Some scholars, such as Finkelstein, who gives greatest credence to the omen tradition, deny that there were any significantly

---

168 Jacobsen, *Sumerian King List*, 206–07. For a list of the inscriptions of these last kings of the Akkad dynasty, see Gelb, *Old Akkadian Writing*, 205 and Hirsch, "Die Inschriften," 31–32.
169 Jacobsen, *Sumerian King List*, 206–07.
170 Poebel, *Historical Texts*, 173–77; Legrain, *Royal Inscriptions and Fragments*, 12–25.
171 The mention of Sharkalisharri as the "builder of the temple of Enlil" (see Jacobsen, "Iphur-Kīshi," 14, n. 57) is not decisive, since this appellation often refers to general restoration work as well.
172 Falkenstein, "Fluch über Akkade," 48.
173 Oppenheim, *Ancient Mesopotamia*, 155.

untoward events during the reign of Naram-Sin.[174] Others, like Speiser, are more inclined to extract latent historical elements from the *Cuthean Legend*'s account. For example, the leader of the enemy coalition is named Anubanini (line 39) who can be readily identified with the historical figure of the same name appearing in documents contemporary with Naram-Sin as king of the powerful Lullu tribe.[175] Also, the fact that the course of the enemy invasion appears to have been from the north-northwest to the southeast lines up with the historical direction of Naram-Sin's major campaigns, which took him primarily to the north and northwest.[176] In addition, the *Cuthean Legend*'s portrayal of a general attack against Naram-Sin which left him weakened but intact is at least partially mirrored in the text published by Grayson and Sollberger,[177] which was unavailable to either Finkelstein or Speiser.

I am therefore inclined towards Speiser's position. In practice, this means that my analysis of chronological displacement in the literary sources will focus exclusively on the *Curse of Agade* and the *Weidner Chronicle*. Why would these particular texts, or the traditions they were based on, have antedated the climactic fall of Akkad at the hands of the Gutians to the reign of Naram-Sin?

According to Finkelstein, the phenomenon in question is to be attributed merely to the passage of time which resulted in popular ignorance of the true historical picture. In other words, the authors of the "literary tradition," whom Finkelstein presumes spun their works de novo, were no longer aware of the few unexceptional kings who followed Naram-Sin. In his words:

> It was Naram-Sin's misfortune, so to speak, to have come after Sargon, and it was precisely because he became such a ruler of such great renown that only his name, besides Sargon's, came down in the folk tradition whereas those of his two predecessors and those of his successors disappeared. And it was only natu-

---

[174] Finkelstein, "Mesopotamian Historiography," 469–70.
[175] Speiser, "Some Factors in the Collapse of Akkad," 99; Jacobsen, "Iphur-Kīshi," 14, n. 58.
[176] Speiser, "Some Factors in the Collapse of Akkad," 99.
[177] Above, n. 163. One major difference between the *Cuthean Legend* and the Grayson text is the role assigned to the Gutians. In the *Cuthean Legend* as we have noted above, the Gutians appear only as victims, while in the Grayson text, they are active members of the coalition fighting Naram-Sin.

ral, therefore, that the downfall of the Akkad dynasty—the exemplar of all such political and social calamities in subsequent Mesopotamian history—should be attached to Naram-Sin's personality, transfiguring it, and causing his real achievements to be ignored.[178]

Thus, in Finkelstein's opinion, the phenomenon in question should be viewed more as a case of chronological misplacement than as one of chronological displacement. In such a case, the Naram-Sin "literary tradition" could not be used to illustrate our topic. To be sure, Finkelstein's explanation may have some application in other cases from later periods of ancient Near Eastern history. For example, classical writers attached the fall of the Neo-Assyrian empire to one "Sardanapallus" (possibly Assurbanipal), in apparent disregard of the last few luckless Assyrian kings who were forgotten in the mist of time.[179] In our particular case, Finkelstein's approach might be appropriate for the *Weidner Chronicle*, which passes over a fair number of the early (pre-Babylonian) kings. However, as far as the *Curse of Agade* is concerned, Finkelstein's approach is called into question by the fact that the text was composed, at the very latest, only 150 years after the fall of the Old Akkadian dynasty (see above, pp. 45, 48) and in a cultural and geographical milieu not far removed from the events it was describing. Hence, it is preferable to look for explanations which seek to account for the chronological framework presented by the *Curse of Agade* in terms of intentional displacement rather than ignorant misplacement.

Such an explanation could be derived from Falkenstein's contention that the *Curse of Agade* displays an anti-Akkad stance. Falkenstein sees this bias in the composition's stark description of Naram-Sin's rape of the Ekur (lines 128–129), and its bleak ending section (as opposed to the

---

[178] Finkelstein, "Mesopotamian Historiography," 470. The same type of explanation was given already by Güterbock, "Die historische Tradition," 75f.

[179] Güterbock, "Die historische Tradition," 75–76. The Sardanapallus saga appears in its fullest form in Diodorus II, 23–28 (Loeb Classical Library ed., Vol. 1, 425–45). Cf. also Herodotus II, 150 (Loeb Classical Library ed., Vol. 1, 461). The identity of Sardanapallus is debated. Drews ("Sargon, Cyrus," 393, n. 31) takes it as a hybrid form combining the names of Esarhaddon and Assurbanipal. However, Weissbach, "Sardanapallus," 2463–65, dismisses any connection with Assurbanipal. For a list of the Assyrian kings who ruled after Assurbanipal, see Reade, "The Accession of Sinsharishkun," 5. The actual king in 612 when Nineveh fell was Sinsharishkun. Cf. also Hallo and Simpson, *The Ancient Near East*, 63, for the case of misplacement in the Book of Daniel from Nabonidus to Nebuchadrezzar.

Lamentation over the Destruction of Ur and Sumer, which closes with a ray of hope for Ur's ultimate restoration).[180] One could theoretically claim that an anti-Akkad Tendenz is what led the Curse of Agade to exaggerate Naram-Sin's misfortunes. However, there are two fundamental problems with such an approach: 1) Anti-Akkadianism is an unknown factor in Sumerian literature. In general, there is no evidence that the restoration of Sumerian power in the Ur III period evoked a resentment of Akkadians in its wake.[181] 2) This approach evades the issue of why Naram-Sin in particular was singled out as the king who bore the brunt of the Gutian attack which destroyed Akkad.

Naram-Sin's role in the Curse of Agade has received renewed treatment since the studies of both Finkelstein and Falkenstein.[182] Both van Dijk and A. Westenholz[183] attempt to uncover an historical kernel in the Curse of Agade's account by interpreting the composition against the backdrop of Naram-Sin's supposed religious policies. These policies are theorized to have entailed certain innovations (particularly the favoring of Agade over Nippur as a central cult center) which antagonized the Sumerian traditionalists and contributed to a serious uprising against Naram-Sin. Westenholz, in particular, goes out on a limb by specifically attributing historical value to the Curse of Agade's description of the Ekur's destruction,[184] thus implying that this action was part of Naram-Sin's violent reaction to the Sumerian rebellion. Thus, once the fall of Akkad had actually come to pass, conservative circles within Mesopotamian society would have had reason to assign the blame for this occurrence to Naram-Sin, and indeed to antedate it to his reign.

The basic problems with this reconstruction are that it ascribes unwarranted historicity to the portrayal of the Ekur's destruction (which as we have seen above, p. 48, does not concur with the historical evidence), as well as the fact that the actual sources relating to Naram-Sin's internal policies are exceedingly limited. Jacobsen avoids the first problem by suggesting that the destruction of the Ekur is actually only a literary reflex of Naram-Sin's suppression of the rebellion described in the text

---

[180] Falkenstein, "Fluch über Akkade," 49–50. The lamentation to which Falkenstein refers is translated by Kramer in ANET, 611–19.
[181] Cooper, The Curse of Agade, 9.
[182] See the literature cited by Cooper, ibid., 6–7.
[183] van Dijk, "Einige Bemerkungen," 234–35; Westenholz, "The Old Akkadian Empire," 112–13.
[184] Westenholz, "The Old Akkadian Empire," 122, n. 32.

published by Grayson and Sollberger (above, p. 47).[185] However, while the rebellion is firmly documented, establishing a causal or even a temporal link between the rebellion and the *Curse of Agade* still remains a highly conjectural enterprise. The Grayson text mentions areas well beyond the confines of greater Sumer as participating in the rebellion and doesn't give a hint as to what inspired the rebellion. Thus, determining the motivating factors behind the *Curse of Agade*'s overall portrayal of Naram-Sin in general and its chronological displacement in particular, must necessarily remain within the realm of conjecture.

In sum, the "literary tradition" relating to Naram-Sin evidently reflects a mixture of both chronological misplacement and displacement.[186] However, even when it is more likely that we are dealing with displacement, determining the motivation(s) for such appears to be beyond our present reach.

Summary of Chapter One

The results obtained to this point regarding chronological displacements in the Mesopotamian material can be sketched in chart form as follows:

Text	Type of Displacement	Motivation	Method
Sargon II's Nineveh prisms	antedates campaigns by one *palû*	ideological (military—to have a campaign for each and every regnal year)	use of a term with double meaning (*palû*)
Esarhaddon's Babylon inscription	antedates building of Esagila by a number of years to the *rēš šarrūti*	ideological (cultic—to express the king's immediate concern for the gods)	viewing an entire project in terms of an initial intention

---

[185] "Iphur-Kīshi," 8.

[186] In this connection, E. Leichty observes that at least part of the Naram-Sin "literary tradition" might actually have as its original historical reference point the end of the *Old Assyrian* period (mid-nineteenth century), which was also presided over by a much lesser known Sargon and his second successor Naram-Sin. At the same time, Leichty acknowledges that the *Curse of Agade*, at least, goes back to an earlier point than that.

Text	Type of Displacement	Motivation	Method
Assurbanipal annals, edition A	antedates final defeat of Babylon by at least one year	ideological ("prophetic future")	loose terminology—*ina ūmēšu*
Nabonidus's Sippar cylinder, Verse Account, Adad-guppi inscription	antedates building of Ehulhul by circa. ten years (or somewhat less)	ideological (political—to enhance or diminish Nabonidus' reputation as a cultic benefactor)	use of typological formula—*ina šalulti šatti*, blurring the precise date for the actual carrying out of the project
Atraḫasis	postdates creation of barren women until after the flood	exegetical (etiological—to provide a more fitting explanation of the barren woman's origins)	grouping barren women with more similar types (not mentioned in the original text)

Of the five instances of chronological displacement in Mesopotamian texts which we examined (excluding the material relating to Naram-Sin), four were taken from the corpus of royal inscriptions (Sargon II's prisms, Esarhaddon's Babylon inscription, Assurbanipal's annals, edition A, and Nabonidus's Sippar cylinder), and one was taken from a literary work best characterized as a myth of origins (Atraḫasis). Within the first four examples, the cases for displacement were based either on a comparison of the given texts with other texts of the same king (Sargon II's Nineveh prisms vs. his Khorsabad annals, Nabonidus's Sippar cylinder vs. his Harran stele), or with roughly contemporaneous texts which provided more credible chronological details bearing on the issues in question (Esarhaddon's Babylon inscription and Assurbanipal's annals, edition A vs. information gleaned from the Babylonian Chronicles). Interestingly, every one of the cases of chronological displacement from the royal inscriptions which we examined reflects an antedating of the given event. However, it is not always possible to determine the precise span of the antedating. Sargon II's prisms antedate his campaigns by one *palû*, thus by one regnal year. Assurbanipal's edition A (lines 128–135) speaks of the fall of Shamashshumukin in a context of about one year too early. The cases from the inscriptions of Esarhaddon and Nabonidus imply an even greater span of displacement, but without precise information on when the Esagila and Ehulhul projects were carried out, we cannot put an exact figure on those spans.

As for motivations, all of the examples from the royal inscriptions share an ideological focus, though the precise natures of the ideological motivations vary slightly. In the case of Sargon II, the emphasis is more on the military virtues of the king, while in the case of Esarhaddon, the emphasis is placed on the king's alacrity in caring for the cult. The latter theme is present in the case of Nabonidus as well, though with stronger political overtones, namely the apparent attempt at wooing the support of the Babylonian populace or at least staving off their opposition. The case from Assurbanipal's edition A functions as a kind of "prophetic future" in the sense that events that had not yet occurred are spoken of as if they had already come to pass. This mode of expression is meant to place full confidence in the powers of the gods (in this case, Sin) to bring about that which they promised.

In terms of methods, the common thrust of the examples from the royal inscriptions is an eye toward purposeful ambiguity, whether that be accomplished through the use of a double-edged term (*palû* for regnal year or military campaign in the case of Sargon II) or through other loose or typological chronological formulae (*ina ūmēšu* in the case of Assurbanipal, *ina šalulti šatti* in the case of Nabonidus).

The case from *Atraḫasis* differs from the others in a number of ways. The events it purports to describe are primeval rather than actually historical. The direction of the displacement in *Atraḫasis* is a postdating of the event in question. The motivation is closer to the exegetical category in the sense that the author of *Atraḫasis* apparently felt that the creation of barren women was simply better suited for a later point than its point of narration in *Enki and Ninmaḫ*. Finally, the method employed involves more of a recasting of the parent tradition than merely a subtle form of ambiguity.

Chapter II

Biblical Material

Introduction

The examples in the previous chapter culled from the Mesopotamian royal inscriptions provided us with the starkest illustrations of chronological displacement. Texts which were composed fairly shortly after the events they described could nevertheless be shown (through the testimony of other contemporaneous texts) to have placed those events in a non-original context. However, with the examples from the "literary" sources, we moved onto somewhat shakier ground, since the texts which appeared to exhibit chronological displacement were composed long after the events they described. Moreover, the relationship of these texts to the older sources from whose chronological framework they appeared to diverge was not as obviously close as the relationship between royal inscriptions which emerged from the same period and milieu.

A somewhat similar situation to the latter examples applies to those in the present chapter which are drawn exclusively from the synoptic (i.e., parallel) sections of the Books of Samuel and Kings on the one hand and Chronicles on the other hand. There is a wide scholarly consensus that the so-called Deuteronomistic History, which covers the Books of Joshua through Kings (i.e., a period of 600 plus years), was completed in its present form shortly after the last event described therein, namely the reprieve of Jehoiachin in 561 (2 Ki. 25:27–30).[1]

---

[1] See above all Noth, *The Deuteronomistic History*, 12. For theories concerning a pre-exilic edition of the history, see Cross, *Canaanite Myth*, 274–89 and his students,

There is also wide agreement that Chronicles was composed somewhat later during the Persian period.[2] However, what is not agreed upon is the extent to which the Chronicler used Samuel and Kings in their present form as a source or the extent to which he relied on other, non-canonical sources. This question is essential in evaluating the presence of chronological frameworks in Chronicles which diverge from those in Samuel and Kings. We must, therefore, briefly spell out the lines of debate.

Early critical opinion was very unsympathetic toward Chronicles. The Chronicler was viewed as a thoroughly biased reworker of Samuel and Kings whose departures from those sources were due overwhelmingly to ideology and occasionally to misunderstanding.[3] The Chronicler's own testimony to additional source material, such as the Book of Kings of Judah and Israel (2 Chr. 25:26; 28:26; 32:32) and various prophetic collections (1 Chr. 29:29; 2 Chr. 12:15; 13:22), were not taken seriously.[4] This extreme view was somewhat tempered by the recognition that at least some of the material unique to Chronicles, particularly that about royal building projects and wars, is not conditioned by ideology and indeed gives the impression of being drawn from archival sources (e.g., 2 Chr. 11:5–10; 26:6–8; 32:30).[5] Studies on individual pericopes within Chronicles likewise sought to attribute greater credibility to the book as an historical source.[6] However, the most significant challenge to the depreciation of the Chronicler as a potentially reliable historian was not launched until a generation ago with the advent of textual studies encompassing the newly published Qumran material. In 1965, Lemke attempted to demonstrate that many of Chronicles' textual deviations from Samuel, which were formerly attributed to the Chronicler's own Tendenz, were in fact based on ancient readings found in 4QSam^a or

---

including McKenzie, *The Chronicler's Use*, 1–15; Nelson, *The Double Redaction*; Friedman, *The Exile and Biblical Narrative*, 1–43.

[2] E.g., Albright, *The Biblical Period*, 95. Noth's argument for a date no earlier than 300 (*The Chronicler's History*, 73) is based on a misinterpretation of the evidence of Ezra 4 (cf. below, p. 126).

[3] This was the trend from de Wette through Wellhausen and into the beginning of the twentieth century. See Japhet's survey of scholarly opinion in "The Historical Reliability" (Hebrew), 328–33.

[4] E.g., Torrey, *Ezra Studies*, 227–31; Pfeiffer, "Chronicles," 578–80.

[5] See already Winckler, *Alttestamentliche Untersuchungen*, 157–67, followed by Noth, *The Chronicler's History*, 57–60.

[6] See Albright, "The Judicial Reform" and the other literature cited by Japhet, "The Historical Reliability" (Hebrew), 340–41.

kindred Septuagint material.7 This new challenge did not go unchallenged itself, with some of Lemke's very examples being used by Seeligmann to demonstrate how the Septuagint to Samuel could have been influenced by the Chronicler's creative homilies!8

For our purposes, two observations relating to the preceding debate are in order:

1) As a whole, Chronicles appears to have been written as an alternative to the Deuteronomistic History.9 This holds true whether the latter corpus lay before the Chronicler in the exact form in which we have it today or whether it reached him in a slightly variant form.

2) In the places where we have found obvious sequence differences between Chronicles and Samuel-Kings, there are as yet no independent textual witnesses (e.g., from Qumran or the Septuagint) which agree with Chronicles, nor does the Chronicler himself claim to be relying on specific sources in such cases.

When taken together, these two considerations show that as a rule, we ought to regard sequence differences between Chronicles and Samuel-Kings as conscious deviations on the part of the Chronicler. That will be our working hypothesis, unless there are cogent grounds for regarding the sequence in Samuel-Kings as secondary. We now turn to the analysis of specific examples of chronological displacement in Chronicles, in which the Chronicler demonstrably changes the order of events found in the sources which lay before him.

2 Samuel 5–6 and 1 Chronicles 13–15

Setting

The chapters in 1 Chronicles describing David's initial activities following his coronation as king over all Israel exhibit some significant editorial departures from the parallel chapters in 2 Samuel 5–6. In order to appreciate these deviations, we shall first outline the contents of the two sources side by side:

---

7 Lemke, "The Synoptic Problem."
8 Seeligmann, "The Beginnings of Midrash" (Hebrew), 16 with n. 7, 18–19 with n. 12.
9 Freedman, "The Chronicler's Purpose," 437; Friedman, *Who Wrote the Bible?*, 211–13.

	2 Sam. 5–6		1 Chr. 13–15
A.	*5:11–25* delegation from Hiram of Tyre to build David's palace; list of children born to David in Jerusalem; skirmishes with Philistines in Valley of Rephaim.	B1.	*13:1–14* David's first abortive attempt at bringing the ark up to Jerusalem, ending with tragedy of Peretz-Uzza and detainment of ark at home of Obed-Edom the Gittite for three months.
B.	*6:1–23* David's first abortive attempt at bringing ark up to Jerusalem, ending with tragedy of Peretz-Uzza, and followed, after a three-month detainment of ark at the home of Obed-Edom the Gittite, by successful second attempt.	A.	*14:1–16* delegation from Hiram of Tyre to build David's palace; list of children born to David in Jerusalem; skirmishes with Philistines in Valley of Rephaim.
		B2.	*15:2ff.* resumption of ark ceremony after three-month delay and its successful culmination.

As demonstrated by the above chart, the Chronicler places the material parallel to 2 Sam. 6:1–11 before the material parallel to 2 Sam. 5:11–25. After thus splitting the ark narrative, he then resumes with the material parallel to 2 Sam. 6:12–23. The effect of this rearrangement is to have David's recall of the ark figure as his first post-coronation act, with Hiram's delegation and the skirmishes at Baal-Peratzim fitted into the three-month hiatus noted in 2 Sam. 6:11.

It ought to be pointed out here that even the arrangement of 2 Sam. 5:11–25 may not be purely sequential in terms of historical reality. For example, Albright's proposed Assyro-Tyrian synchronism would put Hiram no earlier than 969, which would correspond to David's last decade of rule (at the latest).[10] While this datum remains within the realm of historical reconstruction of which we cannot suppose that the Biblical author was aware, it can surely be said that the Biblical author did not mean to suggest that all of David's Jerusalem-born children were born at this juncture. Thus, a topical arrangement has most often been suggested for the elements within this pericope, with the author concentrating together material related to David's activities in Jerusalem.[11]

---

[10] *Mélanges Isidore Lévy*, 1–9 apud Myers, *I Chronicles*, 106.
[11] E.g., Mazar, "David's Reign in Hebron," 242–43. Cf. Abramsky, "Artistry and Historiography" (Hebrew), 459–62, emphasizing the dynastic aspects of both the building of the palace and Solomon's birth which are recorded in this chapter.

Still, this reasonable conclusion does not affect the issue of conscious chronological displacement, for we cannot prove that the author of Samuel intentionally intended to present events which he knew to be from other periods as if they occurred precisely at the beginning of David's reign. However, chronological displacement certainly does come into play with the Chronicler's presentation, since he has consciously switched the order of a pre-existing source as outlined above.

Motivations

Most commentators have accounted for the displacement under discussion by noting that the Chronicler wished to emphasize David's concern for the cult. According to the Chronicler's conception, David attended to the ark without delay even before entering into other domestic affairs.[12] Thus, the motivation for moving up the ark narrative would be strikingly similar to that found for the displacements noted for Esarhaddon's Babylon inscription and Nabonidus's Sippar cylinder (above, pp. 18, 36–37).[13] This explanation is undoubtedly correct but is incomplete. For the Chronicler could just as easily have delayed the material of 2 Sam. 5:11–25 even further rather than splitting the ark narrative in two. Obviously, the Chronicler saw fit to insert that material (his ch. 14) in the middle of the ark narrative, not simply to fill up the three months intervening between each attempt to bring up the ark,[14] but rather to have David's diplomatic and military successes serve as sure signs to David that God was still with him despite the initial fiasco at Peretz-Uzza. Undoubtedly, the triumphant ring of 14:17, "David became famous throughout the lands, and the Lord put the fear of him in all the nations"—a verse which is unique to the Chronicles version (cf. 2 Sam. 5:25), articulates the idea that Yahweh had not turned his favor from David, and thus a renewed attempt at bringing up the ark would not be in vain.[15]

---

[12] This approach is shared by critical and traditional commentators alike, e.g., Curtis and Madsen, *The Books of Chronicles*, 204; Kil, *Dibrê Hayyāmîm*, 294, 303.
[13] See in particular Cogan, "The Chronicler's Use of Chronology," 199–201, 205–07.
[14] Keil, *The Books of the Chronicles*, 198.
[15] See Rothstein and Hänel, *Das erste Buch der Chronik*, 268; Myers, *I Chronicles*, 105–06.

In sum, two motivations are in evidence for the Chronicler's particular manner of displacement. The first is the ideological concern for having David appear as one who gave cultic matters top priority. This picture is in keeping with the Chronicler's portrayal of David as the king who established the Levitical guilds and was the primary force in making preparations for a permanent temple (1 Chr. 22–29). The second motivation is thematically oriented, with the events of 2 Sam. 5:11–25 serving to offset the feelings of despair that David must have felt after his first attempt to bring the ark up to Jerusalem was aborted.

Methods

The splitting of the ark narrative which the Chronicler effected was his most obvious way of accomplishing his twin purposes. However, there is also a somewhat more subtle way by which the thematic motivation was underscored. In incorporating the events of 2 Sam. 5:11–25 where he does as a means of reconfirming David's chosenness, the Chronicler capitalized on the associative link between the ark narrative and the account of the Philistine battles as expressed in the root *pereṣ* ("to break forth," 2 Sam. 5:20; 6:8). It is very conceivable that already the Samuel version's juxtaposition of the Baal-Perazim and Peretz-Uzza events took its cue from the presence of the root *pereṣ* in each pericope.[16] However, by reversing the order of the stories, the Chronicler went beyond mere word association to have the *pereṣ* motif play a meaningful narrative role. For with the "good *pereṣ*" incident now following the "bad *pereṣ*" incident, David could be fully assured that his temporary setback in bringing up the ark was part of the past, not to be repeated again. The operation which began so auspiciously with the call *niprĕṣāh*—"let us send far and wide"—(13:2), could now resume with full force.[17]

---

[16] On this editorial technique, see Cassuto, *Biblical and Canaanite Literatures* (Hebrew), Vol. 1, 200–04.

[17] See Kil, *Dibrê Hayyāmîm*, 296, n. 4 on the use of *pereṣ* as a *Leitwort*.

1 Kings 2:1–9 and 1 Chronicles 22:5–16

Setting

1 Chr. 22–29 is occupied largely by a description of the preparations which David made on behalf of his son Solomon toward the temple building project. Much of this material is unique to Chronicles, without a parallel version being found in the books of Samuel or Kings. Conversely, Chronicles omits the bulk of the so-called "succession narrative" (2 Sam. 9–20),[18] including the narrative in 1 Ki. 1–2 relating to the tangled court intrigues through which Solomon had to navigate both immediately prior to and following his selection as heir to the throne.[19] These striking omissions of Solomon's bumpy road to the throne are in accord with the Chronicler's belief that Solomon's selection as king was preordained by God (1 Chr. 22:9), and thus could brook no human opposition.[20] This is not to say that the Chronicler was unaware of the realpolitik scenario as put forth in Samuel and Kings, but rather that he was selective with the raw material at his disposal. One way of demonstrating the Chronicler's awareness of the narratives he omits is by taking note of the literary allusions or subtle hints to them embedded in his work. For example, Zalewski points to David's words of praise to God in 1 Chr. 29:11b–12 as representing a backhanded stab at Adonijah's claim to the throne. The verses read: "Yes, all that is in heaven and on earth; to You, Lord, belong kingship and preeminence above all. Riches and honor are Yours to dispense; You have dominion over all; with You are strength and might, and it is in Your power to make anyone great and strong." It is perhaps no coincidence that David attributes the only true expression of preeminence (literally, "self-exaltation," Hebrew *hammitnaśśē'*)[21] to Yahweh, as opposed to Adonijah, of whom it is said in 1 Ki. 1:5, "Now Adonijah son of Haggith went about boasting"

---

[18] The term is most closely associated with the work of L. Rost, *Die Überlieferung von der Thronnachfolge Davids*. BWANT 3/6 (Stuttgart: Kohlhammer, 1926). For the subsequent scholarly debate and discussion of Rost's work, see McCarter, *II Samuel*, 9–13; Ackroyd, "The Historical Literature," 302, with bibliography cited.

[19] On the question of the relationship of 1 Ki. 1–2 to the succession narrative, see above note and add Zalewski, *Solomon's Ascension* (Hebrew), 18–31.

[20] Ibid., 220.

[21] Cf. Num. 16:3.

(Hebrew *mitnaśśē' lē'mōr*).²² A similar intent to exclude Adonijah's claim may be inherent in David's words in 1 Chr. 28:5—"And of all my sons—for many are the sons the Lord gave me—He chose my son Solomon to sit on the throne of the kingdom of the Lord over Israel."²³

Another set of such allusions to the Kings narrative is most relevant to our inquiry, since it touches on the question of narrative sequence. 1 Chr. 21, in parallel with 2 Sam. 24, relates the story of David's census and its aftermath, which resulted in the purchase of Ornan's threshing floor. The next chapter, which opens with David's declaration, "Here will be the House of the Lord and here the altar of burnt offerings for Israel" (22:1), continues with David's testament to Solomon, charging him with the task of building the temple (22:6–16). Although the theme of temple building is not duplicated in David's will as recorded in 1 Ki. 2:1–9, it is still possible to detect allusions to that text in the Chronicler's version.²⁴ David's sense of approaching death implied in 1 Chr. 22:5–6—"For David thought, 'My son Solomon is an untried youth, and the House to be built for the Lord is to be made exceedingly great to win fame and glory throughout all the lands; let me then lay aside material for him.' So David laid aside much material before he died. Then he summoned his son Solomon and charged him (*wayĕṣawwēhū*) with building the House for the Lord God of Israel"—brings to mind the opening line of the pericope in Kings—"When David's life was drawing to a close, he charged (*wayĕṣaw*) his son Solomon as follows" (1 Ki. 2:1). 1 Chr. 22:11–13, in particular, appears to make use of 1 Ki. 2:2–3. The clause "if you observantly carry out the laws (*ḥuqqîm*) and the rules (*mišpāṭîm*) which the Lord charged Moses to lay upon Israel" (1 Chr. 22:13) is highly reminiscent of "and following His laws (*ḥuqqōtāyw*), His commandments (*miṣwōtāyw*), His rules (*mišpāṭāyw*), and His admonitions as recorded in the Teaching of Moses" (1 Ki. 2:3). The roots *ḥzq* ("to be strong") and *śkl* ("to be clever or successful") are both employed in the two sources in similar contexts, *ḥăzaq we'ĕmāṣ* (1 Chr. 22:13) // *wĕḥāzaqtā wĕhāyîtā lĕ'îš* (1 Ki. 2:2); *'ak yitten lĕkā YHWH śēkel ûbînāh* (1 Chr. 22:12) // *lĕmaʿan taśkîl* (1 Ki. 2:3).²⁵ 1 Chr. 23 then opens with the

---

²² Zalewski, *Solomon's Ascension* (Hebrew), 322–23.
²³ Ibid., 289.
²⁴ Ibid., 252–56.
²⁵ See Myers, *I Chronicles*, 154, who writes, "It is obviously his [the writer's] intention to imitate the charge of David to Solomon in 1 Kings 2:1–9." See also Michaeli,

statement, "When David was old, full of years, he made his son Solomon king over Israel" (23:1). Here, the allusions appear to revert back to 1 Ki. 1:1 and 43—"King David was now old, advanced in years"; "Our lord King David has made Solomon king."[26] Thus, by incorporating David's face-to-face exhortation to Solomon before the act of *hamlākāh* (designation/coronation), the Chronicler is reversing the order of Kings in which David's testament to Solomon (1 Ki. 2:1–9) is recorded only after the latter has been crowned (1 Ki. 1:39).[27] Even without the aforementioned verbal similarities between Chronicles and Kings, the Chronicler's relocation of David's private charge to Solomon is demonstrated by the very contents of 1 Chr. 23–29, in which following the charge, David is portrayed as taking on official tasks and making a vigorous public appearance. This contrasts sharply with Kings, in which David's charge is given in the throes of his death (1 Ki. 2:10).[28]

Motivation

The explanation for the Chronicler's placement of David's charge lies not in the portions of it which seem to be derived from 1 Ki. 2, but precisely in those passages which are unique to the Chronicler's version. The first portion of the charge as it appears in Chronicles (1 Chr. 22:7–10) constitutes what has been termed a midrash of Nathan's oracle (2 Sam. 7).[29] David offers his personal explanation for why Yahweh denied him the task of temple building, deferring it instead to the son who only here is specifically identified as Solomon (cf. 2 Sam. 7:12–13). The essence of David's charge as it is adopted from 1 Ki. 2 (1 Chr. 22:11–13)

Les Livres des Chroniques, 117. Both texts in turn appear to allude to Deut. 31 and Josh. 1, see Williamson, "The Accession of Solomon," 353.

[26] Coggins, *Chronicles*, 118.

[27] Zalewski, *Solomon's Ascension* (Hebrew), 210. This holds true whether 1 Chr. 23:1 refers to a private nomination of Solomon as crown prince, as opposed to the more public coronation of chaps. 28–29 (Keil, *The Books of the Chronicles*, 252; cf. Zalewski, *Solomon's Ascension* [Hebrew], 223), or whether it serves as a superscription to the events which are spelled out in chaps. 28–29 (Curtis and Madsen, *The Books of Chronicles*, 260). David's words to Solomon in 28:9–10, 20–21, are spoken publicly, and thus do not correspond to 1 Ki. 2 in the way which ch. 22 does.

[28] Cf. Josephus's harmonization, *Antiq.*, Book 7, chapters 14–15, in which the account of 2 Sam. 24 is followed by those of 1 Chr. 22; 1 Ki. 1; 1 Chr. 23–29 (abridged); and 1 Ki. 2, respectively.

[29] Seeligmann, "The Beginnings of Midrash" (Hebrew), 17–18.

expresses David's injunction to Solomon to carry out his divinely-ordained mission of building the temple (note especially the key addition made by the Chronicler to the Kings material in v. 11b, "You shall build the house of the Lord your God as he has spoken concerning you"). This reorientation of David's charge represents a departure of the highest significance from Kings, in which the focus, outside of Solomon's observance of the law, is directed toward Solomon's cunning disposing of David's political enemies. In other words, David's charge as adopted by the Chronicler is transformed from a catalog of earthly score-settling into a program for cultic enterprise. With this new focus, the charge must be incorporated precisely at the point where it is in the Chronicler's narrative, since it can thus serve as an introduction to David's own frantic efforts to put as much of the preparations for the temple building in order as he could prior to his death. In sum, the Chronicler's motivation in antedating David's charge is largely thematic. Once the focus of the charge has been shifted to cultic concerns, its place within the narrative is also transformed from a parting statement of David to an opening statement introducing his efforts made on behalf of Solomon's sacred task.

Method

Adopting the Kings version of the charge wholesale to the new desired location would have been nonsensical for the Chronicler's purpose. He therefore extracted only those passages (1 Ki. 2:2–3) which could be readily incorporated with the new content and focus of the charge as outlined above. This very selective use of the primary source was essential to the displacement process.

1 Kings 22:49–50 and 2 Chronicles 20:35–37

Setting

An interesting case of sequential divergence between Kings and Chronicles occurs in the episode of Jehoshaphat's maritime ventures to Ophir (1 Ki. 22:49–50; 2 Chr. 20:35–37). According to the Kings version:

Jehoshaphat constructed Tarshish ships to sail to Ophir for gold. But he did not sail because the ships were wrecked at Ezion-geber. Then Ahaziah son of Ahab proposed to Jehoshaphat, "Let my servants sail on the ships with your servants"; but Jehoshaphat would not agree.

The Chronicles version reads:

Afterward, King Jehoshaphat of Judah entered into a partnership with King Ahaziah of Israel, thereby acting wickedly.[30] He joined with him in constructing ships to go to Tarshish; the ships were constructed in Ezion-geber. Eliezer son of Dodavahu of Maresha prophesied against Jehoshaphat, "As you have made a partnership with Ahaziah, the Lord will break up your work." The ships were wrecked and were unable to go to Tarshish.

Two notable discrepancies are discernable between the above accounts: 1) Did the contact between Jehoshaphat and Ahaziah occur before (Chr.) or after (Kings) the ships were wrecked? 2) Did this contact result in Jehoshaphat's aligning himself with Ahaziah (Chr.) or spurning Ahaziah's overtures (Kings)?

Commentators with a harmonistic approach were so baffled by these discrepancies that they presumed either that the two sources were relating similar but separate events,[31] or that the Chronicles version supplies the background to the Kings version, to wit: originally Jehoshaphat entered into an alliance with his northern counterpart, but after the ships broke down, he accepted the rebuke of the prophet Eliezer and refused further assistance from Ahaziah.[32] However, neither of these explanations is convincing. The accounts are too similar to be separated in time, yet different enough to preclude harmonization. Both tell of some connection between the kings of Judah and Israel surrounding Tarshish ships which were wrecked at Ezion-geber. However, in the Kings version, Jehoshaphat quite clearly undertakes the shipping enterprise on his own. The wording of v. 50 indicates that Ahaziah's men were not present

---

[30] Our translation follows NJV. See also Myers, II Chronicles, 113. However, it is also possible to take the subject of the phrase hû' hiršîaʿ laʿăśôt as referring to Ahaziah.
[31] E.g., Metzudat David to 2 Chr. 20:37.
[32] Abravanel, Pērûš ʿal Nĕvîʾîm Riʾšônîm, 602; Keil, The Books of the Chronicles, 394.

when the ships were being outfitted for sea. We have no choice, therefore, but to regard the two versions as reflecting two distinct records or two variant interpretations of the same episode. The ramifications for the issue of chronological displacement are obvious, for if we can establish one version as the more credible, the other version will become suspect of having rearranged the time frame during which the contact between Jehoshaphat and Ahaziah occurred.

In this particular case, priority cannot be automatically conferred on the Kings version. To be sure, many scholars have been tempted to hold the Chronicler responsible for antedating the contact between the two kings. In this view, the Chronicler was simply looking for a way to provide a theological explanation for Jehoshaphat's mishap. This explanation accords with the Chronicler's rigid conception of reward and punishment which finds expression throughout the book.[33] However, it has also been suggested that the Kings version purposely goes out of its way to downplay Jehoshaphat's dishonorable relationship with the north by not admitting that Ahaziah took part in the venture from the start. Thus, the Kings version's historical verisimilitude is not necessarily greater than that of Chronicles.[34] This view assumes that the Chronicler was following a slightly variant and more reliable Vorlage than Kings (with the possible exception of the prophetic speech of Eliezer, which may have been of the Chronicler's own composition).

Motivation

The weakness of the latter point concerning an independent Vorlage alleged to have been used by the Chronicler slightly tips the balance in favor of the first view which grants priority to the Kings version. The Vorlage assumed by the second view is hypothetical, with no extant textual witnesses to support it. Moreover, the theme of retribution is much more dominant in Chronicles[35] than a putative desire of Kings to clear Jehoshaphat's reputation. To be sure, Jehoshaphat is regarded by the Deuteronomist as a righteous king (1 Ki. 22:43), but that does not

---

[33] On this aspect of the Chronicler's theology, see Japhet, *The Ideology of the Book of Chronicles* (Hebrew), 133–54 and passim.
[34] Rudolph, *Chronikbücher*, 264–65. Cf. also Benzinger, *Die Bücher der Chronik*, 108–09.
[35] See n. 33 above.

preclude the writer from reporting Jehoshaphat's joining forces with the Omride kings both before and after the shipping incident (1 Ki. 22:4; 2 Ki. 3:7). In sum, then, the Chronicler's antedating (and recasting) of Jehoshaphat's contact with Ahaziah can be said to reflect an ideological motivation, namely providing an explanation for the failure of Jehoshaphat's shipping expedition. The particular advantage of this explanation is that it stems from the words of the text itself, namely the oracle delivered by Eliezer (2 Chr. 20:37).

Method

An important observation on method in this context is made by Halpern[36] who notes that rather than arbitrarily revising the sequence of 1 Ki. 22:49–50, the Chronicler indeed took his lead from the wording of that passage. 1 Ki. 22:45 already notes that "Jehoshaphat made peace with the king of Israel." This notice indicates that an alliance was already in place even prior to the shipping venture. Thus, when the Chronicler arrived at 22:50, which opens with the words 'āz 'āmar 'ăhazyāhû ("Then Ahaziah proposed"), he could infer that the term 'āz was functioning, as it does elsewhere, to introduce a statement which was not necessarily adhering to a strict sequence.[37] In other words, the Chronicler detected in 22:50a at least an allusion to his point of view that the contact between Jehoshaphat and Ahaziah occurred at the outset of the shipping venture. However, the full elaboration of that view, including the novel suggestion that Jehoshaphat in fact accepted Ahaziah's offer rather than rejecting it, represents the free reconstruction of the Chronicler, which was inspired by his ideological mindset as noted above.

---

[36] "A Historiographic Commentary," 131.
[37] For some examples, see Long, *1 Kings*, 24. Although most examples are formed from 'āz + imperfect, there are also a couple of examples of 'āz + perfect as we have in our case, such as 1 Ki. 9:24; 2 Ki. 14:8.

2 Kings 22–23 and 2 Chronicles 34

Setting

A well-known instance of chronological divergence between Chronicles and Kings is the sequence of events in Josiah's cultic reform, or more precisely the point(s) in Josiah's reign at which the reform process got underway. In the Kings account (2 Ki. 22:1–23:20), there is no record of any of Josiah's actions prior to his eighteenth year. In that fateful year, Josiah undertook a refurbishing of the temple, in the course of which the law book was discovered which inspired Josiah to effect a massive purging of all idolatrous cults in Jerusalem and throughout the land. However, according to the Chronicles account (2 Chr. 34:1–33), Josiah "began to seek the God of his father David" (v. 3) already in his eighth year. Furthermore, the essential aspects of Josiah's cultic reform were enacted and completed in the king's twelfth year, six years prior to the temple repairs and the ensuing discovery of the law book.

As can be expected, attempts have been made to harmonize the two accounts. Thus, for example, Josephus in Antiquities 10:52 appears to portray Josiah's earlier reform efforts as more of a private endeavor, with the wholesale public destruction of idolatrous places and vessels occurring only in the eighteenth year. Radak siezes upon the expression *hēḥēl lĕṭahēr*—"he began to purge"—in v. 3 as indicating that the Chronicler merely set out to describe the beginning stages of Josiah's reform, while agreeing with Kings that the reform process was not culminated until after the discovery of the law book in the king's eighteenth year.[38] Malbim is even more explicit in spelling out the harmonistic approach: "The interpretation is that what is related in Kings was also not all carried out in the eighteenth year, for [Josiah] started this in the twelfth year; just that there [in Kings] everything is arranged around the time of completion, and here [in Chronicles], everything is arranged around the time of commencement."[39]

Now, it is true that the Chronicles text might leave some room for seeing the cultic reforms as extending into the eighteenth year. Besides the expression *hēḥēl lĕṭahēr* ("he began to purge," v. 3) pointed out by

---

[38] Radak to 2 Chr. 34:3.
[39] Malbim to 2 Chr. 34:3; cf. also Keil, *The Books of the Chronicles*, 488.

Radak, the language of v. 8—*ûbišnat šĕmōneh ʿeśrēh lĕmolkô lĕṭahēr ʾet hāʾāreṣ wĕhabbāyit* ("In the eighteenth year of his reign, for purifying the land and the temple")—may imply that the purification efforts were still in progress in the eighteenth year. Although some commentators render the infinitive *lĕṭahēr* as denoting "after purging the land and the temple," thus functioning to separate the periods of cultic reform and temple refurbishing,[40] it is equally possible that the temporal reference of *lĕṭahēr* is meant to be coeval with the eighteenth year. In such a case, the infinitive would be rendered "when he was purging the land,"[41] or "while purifying."[42] Another possible indication that the Chronicler allowed for some reform activity in the wake of the discovery of the law book comes in v. 33—"Josiah removed all the abominations from the whole territory of the Israelites...", although as Cogan notes, this verse, "if not a recap, implies at most further mopping up of stray divergent cults."[43]

However, the above points are insufficient for upholding the harmonistic approach. First, the language of 2 Chr. 34:3–7 is so closely related to 2 Ki. 23:6–20[44] that one has no recourse but to conclude that the Chronicler was in effect assigning the *entire* process of reform, from the demolition of the Baal altars to Josiah's return to Jerusalem, to the twelfth year. Second, the Kings account, on its own terms, contains absolutely no hint whatsoever of describing merely the latter stage of a drawn out process.

As was the case with our previous example (2 Chr. 20:35–37), there is a school of thought which gives priority precisely to the Chronicles account. In other words, instead of viewing Kings as the source from which the Chronicler antedated the reform, some scholars posit that the Chronicler was following an independent, reliable Vorlage from which the author of Kings postdated the reform. These scholars point to the geo-political changes which were taking place in the region during the

---

[40] See Metzudat David to 2 Chr. 34:8; Kil, *Dibrê Hayyāmîm*, 903; NJV; Coggins, *Chronicles*, 293; Myers, *II Chronicles*, 201.
[41] Keil, *The Books of the Chronicles*, 491. Cf. Radak, ad loc.
[42] Curtis and Madsen, *The Books of Chronicles*, 507. In support of these latter alternatives, Curtis and Madsen note that the infinitive construct with *lamed* is not used to express the past perfect. Keil, *The Books of the Chronicles*, 491, adds that the infinitive construct with *lamed* can be used to denote approximate time or an action in progress. See *Gesenius' Hebrew Grammar*, 348 (sec. 114 i).
[43] Cogan, "The Chronicler's Use of Chronology," 205, n. 30.
[44] See Rudolph, *Chronikbücher*, 319.

first half of Josiah's reign.[45] Assyrian power was on an irreversible decline. Josiah took advantage of this situation to assert his independence from Assyria both religiously, by ridding the Judean cultus of Assyrian deities, and politically, by embarking on forays into the Samarian province. Therefore, the earlier dating of Josiah's reforms in Chronicles becomes intelligible in light of the putative nationalistic background of these policies. It is the Kings account that telescopes the events of Josiah's first eighteen years, in order to make it appear that the discovery of the law book played the decisive role in inspiring Josiah's reforms.[46] Another line of argument favoring the Chronicles scheme is that Josiah's interest in repairing the temple, which by all accounts preceded the discovery of the law book, itself intimates a reform process in progress.[47]

However, the above approach is not persuasive. First, the historical argument regarding the Assyrians is not airtight, since Josiah's cultic purges can no longer be viewed as being directed specifically against Assyrian dieties.[48] Second, even if Assyrian political power was on the decline, it is questionable whether Samaria was already up for grabs by 627 (Josiah's twelfth year).[49] Third, the notion that a temple refurbishing necessarily goes hand in hand with a cultic purging is somewhat misleading. In the case of Jehoash, for example,[50] there is no intrinsic connection between the attack on the Baal cult, which was carried out at the time of the rebellion against Athalia (2 Ki. 11:18; 2 Chr. 23:17), and Jehoash's plan to repair the temple, which occurred some time later (2 Ki. 12:5–6; 2 Chr. 24:4–5). In the Chronicles account about Josiah, the cleansing of the temple is mentioned only tangentially, since supposedly, Menasseh had reversed his wicked ways and removed pagan objects from the temple (2 Chr. 33:15–16).[51] Whether this presentation is historical or not, it does show that for the Chronicler, at least, Josiah's temple repairs could have been ordered independently of his cultic cleanup. But most of all, the emphasis of the Kings account on the law book serving as

---

[45] The seminal study in this direction was Cross and Freedman, "Josiah's Revolt."
[46] See Alt, "Die Heimat," 256; Coggins, Chronicles, 291–92; Myers, II Chronicles, 205–06; Nicholson, Deuteronomy and Tradition, 13–15.
[47] McKenzie, The Chronicler's Use, 168–69. Cf. Kil, Dibrê Hayyāmîm, 903.
[48] This is the inevitable conclusion emerging from Cogan's demonstration that the cultic innovations of Ahaz and Manasseh (which Josiah reversed) were not related to Assyrian cults (Imperialism and Religion, 72–88).
[49] Rudolph, Chronikbücher, 319–20.
[50] See Kil, above n. 40.
[51] Michaeli, Les Livres des Chroniques, 243–44; Rudolph, Chronikbücher, 319.

Josiah's real impetus makes good sense, especially in light of the fact that the reforms were undertaken in the spirit of Deuteronomy.[52] Moreover, we have already come across one empirical case of the Chronicler antedating a cultic project (1 Chr. 13), and the motivation for the antedating in that case appears to fit the present case admirably (see below). Finally, the structure of 2 Chr. 34 itself betrays its secondary nature. If indeed serious reforms had been undertaken in Josiah's twelfth year, the panic occasioned by the discovery of the law book would be hard to explain. And even if Josiah was confident of his own merits and was afraid only of the sins of past generations (v. 21), Huldah's words in v. 25 once again put the onus of religious backsliding upon the current generation, without any apparent recognition of the reform efforts which had supposedly been in full gear six years earlier.[53] Thus, we are led to the conclusion that Josiah's reforms indeed began in earnest only in his eighteenth year in the wake of the discovery of the law book, and that the Chronicler displaced the heart of the reform account to an earlier point in Josiah's reign.

Motivation

By antedating the reforms to the first half of Josiah's reign, the Chronicler not only portrays Josiah as one who followed the right path from a young age, but as one who did so independently of the demands of the law book. As Cogan notes, "The schematic nature of the Chronicler's chronology and its historiographic underpinnings are readily discernable: they are designed to show the earliness and self-motivation of the king's piety."[54] To be sure, the choice of the "eighth year" and the "twelfth year," as opposed to the "first year" or "the beginning of his reign," could diminish the argument that the Chronicler is constructing

---

[52] See Kaufmann, "The Book of Deuteronomy" (Hebrew), especially 164–66.

[53] J. Tigay, oral remarks cited in Cogan, "The Chronicler's Use of Chronology," 204, n. 30; Rudolph, *Chronikbücher*, 319. Nicholson, *Deuteronomy and Tradition*, 13–15, offers the weak explanation that Huldah's diatribe ignored earlier reform efforts, since those efforts were only politically and not religiously motivated.

[54] Cogan, "The Chronicler's Use of Chronology," 204–05. Cogan also compares the motif of the king's youthful piety to a similar passage in an inscription of Esarhaddon (ibid., n. 31). See also Curtis and Madsen, *The Books of Chronicles*, 502; Rudolph, *Chronikbücher*, 321.

a typological scheme.⁵⁵ However, considering that Josiah took over the kingship when he was a mere boy of eight, it is quite likely that the operation of the government was entrusted for some time to an authoritative council. Thus, the "eighth year," when Josiah turned sixteen, might represent the earliest age at which Josiah was ruling independently. The "twelfth year," when Josiah turned twenty, might represent Josiah's attainment of official majority.⁵⁶

Method

One can always surmise, as we did regarding Esarhaddon's scribes (above, p. 18), that the Chronicler rationalized his antedating by thinking in terms of Josiah's early good *intentions*. However, the Chronicler made a greater effort than that to adapt his scheme to the historical record. The opening description of the twelfth year—"he began to purge" (v. 3)—together with the ambiguous infinitive in v. 8 and the summary notation in v. 33 (above, p. 69), all represent the Chronicler's attempt to soften the impact of his displacement. Although on the one hand, the Chronicler's primary purpose, namely glorifying Josiah, was accomplished by transposing the events of the eighteenth year in their entirety to the twelfth year, on the other hand, the Chronicler's sensitivity to the actual course of events as portrayed by Kings, may have led him to open the door, if ever so slightly, to the harmonistic approach referred to above.

Ezra 4:6–24

The inclusion of documents from the times of Xerxes and Artaxerxes in an earlier context between the reigns of Cyrus and Darius is a prime example of intentional chronological displacement in the Bible which can most likely be demonstrated empirically. However, since the analysis of this passage is so inherently intertwined with the post-Biblical treatments of the same material, we shall be postponing our discussion until chapter three which deals with post-Biblical sources (below, pp. 125–31).

---

⁵⁵ See the reservations of Halpern, "A Historiographic Commentary," 131.
⁵⁶ Cogan, "The Chronicler's Use of Chronology," 204.

Summary of Chapter Two

The results obtained from the analysis of chronological displacements in Chronicles vis-a-vis Samuel and Kings can be summarized in chart form as follows:

Text	Type of Displacement	Motivation	Method
1 Chr. 13–14	a) antedates first installment of David's bringing ark to Jerusalem to before Hiram's delegation and Philistine battles	a) ideological (cultic): to express David's immediate concern for Yahweh	reinterpretation of associative link *pereṣ*
	b) postdates the latter events to middle of ark story	b) thematic: emphasizing that David's setback was only temporary	
1 Chr. 22:5–16	antedates David's charge to Solomon to before the latter's coronation	thematic: to have the charge serve as introduction to David's energetic preparations for temple project	selective use of original text (1 Ki. 2:1–9)
2 Chr. 20:35–37	antedates Jehoshaphat's contact with Ahaziah to before shipwreck	ideological (religious): to provide explanation according to doctrine of retribution	reinterpretation of term '*āz* in 1 Ki. 22:50
2 Chr. 34	antedates the bulk of Josiah's reform by six years	ideological (cultic): to express Josiah's immediate concern for Yahweh	muddling effect of ambiguous infinitive in v. 8, summary notation in v. 33.

In this chapter, we analyzed four cases of chronological displacement in the Book of Chronicles. As was the case with the examples in chapter one from the Mesopotamian royal inscriptions, the direction of the displacements in Chronicles reflects antedating, although in the first example (1 Chr. 13–14), antedating and postdating can be viewed as two sides of the same coin. Only one case provides a clear measurement of the length of time which the displacement compresses (six years in the case of 2 Chr. 34). The other cases provide too little chronological information to measure the extent of the displacements.

The Chronicler's motivations present a combination of ideological and thematic considerations. In certain cases, the focus of the ideological concern corresponds to what was found in Mesopotamian texts (cf. Cogan's insightful comparison of 1 Chr. 13 and 2 Chr. 34 with Esarhaddon's Babylon inscription.)[57] In another case, the ideological concern is unique to the Chronicler's perspective (2 Chr. 20:35–37). The thematic motivations identified here reflect the Chronicler's literary skill in reorganizing his materials to suit his particular historiographic format. The most noteworthy example in this regard is the Chronicler's use of David's charge to Solomon as an introduction to the energetic preparations for building the temple rather than as the political testament of a dying king.

The Chronicler's methods also overlap only partially with those that we encountered in the Mesopotamian material. The possible muddling of sequences in 2 Chr. 34:8, 33 is most similar to the pattern of the royal inscriptions. The very selective use of an original text in 1 Chr. 22:5–16 is somewhat reminiscent of *Atraḫasis*'s omission of the various types mentioned in its parent text. However, the Chronicler's originality stands out in his adaptation of the associative link *pereṣ* from 2 Sam. 5–6 in the case of 1 Chr. 13–14 and in his reinterpretation of *'āz* from 1 Ki. 22:50 in the case of 2 Chr. 20:35–37. This type of detailed engagement of earlier sources (which, to be sure, is never far removed from the Chronicler's ideological motivations) indeed points to the Chronicler's historiographical sophistication.

---

[57] "The Chronicler's Use of Chronology."

Chapter III

Post-Biblical Material

Introduction

In the empirical examples of chronological displacement studied so far, we have come across various types of relationships between the texts which provide opposing chronological frameworks for the same event(s). In the first chapter, we dealt primarily with texts which were contemporaneous with the events which they described and which emanated from the same milieu as each other. Thus, one or the other of the opposing chronological frameworks found in these texts perforce had to represent conscious displacement (e.g., the Nabonidus inscriptions). In the second chapter, we took up texts which were composed much later than the events which they describe and which emanated from disparate literary circles. Nevertheless, since Chronicles was composed as an alternative history to Samuel-Kings, we could generally assume that the author of Chronicles, in presenting an alternative chronological scheme to that of Samuel-Kings, was consciously revising that scheme. In the present chapter, the net is spread much wider to include such diverse materials as the Septuagint (hereafter, LXX), the Apocrypha, Josephus's *Antiquities*, and Rabbinic literature. Each of these sources has a long and complex history and a different type of relationship to the Masoretic text (hereafter, MT).

The LXX is recognized in modern scholarship as containing a variety of translation strata, some of which reflect Hebrew *Vorlagen* older than and independent of those represented by the MT, and others of which reflect greater adherence to MT-type *Vorlagen*.[1] These general conclusions are substantiated both by the findings of diverse "text-types" among the Qumran scrolls,[2] and by text-critical methodologies, such as the study of "translation technique."[3] Given this state of affairs, sequence differences between the LXX and the MT can by no means automatically indicate the priority of the latter's chronological framework over that of the former. In other words, even though the LXX is popularly conceived of as a translation of "the Bible," it is by no means certain that an alternative chronological scheme found in the LXX is secondary to the MT; it could, rather, reflect an ancient, authentic Hebrew tradition whose order of events was changed by the MT.

The books of the Apocrypha and Pseudepigrapha were composed over a long period of time (approximately 350 B.C.E.–150 C.E.)[4] This roughly corresponds to the time when the Biblical text itself was being gradually standardized and canonized.[5] Thus, in theory, when recounting Biblical tales, the authors of the apocryphal and pseudepigraphical books could have drawn from materials akin to the developing MT (so-called "proto-Masoretic" traditions), from rival, ancient traditions embedded in the LXX, from sources outside of both the MT and LXX, or simply from their own creative imagination. Each of these possibilities must be considered in accounting for sequence differences between apocryphal-pseudepigrahical material and the MT.

A similar situation applies to Josephus's *Antiquities*. Modern study of the question of Josephus's sources has established quite clearly that in

---

[1] That the LXX of Kings is based on various recensions of the Hebrew text was first observed by Thackeray, "The Greek Translators," who concluded that the translation to 1 Kings diverges widely from the MT, but that the translation to 2 Kings reflects a later recension which brought the (presumed) original translation into greater harmony with the proto-Masoretic text. Cf. also Shenkel, *Chronology and Recensional Development*, 5–21.

[2] E.g., Cross, "The History of the Biblical Text" and "The Contribution of the Qumran Discoveries."

[3] E.g., Tov, "The Composition of 1 Samuel 16–18;" Kraft, "Septuagint, Earliest Greek Versions," 813–14.

[4] Licht, "*sĕpārîm ḥîṣônîm ûgĕnûzîm*," 1104.

[5] On the standardization of the text, see Cross, "The Contribution of the Qumran Discoveries." On the canonization process, see Leiman, *The Canonization of Hebrew Scripture*.

addition to the MT,[6] Josephus's presentation derives from the LXX,[7] apocryphal and pseudepigraphical traditions,[8] Jewish midrashic tradition,[9] or from his own free composition based on Greek historiographic methods and his own overall *Tendenz*.[10] This conclusion holds true despite Josephus's statement in *Antiquities* 1:17 that he will set forth "in the proper place the precise details of what is in the Scriptures...neither adding nor omitting anything."[11] On the surface, Josephus would appear to preclude anything but a literal recapitulation of the Biblical narrative. There would be no room for variant traditions, chronological rearrangement, and the like. However, Josephus's disclaimer could be just a stereotypical expression, intended to establish his authenticity.[12] Or he may be using the term "Scriptures" in a wide sense to include not only the written Bible but Jewish tradition generally, including such sources as the Jewish *midrashim*.[13] Moreover, Josephus is sensitive to Greek historiographic method, which allowed for the embellishment and polishing of one's sources in order to produce greater coherence and thematic unity.[14] Indeed, Josephus himself admits that certain of Moses's writings would require rearrangement by subject (*Antiq.* 4:197).[15] Thus, instances of chronological variance between Josephus and the Bible could be explained either as a reflection of alternative sources or as independent revisions.

Rabbinic literature, although occasionally preserving ancient traditions in a more explicit fashion than the Bible itself,[16] is most likely

---

[6] For evidence of the canonization prior to Josephus, see Leiman, *The Canonization of Hebrew Scripture*, 31–34; idem, "Josephus and the Canon of the Bible."

[7] See the bibliography cited by Feldman in *Josephus and Modern Scholarship*, 131–33, 165–70.

[8] E.g., Feldman, "Josephus' *Jewish Antiquities* and Pseudo-Philo's *Biblical Antiquities*," 67.

[9] Ibid., 63. Cf. idem, "Prolegomenon" to the reissue of M.R. James's *The Biblical Antiquities of Philo*, The Library of Biblical Studies, (New York: KTAV, 1971), LX–LXI.

[10] See Heinemann, "Josephus's Method in the Description of the Antiquities of the Jews" (Hebrew); idem, *Darkê Hā'aggādāh*, 45–46, 145–46; Shaye J.D. Cohen as summarized by Feldman, *Josephus and Modern Scholarship*, 130. For specific examples, see Feldman, "Josephus' *Jewish Antiquities* and Pseudo-Philo's *Biblical Antiquities*," 73–75.

[11] See Josephus, Loeb Classics ed., Vol. 4, 9; Cohen, *Josephus in Galilee*, 24.

[12] Cohen, *Josephus in Galilee*, 27–29.

[13] For a survey of opinions, see Feldman, *Josephus and Modern Scholarship*, 121–24.

[14] Cohen, *Josephus in Galilee*, 29–33.

[15] Ibid., 32–33.

[16] See Cassuto's remarks on the Rabbinic reflexes of the myth of the primeval battle between Yahweh and the sea, which, he argues, go back to the Ugaritic Ba'al

functioning as a commentary on the received MT. This, after all, was the guiding force behind the entire Rabbinic enterprise, namely to elucidate the Bible in its accepted form.

In sum, in evaluating the relative priority of and relationship between opposing chronological schemes found in the MT and post-Biblical sources, three possibilities present themselves:

1) The post-Biblical sources represent or rely on an ancient line of tradition, which reflects the original sequence of events. In such a case, the MT would have to be regarded as the locus of displacement, having modified the order of the original sequence. This scenario is relatively most likely for alternative chronological schemes found in the LXX, less likely for those found in the Apocrypha and Josephus, and least likely for those found in Rabbinic literature.

2) The chronological framework found in the MT reflects the original sequence. The post-Biblical sources (or their sources) consciously modified this sequence.

3) The chronological framework found in the MT is ambiguous or otherwise problematic. The post-Biblical sources used their own judgement in making a determination. Thus, while it may be impossible to arrive at the original sequence of events, we would still be able to point to an empirical displacement of the MT's presentation by the post-Biblical sources, resulting from what they perceived to be the MT's own internal displacement.

One can also not exclude a combination of the above possibilities, for example, in a situation where only part of the MT presentation is either non-original or problematic. In such a case, the corresponding post-Biblical presentation could reflect a combination of an ancient tradition together with ad hoc exegetical resolutions.

Our analyses of sequence variations in post-Biblical sources will proceed according to the order of the material as it appears in the Bible, with our first example taken from material in Genesis which is paralleled in the pseudepigraphical Book of Jubilees.

---

epic: Cassuto, *Biblical and Canaanite Literatures*, Vol. 1, 71–72. For a full discussion of the Ugaritic material, see Day, *God's Conflict*, 4–18.

Genesis 35–41 and Jubilees 34–41

Introduction

The Book of Jubilees is a pseudepigraphical work evidently composed in the second half of the second century B.C.E.[17] It recounts the episodes contained in the Biblical book of Genesis according to a formal chronological structure, dating each event by the year of the jubilee cycle in which it occurred. Although the book draws mostly from Genesis, it also shares certain traditions found only in other pseudepigraphical literature. For example, Jubilees 4:17–26 summarizes the Book of Enoch.[18] The wars of Jacob's sons described in Jubilees 38 are reminiscent of material found in the Testament of Judah.[19] However, such links hardly increase the historical veracity of the traditions involved. For example, the wars just mentioned have been shown to reflect those of John Hyrcanus against Edom. In other words, Jubilees' description of the wars between the sons of Jacob and Esau is colored by the second century struggles between Judea and Edom.[20] In addition, the author of Jubilees is not averse to composing material from his own imagination for the sake of artistic expansion, such as the details of Reuben's infatuation with Bilhah (Jub. 33:2–6).[21] Thus, the probability of Jubilees preserving authentic ancient traditions independent of the Biblical Genesis is extremely slim, and we shall proceed from the assumption that chronological divergencies between Genesis and Jubilees reflect conscious displacements by the latter.

Setting

The Book of Jubilees makes two significant rearrangements of the material parallel to Gen. 35 (end) through Gen. 41. First, in contrast to Genesis, which records the death of Isaac (Gen. 35:29) before the sale of

---

[17] See Charles, *Apocrypha and Pseudepigrapha*, Vol. 2, 6; Metzger, *The Apocrypha* (RSV), xix; Goldman in A. Kahana (ed.), *Hassĕpārîm Haḥîsônîm*, Vol. 1, 217–18.
[18] Charles, *Apocrypha and Pseudepigrapha*, 7.
[19] Licht, "Yôblîm," 585.
[20] Klein apud Licht, ibid.
[21] Ibid., 583.

Joseph (Gen. 37), Jubilees reverses the order and explicitly dates Isaac's death thirteen years after Joseph's sale. Specifically, Joseph's sale is said to have occurred in the seventh year of the sixth "week" (cycle), i.e., in the forty-second year of the forty-fourth jubilee (or A.M. 2149; Jub. 34:1, 10; cf. 30:1), while Isaac's death followed in the sixth year of the first "week" of the forty-fifth jubilee (or A.M. 2162; Jub. 36:1, 18; cf. 35:1). Second, in contrast to Genesis, which tells about Judah and his family (Gen. 38) before the experiences of Joseph in Egypt through the time he was appointed viceroy (Gen. 39–41), Jubilees first tells of Joseph's experiences in Egypt (Jub. 39–40) and only then moves on to the events concerning Judah's family (Jub. 41), which it explicitly dates to after the time when Joseph achieved his high position. Specifically, Joseph's elevation is said to have occurred in the same year that Isaac died (Jub. 40:11–12), i.e., in the sixth year of the forty-fifth jubilee (A.M. 2162; see above), while the events in Judah's family are said to have begun in the ninth year of that jubilee (A.M. 2165; Jub. 41:1) and to have lasted over the next five years (41:7–8, 21).

In sum, then, the presentation of Jubilees 34–41 (not including the additional material not found in Genesis) reflects a sequence Gen. 37:12–35; 35:29; 36:31–43; 37:1–2a (used as a linking device; see below n. 25); 39–41; 38. Thus, Gen. 35:29 (the death of Isaac) and Gen. 38 (the events in Judah's family) are seen to be displaced from their original context in Genesis.

Motivations

Since the Book of Jubilees purports to present events according to a strict chronological framework, the first motivation to come to mind in accounting for a chronologically-related divergence from the Bible is that the author of Jubilees was attempting to rectify what he perceived to be an internal Biblical displacement. This explanation is indeed convincing in connection with Jubilees' placement of the death of Isaac. Rashi, in his commentary to the Pentateuch, makes the most detailed case for Gen. 35:29 being internally displaced according to the Bible's own sequence:

And Isaac expired: There is no such thing as "earlier" or "later" (chronological order) in the narratives of the Torah, and the sale of Joseph preceded Isaac's death by twelve years. Thus: at Jacob's birth Isaac was sixty years old...(Gen. 25:26). Isaac died when Jacob was 120, for if you deduct 60 from 180 (Isaac's age when he died), you have left 120. Joseph was 17 years old when he was sold (Gen. 37:2), and that year was the one hundred and eighth of Jacob's life. This may...be derived...from Scripture thus: From the time when Joseph was sold until the time when Jacob came to Egypt was 22 years, for it is said (Gen. 46:46), "And Joseph was 30 years old [when he stood before Pharaoh]" (and therefore he had been in Egypt 13 years, as he was 17 when he was sold), and the seven years of plenty and two of famine had elapsed before Jacob came to Egypt (cf. Gen. 45:6), making 22 years. And it is written (Gen. 47:9) that Jacob on his arrival in Egypt said to Pharaoh, "The days of the years of my sojournings are a hundred and thirty years." It follows that at the time when Joseph was sold Jacob was 108 years old.[22]

It is most interesting to note how Jubilees' reckoning of a thirteen year separation between Joseph's sale and Isaac's death comes out to just about the same total as Rashi's computations (twelve years). Thus, it is quite likely that the author of Jubilees was likewise engaging in a processing of the Biblical data, and that his presentation reflects an exegetical conclusion similar to Rashi's. We shall return to consider the motivation for the internal Biblical displacement noted here in the last chapter of the book (see below, pp. 151–52).

By contrast, Jubilees' placement of Gen. 38 does not appear to be governed by strict chronological calculations. To be sure, many commentators have noted that Gen. 38 interrupts the flow of the Joseph story and is only loosely connected to it sequentially through the vague formula *wayĕhî bā'ēt hahî'* ("About that time"—Gen.38:1).[23] Nevertheless, the way in which Jubilees squeezes the entire scope of Gen. 38:6–30 into a mere five years hardly seems chronologically credible (cf.

---

[22] The translation of Rashi follows the Rosenbaum and Silbermann English edition, *Pentateuch with Rashi's Commentary*, Vol. 1, 173.
[23] But cf. Alter's critique and discussion in *The Art of Biblical Narrative*, 3–12.

in particular Gen. 38:12, which speaks in terms of "a long time afterward"). Moreover, if all or some of the events of Gen. 38 are to be relocated anywhere, the more appropriate place (chronologically speaking) would be *before* the sale of Joseph rather than sixteen years after it. As Ibn Ezra astutely points out, the twenty-two years allowed for by Biblical chronology between Joseph's sale and the arrival of Jacob's family in Egypt (see Rashi's comment above) would hardly leave enough time for Judah to have produced grandchildren from Peretz (cf. Gen. 46:12) who himself was born only after a lengthy interval following the death of Judah's two elder sons (Gen. 38:12–30).[24] Actually, the Bible's apparent internal displacement is only partial, since only some of the interval covered in Gen. 38 must have preceded Joseph's sale. Here, however, where the focus is on the motivation for Jubilees' displacement, it is worth noting once again how the author of Jubilees chooses to be oblivious to the long span of time presupposed by Gen. 38. The precise motivation for Jubilees' dating of this material might be hinted at in Jub. 41:22, where it is stated that the five years which Jubilees allows for the events of Gen. 38 overlapped with the seven years of plenty following Joseph's elevation (cf. also 41:1,, 21; 42:1). The Bible itself provides little detail about the seven years of plenty (Gen. 41:47–53). The author of Jubilees could have been siezing upon the Judah narrative, which is not clearly dated in the Bible, in order to fill in this tantalizing gap. Thus, the motivation for the displacement in this case could derive from Jubilees' penchant for providing as much narrative detail as possible for those years which are only scantily documented in the Bible.[25]

---

[24] Ibn Ezra to Gen. 38:1. Cf. Talmon, "The Presentation of Synchroneity," 18–19.

[25] The motivation cannot be said to be simply to keep the Joseph narrative uninterrupted, since if that were the case, Jubilees still could have placed the Judah narrative where it does but assigned it to an earlier year. Jubilees doesn't hesitate to jump back and forth between earlier and later events. For example, the death of Isaac (36:1–18) is followed in the narration by Leah's death five years later (36:21–24), after which the narration reverts back to the squabbles that ensued immediately following Isaac's death (chs. 37–38). Likewise, Jubilees tells of Joseph's sale in 34:10–14 but then briefly recapitulates it in 39:1–2 (by quoting Gen. 37:1–2a; 39:1) in order to proceed with the Joseph narrative, despite having covered events that followed Joseph's sale in the interim (chs. 35–38).

Methods

Jubilees' dating of events according to the jubilee cycle provided a built-in method for the author to arrange and rearrange the sequence of events. Whether the (re)arrangement reflected bona fide calculations (as with Isaac's death) or creative manipulation (as with the Judah episode) didn't matter as much as the impression of authenticity generated by the jubilee dates. In addition, as we have already noted for the material from Gen. 38, the author of Jubilees could capitalize on the inherent vagueness of the Biblical text regarding the proper sequential relationship of the Judah episode to the Joseph narrative. The average reader of the Biblical text would probably notice that Gen. 38 interrupts the flow of Gen. 37, 39ff. But only the very astute reader would realize (as Ibn Ezra did) that the events of Gen. 38 could not possibly belong, at least in their entirety, to the period following Joseph's sale, much less to the period following his elevation.

Joshua 8:30–35; Tôseftā' Sôṭāh 8:7–8; and Josephus, Antiquities 5:68–70

Setting

Josh. 8:30–35 tells of Joshua's building of an altar in the vicinity of Mt. Ebal, offering sacrifices and inscribing a "copy of the teaching of Moses" thereon, and reciting the blessing and curse formulas—all in accordance with the commands of Moses in Deuteronomy 27. In the MT sequence, the section appears after the narrative of Joshua's successful counterattack against Ai, the second of the great battles of conquest (Josh. 8:1–29). By contrast, the; Tôseftā' Sôṭāh 8:7–8 locates the event described in our section earlier, immediately after the Israelites crossed the Jordan into Canaan:

> Come and see how many miracles were done for Israel on that (very) day. They crossed the Jordan and came to Mt. Gerizim, a distance of sixty *mil*, and no one stopped them…They brought the stones which they had taken from the Jordan, built the altar (with those stones), and offered on it burnt and peace sacri-

fices. They took down the stones and came and slept in their encampment...in Gilgal, as it is written, "These twelve stones which the children of Israel took, Joshua erected in Gilgal" (Josh. 4:20), which teaches that they put up (the stones) in Gilgal.[26]

Specifically, then, this Rabbinic tradition would locate the events of Josh. 8:30–35 between Josh. 4:19 (the crossing of the Jordan) and 4:20 (the erection of the stones at Gilgal). This is also the implication of the Mishnah Sôṭāh 7:5, which describes the blessing and curse ceremony and the altar construction in very similar terms (including the dismantling of the altar and the return to Gilgal), although the Mishna doesn't use the specific phrase "on that (very) day." The other relevant Rabbinic source is in the Jerusalem Talmud, Sôṭāh 7:3 (p. 30a–b), in which Rabbi Judah and Rabbi Elazar clash over whether the Israelites actually made a 120 mil round trip to Mt. Gerizim on the day they crossed the Jordan, or whether they held the blessing and curse ceremony in the vicinity of Gilgal under the shadow of *artificial* mounds which they called "Gerizim" and "Ebal." Both positions presuppose that the events of Josh. 8:30–35 occurred on the day that the Israelites crossed the Jordan. They only differ on the specific locale of the events.

An alternative position is espoused by Rabbi Ishmael (as explained by Rabbi Mana), who holds that at most, only a part of Moses's commands in Deut. 27 was executed immediately, namely the erecting of stones (Deut. 27:2). The remaining commands, namely the blessing and cursing ceremony, occurred only after the conquest was completed.[27] Thus, according to Rabbi Ishmael, Josh. 8:30–35, if anything, reflects events which occurred later than its setting in the Book of Joshua.

Finally, Josephus places the ceremony described in Josh. 8:30–35 after his account of Joshua's last battle and in conjunction with the material found at the beginning of Josh. 18 concerning the establishment of the Shiloh shrine (*Antiq.* 5:68–70). Josephus's position is thus similar to that of Rabbi Ishmael, although Josephus goes even further by presenting the original command of Moses in Deut. 27 as referring specifically to the time when the Israelites will have taken possession of the land of

---

[26] Zuckermandel ed., 311. Cf. the parallel in B. Sôṭāh 36a.
[27] P. Sôṭāh 7:3. Also *Midraš Tannā'îm*, 58, cited by Lieberman, *Tôseptā' Kipšûṭā'* Vol. 8 (New York: Jewish Theological Seminary of America, 1973), 697.

Canaan, and will have destroyed the whole multitude of its inhabitants (Antiq. 4:305).

In evaluating the relative priority of the variant sequences based on the possibilities outlined above (p. 78), it is practically certain that neither the Rabbinic sources nor Josephus reflects the original order of events. For one, the sequences they suggest have no precedent in the LXX or other versions, all of which agree, with slight variations, with the MT's order.[28] Even the supposition that the sequences in the Rabbinic sources and Josephus might be based on ancient oral traditions can be discounted, since as we shall see (below, pp. 86–88), these sequences are designed to address tensions in the Biblical text itself regarding the time frame of the event described in Josh. 8:30–35. It is necessary, then, to question whether or not the MT appears to reflect an original sequence in order to understand why the rabbis and Josephus deviated from it. Modern scholarship has by and large treated Josh. 8:30–35 as an interpolation which doesn't sit well in its present location. The reasons adduced for this conclusion can be labeled as textual, geographical-historical, and typological.[29]

a) *Textual.* The section, along with 9:1–2, appears to be parenthetical, interrupting the flow between 8:29 and 9:3.[30] This impression is strengthened by the vague opening chronological term 'āz ("then," 8:30) and by the variant location of the section in LXX (*after* 9:2), which suggests a fluidity regarding the section's proper placement.[31]

b) *Geographical-historical.* It is unlikely that Joshua and the people would have made the trek from Ai to Shechem (some 20 miles north) at this juncture, particularly when the intervening territory of Mt. Ephraim is not yet said to have been under Israelite control.

c) *Typological.* The section describes a quintessential covenant-ratifying ceremony in the area of Shechem. As such, it is best treated in

---

[28] LXX[B] puts the section Josh. 8:30–35 following 9:2. However, this variance doesn't essentially affect the *chronological* placement of the event. See Boling, *Joshua*, 246.

[29] The textual and geographical-historical claims were made as early as the first half of the nineteenth century (see the opinions quoted in Keil, *Joshua*, 218–19) and have been repeated ever since without much variation, e.g., Bright, *The Book of Joshua*, 595. The typological argument is of more recent vintage, stemming from the tradition-history school (see below, notes 32 and 34).

[30] The latter verse refers directly back to the events culminating in 8:29, introducing the episode of the Gibeonite deception as the the result of the fear inspired by the fate of Jericho and Ai.

[31] See most recently Tov, "Some Sequence Differences," 152–54.

conjunction with the last chapter of Joshua (ch. 24), which describes just such a ceremony at a more appropriate occasion, i.e., prior to Joshua's death.[32]

Of the above arguments, the textual ones do not really affect the question of *chronological* displacement. Just because a section may be a later addition does not necessarily mean that the events it describes are out of sequence with the surrounding context. The geographical-historical and typological arguments are rather weak. Mt. Ephraim was either sparsely populated (Josh. 17:14–18) or occupied by inhabitants friendly to the Israelites.[33] In any event, the book of Joshua has no record of this area being conquered by the Israelites, presumably because that was unnecessary. The putative connection of 8:30–35 with ch. 24 is purely conjectural and even arbitrary in view of the facts that both events are treated as separate one-time affairs and Shechem is not even mentioned by name in our section.[34]

If, then, the authenticity of the MT's chronological framework isn't in serious doubt, what would have inspired the rabbis and Josephus to offer divergent sequences? We now turn to this question.

Motivations

There is one overriding factor which guided the rabbis and Josephus in their treatment of Josh. 8:30–35, and that is the relationship of the passage to Deut. 27. The latter chapter, particularly its first eight verses, present an array of problems, including the repetition of some of the prominent commands. The erecting of stones which are are to be coated with plaster is commanded in vv. 2 and 4. The inscribing of "all the words of this teaching" on the stones is commanded in vv. 3 and 8.

---

[32] Soggin, *Joshua*, 220f. Cf. Keller, "Über einige alttestamentliche Heiligtumslegenden I," 146.

[33] Albright, cited in Bright, *The Book of Joshua*, 595.

[34] Kaufmann, *Sēper Yĕhôšuʿa*, 132. For the same reasons, I shall leave Soggin's explanation for the present placement of the unit 8:30–35 out of consideration. He claims ("Zwei umstrittene Stellen," 87) that the Shechem-connected event in 8:30–35 was combined with the Ai tradition (8:1–29) to which Bethel traditions were mistakenly transferred. This explanation depends on Alt's imaginative reconstruction of a regular pilgrimage between Bethel and Shechem which is supposedly embedded in the text of Gen. 35:1–5 (Alt, "Die Wallfahrt von Sichem nach Bethel," *Kleine Schriften zur Geschichte des Volkes Israel* [Munich, C.H. Beck, 1953], Vol. 1, 79–88).

These repetitions, noted already by the traditional medieval commentators,[35] have led most modern scholars to treat vv. 2–3a as a separate unit, presumably once independent of vv. 4–8.[36] Vv. 2–3 stand out in two more crucial ways. First, only v. 2 specifies that the stones are to be erected on the very day (*bayyôm*) that the people cross the Jordan,[37] as opposed to the more general "upon your crossing the Jordan" of v. 4. Second, vv. 2–3 do not single out Mt. Ebal as the site for erecting the stones as does v. 4. Many intricate historical-critical explanations have been offered by modern scholars for these differences.[38] However, the rabbis, for whom the Torah text represented a unified whole, were bound to take account of the oddities of vv. 2–3 in explaining how Joshua indeed carried out everything which Moses commanded. Thus, the dominant opinion, namely that the events of Josh. 8:30–35 were accomplished on the very day of crossing the Jordan, stems from the conception that Deut. 27:2 was enacted literally (even if this necessitates presuming a journey of miraculous proportions on the one hand, or a far-fetched interpretation of the geographic indicators "Mt. Gerizim" and "Mt. Ebal" on the other hand). The minority opinion of Rabbi Ishmael (as explained by Rabbi Mana), according to which the events of Josh. 8:30–35 occurred only at the end of the conquest period, is forced to conclude that the time limitations of Deut. 27 refer exclusively to the erection of stones. However, this approach essentially avoids the problem of repeti-

---

[35] E.g., Abravanel, *Pērûš ʿal Hattôrāh*, Vol. 3, 240.

[36] Cf. Driver, *Deuteronomy*, 295; von Rad, *Deuteronomy*, 165; Rofé, *Introduction to Deuteronomy* (Hebrew), 19. For overall literary-critical treatments of vv. 1–8, see Nielsen, *Shechem*, 52–55.

[37] It is Driver, *Deuteronomy*, 295, who argues forcefully that *bayyôm* must be taken literally as per its usage in 2 Sam. 19:20; Esth. 9:1; as opposed to the more general *běyôm* followed by an infinitive construct or the like (e.g., Gen. 2:4; Num. 3:1), which can mean "in the time when."

[38] According to Eissfeldt ("Gilgal or Shechem?," 96–97), vv. 2–3 are the original kernel of a command to build an altar at Gilgal. These verses were overlaid by vv. 4–8, which refer secondarily to the Shechem area under the influence of the once separate command to hold a blessing and curse ceremony in that region (cf. Deut. 27:11–13; 11:29–32). Eissfeldt's position is a variation of those of Meyer and Mowinckel, which are adopted by Nielsen, *Shechem*, 65–66. According to Rofé (*Introduction to Deuteronomy* [Hebrew], 19, 24), vv. 2–3 are the later revision of vv. 4–8 by a Deuteronomic compiler who was uncomfortable with the notion of singling out Mt. Ebal as the site for a cultic ceremony. This same compiler was at work in tampering with the text of Deut. 11:30, specifically by adding the problematic phrases *bě'ereṣ hakkěnaʿănî hayyōšēb bāʿărābāh mûl haggilgāl* ("in the land of the Canaanites who dwell in the Arabah, near Gilgal"), which remove the focus from the Shechem area. But cf. Kaufmann, *Sēper Yěhôšuʿa*, 132.

tion between vv. 2–3 and 4–8 and even exacerbates it. Were the words of the "Torah" to be inscribed on stones immediately after crossing the Jordan (vv. 2–3) as well as on the stones of the altar to be set up later on Ebal (v. 8)? And were both sets of stones to be coated with plaster (vv. 2, 4)? Tellingly, the text itself referring to the stones erected immediately at Gilgal (Josh. 4:20) has absolutely nothing to say about them being inscribed or plastered.

Nevertheless, as far removed as the Rabbinic interpretations seem to be from the plain meaning of Scripture, their motivation is eminently clear, namely to harmonize the actions of Joshua with the instructions of Moses. Ironically, this was probably the intention of the Biblical author/redactor himself who inserted the narrative of Josh. 8:30–35 at the first possible point that it could have occurred given the geo-military situation facing Joshua.[39] Perhaps the use of the vague 'āz ("then") in v. 30 was meant precisely to mitigate the temporal gap between the ideal of Moses's command bayyôm ("on that very day"—Deut. 27:2) and the geo-military reality, which forced Joshua to delay the ceremony until a slightly later time.

As for Josephus, who did not have the same qualms as the rabbis about altering the Biblical text, the whole matter of relating Josh. 8:30–35 to Deut. 27 could be dealt with in what seemed to be the most rational way from an historical and military standpoint.[40] Josephus's wholesale revision of Deut. 27, in which he not only dispenses with the problematic bayyôm of v. 2 but spells out a time frame subsequent to the conquest, represents no more than the personal judgement of Josephus as an historian as to when the provisions of Deut. 27 would have been most appropriate. In this regard, Josephus somewhat anticipates those modern scholars who feel that the entire episode of Josh. 8:30–35 fits better with a period later in Joshua's career. Thus, Josephus's motivation can be described as historical-exegetical, to the extent that he felt that his proposed sequence was clarifying and indeed improving on the sequence reflected by the MT.

---

[39] Kaufmann, Sēper Yĕhôšuʿa, 132, Noth, Das Buch Josua, 52.
[40] Josephus's military perspective as a professional army commander is well known.

Methods

The methods of the rabbis and Josephus are in consonance with their presuppositions and motivations. The rabbis, for whom the Joshua narrative had to be read as a literal fulfillment of Deut. 27, forced one text or the other into the procrustean bed of harmonization (either Josh. 8:30–35 occurred on the *bayyôm* of Deut. 27:2, or the *bayyôm* of Deut. 27:2 is to be severed from its overall context which refers to the building of an altar, blessings and curses, etc.). Josephus, for whom historical and military logic was paramount, took the liberty of recasting both Moses's command and Joshua's fulfillment of it in order to put the spotlight on the period following the conquest, for which Josephus deemed the events in question to be best suited.

Judges 17–21; Sēder ʿÔlām, ch. 12; and Josephus, Antiquities 5:132–179

Setting

The last five chapters of the book of Judges narrate the following events: The incident of Micah's idol (ch. 17) leading into the story of the Danites' resettlement in northern Israel (ch. 18) and the incident of the atrocity committed by the people of Gibeah in Benjamin against an innocent man's concubine (ch. 19), leading to full-scale civil war between the Benjaminites and the other tribes of Israel (chaps. 19–20). The LXX follows the MT, with the events of Judges 17–21 appearing at the end of the book. However, other post-Biblical sources arrange the material in different ways. Pseudo-Philo follows the order of the MT, but omits Judges 18 (the Danite migration). In other words, his order is Judges 1–17, 19–21. *Sēder ʿÔlām Rabbāh* (a second century C.E. Midrashic chronology, hereafter referred to as S.O.)[41] has the events of Judges 17–21 occurring earlier, in the time of Cushan-Rishatayim, reflecting the order Judges 1:1–3:11; 17–21; 3:12–16:31. Josephus has the events of Judges 18–21 (omitting ch. 17 and those parts of ch. 18 relating to Micah's idol) occurring even earlier, before the time of Cushan-Rishatayim. Josephus also takes up the concubine incident (chaps. 19–

---
[41] See Milikowsky, "Seder Olam," 12–17.

21) before the Danite migration (ch. 18). Thus, he reflects the order Judges 1:1–2:3; 19–21; 18 (selected portions); 3:7–16:31.

In evaluating the relative priority of these variant time frames and their relationship to each other, we return to the three possibilities outlined at the beginning of this chapter (above, p. 78). Either (a) S.O. and/or Josephus preserve the original sequence of events which is reversed by the MT, or (b) the MT preserves the original sequence which is reversed by S.O. and/or Josephus, or (c) S.O. and/or Josephus attempt to clarify the MT's sequential ambiguity. Of these three possibilities, the latter one is the most appropriate to choose as a working hypothesis. The first possibility is weakened by the overall tendency of S.O. to operate as a commentary on the Bible rather than as an independent rendition.[42] As for Josephus, the agreement of LXX with the MT in our case all but precludes the possibility that he was drawing from an independent textual prototype. Whatever independent *oral* tradition Josephus may have had is obviously beyond recovery. Thus, the assumption that Josephus's modification of the MT's sequence relies on ancient oral tradition would take us beyond the range of empiricism. All we can say is that with or without such an oral tradition, Josephus winds up altering the sequence of the Masoretic text with which he was clearly familiar. The second possibility is weakened by the very suggestive, though not independently verifiable, arguments against the sequence found in the MT. Indeed, some of these arguments serve as linchpins for the presentations of S.O. and Josephus (see presently), a fact which heightens our preference for the third possibility stated above.

The key factor in substantiating the third possibility is analyzing how S.O. and Josephus themselves justify their presentations. Although the apparent reasonings of S.O. and Josephus are noticeably different, they do share the common denominator of being spurred by considerations derived from the material itself. The source in S.O. (ch. 12) reads:

> In the days of Cushan-Rishataim was Micah's idol as it says, "And the Danites set up the idol for themselves," etc. [Judges 18:30. The rest of the quoted verse reads: "and Jonathan son of Gershom son of Manasseh, and his descendants, served as priests to the Danite tribe until the land went into exile."] And

---

[42] Cf. ibid., 1–2.

in his [Cushan-Rishataim's] time was the (incident of the) concubine in Gibeah; "He rose up and departed and arrived opposite Jebus, that is, Jerusalem. And his master said to him…" [Judges 19:10, 12. The rest of the latter verse reads: "We will not turn aside to a town of aliens who are not of Israel, but will continue to Gibeah."]⁴³

In quoting Jud. 18:30, S.O. appears to be relying on the tradition that Jonathan son of Gershom son of Manasseh was none other than the grandson of Moses.⁴⁴ In such a case, the events of Judges 17–18 must have occurred closer to the conquest period than to the close of the Judges period. In fact, the only likely reason why S.O. assigns the events precisely to the days of Cushan-Rishatayim rather than even earlier is because of the Biblical testimony that "The people served the Lord during the lifetime of Joshua and the lifetime of the elders who lived on after Joshua" (Judges 2:7).⁴⁵ The same reasoning holds true for an alternative version of S.O., which brings Jud. 18:31 as a prooftext rather than Jud. 18:30.⁴⁶ This verse reads: "They [the Danites] maintained the sculptured image that Micah had made throughout the time that the House of God stood at Shiloh." Now, we do not know precisely when the Shiloh temple was erected, but S.O. (end of ch. 11) clearly connects this event with the housing of the tabernacle at Shiloh in the time of Joshua (Josh. 18:1).⁴⁷ As we have just observed, since S.O. cannot countenance such apostasy as we encounter in Jud. 17–18 during the days of Joshua, the second version too (quoting Jud. 18:31) appears to zero in precisely on the days of Cushan-Rishatayim, since that was the first opportunity for apostasy during "the time that the House of God stood at Shiloh."

As for the time frame of the concubine incident, we must presume that S.O. *a priori* viewed it as closely linked with that of Micah's idol, since the Bible itself places the two episodes virtually back to back. And

---

⁴³ Ibid., 482–83.

⁴⁴ The reading "Manasseh" is only the result of a "suspended *nun*" added to the name "Moses" in order to protect Moses' honor. See Ginsburg, *Introduction to the Massoretico-Critical Edition*, 334–38; Smith, *The Early History of God*, 35, n. 66.

⁴⁵ Although there is a midrashic tradition that Micah's idol was already in existence prior to the Israelites' departure from Egypt, this is still not the same as public worship of the idol in its own special temple. See Ginzberg, *Legends of the Jews*, Vol. 4, 49–50 with notes 127–128 in Vol. 6, 209–10.

⁴⁶ See Ratner ed., 52, n. 7; Rashi to Jud. 17:1.

⁴⁷ Milikowsky ed., 481–82. See also Radak to Jud. 17:1.

indeed, S.O. cites a prooftext (Jud. 19:10,12) by which it intends to demonstrate the early time frame of the narrative. The reasoning of S.O. here is that Jebusite control of Jerusalem as reflected in the narrative presupposes a context earlier than the Judean capture of the city recorded in Jud. 1:8. As was the case with Micah's idol, assigning the notorious concubine incident precisely to the days of Cushan-Rishatayim rather than even earlier probably derives from the notion of the impossibility of such an ignominous event taking place during Joshua's stewardship. Thus, S.O. singles out the reign of Cushan-Rishatayim as the time frame of the concubine incident, since those years marked the sole period between Joshua's death on the one hand, and the Judean conquest of Jerusalem on the other hand.[48]

Josephus, for his part, operates out of an entirely different frame of reference than S.O. In keeping with his historiographic tendency of highlighting the political and military angle of events,[49] Josephus links the concubine incident directly with the indolence which prevailed among the Israelites at the beginning of the Judges period. According to Josephus, this indolence led to corruption which took on the form of political anarchy:

> But the Israelites, while despondent at this message from God, were yet ill-disposed for warfare, for they had won much from the Canaanites and luxury had by now unnerved them for fatigues. Aye, even that aristocracy of theirs was now becoming corrupted: no more did they appoint councils or elders or any other of those magistracies beforetime ordained by law, but lived on their estates, enslaved to the pleasures of lucre. And so, by reason of this gross listlessness, grave discord again assailed them and they were launched into civil war through the following cause...(*Antiq.* 5:134-35)[50]

In other words, Josephus views the beginning of the Judges period as the most likely occasion for the Bible's description, "In those days there was no king in Israel; every man did as he pleased" (Jud. 17:6; 21:25; cf.

---

[48] To be sure, strictly speaking, the notice of Jud. 1:8 precedes the ascension of Cushan-Rishatayim in ch. 3. However, in S.O.'s terms, Cushan-Rishatayim immediately followed Joshua (see S.O., beginning of ch. 12 commenting on Josh. 24:31) and thus the events of Jud. 1 do not necessarily appear chronologically.
[49] See above, notes 10 and 40.
[50] Josephus, Loeb Classics ed., Vol. 5, 63.

also 18:1 and 19:1). The concubine incident served as a fitting illustration of this anarchy, and Josephus incorporated it for its political and military interest despite his tendency to omit episodes which could cause the Jews embarrassment. This latter tendency shows itself in Josephus's omission of the incident of Micah's idol and its subsequent expropriation by the migrating Danites. For Josephus, the setting of the Danite migration is not determined by hints stemming from the incriminating verses 18:30–31, but rather by geo-political considerations coupled with the principle of analogy. Josephus introduces the Danite migration with the statement, "Now it happened that the tribe of Dan suffered in like manner with the tribe of Benjamin" (Antiq. 5:175). Just as the Benjaminites were a small tribe facing an overwhelming multitude, so were the Danites left on their own against the might of the Canaanites. Josephus continues, "They [the Canaanites] also forced the Danites to fly into the mountainous country, and left them not the least portion of the plain country to set their foot on" (5:177). This formulation is highly reminiscent of Jud. 1:34, "The Amorites pressed the Danites into the hill country; they would not let them come down to the plain." Apparently, Josephus took this early (i.e., pre-Philistine) oppression of the Danites to be the direct cause of the tribe's migration.[51] Thus, the Danite migration is presented as part of the early history of the Judges period, although its precise setting after the concubine incident is determined by analogy.

Interestingly enough, every one of the factors underlying S.O.'s and Josephus's antedating of the Danite migration, though not their antedating of the concubine incident, was taken up by the medieval Jewish commentators, and/or found its way into the modern scholarly debate of the issue.

1) As for the genealogy of Jud. 18:30 ("Jonathan son of Gershom son of Manasseh"), there is near universal acceptance of the tradition which takes "Manasseh" as referring to Moses.[52] Furthermore, some scholars accept the genealogy literally, taking it as evidence for an early date for the Danite migration.[53] However, others view the three-generation scheme as merely typological. These scholars maintain that, given

---

[51] This is also the implied view of the LXX to Josh. 19:47 which is preceded by a paraphrase of Jud. 1:34.
[52] E.g., Moore, *Judges*, 400–02; Boling, *Judges*, 266; Soggin, *Judges*, 268–69.
[53] E.g., Aharoni, *The Land of the Bible*, 221; Talmon, "In those Days There Was No King" (Hebrew), 140–41; idem, comments to B.Z. Luria's "The Settlement of the Tribe of Dan" (Hebrew), 265; Gevaryahu, "Micah's House of God" (Hebrew), 561.

the likelihood of generational telescoping, no firm chronological conclusions can be drawn regarding the setting of the migration.[54]

2) The deduction made from the formulation of Jud. 18:31 ("all the days that the House of God stood at Shiloh") regarding the early setting of the Danite migration is accepted by Rashi.[55] Even a modern scholar such as Burney takes the key phrase as harking back to an early period, though he does not spell out his views regarding the time frame of the entire episode.[56] Contrariwise, Radak and Abarbanel demur from the literal interpretation of kol yĕmê ("all the days..."). They argue that the phrase does not require us to suppose that the presence of Micah's idol in the Danite temple overlapped with the *entire* period of the Shiloh temple, but only that from the time of the idol's construction, it overlapped with the existence of the Shiloh temple until the latter's destruction.[57]

3) Josephus's characterization of the beginning of the Judges period as the high point of internal Israelite anarchy is accepted by Ralbag[58] and Talmon,[59] both of whom assign the episodes of Jud. 17–21 to the earlier time frame for that reason. However, Radak insists that the same can be said for the period between Samson and Eli, namely the end of the Judges period.[60]

4) For some commentators (e.g., Rashi,[61] Ralbag,[62] Elitzur[63]), the very fact that the Danites were still searching for an inheritance conjures up the flavor of an early period. This holds true especially if the Danite migration is seen in conjunction with the Amorite oppression of Jud. 1:34, as suggested by Josephus.[64] On the other hand, Jud. 1:34 can be taken to reflect merely the first stage of oppression which drove the Danites from the coastal areas into the central hill country. The migration to the north, however, would occur only at a later stage due to the

---

[54] Malamat, "The Danite Migration," 13; idem, "The Period of the Judges," 132; de Vaux, *Early History*, 780; Yeivin, comments to Y. Aharoni's "The Stories of Samson" (Hebrew), 451.
[55] Rashi to Jud. 18:31.
[56] *The Book of Judges*, 436.
[57] Radak to Jud. 17:1; Abravanel, Pērûš ʿal Nĕvî'îm Ri'šônîm, 142.
[58] Ralbag to Jud. 18:6.
[59] "In Those Days There Was No King" (Hebrew), 140–41.
[60] Radak to Jud. 18:1.
[61] Rashi to Jud. 18:1.
[62] Ralbag to Jud. 17:6.
[63] Sēper Šôpĕṭîm, 156.
[64] Talmon, comments to B.Z. Luria's "The Settlement of the Tribe of Dan" (Hebrew), 265. Cf. also n. 51 above on the LXX to Josh. 19:47.

influx of the Philistines or Sea Peoples.[65] Still another caveat is the possibility that Judges 1 constitutes a catalog of notices, which do not necessarily fall squarely into the period immediately following the death of Joshua.[66] Thus far, we have elucidated the various points adumbrated by the chronological presentations of S.O. and Josephus. However, there are even more factors which enter exclusively into the modern scholarly discussion. They run as follows:

5) In the present arrangement of the MT, the chapters describing the Danite migration (Judges 17–18) are immediately preceded by the exploits of Samson, who is said to be of Danite extraction (Jud. 13:2) and residing in the mountainous country near Philistine territory (Jud. 13:25–14:1). On the surface, therefore, the text would have us believe that the Danite migration did not occur until after the death of Samson when Philistine domination became too unbearable.[67] A common explanation for supporters of an early date for the migration is that not all of the Danites threw in their lot with the movement northward, and Samson's family could have been among those who remained in their southern holdings. Talmon argues for the partitive use of the preposition *mi* in 18:11, with the resulting interpretation being, "They departed from there, some of the clan of the Danites." In other words, only part of the tribe is said to have migrated.[68] Aharoni notes how the Danites of the Samson cycle appear to be amalgamated into the Judean sphere of influence (cf. Jud. 15:9–11). This, he believes, was the fate of the Danites who remained after the earlier migration.[69] Actually the issue is not clear cut, since 18:1 and 18:30 express more of a pan-Danite perspective, implying that the entire tribe acted as a united whole.[70]

6) The cryptic verse relating to Dan in the Song of Deborah has occasionally been brought into the discussion of the date of the migration. The verse reads: "Gilead tarried beyond the Jordan; and Dan—why did

---

[65] Yeivin, "Dān," 680.

[66] See in particular Wright, "The Literary and Historical Problem," 109.

[67] That is, unless the entire Samson cycle is to be placed at the beginning of the Judges period (so Kaufmann, *Sēper Šôpĕṭîm*, 56). However, this far-reaching suggestion lacks further internal support.

[68] Talmon, comments to B.Z. Luria's "The Settlement of the Tribe of Dan" (Hebrew), 266; Gevaryahu, "Micah's House of God" (Hebrew), 579–80.

[69] Aharoni, "The Stories of Samson" (Hebrew), 439–41; idem, comments to B.Z. Luria's "The Settlement of the Tribe of Dan" (Hebrew), 268.

[70] D. Ben-Gurion, comments to H. Gevaryahu's "Micah's House of God" (Hebrew), 566, 576.

he linger by the ships?" (Jud. 5:17). On the exegetical level, the location of these ships has been seen as either the Mediterranean near Joppa,[71] the Mediterranean near Sidon,[72] the Hulah swamp,[73] or the Jordan River.[74] On the geo-historical level, scholars on both sides of the debate over the date of the Danite migration have attempted to extrapolate proof for their position from this verse. Aharoni, siding with the exegetes who refer the verse to a northern location, claims that it points to an early date for the migration,[75] while Yeivin, siding with those who refer the verse to a southern location, claims that the verse points to a later date for the migration.[76] Both scholars evidently assume that the Song of Deborah reflects an early state of affairs. However, this assumption is not universally accepted,[77] and in any event, the exact intent of the verse remains eminently unclear.[78]

7) Even the findings of modern archaeology do not shed conclusive light on the date of the Danite migration. The destruction level VI at Tel Dan appears to be from the end of the twelfth or the beginning of the eleventh century. Were the Danites to be identified as the destroyers, this would date the migration to that time and would bring us down to a comparatively late date in terms of scholarly assessments of the chronological framework of the Judges period.[79] However, there is no positive evidence for associating the Danites with any particular settlement level.[80]

Scholarly assessments of the time frame of the concubine incident are even more tenuous. On the one hand, the mention of Phinehas in an active role as high priest (Jud. 20:28) would appear to indicate an early setting, since Phinehas had already come of age by the end of the desert

---

[71] Elitzur, Sēper Šôpĕṭîm, 70.
[72] Moore and Meyer, cited by B.Z. Luria, "The Settlement of the Tribe of Dan" (Hebrew), 251–52.
[73] Vilnai, comments to Luria, ibid., 260.
[74] Targum Jonathan, Rashi, and Radak to Jud. 5:17.
[75] "The Settlement of Canaan," 119; comments to B.Z. Luria's "The Settlement of the Tribe of Dan" (Hebrew), 269.
[76] "Dān," 680; comments to Y. Aharoni's "The Stories of Samson" (Hebrew), 451.
[77] See Malamat, "The Period of the Judges," 136–37.
[78] de Vaux, Early History, 778–79.
[79] The Judges period encompasses roughly the beginning of the twelfth century through the middle of the eleventh century.
[80] de Vaux, Early History, 780–81; Malamat, "The Danite Migration," 14, n. 1.

wanderings (Num. 25:7).[81] On the other hand, the sorry state in which the Benjaminites found themselves after the civil war and that tribe's special relationship with Jabesh Gilead (Jud. 21) might fit more readily into the period immediately prior to Saul's ascendance (cf. 1 Sam. 9:21; 11:1–11).[82] Furthermore, the mention of Phinehas could be motivated more by tendentious desires to have him appear in various ark traditions than by precise chronological considerations.[83] Even the text's presupposition that the Danite migration had already taken place—viz. the geographical merismus "from Dan to Beersheva" (Jud. 20:1)—does not help a great deal so long as the date of the migration remains in doubt.

The result of all of the above points is that the case for viewing Jud. 17–21 as internally displaced in the Bible is plausible but highly equivocal, since it is based on the cumulative evidence of hints scattered throughout the book of Judges, rather than on clear-cut external references to the circumstances of the events in question. In other words, the case for the chronological displacement of these chapters within the flow of the Biblical narrative is at best "non-empirical," and I shall therefore not attempt to offer explanations for this possible displacement until the last chapter of the book when I take up some non-empirical cases (see below, pp. 157–62). At the same time, the difference in arrangement between the MT on the one hand and S.O. and Josephus on the other hand remains an empirical fact. Since neither arrangement appears conclusively to be original, our working hypothesis, namely that the post-Biblical versions reflect judgemental determinations of how the ambiguous Biblical evidence is best treated (above, p. 90), is validated. We shall now recapitulate the precise nature of these determinations.

---

[81] Cf. Talmon, comments to B.Z. Luria's "The Settlement of the Tribe of Dan" (Hebrew), 266.
[82] Malamat, "The Period of the Judges," 132, 161–62.
[83] Ibid., 323, n. 87.

Motivations

For S.O.'s arrangement, the dating of Micah's idol back to the early period of the Judges stems from a close reading of Jud. 18:30 or 31 ("Jonathan son of Gershom son of Manasseh;" "throughout the time that the House of God stood at Shiloh"), both of which bring us back to an early period. The testimony of Josh. 24:31//Jud. 2:7 concerning the people's religious fidelity during the lifetime of Joshua leads to the choice of Cushan-Rishatayim's days as the background for Jud. 17–18. Thus, S.O.'s motivation can fairly be described as exegetical, to the extent that it attempts to create an historical flow out of seemingly disparate and displaced pieces of evidence. S.O.'s assigning of the concubine incident to the same early period stems from the juxtaposition of chaps. 19–21 to chaps. 17–18, as well as from the setting which S.O. understood 19:10, 12 to reflect.

As for Josephus's arrangement, we have already called attention to the omission of the embarrassing narrative of Jud. 17 and the related portions of Jud. 18. The concubine incident, though, despite its poor reflection on the Jews, was useful enough for Josephus to include in his history. What, then, lies behind Josephus's particular placement of this incident? Spiro and Thackeray both suggest wholly exegetical motivations. According to Spiro, Josephus must have realized that Phinehas could not possibly have been alive at the end of the Judges period. This would explain the dating of the story in Josephus as well as in S.O.[84] However, it is doubtful that Phinehas's lifespan was a major consideration for Josephus. Josephus never makes particular note of Phinehas's age, and does not include a death notice for Phinehas such as we find in the LXX.[85] According to Thackeray, Josephus was concerned to allow enough time to elapse between the virtual destruction of the Benjaminites in the civil war and Saul's ascendance.[86] However, the same concern would be even more acute were the civil war to be dated shortly before the exploits of the Benjaminite Ehud as Josephus has it. Besides, as we have noted above (p. 97), Saul's statement in 1 Sam. 9:21 can well be viewed against the background of a recent disaster suffered by

---

[84] Spiro, "Rewriting Biblical History," 234.
[85] See ibid., 232.
[86] Josephus, Loeb Classics ed., Vol. 5, 62–63. Cf. also Whiston ed., 152, note.

his tribe. Given these objections to the exegetical explanations, I prefer the approach of Attridge, who favors a thematic explanation.[87] Attridge notes how Josephus's transitional passage introducing the concubine incident (*Antiq.* 5:134–135, quoted above p. 92) follows immediately upon the heels of a divine admonition based on Jud. 2:1–3. Josephus probably realized that the state of anarchy epitomized by the Bible's statement "In those days there was no king in Israel" applied well beyond the beginning of the Judges period. However, a thematic presentation of history would be most effective by immediately recounting the deplorable results of the people's shunning of God's word. In this way, the reader could come away with a conscious impression of historical cause and effect. Josephus's use of the thematic approach here accords with general Greek historiographic practice, as well as with his own declaration in *Antiq.* 4:197 that certain of Moses's writings would require rearrangement by subject (see above, p. 77). This same technique guides Josephus in his opening remarks concerning the Danite migration. Josephus attributes the Danites' predicament to the same condition which brought about the civil war, namely the inertia of the Israelites and their failure to dislodge the Canaanites, with all of the ensuing ramifications. To be sure, Josephus may very well have taken his cue for the early dating of the migration from Jud. 1:34 as noted above (p. 93), but his specific analogizing of the Danites' situation with that of the Benjaminites is decidedly thematic.

Methods

S.O. adheres to a set chronographic form in which all events are related as part of an overarching chronological scheme, with the specific figures and computations being drawn from the Biblical text. However, since the Bible does not attach precise numbers (in terms of years or sequence) to the Danite migration and concubine incident, S.O. could insert them conveniently in their presumed time slot without altering its computations in any way. Specifically, S.O. posits 369 years during which the Israelites worshipped at the Shiloh shrine.[88] These 369 years run from the shrine's construction during the tenure of Joshua through

---

[87] Attridge, *The Interpretation of Biblical History*, 133–36.
[88] S.O. ch. 11, Milikowsky ed., 481–82.

its destruction in the days of Eli, with some modifications allowed to exclude periods of foreign oppression (during which the Israelites presumably did not have access to the shrine) and years which overlapped more than one judge.[89] Although S.O.'s reckonings are pliable enough to allow for a few years at the end of the Judges period for the events of Jud. 17–21 to have occurred,[90] the fact that these events were not treated in the Bible as part of the running sequential framework of the Book of Judges meant that practically, S.O. could include them just about anywhere. The decision to include them during the eight years of Cushan-Rishatayim's oppression was made, as we have seen, on the basis of internal exegetical determinations.

Josephus's method is a natural outgrowth of his conception of how a good history should be presented. Establishing thematic links and analogies between comparable events, even if they were originally transmitted separately, was surely viewed by Josephus not as a departure from historical authenticity, but as an improvement on the effectiveness and aesthetic quality of his sources.

1 Kings 14:1–18 and LXX 3 Reigns 12:24g–n

Setting

The LXX^B (Codex Vaticanus) to 1 Kings, which with the exception of ch. 1:1–2:11 and ch. 22 reflects the Old Greek stratum of translation,[91] exhibits a number of textual additions to the MT.[92] The most lengthy and controversial of these additions is the section following MT 12:24. This section, numbered as 12:24a–z in Rahlfs' edition, forms a duplicate account of the events already related in 11:26–12:24 and those still to be related in 14:1–18. The events in 11:26–12:24 include Jeroboam's rebellion, his flight to Egypt and return home, and the proceedings at Shechem which resulted in the ten tribes' schism from the

---

[89] S.O. ch. 12. Generally speaking, S.O. considers the years given in the Book of Judges for each of the judges' reigns to have been consecutive rather than overlapping as most modern scholars would suppose. For details, see Fendel, *Legacy of Sinai*, 67, 282–83.
[90] See Radak to Jud. 18:1.
[91] See Shenkel, *Chronology and Recensional Development*, 5–21.
[92] For full studies of the additions in 1 Ki. 2, see Gooding, *Relics of Ancient Exegesis*; Tov, "The LXX Additions."

Davidic kingdom. 14:1–18 narrates the story of Jeroboam's sick child Abijah, culminating in the prophetic renunciation of Jeroboam and his household. Indeed, it is the repetition of these events in a somewhat different form from the MT which sets apart 12:24a–z (henceforth Version 2, or V2) as a distinct literary unit from the surrounding LXX text (henceforth Version 1, or V1), which closely follows the MT practically verse by verse.[93] Within V2, however, the section 12:24g–n, which contains the material parallel to MT 14:1–18, stands in a class by itself. First, unlike the rest of V2 which covers events already related in the MT (and the corresponding LXX translation in V1), 12:24g–n relates the story of the sick child before it has appeared in the MT and places it in a much earlier context altogether. While in the MT the story appears at the end of Jeroboam's reign and as a prelude to his imminent demise, in V2 it appears immediately after Jeroboam's return from Egypt and prior to the Shechem proceedings, before Jeroboam has even assumed the kingship. Second, while the rest of V2 constitutes a duplicate to what appears previously in V1, the story of the sick child is omitted in the Old Greek at the point in which it appears in the MT (i.e., MT 14:1–18), and is appended only secondarily by manuscripts which reflect a somewhat later stage of Greek textual development (e.g., Codex Alexandrinus, manuscript c2, the Syro-Hexapla, etc.) in an effort to bring the Greek Bible into greater conformity with the MT.[94] This literary and textual state of affairs necessarily raises the same general questions we posed for all post-Biblical divergencies from the MT (above, p. 78), namely can the post-Biblical witness (in this case 12:24 g–n) be said to reflect an original sequence from which the MT (or its *Vorlage*) deviated? Or should the MT sequence be taken as original and the deviation be ascribed to V2? Or could the originality of both sequences (the MT and V2) be indeterminate?

The actual historical juncture of Abijah's illness is obviously impossible to recover. We are thus left in an either/or situation. Which of the sequences (the MT or V2) appears to be more original, if not from an historical then at least from a literary point of view? To a large extent, this question revolves around the more general issue of V2's nature and degree of reliability. This issue has been hotly debated for over a century. By 1914, Olmstead could already produce an impressive register of emi-

---

93 Talshir, *The Duplicate Story* (Hebrew), 137.
94 Olmstead, "Source Study," 28; Montgomery, *Kings*, 265.

nent scholars who came down on either side of the debate.[95] The lines of argument have not been significantly altered since then. Those who look favorably on V2 as a reliable source point to the following features:

1) The Hebraisms embedded in V2's translation indicate that V2 goes back to a pre-exilic Hebrew *Vorlage* whose language resembled that of the north-Israelite prophetic stories.[96]

2) 12:24b gives a more elaborate historical picture of Jeroboam's rebellion than the cryptic version of MT 11:27. V2 also preserves isolated historical notices which are not paralleled in the MT (e.g., 12:24f, which tells of Jeroboam building a fortress in Sarira).[97]

3) 12:24b–c is also shown to be more original than the MT by the fact that it doesn't include the prophecy of Ahijah, which is largely made up of (secondary) Deuteronomistic material. Rather, it reflects a stage of the text in which MT 11:28 was continued directly (and more naturally) by 11:40.[98]

4) The story of the sick child in V2 is similarly free of Deuteronomistic phraseology (except for 12:24m) and preserves a form of the story that originally fit better into its context than the MT version does in its context.[99] To this one can add the consideration mentioned above that the story does not reappear in the consecutive parallel text of the Old Greek to MT ch. 14, thus further supporting the originality of V2's placement of the story. For if the MT's placement were original, the Greek text would have repeated the story twice, once in V2 and once it its original place (ch. 14), just as it repeats the material relating to the schism twice. Furthermore, even the later Greek manuscripts which do record the story at the point equivalent to MT ch. 14 show some affinities with the text of V2.[100]

---

[95] Olmstead, "Source Study," 15–17.
[96] Ibid., 20.
[97] E.g., Stanley and Cheyne (cited in Olmstead, ibid., 15–16) and more recently Seebass, "Zur Königserhebung Jerobeams I," 325–26.
[98] Olmstead, "Source Study," 23 (following van Ranke) and more recently Debus, *Die Sünde Jerobeams*, 84–85.
[99] Winckler, *Alttestamentliche Untersuchungen*, 12–14; Olmstead, "Source Study," 23; Seebass, "Die Verwerfung Jerobeams I," 164–67, 182; Burney, *Notes*, 167.
[100] E.g., manuscript C2 includes the name Ano for Jeroboam's wife; the Hexapla reads "and the man was old" in 14:4 (= V2, 12:24i). See *BHS* ad loc.

The counterattack, which I find more convincing, runs as follows:

1) The notion of a Hebrew *Vorlage* to V2 can be granted without presupposing that such a *Vorlage* necessarily takes priority over the MT's *Vorlage*.[101]

2) The more expansive notices in V2, particularly those concerning Jeroboam's rebellion, are more likely the product of a creative imagination than the preservation of authentic traditions. 12:24b identifies Jeroboam's mother as a harlot while omitting his father's name. Such a stab at Jeroboam, were it part of an original version, would hardly have been changed for the better by the Deuteronomistic editor of the MT.[102] Furthermore, 12:24b claims that Jeroboam had three hundred chariots of horses at his disposal, a fantastic number considering Jeroboam's subordinate position in Solomon's kingdom, and more likely a literary flourish (cf. 2 Sam. 15:1; 1 Ki. 1:5).[103] Finally, the wording of the last clauses in 12:24b ("he built the citadel...") appears to be a deliberate re-interpretation of MT 11:27, by which the subject of the actions described is changed from Solomon to Jeroboam.[104] Not only that, but the specific action of Solomon in repairing the breach of the city (*sāgar 'et pereṣ ʿîr dāwîd*) is deliberately recast from enclosing the city to Jeroboam's blocking it off as an act of defiance.[105]

3) The issue of the placement and makeup of Ahijah's prophecy in the MT is extremely complex.[106] However, any hasty verdict in favor of 12:24b–c (which is already weakened by the considerations just noted)

---

[101] Talshir, *The Duplicate Story* (Hebrew), 243–46.

[102] Talshir, ibid., 169; Gordon, "The Second Septuagint Account," 377–78. The attempt of Aberbach and Smolar to deflect this argument ("Jeroboam's Rise to Power," 70–71) is weak and unconvincing.

[103] Talshir, *The Duplicate Story* (Hebrew), 170–71; Gordon, "The Second Septuagint Account," 380.

[104] Gordon, "The Second Septuagint Account," 383–84.

[105] Montgomery, *Kings*, 251; Gooding, "The Septuagint's Rival Versions," 187 and "Problems of Text and Midrash," 12; more cautiously Talshir, *The Duplicate Story* (Hebrew), 49. The Greek verb used in both 11:27 and 12:24b (*sug-kleistos*) is the same, meaning to shut up or enclose (see Liddel and Scott, *A Greek-English Lexicon*, 1665). However, while in 11:27 the enclosing refers to the city wall (or fortification), in 12:24b it refers to the city itself! Moreover, 12:24b is capped off by the phrase "and he [Jeroboam] aspired to the kingdom," which is reminiscent of the phrase used in connection with Adonijah in 1 Ki. 1:5 (see Gordon, "The Second Septuagint Account," 382, n. 78; Talshir, *The Duplicate Story* [Hebrew], 50). These latter explanations are in opposition to Olmstead, who in attempting to show how V2 is in fact *sympathetic* toward Jeroboam, offers the dubious translation "he repaired the city of David and was exalted over the kingdom" ("Source Study," 17).

[106] See the standard commentaries ad loc.

must be tempered by the recognition that V2 does in fact contain a reflex of this prophecy in 12:24o, where it is put in the mouth of Shemaiah at the outset of the Shechem proceedings. The extreme abridgement of the prophecy and its variant setting, rather than unequivocally demonstrating the secondary nature of MT 11:29–39, only complicates the issue. For it is highly possible that V2 itself reflects a reaction to the MT which is guided by ideological considerations. For example, the omission of the patently Deuteronomistic material from the prophecy could be due to V2's desire to keep the spotlight off of Solomon's sins.[107] Indeed, Solomon isn't mentioned at all in 12:24o, nor is the favorable conditional promise to Jeroboam (MT 11:38), which further raises the suspicion that V2 is deliberately suppressing elements which shed any positive light on Jeroboam.[108] In like manner, V2's mention of the prophecy only at a later stage than the MT (and indeed immediately following Jeroboam's censuring by Ahijah) has the effect of diminishing the degree of prophetic support which Jeroboam enjoyed from the very outset of his career.[109] In sum, V2's omission of Ahijah's oracle from its MT position is at best inconclusive and at worst detrimental to those who would argue for V2's primacy. 4) The claim made concerning the original form of the story of the sick child is inherently weak since it steps into the highly speculative arena of the pre-history of the text. Those who argue in favor of V2's presentation must assume as a matter of course that 12:24m is a later harmonistic addition influenced by the present form of the MT. This is because 12:24m, which *does* in fact go hand in hand with the Deuteronomistic perspective of Jeroboam, stands out starkly in its complete renunciation of Jeroboam, as opposed to the rest of the story in which Jeroboam is simply the luckless victim of a personal tragedy.[110] Seebass, in particular, goes much further in arguing that V2, once excised of its few references

---

[107] Cf. Gooding, "The Septuagint's Rival Versions," 188.

[108] Montgomery, Kings, 253.

[109] See Montgomery, ibid., 266. This conclusion can essentially hold true even if one is to assume with Talshir (*The Duplicate Story* [Hebrew], 152, 167) that 12:24o is worded as a flashback to some previous, unspecified time, rather than representing a true chronological displacement as I have been using the term. Like Talshir, I have not treated 12:24o as an independent case-study for the phenomenon of chronological displacement. However, even the fact that 12:24o only "flashes back" to an unspecified time rather than specifically to the reign of Solomon (as 12:24b–c does) detracts from the strong basis of prophetic legitimacy which the MT grants to Jeroboam from the start.

[110] See n. 99 above.

to Ahijah and his poor sight (and of course, 12:24m), preserves the original folk story of the visit of Jeroboam's wife to a holy man, which originally had nothing to do with Jeroboam's rejection.[111] However, the alleged textual anomalies on which Seebass bases his elaborate traditio-historical reconstruction (e.g., the interchange between the designations "Ahijah" and "the man of God") are exaggerated and can sustain more conventional literary explanations. Moreover, the absence of the Deuteronomistic verses MT 14:7–10, 14–16 from V2's account in no way points to an earlier text-type, since these verses, which refer to Jeroboam's actions after he became king and his religious legacy, could simply not be incorporated logically into V2, in which the story unfolds before Jeroboam has even become king.[112] For this very reason, V2 also had to dispense with such non-Deuteronomistic elements as MT 14:2b, "[Ahijah], the one who predicted that I [Jeroboam] would be king over this people," MT 14:13, "And all Israel shall lament over him [Abijah]," and the disguise of Jeroboam's wife (since according to V2's sequence, she was not yet a queen who would be recognized).[113] Finally, the fact that the story is not included in the Old Greek in its MT position could reflect a technical editorial decision by the interpolator of V2 not to duplicate material found in the MT after the point of interpolation (even though he retained duplicate material which stood before the point of interpolation).[114] The omission of MT 14:19–20 (Jeroboam's summation and death formulae) from the Old Greek as well, apparently by accident, also points to secondary tampering with a consecutive Greek text that once included all of MT 14:1–20, since no *Vorlage* would have deliberately omitted the latter two verses.[115] As for the textual affinities of the later Greek versions (to MT ch. 14) with V2, these can be viewed as part of an internal Greek redaction process designed to assimilate V2's text with the MT where possible.[116]

There are still more reasons for viewing V2 as a relatively late development (as compared to the MT). These include V2's use of the judgemental formula "And he [Rehoboam] did that which was evil in the

---

[111] "Die Verwerfung Jerobeams I," 164–66.
[112] Montgomery, *Kings*, 265–66; Talshir, *The Duplicate Story* (Hebrew), 179.
[113] Montgomery, *Kings*, 265–66; Talshir, *The Duplicate Story* (Hebrew), 217.
[114] Gooding, "Problems of Text and Midrash," 12–13; Talshir, *The Duplicate Story* (Hebrew), 138–39.
[115] See previous note.
[116] Talshir, *The Duplicate Story* (Hebrew), 234–37.

sight of the Lord, and walked not in the way of David his father" (12:24a), which is characteristic of the crystallized (Deuteronomistic) edition of MT Kings.[117] Also, V2's apparent transferal of part of the Hadad story (MT 11:19–22) to Jeroboam (12:24d–e) betrays its secondary nature; its supposition that the Pharaoh would have given his sister-in-law to a commoner stretches the imagination.[118] All in all,[119] we are on safe ground in postulating that V2 is the source responsible for the chronological displacement of the story of the sick child from MT 14:1–18. We now turn to explaining the motivation for this displacement.

Motivation

One's initial tendency in defining a Biblical writer's motivation is to steer away from simplistic labels which aim to identify the writer's personal biases. This is because Biblical narrative, as a rule, does not judge its characters overtly,[120] so the assigning of such labels as "pro-David" or "anti-David" etc. can be notoriously equivocal. For example, many scholars have viewed David's dying charge to Solomon (1 Ki. 2:1–9) as reflecting poorly on him, since his dying concerns revolve around personal vendettas. Yet, Zalewski has argued (in my opinion, satisfactorily) that a close reading of the text yields just the opposite conclusion.[121] The same problem presents itself in evaluating the LXX to 1 Kings. Wevers notes several examples of how he believes the LXX goes out of its way to favor Solomon.[122] At the same time, Gooding makes the case that the LXX's arrangement of its material at times puts Solomon in a

---

[117] Ibid., 161.
[118] Ibid., 173; Gordon, "The Second Septuagint Account," 385; Montgomery, *Kings*, 253.
[119] For even more arguments for V2's secondary nature, see Talshir, *The Duplicate Story* (Hebrew), 162; Gordon, "The Second Septuagint Account," 375–76.
[120] Cf. Bar-Efrat, *The Art of the Biblical Story* (Hebrew), 110–111.
[121] *Solomon's Ascension to the Throne* (Hebrew), 93–109.
[122] "Exegetical Principles," 307–09. Examples include 5:1, where Hiram is said to have sent servants to Solomon's coronation rather than just hearing about it after the fact (as in the MT). Also 11:33, where Solomon is said only to have made idols of Astarte and Chemosh, but not to have bowed down to them (as in the MT).

negative light.[123] For our present purpose, the debate over whether V2 is (or ever was) sympathetic or hostile toward Jeroboam is practically as old and long-standing as the debate over V2's reliability.[124] Perhaps the pitfalls of subjective interpretation are what led Talshir, in her recent book-length study of V2, to conclude emphatically that the author of V2 had no particular *Tendenz* other than to write a good story.[125] Commenting specifically on the placement of the story of the sick child, Talshir says that the imagination of V2's author was kindled by the opportunity to construct a "full novella" about Jeroboam's son, and that the resulting position of the oracle of doom (12:24m) was just an ensuing by-product.[126]

Nevertheless, with all due reserve, I find the case for V2's anti-Jeroboam stance to be too strong to push aside. The arguments for viewing V2 as sympathetic toward Jeroboam are rather tenuous, being based on a questionable interpretation of 12:24b[127] and on the assumption that V2, in its present state, has been reworked from its pristine form.[128] On the other hand, the points which illustrate an anti-Jeroboam tendency are solid and defensible. We have already commented on 12:24b, which indulges in midrash-like amplification to denigrate Jeroboam's pedigree and to underscore his rebelliousness (above, p. 103). The transfer of part of the Hadad episode to Jeroboam (12:24d-e), which a few scholars have interpreted as enhancing Jeroboam's prestige (since it is now he who married the Pharaoh's sister-in-law)[129] is actually a continuation of the same tendency noted for 12:24b. For now, Jeroboam is cast as the rebel *par excellence*, who goes so far as to marry into the family of the hostile Pharaoh, who is tellingly identified only in V2 as Shishak (the same king who would later raid Jerusalem—1 Ki. 14:25–26). Jeroboam's first action upon returning home is to build a fortress in Sarira (12:24f), again a sign of his pernicious intentions. But above all,

---

[123] "Solomon's Misconduct," 325–35. For example, the LXX's transferal of MT 9:24a to immediately after 9:9 foreshadows the negative links made in the Midrash between Solomon's completion of the temple and his marriage to Pharaoh's daughter.
[124] On the sympathetic side are Kuenen apud Burney, *Notes*, 169–69; Olmstead, "Source Study," 22; and to a limited extent Aberbach and Smolar, "Jeroboam's Rise to Power," 72. On the hostile side are Kittel, *Geschichte*, Vol. 2, 206f.; Montgomery, *Kings*, 253; Gooding, "The Septuagint's Rival Versions," 187–88.
[125] Talshir, *The Duplicate Story* (Hebrew), 247.
[126] Ibid., 177, 247.
[127] See in particular Olmstead's position, above, n. 105.
[128] Cf. above, note 99.
[129] Kuenen (above, n. 124); Aberbach and Smolar, "Jeroboam's Rise to Power," 72.

we can concur with Gooding that the chronological displacement of the story of the sick child was meant to demonstrate that Jeroboam's potential for evil was recognized by Ahijah from the outset. In Gooding's words: "It was not a case of a reasonable man being corrupted by power; he [Jeroboam] was incurably wicked before he came to power!"[130] To this, Talshir objects that if the whole point of bringing the story early were to vilify Jeroboam even before he took office, V2 would not have dropped the material from the MT which spells out Jeroboam's sins (e.g., 14:9).[131] However, this problem has been dealt with by Talshir herself, who says elsewhere that V2 was constrained from including the bulk of the accusations against Jeroboam, since they would not fit into the story's new context, i.e., Jeroboam's actions after he became king could not be incorporated into a context before his rule (see above, p. 105 and n. 112). Talshir also attempts to shift the focus away from an anti-Jeroboam bias in V2 by pointing out that Rehoboam too is described unfavorably in 12:24a and 12:24p–u (note especially the addition in 12:24t, "for this man is not for a prince or a ruler over us.")[132] However, in my opinion, the effect of V2's negative appraisal of Rehoboam is not to lighten the accusations against Jeroboam, but rather to divert attention from *Solomon's* role in the splitting of the kingdom. This role is very explicit in the original oracle of Ahijah in MT 11:33, but is intentionally dropped, along with all other references to Solomon, in the truncated reflex of the oracle in 12:24o (above, pp. 103–04). In sum, the outlook of V2, as also reflected by the chronological displacement under discussion, is rather similar to that of the Chronicler. The Chronicler never accepts the legitimacy of the northern kingdom (2 Chr. 13:4–12), but at the same time is loath to incriminate David or Solomon for any wrongdoing, making only a passing reference to Ahijah's oracle (2 Chr. 10:15) in accounting for the schism.

Methods

What Talshir regards as a motivation, namely the opportunity afforded to the author of V2 by the story of the sick child to construct a

---

[130] "Problems of Text and Midrash," 12.
[131] Talshir, *The Duplicate Story* (Hebrew), 199, n. 26.
[132] Ibid., 247.

"novella" about Jeroboam's son,[133] I would regard as a method. The author of V2 did his very best to integrate the condemnation of Jeroboam into its artificially early context by giving the appearance of a natural link between the birth of Abijah in Egypt and his subsequent illness upon his parents' return to Mt. Ephraim.[134] To the same end, he touched up the story itself, removing the notion of any previous acquaintance between Ahijah and Jeroboam, dispensing with Jeroboam's wife's disguise, and omitting the (Deuteronomistic) verses which presuppose Jeroboam's attainment of the kingship (above, p. 105). All in all, a skillful editing job, which rendered the seemingly impossible objective of condemning Jeroboam's line before he had even ascended to the throne at least passingly tolerable.

1 Kings 20–22 and LXX 3 Reigns 20–22

Setting

A well known sequence difference with chronological overtones between the MT and the LXX is found in the alternative locations of the Naboth story. In the MT, it appears as ch. 21, coming in between the two chapters dealing with Ahab's wars against Ben-Hadad and the Arameans (chaps. 20, 22). However, in the LXX, the Naboth story precedes the material of MT ch. 20, with the result that the chapters concerning the Aramean wars appear back to back. Thus, the order of MT chapters 20, 21, 22, appears in the LXX as 21, 20, 22. Josephus, likewise, follows the order of the LXX (*Antiq.* 8:355ff.). Although there has been much scholarly discussion regarding the original historical setting particularly of chaps. 20 and 22, I shall limit myself to a comparison between the arrangements of the MT and the LXX as they now stand. This is because the various historical considerations which are brought to bear by modern scholars are either too equivocal or, in any case, are not likely to

---

[133] Ibid., 177.
[134] Olmstead ("Source Study," 21) falls into the trap by taking this linkage at face value, stating that the long journey back from Egypt and the unsanitary character of the camp caused the boy Abijah to fall sick. Olmstead's perception of the journey is, of course, arbitrary. One could argue just as well that Jeroboam was well-supplied with necessary nutritional and medical provisions by his father-in-law the Pharaoh for the return trip to Israel.

have been fully known or recognized by the compiler of the stories or the redactor(s) of Kings.[135]

The case for the LXX's priority has been made by Benzinger,[136] Kittel,[137] Burney,[138] and to a certain extent Eissfeldt.[139] The thread uniting their positions is that chaps. 20 and 22 ought to be seen as a unit distinct from ch. 21 and therefore grouped together as in the LXX. There is much to be said for this approach. Both chapters 20 and 22 deal with

---

[135] The approach which advocates an historical setting for 1 Ki. 20 and 22 later than the time of Ahab was initially put forward by Jepsen, ("Israel und Damaskus") and was taken up in variant or expanded form by Whitley ("The Deuteronomic Presentation"), Miller ("The Elisha Cycle" and "The Rest of the Acts"), and Lipinski ("An Assyro-Israelite Alliance"). Its strongest point centers on the gross disparity between the depiction of a pathetically weak Samarian kingdom in 20:1, 15 (especially if this story is to be understood in the chronological context of three years before Ahab's death, cf. 22:1) and the evidence of Shalmaneser's Black Obelisk, which lists Ahab as the foremost military power in the Fertile Crescent in 853, that is, one year before Ahab's death. Added to this are the observations that the story of 1 Ki. 20 appears to manifest links with the reign of Jehoahaz son of Jehu (cf. 1 Ki. 20:15 with 2 Ki. 13:7; 1 Ki. 20:26, 30 with 2 Ki. 13:17; 1 Ki. 20:34 with 2 Ki. 13:25) and that Ahab's identity in the story is spelled out explicitly only in vv. 2 and 14 (elsewhere, the story refers anonymously to "the king of Israel"). However, the true extent of Ahab's military might as exemplified by the Assyrian source could very well have been lost upon the compilers of the prophetic tale, not to mention the much later Judean editor(s) of Kings. The alleged "doublets" with 2 Ki. 13 are insufficient to prove that 1 Ki. 20 is displaced from its original context, and the anonymous references to the "king of Israel," as in ch. 22, could be a stylistic peculiarity of the prophetic circles that produced the stories.

The arguments concerning ch. 22 are still more problematic. The assumption that two erstwhile allies (Israel and Aram) wouldn't have been fighting each other only one year after joining forces (cf. Miller, "The Elisha Cycle," p. 444) is subjective and disproven by modern Middle Eastern politics. Without downplaying the possible problematic implications of 22:40 (if the formula šākab ʿim ʾăbōtāyw indeed is restricted to a natural death, see ibid.), the suggestions to understand the chapter as reflecting the death of Jehoram son of Ahab (Whitley, Lipinski) or as a composite of the deaths of that Jehoram and Jehoahaz son of Jehu (Miller) create more problems than they solve. Jehoram already controlled Ramot Gilead (2 Ki. 9:1, 4, 14) and would have had no reason to "restore" it to Israelite hands (cf. 1 Ki. 22:3. The argument that this statement couldn't apply to Ahab either is indecisive. Perhaps the Arameans failed to keep their part of the bargain in returning certain cities, [cf. 20:34]. Jehoram's possession of Ramot Gilead would mean that the Israelite effort to regain the city as described in 1 Ki. 22 was evidently successful, even though Ahab lost his life in the process). Miller, who recognizes this problem, refers the chapter, at least in part, to the cycle of victories predicted by Elisha in 2 Ki. 13. But that Elisha's name has not survived in the context of such an alleged setting is surprising to say the least.

[136] *Könige*, 114.
[137] *Könige*, 155–56.
[138] *Notes*, 210.
[139] *Introduction*, 292.

the same subject matter, namely the cycle of wars between Israel and Aram. The opening verse of ch. 22, "They remained thus for three years without war between Aram and Israel," even implies a direct continuation from a preceding war account. Both chapters appear to stem from the same circles, namely the anonymous prophetic schools of the north. No mention is made of Elijah or of his titanic struggle against Ahab's religious policies. By contrast, ch. 21, in which Elijah plays a prominent role, is more closely linked with the narratives of chaps. 17–19. Finally, the oracle against Ahab in 20:42, "Your life shall be forfeit for his life," leads directly into the account of Ahab's death in ch. 22.

Arguing for the primacy of the MT arrangement are Montgomery and Gooding. Montgomery summarily dismisses any LXX arrangement as unreliable.[140] Such a verdict, however, is too hasty in light of the points just mentioned. Gooding[141] takes a more analytical approach by claiming that the LXX's positioning of ch. 21 is a function of its tendency to put Ahab in a sympathetic light. This tendency is underscored by the LXX's additions in 21 (LXX 20):16, 27 concerning Ahab's expressions of grief on the day that Naboth was killed[142] and by the passive formulation "he was sold (to do evil)," as opposed to the MT's reflexive form "he sold himself," in rendering the verb *hitmakkēr* in v. 25.[143] Once the LXX had softened Ahab's image, it could not countenance placing the story of his bitter end (ch. 22) so soon after his show of contrition (21:27–29). It therefore moved ch. 21 ahead of ch. 20 so that Ahab's death would be seen as the result of yet another backsliding, namely the leniency he showed toward Ben-Hadad (20:32–43).[144] However, while Gooding's observations concerning the LXX's treatment of Ahab in the Naboth episode are well taken, his actual explanation for the LXX's alleged reordering rests on the assumption that the LXX misunderstood the terms of the respite granted to Ahab in 21:29 ("Because he [Ahab] has humbled himself before Me [Yahweh], I will not bring the disaster in his lifetime; I will bring the disaster upon his house in his son's time"), applying it mistakenly to Ahab personally instead of to his dynasty.[145] In other words, the LXX would only have had reason to switch the order of MT

---

[140] *Kings*, 319.
[141] Gooding, "Ahab According to the Septuagint," 269–80.
[142] Ibid., 272–73.
[143] Ibid., 279.
[144] Ibid., 277 and more explicitly in "Problems of Text and Midrash," 26.
[145] "Ahab According to the Septuagint," 277.

chaps. 20 and 21 if it believed (mistakenly) that 21:29 removed the threat of death from Ahab himself. However, there is no reason to assume such a misinterpretation on the part of the LXX. One can admit to the sympathetic picture of Ahab in the LXX's Naboth story without also supposing that the LXX's arrangement of MT chaps. 20–21 is secondary.

One final point which could be brought in favor of the MT's arrangement is the resulting proximity between the oracle of 21:19, "In the very place where the dogs lapped up Naboth's blood, the dogs will lap up your blood too," and its fulfillment in 22:38, "Thus the dogs lapped up his [Ahab's] blood." However, whatever connection may exist between these two verses is somewhat forced and possibly secondary, since the location of the scene in 22:38 (the pool of Samaria) is not the same as the one in 21:19 (Naboth's vineyard).[146] Besides, as we have mentioned above, there already is a natural connection between the oracle of Ahab's doom in 20:42 and the narrative of ch. 22.

In sum, the weight of probability favors the originality of the LXX's *Vorlage*, with the MT representing a displacement from that *Vorlage*. We now turn to explaining the motivation for that displacement.

Motivation

Even though the MT separates ch. 21 from the other narratives dealing with Elijah (chaps. 17–19), its arrangement is thematically very climactic. As opposed to the anonymous prophet in 20:42 or even Micaiah son of Imlah in 22:17–23, both of whom address Ahab's personal fate, Elijah's role in ch. 21 is to announce the impending downfall of the entire Omride dynasty. The Naboth incident is placed where it is, even though it belonged earlier, because it served as a paradigmatic example of all that was wrong with Ahab's rule and as a justification for the fate decreed against his entire household. In its thematic role as a climactic unit, the incident of Naboth's vineyard belongs in the last possible spot before the account of Ahab's demise. To this end, 21:25–26 functions as a final summation notice: "Indeed, there never was anyone like Ahab, who committed himself to doing what was displeasing to the Lord, at the instigation of his wife Jezebel. He acted most abominably,

---

[146] See Burney, *Notes,* 212, and the discussions of Napier, "The Omrides of Jezreel," 366–74, and Miller, "The Fall of the House of Ahab," 307–17.

straying after the fetishes just like the Amorites..." These verses are made extra conspicuous by the fact that they interrupt Elijah's actual announcement (vv. 21-24) and Ahab's reaction (v. 27). Even if they do not belong to the original text of the story,[147] the redactor who inserted them intended to underscore the very motivation which guided the placement of the story as a whole, namely closing the circle not only on Ahab personally but on his dynasty.

Methods

The MT's insertion of the Naboth incident between the two chapters dealing with the Aramean wars was facilitated by the stated lapse of three years between the war at Aphek (20:26) and the resumption of hostilities at Ramot Gilead (22:1). The redactor could thus make it appear that the Naboth incident occurred sometime within these three years. Another chronological linkage technique adopted by the MT was the use of the vague formula ʾaḥar haddĕbārîm hāʾēlleh ("After these matters," 21:1). These words do *not* appear in the LXX version, possibly because the positioning of the story in the LXX (following ch. 19) does not necessitate the same kind of sequential fudging as does the MT arrangement. Now as Benzinger astutely points out, the formula itself need not be taken as secondary. However, the way it is made to refer back to the events of ch. 20 most surely is.[148] In other words, the redactor of the MT (or its *Vorlage*) could have adopted the already existing formula ʾaḥar haddĕbārîm hāʾēlleh, which originally may have had some unknown referent, and made it to refer to the events of ch. 20 by placing ch. 21 in its present location.

Ezra 1-6; 1 Esdras 2-7; and Josephus, Antiquities 11:1-113

I. *Outline of the material*

A relatively large body of material which provides fertile ground for empirical analysis of variant chronological sequences is represented by

---

[147] See standard commentaries ad loc.
[148] Benzinger, *Könige*, 114.

the accounts of early post-exilic history found in the Biblical books of Ezra-Nehemiah, the apocryphal book 1 Esdras, and Josephus's *Antiquities*, Book 11, respectively. There are two basic issues in which the question of chronological displacement is most prominent:

1) The sequence of the early returns of the Jews from Babylonia to Judah during the reigns of Cyrus (539–530)[149] and Darius (522–486). Specifically, this issue entails determining which Jewish leaders led the early waves of immigration, and what they accomplished.

2) The sequence of the attempts by the Jews' enemies to interfere with progress that was being made on work relating to the rebuilding of Jerusalem and its temple.[150]

In setting out and analyzing the sequence differences found in the primary sources, we shall keep in mind the methodological tasks of establishing which version appears to represent a more original order of events, determining the degree of dependency between the various versions, and defining the particular motives which might have inspired shifts from either the original historical sequence or from previous written traditions. The sequential differences we shall take up presently can best be outlined in chart form as follows: (The reader may also refer to a list with the dates of the Persian kings who reigned during the period of the Jews' early returns to Judah, below, p. 191).

---

[149] The starting date for Cyrus given here is the year in which he took over as king of Babylonia (in addition to Persia). See Hallo and Simpson, *The Ancient Near East*, 149. A new count starting from the conquest of Babylon is also reflected by Ezra 1:1.

[150] An additional case of displacement is often alleged to be found in the sequence of the returns and activities of Ezra and Nehemiah as portrayed by the book bearing their names. Although this issue has generated a tremendous amount of scholarly literature (see references in Rowley, "The Chronological Order"), I shall not be taking it up here since the grounds adduced for the alleged displacement are clearly nonempirical, i.e., they are based primarily on internal, literary anomalies or conjectural historical premises (see succinctly Demsky, "The Age of Ezra and Nehemiah" [Hebrew], 41), which however, can sustain explanations other than the presence of chronological displacement. The only argument which even approaches empirical status is that which would place Neh. 8 before Neh. 1–7 in light of the arrangement reflected by 1 Esdras, which brings Neh. 8 in immediate conjunction with Ezra 7–10. However, in view of the fact that 1 Esdras is, after all, a composition devoted to Ezra, the omission of the material relating exclusively to Nehemiah (Neh. 1–7) cannot be used convincingly in reconstructing the literary history of Neh. 8.

	Ezra	1 Esdras[151]	Josephus[152]
A.	1	2:1–15	11:1–11
A′.	—	—	11:12–18
B.	(appears later in 4:7–24)	2:16–30	11:19–30
C.	—	3:1–5:6	11:31–67
D.	2	5:7–46	brief summation notice at end of 11:18 resumed again in 11:68–74.
E.	3	5:47–65	11:75–83
F.	4:1–5	5:66–73	11:84–87
G.	4:6	—	—
G′.	4:7–24	(appears earlier in 2:16–30)	(appears earlier in 11:19–30)
H.	5–6	6–7	11:88–113

Before proceeding with a detailed resume of the material, we can briefly sum up the outstanding sequence differences between the sources as follows:

1) According to MT Ezra, Zerubbabel returned to Judah and laid the temple foundations in the early years of Cyrus (Ezra 2:1–2; 3:1–13). 1 Esdras, however, by including the three guardsmen story (1 Esd. 3:1–4:63), presents these same events (1 Esd. 5:1–8, 47–65) within the scope of the early years of Darius (a difference of some 16–18 years, see below p. 191, appendix). Josephus appears to combine both positions by having Zerubbabel return to Jerusalem twice, once in the reign of Cyrus (*Antiq.* 11:13–14) and once in the reign of Darius (*Antiq.* 11:32, 59–83).

2) Even though, historically, Artaxerxes' reign did not begin until twenty-two years after Darius's ended, both MT Ezra and 1 Esdras place the episode of the correspondence to Artaxerxes between the early years of Cyrus and the second year of Darius (Ezra 4:7–24; 1 Esd. 2:16–30). However, in MT Ezra, the narration of the episode follows the arrival and activities of Zerubbabel (Ezra 2:1–4:5), whereas in 1 Esdras, the episode precedes the arrival and activities of Zerubbabel (1 Esd. 5:7–73), coming on the heels of the material parallel to MT Ezra ch. 1 (1 Esd.

---
[151] The verse numbering follows RSV.
[152] The numbering follows Loeb Classics edition.

2:1–15). Josephus places the episode in between Zerubbabel's two missions to Jerusalem and gives the name of the king as Cambyses rather than Artaxerxes (Antiq. 11:19–30).

We now turn to an in-depth explication of the above points.

A + A´. All versions contain an account of Cyrus's decree, promulgated in his first year, which permitted the Jews to return to Jerusalem to rebuild the temple. Ezra and 1 Esdras agree that the temple vessels, after being released by Cyrus to Mithredath, the treasurer, were delivered to Sheshbazzar, who then carried them from Babylon to Jerusalem. Josephus differs in two respects. First, he does not say explicitly that Sheshbazzar ("Sanabassar") came from Babylon with the vessels. Second, he adds what looks like a paraphrased and expanded version of Ezra 6:3–5 (a record of Cyrus's edict supposedly found years later by Darius), couching it in the framework of an epistle which Cyrus actually sent to his governors in Syria at the time of the Jews' first return to Jerusalem (Antiq. 11:12–18). Josephus inserts this long addition in his account of Cyrus's reign, in between his equivalents of Ezra 1:8 and 1:9, since this is where Cyrus's first-year act, which is mentioned only retrospectively by MT Ezra 6:3, belongs sequentially.[153] Although Josephus later repeats the basic contents of Ezra 6:3–5 when he gets to that point in his narration (Antiq. 11:99–103), the chronological significance of his insertion in 11:12–18 is that in contrast to Ezra 6:3–5 which doesn't mention any names, Josephus explicitly introduces Zerubbabel (not Sheshbazzar) as the person who, along with Mithredath, was sent by Cyrus to restore the temple vessels to their proper place and to rebuild the temple.

B. 1 Esdras recounts essentially the same information found in Ezra 4:7–24, namely the dispatching of correspondence by Rehum and Shimshai to King Artaxerxes, and the latter's response, which put a halt to the Jews' building activity in Jerusalem. As mentioned above, both Ezra and 1 Esdras put Artaxerxes in an earlier context than he belongs in historically. However, an important difference between 1 Esdras and

---

[153] The phenomenon of amplifying a given context on the basis of retrospective references at a later point in the text is well known from the Samaritan Pentateuch. For example, the Samaritan Pentateuch repeats the text of MT Gen. 31:11–13 (Jacob's retrospective report of an angel's message) following Gen. 30:36, which is where the angel's message belongs sequentially. Similarly, the Samaritan Pentateuch amplifies the description of the theophany in Exod. 20:15–18 (18–21) by inserting the relevant descriptions of the same occasion found in Deut. 5:21–28; 18:18–22. See Tigay, "An Empirical Basis," 336–37.

Ezra, besides the obvious disparity in the specific literary placement of the correspondence, is that only 1 Esdras (2:18) specifically mentions the laying of the *temple* foundations as well as the city wall in the context of the accusations made by Rehum and his cohorts. Ezra 4 speaks only of the foundations laid for the city wall.[154] Josephus's version represents an even more radical difference, since by its account, the king to whom the correspondence was addressed was not Artaxerxes, but Cambyses, Cyrus's successor. Josephus lines up with 1 Esdras in stating that the laying of the temple foundations, as well as the setting up of Jerusalem's walls, fueled the concerns of the Jews' rivals and prompted them to contact the Persian king. All three versions close out the account of the correspondence by stating that work on the temple was held up until the second year of Darius by written order of the Persian king (either Artaxerxes or Cambyses).

C. The long section which follows in 1 Esdras and Josephus, which has no parallel in Ezra, is commonly referred to as the story of the three guardsmen. It narrates the story of Zerubbabel's rise to prominence in the court of King Darius, culminating with Darius's permission to Zerubbabel to go build the temple in Jerusalem. Thus, Zerubbabel's mission to Jerusalem is firmly set in the beginning of Darius's reign (1 Esd. 3:1; 5:5–6; *Antiq.* 11:33, 64–67). Up to this point in the narration, 1 Esdras has not stated anything which could contradict this chronological reference point. However, according to Josephus's account, Zerubbabel had already arrived in Jerusalem in the wake of Cyrus's edict. In order to account for the reappearance of Zerubbabel in the Persian court, Josephus adds the information that Zerubbabel returned from Jerusalem to congratulate Darius upon the latter's ascension to the throne (*Antiq.* 11:32). Thus, according to Josephus, when Zerubbabel accompanied the immigration wave sanctioned by Darius following the guardsmen episode, he was participating for the second time in a mass movement of returnees from Babylon to Jerusalem.

D. The Ezra narrative picks up with a list of the "people of the province" who went up to Jerusalem under the leadership of Zerubbabel. Ostensibly, this is a direct continuation of chapter 1 (cf. 1:11—"when the exiles came back from Babylon to Jerusalem," and 2:1—"These are the people of the province who came up from among the captive ex-

---

[154] Cf. below, p. 125.

iles...who returned to Jerusalem and Judah"). In such a case, ch. 2, like ch. 1, would be rendering an account of the events which occurred in the first year of Cyrus. However, in 1 Esdras, where the same list follows the three guardsmen story, the context spoken of is clearly the beginning of Darius's reign, for it was he who had just granted permission to Zerubbabel and company to return to Jerusalem. In Josephus, the situation is somewhat confusing. On the one hand, at the end of *Antiq.* 11:18, Josephus speaks of a large group which returned from captivity at the beginning of Cyrus's reign, and which numbered 42,462 (a difference of a mere 102 from the figure given in Ezra 2:64). On the other hand, in *Antiq.* 11:68–74, Josephus gives a version of the list in Ezra 2; though it is much abridged, with the omission of all the specific family names, Josephus is clearly adhering to the structure of the list and using some of the same numerical figures,[155] all the while referring to the chronological context of the beginning of Darius's reign, as in 1 Esdras. Perhaps this is Josephus's way of harmonizing Ezra and 1 Esdras, namely by positing two separate migrations of practically equal number.

E + F. The account in Ezra 3:1–4:5 of the laying of the temple foundations by Zerubbabel and Jeshua, and the subsequent altercations with the "adversaries of Judah and Benjamin," gives every indication of being set in the early period of Cyrus's reign. First, the opening verse of ch. 3 ("When the seventh month arrived—the Israelites being settled in their towns...") reads as a direct continuation of ch. 2 ("and all Israel in their towns"—2:70), which in turn forms a link back to ch. 1 (see above, section D). Second, the direct authority of Cyrus is invoked on two occasions to justify the activities of the returnees (3:7; 4:3). Finally, the summary verse in 4:5 explicitly bridges the present time, i.e., the reign of Cyrus, with a time which lies beyond the horizon of the immediately preceding narrative, i.e., the reign of Darius.

1 Esdras, which displays essentially the same text as MT Ezra throughout these sections, winds up with a grave inconsistency. For at the same time that 1 Esd. 3:1–5:6 (above, section C) would lead us to believe that Zerubbabel's return and subsequent activities took place in

---

[155] E.g., like Ezra 2, Josephus first gives the population figures for the lay and Levitical families, then the temple servants and those with questionable genealogical status, and finally the servants and animals. Josephus's sum totals for the temple servants (392), those of questionable status (652), servants (7337), and camels (435) are the same as those given in Ezra 2:58, 60, 65, 67. However, some of his other sum totals are different from Ezra 2.

Darius's second year and thanks to Darius's backing, 5:55 and 71–73 (which parallel Ezra 3:7 and 4:3–5, respectively), appear to throw Zerubbabel and his mission back to the reign of Cyrus! Indeed, the connection these verses make between Zerubbabel's mandate and the terms of Cyrus's edict is entirely out of place in the context of 1 Esdras, since according to the three guardsmen story, Zerubbabel had obtained precisely the same guarantees from the reigning king, Darius. In other words, 5:55 and 71–73 seem to be oblivious to 4:47–57.[156] Moreover, the spanning of the periods, which brings the narrative from the lifetime of Cyrus up until the reign of Darius (5:73), is entirely nonsensical if the preceding narrative has *already* been taking place in the reign of Darius!

Josephus also relates the events of Ezra 3 and the beginning of Ezra 4 within the time frame of the first years of Darius. However, he overcomes the difficulties which remain in 1 Esdras by adding "and what was now done at the command of Darius"; "and now by Darius," to his versions of Ezra 3:7 and 4:3, respectively (*Antiq.* 11:78 and 86), and by dropping Ezra 4:4–5 altogether. Thus, Josephus anchors the events into the context of Darius's reign more successfully.

G + G′. See the discussion in section B, above. The only other noteworthy difference between the versions is that neither 1 Esdras nor Josephus mentions the letter of accusation which was written to Xerxes (Ezra 4:6).

H. With the opening of Ezra 5, the scene has already shifted to the reign of Darius (see 4:24). A further challenge against the Jews' renewed building efforts is raised by Tattenai, the governor of the province "beyond the river,"[157] and Shethar-bozenai. They take up the matter through correspondence with Darius, who upon investigation, discovers that his predecessor Cyrus had granted the original permission for the Jews to build the Jerusalem temple. This is a reasonably believable account, since given the passage of time and the instabilities which rocked the Persian empire with the ascendance of Darius,[158] Cyrus's edict concerning the Jews could well have been relegated to the bottom of the

---

[156] 4:57 in turn, appears to be oblivious to 2:10–15. If the temple vessels had already been taken to Jerusalem under Cyrus's decree, there would be no place for Darius to give the same order. See Eissfeldt, *Introduction*, 576; Metzger, *Introduction*, 17.

[157] On the use of the term as a geographic referent in the inscriptional evidence, see Rainey, "ʿēber hannāhār."

[158] See Bright, *History*, 369.

court's concerns, if not completely forgotten. However, the fact that 1 Esdras incorporates the same text as Ezra again makes for an intolerable internal inconsistency. For according to 1 Esdras, Darius had *himself* already given direct authorization to Zerubbabel to build the temple and had ordered all his imperial officials to support the project (4:47–57). In such a case, Tattenai (Greek Sisinnes) would not have had any grounds on which to challenge the Jews, and the Jews would not have had to submit any such challenge to royal arbitration. Certainly Darius himself would not have had to make such a thorough investigation of past edicts permitting the Jews to return had he himself issued such an edict! Indeed, 4:57 may be taken to imply that Darius was well aware of Cyrus's edict when he issued his own.[159]

Josephus agrees with 1 Esdras that Darius had previously given his blessings to the Jews who were returning to Jerusalem to build the temple (see section C, above). However, he skirts the serious difficulty which the Tattenai episode poses for this premise by recasting the nature of Tattenai's complaint. According to Josephus, Tattenai was not challenging the Jews' right to build the temple, but only the *manner* in which they were building it, to resemble a citadel (*Antiq.* 11:89). Darius, for his part, acted not out of ignorance of the permission he previously granted to Zerubbabel, but from a temporary reconsideration of his policy in light of Tattenai's specific complaint, backed up by the epistle of Cambyses (section B, above), to which Darius was evidently being exposed for the first time (*Antiq.* 11:97).

II. Analysis of the chronological difficulties in Ezra 2:1–4:24

A. Setting

Having completed a basic outline of the material, we now turn to the question of which of the versions, if any, most likely reflects the original order of events. We shall take up each source individually on its own merits, beginning with MT Ezra 1–6. Within our extended discussion of Ezra, we shall consider the chronological problems of 4:6–24 separately, since this passage appears to represent a time frame which is

---

[159] The above problems are set forth by Segal, "ʿEzrāʾ ûNĕḥemyāh," 145; Kaufmann, *Tôlĕdôt*, Vol. 8, 543.

widely separated from the rest of the material. Of the remaining material, ch. 1 clearly refers to events of Cyrus's first year (1:1), and chaps. 5–6 clearly refer to events of Darius's early years (5:5; 6:15). The problems arise only in regard to 2:1–4:5.

On the surface, Ezra 1:1–4:5 reads as a chronological continuum. As we have noted in our outline above, Cyrus's decree in his first year is put into practice with the mobilizing of an immigration wave led by Sheshbazzar, the *nāśî'* of Judah.[160] Chapter 2 then records the names of those who returned with Zerubbabel and Jeshua. Although the latter two figures have not been mentioned previously, and no absolute date is provided, the unwitting reader would conclude that the names listed in ch. 2 are those of the returnees who heeded Cyrus's call in ch. 1.[161] Chapter 3 picks up where ch. 2 left off, with "all Israel in their towns." It records the altar building undertaken by Zerubbabel and Jeshua in "the seventh month," and the actual foundation which took place "in the second year after their arrival at the House of God, at Jerusalem, in the second month." Chapter 4:1–5 records Zerubbabel's and Jeshua's rebuff of the "adversaries of Judah and Benjamin," and the resulting enmity which lasted "all the years of King Cyrus of Persia and until the reign of King Darius of Persia." The total impression created by 1:1–4:5 is, therefore, that both Zerubbabel's immigration and his laying of the temple foundations took place early in the reign of Cyrus.

However, while the account of 1:1–4:5 is presented as a chronological continuum, critical analysis puts this conclusion in serious doubt. Perhaps the most striking feature of the account is the sudden disappearance of Sheshbazzar after ch. 1, and his evident replacement as head of the people by Zerubbabel and Jeshua. In fact, the sole reference to Sheshbazzar from this point on comes in 5:15–16, where the Jews of Darius's time are quoted as saying: "He (Cyrus) said to him (Sheshbazzar), 'Take these vessels, go, deposit them in the temple in Jerusalem, and let the House of God be rebuilt on its original site.' That

---

[160] On the title *nāśî'* with reference to Sheshbazzar, see Liver, "*nāśî'*." A common theory equates Sheshbazzar with Shenazzar, the son of Jehoiachin (1 Chr. 3:18), e.g., Freedman, "The Chronicler's Purpose," 439, who notes that both names are apparently corruptions of an original Sinabusur.
[161] See *Sēder 'Ôlām Zûṭā'* ch. 7 which says explicitly, "Zerubbabel went up to Jerusalem with his repatriates in the first year of Cyrus king of Persia" (Grossberg ed., 23).

same Sheshbazzar then came and laid the foundations for the House of God in Jerusalem..." Thus, we have evidence from elsewhere in Ezra itself that Sheshbazzar (rather than Zerubbabel and Jeshua) was responsible for the original foundation laying during Cyrus's reign.

This datum creates the impression that 1:1–4:5 reflects an artificial fusion of the careers of Sheshbazzar and Zerubbabel and of the events in the reigns of Cyrus and Darius. This impression appears to be strengthened by the prophecies found in the books of Haggai and Zechariah. These prophets were active during the reign of Darius (which the book of Ezra recognizes as being later than Cyrus, see 4:5; 6:14), and contemporaneous with the building activities of Zerubbabel and Jeshua (cf. Ezra 4:24b–5:2). In a prophecy dated to the twenty-first day of the seventh month in Darius's second year, Haggai encourages Zerubbabel and Jeshua to proceed with the building of the temple (Hag. 2:1–9). Two months later, on the twenty-fourth day of the ninth month, Haggai declares, "And now take thought, from this day backward: As long as no stone had been laid on another in the House of the Lord.... Take note, from this day forward—from the twenty-fourth day of the ninth month, from the day when the foundation was laid for the Lord's Temple..." (Hag. 2:15, 18). Zechariah says in the same year, "Zerubbabel's hands have founded this House and Zerubbabel's hands shall complete it" (Zech. 4:9). Thus, we have what appear to be explicit references to a foundation under Zerubbabel and Jeshua taking place only later, during the reign of Darius, rather than at the beginning of the reign of Cyrus.[162]

In sum, the probability that Ezra 2:1–4:5 reflects a temporal context *later* than the early days of Cyrus is borne out most strongly by the combined evidence of:

1) Ezra 5:16, which assigns the role of earliest foundation layer to Sheshbazzar.

2) The absence of Sheshbazzar in Ezra 2:1–4:5, and the assumption of his role by Zerubbabel.

---

[162] Some scholars feel that Ezra 5:16 and the evidence from Haggai and Zechariah are mutually exclusive, i.e., that Haggai and Zechariah don't leave room for any prior foundation laying whatsoever. However, I agree with those scholars who give a wider interpretation to *ysd* so that it can refer not only to the original foundation laying, but also to the inauguration of continuous building or to building in general. This is the case especially in Late Biblical Hebrew (cf. Isa. 44:28; 2 Chr. 24:27). See Batten, *Ezra and Nehemiah*, 119; Segal, "ʿEzrāʾ ûNěhemyāh," 145; Halpern, "A Historiographic Commentary," 103; Talshir, "The Description of the Second Temple's Foundation" (Hebrew), 350–53. Cf. Blenkinsopp, *Ezra-Nehemiah*, 102–04.

3) The prophecies of Haggai and Zechariah, which set the activities of Zerubbabel and Jeshua squarely in the second year of Darius.

Thus, Ezra 2:1–4:5, which describes the return and activities of Zerubbabel and Jeshua as part of the original movement under Sheshbazzar, suggests the fusion of different time frames. Additional support for the conclusion that Ezra 2:1–4:5 reflects events from no earlier than the early days of Darius (rather than the early days of Cyrus) comes from the following points:

4) The enemies mentioned in Ezra 4:1–5 as being present throughout the reign of Cyrus appear to be unknown to Haggai, who blames the neglect of the temple building project during the reign of Cyrus solely on the people's lethargy (Hag. 1:3–11). Ezra 4:1–5 would thus appear to reflect a situation which prevailed later than the reign of Cyrus.[163]

5) The description in Ezra 3:12–13 of intermingled joy and sorrow at the temple's foundation appears to take its cue from Hag. 2:3, which is addressed to the people of Darius's period.[164]

6) Zerubbabel's age in 538 (the year of the first return, under Cyrus) can be estimated at about 25 if not lower.[165] Such a young man would not likely have yet attained a high leadership position.

To be sure, there are scholars who dispute some or all of the above points. Regarding points 1, 2, and 3, M.H. Segal and Y. Kaufmann both claim that Zerubbabel was in fact the one who laid the foundations during Cyrus's reign, but that in an official context such as Ezra 5:16, credit had to be given to Sheshbazzar, who was the governor designated by the Persian authorities.[166] Haggai and Zechariah's prophecies from Darius's second year refer to a second attempt by Zerubbabel and Jeshua to get the temple building project underway after years of inactivity (cf. Ezra

---

[163] See Halpern, "A Historiographic Commentary," 104.
[164] Rudolph, *Esra und Nehemia*, 31; Williamson, "The Composition of Ezra i–vi," 25.
[165] This would be especially true if Zerubbabel was the great-grandson of Jehoiachin (cf. 1 Chr. 3:17–19, which might imply that Shaltiel was Zerubbabel's grandfather, rather than his father as he is generally identified, e.g., Hag. 1:1). Jehoiachin was 18 years old in 597 when he was exiled and apparently childless (2 Ki. 24:8, 12). Allowing twenty years per generation, Zerubbabel's birthdate would thus come out to circa. 555 (thus Ben-Yashar, "The Problem of Sheshbazzar and Zerubbabel" [Hebrew], 56, n. 60). Halpern ("A Historiographic Commentary," 129) argues that even were Zerubbabel to be taken as Jehoiachin's grandson, 565 would seem to be the earliest possible date for his birth, given the infant mortality rate and the "disruptions in domestic life occasioned by the exile."
[166] Segal, "'Ezrā' ûNĕḥemyāh," 146; Kaufmann, *Tôlĕdôt*, Vol. 8, 212.

5:1–2). Regarding point 4, Kaufmann goes on to say that the rebuke contained in Haggai 1:3–11 does not deny the existence of external restraints, but still places some of the onus on the people, who were, after all, in a secure enough position to construct paneled homes for themselves (Hag. 1:4).[167] As for point 5, Hag. 2:3 refers not to a specific event, but to a general feeling of wistfulness among the elders, while Ezra 3:12–13 describes the weeping of a particular time and place, which was brought on not so much by wistfulness as by the recollection of recent tragedies.[168] Point 6 is not unimpeachable, since according to the palace text of Nebuchadnezzar published by Weidner, Jehoiachin's five eldest sons were all born by 592, so Zerubbabel could easily have been born by 570.[169]

Other scholars attempt to salvage the chronological integrity of Ezra 2:1–4:5 by identifying Sheshbazzar and Zerubbabel as one and the same person, or at least attributing such an identification to the author of Ezra.[170] If this proposed identification could stand, the problems involved in combining the various chronological reference points would be somewhat tempered. Sheshbazzar = Zerubbabel could be viewed as the one who led the original return and first temple foundation efforts (Ezra), as well as the one who years later, picked up where he had left off (Haggai and Zechariah).

I am inclined to grant Kaufmann his position on points 4 and 5 listed above.[171] I also agree that Haggai and Zechariah could be referring to a renewal of temple-building activities after a long hiatus. The act of *ysd* ("foundation" or "founding") was not necessarily a one-time affair, and the silence of Haggai and Zechariah about events in the reign of Cyrus does not mean that no attempts were made at that time to start

---

[167] Kaufmann, *Tôlĕdôt*, Vol. 8, 196.
[168] Ibid., 193.
[169] Albright, *The Biblical Period*, 88; Rudolph, *Esra und Nehemia*, 19. For the palace text, see Weidner, "Jojachin, König von Juda, in babylonischen Keilschrifttexten," in *Mélanges syriens offerts à Monsieur Rene Dussaud*, II (Paris: 1939), 923–35; *ANET*, 308.
[170] See already the commentary attributed to Ibn Ezra on Ezra 1:8 and more recently Bartal, "And Again—Who is Sheshbazzar?" (Hebrew) with further literature. Cf. Rudolph, *Esra und Nehemia*, 7, 18, 29, 62; Myers, *Ezra-Nehemiah*, 15.
[171] Interestingly, Kaufmann's position on point 4 can be supported by our discussion of Nabonidus's Sippar cylinder and Harran stele, wherein both reasons given for the delay of the temple building (external restraints and internal opposition) are essentially true (see above, p. 39).

work on the temple.[172] However, the crucial point still remains intact, namely that in both Ezra and Haggai-Zechariah, there remain clear distinctions between the persons and periods of activity of Sheshbazzar and Zerubbabel. In Ezra 5:14, 16, we find the elders contemporary with Zerubbabel and Jeshua referring to Sheshbazzar in the third person and as a figure from beyond the very recent past.[173] Although Sheshbazzar is not mentioned in Haggai and Zechariah, Japhet notes correctly that, "The general impression…arising from the way Zerubbabel is presented and referred to [in Haggai and Zechariah]…is that Zerubbabel's star has just now risen."[174]

As regards Ezra 4:6–24, the overwhelming majority of scholars regard it as displaced material.[175] The following reasons support this claim:

1) The historical order of the pertinent Persian kings was Cyrus, Cambyses, Darius I, Xerxes, Artaxerxes I, whereas Ezra 4 presents them in the order Cyrus, Xerxes, Artaxerxes, Darius. Unless there is strong evidence to the contrary, we should presume that the historical order was familiar to the author of Ezra (who was evidently active during the Persian period)[176] and that Ezra 4:6–24 represents an intentional displacement. Indeed, Ezra 6:14 does mention Cyrus, Darius, and Artaxerxes in the proper order and Ezra 7:1 recognizes Artaxerxes as belonging to a period later than both Cyrus and Darius.

2) The section 4:6–24 is framed by a "resumptive repetition," namely the mention in both verses 5 and 24 of inactivity in the building project up until the reign of Darius. This type of repetition is often a literary device designed to smoothen the inclusion of material which is chronologically or otherwise parenthetical.[177]

3) The content of the letter to Artaxerxes never mentions the temple, but rather objects to the building of the city walls. This fact accords better with the period after Darius when the temple had already been completed (Ezra 6:15; cf. Neh. 1:3).

4) A royal order which prohibited further work on the temple could hardly have been made prior to Darius's reign (as 4:23–24 implies), since

---

[172] See above, n. 162.
[173] Ben-Yashar, "The Problem of Sheshbazzar and Zerubbabel" (Hebrew), 47.
[174] Japhet, "Sheshbazzar and Zerubbabel," 90.
[175] See commentaries.
[176] See Demsky, "The Age of Ezra and Nehemiah" (Hebrew), 42.
[177] See e.g., Long, "Framing Repetitions," 385–86 with references.

Tattenai, the regional governor, is obviously unaware of such an order when he registers his complaint to Darius against the Jews for their continued work on the temple (Ezra 5:6–17).[178] Furthermore, had such an order been in place, Haggai and Zechariah could hardly have taken the people to task for not proceeding with the temple work (Hag. 1:3–11) and even if they had, it is doubtful that the people would have responded positively (Ezra 5:1–2, 5).[179]

At least two detailed arguments by modern scholars have taken exception to the notion that our section exhibits an intentional chronological displacement.[180] Y. Kaufmann[181] dismisses vv. 6–7 as a secondary scribal gloss of no chronological significance and takes "Artaxerxes" of vv. 8ff. to refer to Cambyses. The latter claim is essentially a reading back into the Biblical text of Josephus's position (above, p. 117, section B). Moreover, Kaufmann denies the claim that the content of the letter to "Artaxerxes" reflects a period following the temple's completion. He interprets the adversaries' accusation to be that the Jews were going beyond their limited mandate to build the temple by constructing houses in and around the city. Kaufmann is also not impressed by the literary ramifications of v. 24's connection with v. 5. He argues that v. 24, which continues in the Aramaic of vv. 8–23, and opens with the preposition *bēʾdayin* (then), serves as a direct continuation of what precedes, rather than as a framework for bracketing vv. 6–23. Actually, as we shall see (below, p. 129), v. 24 is meant to serve both functions. However, Kaufmann's other points are wholly arbitrary (e.g., the identification of Artaxerxes with Cambyses) or unconvincing (e.g., the roundabout manner in which he claims that the adversaries presented their case for halting work on the temple).

The other approach which denies the presence of intentional chronological displacement in our section argues that in fact, Ezra 4:6–24 serves as an example of chronological *misplacement*. In other words, the editor, who mistakenly considered the building of the city to be part and parcel of the building of the temple, wound up with a non-historical sequence simply because he didn't know any better. The placing of Darius after Artaxerxes (4:24) would most probably reflect a confusion of Darius

---

[178] Japhet, "History and Literature," 180.
[179] Ibid., 179–81.
[180] I am just citing representative examples. For full bibliography, see H.H. Rowley, "Nehemiah's Mission," 219–27.
[181] *Tôlĕdôt*, Vol. 8, 209, 522–27.

I with Darius II (the latter having indeed followed Artaxerxes I), while the mention of an even later Artaxerxes in the time of Ezra (Ezra 7:1) would reflect a confusion of Artaxerxes I with Artaxerxes II (the latter having indeed followed Darius II).[182] This approach is championed in greatest detail by Torrey, who makes the case that Ezra 4 follows the same non-historical sequence of Persian kings evidenced by Jewish apocalyptic and midrashic literature, particularly the Book of Daniel and Sēder ʿÔlām Rabbāh.[183]

However, the argument for chronological misplacement in our section is weakened not only by the particular literary structure of Ezra 4 (above, p. 125, point 2), but by the probability that the blending of the city and temple building projects is the result of an intentional historiosophic aim rather than an ignorant confusion (see below, p. 129). Moreover, Torrey's particular reconstruction of the (pseudo)-chronological framework of Ezra 4:6–24, although intricately worked out and presented, is ultimately unconvincing.[184] His only specific argument which merits special attention is similar to Kaufmann's claim that the absence of explicit reference to the temple in the letter to Artaxerxes does not necessarily indicate a much later setting. In Torrey's words:

> This king...the Artaxerxes of Ezra 4:7–24, had permitted the Jews to build their temple; until the lying report of their enemies, the Samaritans, that they were building *the wall of the city*, caused him to give an order under cover of which these enemies proceeded by force to stop the building of *the temple*. A well-told story of a successful trick.[185]

Torrey's formulation, while clever, perhaps presupposes a bit too much daring on the part of the Jews' adversaries. After all, it was not only the Samaritans who were bringing charges, but the local Persian officials as well. The Jews could easily have countered and exposed these officials' lies, thereby putting their very positions at risk. Besides, the cumulative evidence pointing to the chronological displacement of Ezra 4:6–23 is altogether stronger than Torrey's interpretation.

---

[182] Noth, *The Chronicler's History*, 72–73. Cf. Liver, "The Order of the Persian Kings" (Hebrew), 270–75.
[183] Torrey, "Medes and Persians," *JAOS* 66 (1946), 1–15.
[184] For a full elaboration of Torrey's thesis and its weaknesses, see the appendix.
[185] Torrey, "Medes and Persians," 2.

At this point, it must be stressed that the non-chronological features which we have detected in Ezra 2:1–4:5 do not derive from the same empirical basis as the displacement noted for 4:6–24. While the case for chronological displacement in 4:6–24 is made evident by the deviation from the known sequence of Persian kings, the argument in the case of 2:1–4:5 rests on evidence from within the same book (Ezra 5:16) and from material (Haggai and Zechariah) that, however suggestive, does not cover the period which Ezra 2:1–4:5 purports to describe, namely the reign of Cyrus. This being the case, I shall defer more precise study of, and explanations for, the displacement represented by 2:1–4:5 until the last chapter of the book (non-empirical examples, below, pp. 167–74), concentrating here only on the explanation for the displacement in 4:6–24.

B. *Motivation*

One explanation for the inclusion of material from a later period in Ezra 4:6–24 is that the mention of enemy interference in the days of Cyrus and Darius (4:5) led the editor to include historically later examples of such interference by way of association. For example, Blenkinsopp writes: "Having just dealt with opposition under Cyrus, he [the author] simply wished to carry this theme through the reigns of Darius (4:5), Xerxes (4:6), and Artaxerxes (4:7–23) in the correct chronological order."[186] However, while the associative-topical explanation is legitimate, it is still preferable to seek a deeper narrative meaning to the way in which the digression of 4:6–24 functions. This meaning is expressed well by Williamson:

> It is not difficult to explain why the writer should have wanted to include the digression here. He had just recorded an apparently harsh rejection of an offer to help with the rebuilding of the temple. Here, he has sought to justify this by showing how, in the light of history, his earlier designation of this group as "the enemies of Judah and Benjamin" (4:1) was entirely justified.[187]

---

[186] *Ezra-Nehemiah*, 106.
[187] Williamson, *Ezra, Nehemiah*, 57.

Williamson's understanding of the displacement moves beyond the technical associative explanation offerred by Blenkinsopp. For Williamson, the record of the later accusations made by the Jews' enemies was not included merely out of antiquarian interest, but because it contributed directly to an appreciation of the circumstances faced by Zerubbabel and Jeshua. As such, the motivation to which Williamson attributes the displacement can be labeled as exegetical.

However, this approach too is insufficient, since in 4:6–24 we are dealing not merely with historical analogy, but with an ideologically motivated blending of time frames. Kaufmann's observation on v. 24 (above, p. 126) is of special import here. For while, on the one hand, the author does step beyond the Cyrus-Darius period by mentioning Xerxes and Artaxerxes (vv. 6–7), on the other hand, vv. 23–24 invite us to read in a cause and effect relationship between the interruption of work on the city walls and the interruption of work on the temple, even though in historical reality, the latter interruption was almost surely resolved by the time of the former interruption. The notice of the temple work being completed in Darius's sixth year (6:15), i.e., well before the reign of Artaxerxes, testifies to an awareness of this reality on the part of the author. Nevertheless, it appears that in our chapter, the author is siezing upon admittedly later events, not so much to justify the Zerubbabel-led community's original rejection of the "adversaries," as to beef up the apology for that community's inability to carry out their sacred task of temple-building. In this understanding of the author's underlying motivation, we are following Halpern's lead. Halpern picturesquely describes the author's blending together of the actual temple-building and the (later) wall fortifications as "cloaking the latter in the shining raiment of sacred duty that distinguished the former."[188]

C. Methods

How did the author manage to include wall-building of a later time period under the rubric of temple-building of an earlier time period? Three avenues are in evidence here:

1) The thematic and ideological connection between the temple proper and the city as a whole is not something contrived by the author

---

[188] Halpern, "A Historiographic Commentary," 112.

of Ezra 4, but is drawn from the well-established "sacred precinct" motif, in which the temple's holiness is extended to the entire surrounding locale.[189] Eskenazi notes how this motif dominates the entire book of Ezra-Nehemiah.[190] For our purposes, it is sufficient to point to Ezra 6:14, where Artaxerxes, who was to allow Nehemiah to go and build the city walls, is mentioned as one of the Persian kings who sponsored the temple-building. The inclusion of Artaxerxes (who reigned long after the temple-building was completed) is explainable on the grounds that for the author of Ezra, the wall-building ultimately represented the climactic conclusion of the temple-building.[191] Thus, the two could be juxtaposed non-sequentially from even the earliest periods onward.

2) Although the oft-noted use of "resumptive repetition" found in the closing phrases of vv. 5 and 24 sets apart the intervening material as a parenthetical unit,[192] we must also take note of the connection between vv. 23 and 24 signified by the flexible temporal indicator $bē'dayin$ (//Hebrew $'āz$, "then"), which appears at the beginning of v. 24. This term functions as a loose temporal connector between the action it introduces and the immediately preceding action, without, however, establishing the same sequential precision as an explicit dating formula. By resorting to a vague chronological term, the author bridges the large chronological gap between the temple and wall-building projects, bringing them in juxtaposition, even as he formally acknowledges their chronologically separate backgrounds (vv. 6–7).

3) The above dichotomy could have been overcome in the author's mind by bona fide historical speculation. Although the recorded instances which reached him of external interference in the wall-building endeavor postdated the completion of the temple, there was nothing preventing the supposition that earlier attempts at wall-building with similar results had been undertaken previously. At least in ideal terms, such attempts should have been made. Thus, even the hypothetical possibility of wall-building as far back as the time of Zerubbabel allowed the

---

[189] In the Bible, this motif is intimately connected with the so-called "Zion tradition," see e.g., Levenson, *Sinai and Zion*, 156–65. Halpern, "A Historiographic Commentary," 115, notes how the linkage between temple building and wall building is already intimated in Isa. 44–45; Zech. 1–6. He evidently has in mind Isa. 45:13; Zech. 1:16–17; 2:9.

[190] *In an Age of Prose*, 55–56, 120–21.

[191] Ibid., 59–60.

[192] See above, n. 177.

author to use later, specific illustrations of the kind of obstacles that could have thwarted the noble efforts of the original community as well.

In sum, the appropriation of a widespread motif, the skillful use of a vague chronological term, and creative historical speculation, all allowed for a smooth transposition of the displaced material 4:6–24 into its current location.

III. Analysis of the sequence differences in 1 Esdras 2–7

A. *Setting*

As noted above (pp. 115–16), the sequence differences between 1 Esdras and Ezra boil down to two matters: 1) The addition of the three guardsmen story, which traces the rise of Zerubbabel in the court of Darius, and by extension, focuses the rest of Zerubbabel's career (including the material parallel to Ezra 2:1–4:5) within the framework of the early years of Darius. 2) The placement of the Artaxerxes correspondence (with slight but significant adjustments) in an earlier context, immediately following the material parallel to Ezra 1.

At the focus of our methodological concerns is whether these differences represent alternative independent traditions, which are more faithful to the actual course of events than those in MT Ezra. Or does the evidence indicate that 1 Esdras's presentation is still ultimately dependent on the MT, which we have demonstrated to be non-chronological? If, as shall become clear very soon, the latter possibility is correct, how are the existing (empirical) divergencies of 1 Esdras from Ezra to be explained? Can they be said to reflect either literary-thematic, interpretive-exegetical, or ideological concerns? The following chart is meant to address both the issue of 1 Esdras's literary dependency on Ezra, as well as the issue of possible explanations for 1 Esdras's divergencies from Ezra.

Problems in Ezra	Resolutions in 1 Esdras	Inconsistencies in 1 Esdras
A. Zerubbabel and Jeshua's return and activites (2:1–4:5) are presented in the context of the first immigration wave during the early years of Cyrus, as against the combined evidence of Ezra 5:16, the absence of Sheshbazzar in 2:1–4:5, and the prophecies of Haggai and Zechariah, which all suggest that Zerubbabel's and Jeshua's return and activities should be located later on.	The three guardsmen story explains the return of Zerubbabel as the result of his dealings with Darius, thus ostensibly presenting the events paralleling Ezra 2:1–4:5 against the backdrop of the early years of Darius.	1) The three guardsmen story implies that the temple vessels were being sent back to Jerusalem for the first time by Darius (4:43–44, 57). This contradicts 2:14–15 (Ezra 1:11), according to which they were sent back by Cyrus.
		2) 5:55, 71–73 (Ezra 3:7; 4:3–5) once again throw Zerubbabel and his mission back to the reign of Cyrus, in total disregard of 4:47–57.
		3) Chaps. 6–7 (Tattenai correspondence and responses) is oblivious to Darius's supposed prior support for the temple building project as recorded in 4:43–57 (the end of the three guardsmen story).
		4) 6:18, which suggests that Sheshbazzar and Zerubbabel returned at the same early date. (This verse, however, is anomalous even within its own context).

Problems in Ezra	Resolutions in 1 Esdras	Inconsistencies in 1 Esdras
B. A letter, which is addressed to a king later than Darius, and whose contents reflect a period later than Darius, is interpolated into the section which bridges the reigns of Cyrus and Darius (4:7–24).	The earlier literary placement of the letter together with an adjustment of its contents (mention of the temple foundations in 2:18, 20) make it better suited for the period between Cyrus and Darius. A greater time span is allowed for between the first attempt at foundation laying (implied in 2:18) and Zerubbabel's arrival, with an explanation provided for the hardships and delays that befell the first group of returnees.	5) The initiators of the correspondence (Rehum, Shimshai) and the king to whom it was addressed (Artaxerxes) are the same historically later figures as in Ezra (1 Esd. 2:16–30//Ezra 4:7–24).

In the first half of the chart (A), it will be noticed that 1 Esdras's resolution as well as the resulting inconsistencies arise from two factors: a) the inclusion of the three guardsmen story. b) 1 Esdras's repetition, essentially verbatim, of the material found in Ezra 2:1–4:5; 5–6. It will further be noticed that from a logical standpoint, these two factors clash with each other. In other words, the chronological picture emerging from the three guardsmen story could only be maintained if the ensuing material, namely 5:7–7:15 (i.e., the material parallel to Ezra 2:1–4:5; 5–6) had been modified, which it was not. Conversely, the chronological picture emerging from 5:7–7:15 could only be maintained if the three guardsmen story were eliminated, which it was not. This in turn leads to two conclusions: a) The three guardsmen story was deemed by the redactor of 1 Esdras to be of great importance, since he included it despite the problems it caused. b) The redactor of 1 Esdras felt bound to preserve a *Vorlage* akin to the MT largely intact with minimal modifications, despite the internal inconsistencies which this constraint produced for his overall presentation.

B. Motivations

1 Esdras's fidelity to the MT-type *Vorlage* does not, in and of itself, impinge upon the possible historical worth of the sequence represented by the three guardsmen story. That episode could theoretically preserve the kernel of an authentic tradition according to which, Zerubbabel's mission was sponsored by Darius. Such a tradition, clearly separating Zerubbabel's activity from the early return under Sheshbazzar, would line up with the evidence of Ezra 5:16 and Haggai and Zechariah, and remove the chronological displacement which we have hypothesized for Ezra 2:1–4:5. By incorporating the three guardsmen story, the redactor of 1 Esdras could have been seeking to partially rectify the MT's displacement without altering the MT itself. In such a case, the motivating factor for 1 Esdras's inclusion of the three guardsmen story could be seen as exegetical.

Nevertheless, there are indications that the sequence represented by the three guardsmen story is conditioned more by ideological factors than by the authentic course of events. First, the very connection of Zerubbabel with the three guardsmen story looks like a secondary revision of the story (cf. the almost incidental introduction of Zerubbabel in 4:13—"Then the third, that is Zerubbabel...").[193] Second, the story's apparent disregard of any previous Jewish return to Jerusalem during the reign of Cyrus (4:43–57; cf. chart above, p. 132, section A, inconsistency 1) weakens our confidence in its historical character, since such a return is clearly indicated by Ezra 1 and 5:13–16.[194] Third, Zerubbabel's return, while not simultaneous with that of Sheshbazzar, may still very well have occurred sometime during the later years of Cyrus (or the reign of Cambyses), since by Darius's second year, Zerubbabel was already well established as a respected public figure in Judah (Haggai 1:12–15; 2:20–23).[195] Finally, the three guardsmen story's account of Darius's personal involvement in sponsoring the Jewish immigration movement creates intractable difficulties with the tradition of the Tattenai correspondence (see chart above, p. 132, section A, inconsistency 3). Since the historical

---

[193] Torrey, *Ezra Studies*, 25–28; Eissfeldt, *Introduction*, 576.
[194] Cf. Torrey, "A Revised View," 398; Eissfeldt, *Introduction*, 576.
[195] See Ben-Yashar, "On the Problem of Sheshbazzar and Zerubbabel" (Hebrew), 52.

character of the three guardsmen story is so doubtful, I am inclined to side with the approach voiced most recently by Eskenazi, namely that 1 Esdras's primary purpose in incorporating the three guardsmen story was to highlight the mission of Zerubbabel as one of grand and unobstructed progress.[196] Thus, the motivation for the resulting chronological displacement (from MT Ezra) should be viewed as ideological.

This same explanation, of course, applies, at least in part, to 1 Esdras's placement of the Artaxerxes correspondence.[197] This section fits so well into its context in 1 Esdras that some scholars have even been tempted to take it as a running historical account, for example, by supposing that the author of 1 Esdras already identified "Artaxerxes" with Cambyses.[198] I see no evident support for this approach. 1 Esdras is just as aware as Ezra of the true historical position of Artaxerxes (7:4//Ezra 6:14), and thus of the true later setting of the correspondence. Still, the redactor of 1 Esdras evidently realized (like the author of Ezra before him) that the Artaxerxes correspondence could be used by way of historical apologetic, i.e., drawing upon later events in order to justify an earlier situation. Just as enemy interference was to hold up work on the city walls during the reign of Artaxerxes, so the same obstacle could be cited in order to explain the delays surrounding the early work on the temple. This would explain the (non-chronological) linkage expressed in 1 Esd. 2:30 (//Ezra 4:24) between the aftermath of the Artaxerxes correspondence (which historically speaking, brought a halt to work on the city walls many years after the temple was completed), and the delay of the temple building project. The difference between Ezra and 1 Esdras is not in their analogical use of the Artaxerxes correspondence, but rather in how far back the analogy is taken. In Ezra, the delays in building the temple, which are illustrated by way of historical analogy through the Artaxerxes correspondence, occurred after Zerubbabel and Jeshua had arrived on the scene. However, in 1 Esdras, the delays all preceded the climactic arrival of Zerubbabel and his group of returnees. Thus, it is certainly possible, following Eskenazi (above) to view 1 Esdras's placement of the correspondence as another indication of the ideal picture which 1 Esdras was trying to paint of Zerubbabel's mission.

---

196 Eskenazi, *In an Age of Prose*, 173.
197 Ibid.
198 E.g., Ben-Yashar, "On the Problem of Sheshbazzar and Zerubbabel" (Hebrew), 48, n. 17.

At the same time, the placement of the correspondence in 1 Esdras also has salutary exegetical effects. As noted in our chart (above, p. 133, section B, resolutions), 1 Esd. 2:16–30 helps to widen the temporal distance between the arrival and (bad) fortunes of the original group of returnees (i.e., those who came with Sheshbazzar at the beginning of Cyrus's reign) and the group which came with Zerubbabel at a somewhat later point.[199] In this way, 1 Esd. 2:16–30 serves to ameliorate the basic non-chronological feature which I hypothesized for MT Ezra, namely the blending together of the return and activities of Sheshbazzar with those of Zerubbabel and Jeshua (see chart above, p. 132, section A, problems). Interestingly, the textual pluses in 1 Esd. 2:18, 20, referring to the original temple foundations being laid in a context prior to Zerubbabel's arrival, tacitly support the (historical) tradition of Sheshbazzar's role in that effort (Ezra 5:16//1 Esd. 6:20).

In sum, the empirical differences between Ezra and 1 Esdras as regarding the time of Zerubbabel's return and the placement of the Artaxerxes correspondence sustain a two-pronged explanation. 1 Esdras's description of Zerubbabel's return under the sponsorship of Darius, as reflected by the three guardsmen story, is decidedly ideological in its motivation. Although Zerubbabel's return according to the three guardsmen story is widely separated from the non-chronological date of Cyrus's first year implied in Ezra, the three guardsmen story betrays its own unhistorical character by seeming to deny any previous immigration wave during Cyrus's reign, by overly postdating Zerubbabel's return, and by overstating Darius's involvement in supporting the Jews' cause. All this leads to the conclusion that 1 Esdras's interest in the three guardsmen story (and ergo its dating of Zerubbabel's return) was kindled primarily by the aura of grandeur and success which accompanied Zerubbabel's rise to prominence and his subsequent mission.

The placement of the Artaxerxes correspondence in 1 Esdras, which, to be sure, contributes to an ideal portrayal of the Zerubbabel mission by assigning most of the major external impediments to an earlier period, can also be seen as reflecting an attempt at exegetical revision. The subtle additions in 2:18, 20, taken together with the section as a whole, provide an historically justified separation of the earliest doomed efforts of Sheshbazzar from the somewhat later arrivals and ac-

---

[199] On this point, see Licht, "*ʿezrāʾ hahîṣônî*," 153; Talshir, "The Description of the Second Temple's Foundation" (Hebrew), 358–59.

tivities of Zerubbabel and Jeshua. Thus, the placement of the Artaxerxes correspondence in 1 Esdras may also have been intended as a partial rectification of the chronological amorphousness which emerges from Ezra 2:1–4:5.

C. Methods

1 Esdras's manner of incorporating the three guardsmen story into the flow of the Ezra narrative was relatively conservative, given the fact that it did not result in meaningful alterations of the material parallel to MT Ezra 3:1–4:5; 6–7. It was simply a matter of placing originally independent material (i.e., the guardsmen story) at the least inappropriate juncture of the existing narrative and letting the chips fall where they may. Contrariwise, the anchoring of the Artaxerxes correspondence in its present location in 1 Esdras was more thorough, due to the recognition that an early foundation laying for the temple had taken place under Sheshbazzar (Ezra 5:16//1 Esd. 6:20), to which the correspondence pericope could serve as an indignant enemy reaction.

1 Esdras's lifting of the correspondence from its displaced position in Ezra 4 to an even earlier historically displaced point might also have been facilitated by the opportunity for creative textual interpretation posed by Ezra 4:14. The beginning of that verse reads kěʿan kol qěbel dî mělaḥ hêklāʾ mělaḥnāʾ ("Now since we eat the salt of the palace..."). On the surface, 1 Esdras's version of this verse, which reads, "And since the building of the temple is now going on..." (1 Esd. 2:20) would appear to be completely unrelated. However, the possibility exists that the original Aramaic mělaḥ hêklāʾ suggested to the author of 1 Esdras the reading měleʾket hahêkāl ("the building of the temple"), with the rare and misunderstood expression mělaḥ being replaced by the orthographically similar and more familiar term mělāʾkāh, and hêklāʾ being taken as a synonym for the temple.[200] Of course, this suggestion is based only on a hypothesized Hebrew retroversion of the Greek text of 1 Esdras[201] (the original Hebrew having been lost). However, its appeal lies in the fact that were it correct, we would not have to suppose that 1 Esdras's method in repositioning the Artaxerxes correspondence was so much more radical

---

[200] J. Tigay, oral communication.
[201] Kahana, Hassěpārîm Haḥîṣônîm, Vol. 1, 586.

than his treatment of Ezra 3:1–4:5; 6–7. The repositioning, which was done for a combination of ideological and exegetical purposes, as noted above, would have been effected by a sincere, if incorrect, understanding of the MT-type *Vorlage* represented by Ezra 4:14, rather than by an intentional revision of that *Vorlage*.

IV. Analysis of the sequence differences in Antiquities 11:1–113

A. Setting

If 1 Esdras's presentation can be viewed in part as an attempted solution to the chronological perplexities of MT Ezra, the sequence differences in Josephus add up to a systematic attempt at unraveling the intricate pseudo-chronological tapestry of both Ezra and 1 Esdras. We have already taken note in our outline of the material (above, pp. 116–20) of Josephus's treatment of the individual pericopes which make up the accounts of Ezra 1–6 and 1 Esd. 2–7. At this point, we shall recapitulate Josephus's two major sequential departures from both Ezra and 1 Esdras, which relate back to the problems outlined in our chart (above, pp. 132–33).

A. Josephus has Zerubbabel participating in two mass immigration movements to Jerusalem—one at the beginning of Cyrus's reign and reflecting the events of Ezra 1; the other at the beginning of Darius's reign and reflecting the events of 1 Esd. 3:1–4:3 (the three guardsmen story) and Ezra 2:1–4:3 (with the attendant textual modifications made for Ezra 3:7; 4:3—see above p. 119).

B. Josephus identifies the king to whom Rehum and Shimshai (Greek Rathumus and Semellius) wrote as Cambyses, thus maintaining the strict chronological sequence of Persian kings throughout the narrative.

B. Motivation

As was the case with 1 Esdras's divergencies from Ezra, the basic methodological question arises as to whether the sequence differences in Josephus can be said to represent authentic chronological traditions, which would empirically demonstrate the secondary nature of the presentations in Ezra and 1 Esdras. Or do Josephus's sequence differences themselves give the appearance of being secondary alterations of the previous textual traditions, in which case we would have to account for Josephus's motivation(s) in devising these alterations?

Closer investigation emphatically bears out the latter possibility. Josephus's portrayal of Zerubbabel participating in two separate returns seems artificial for the following reasons:

1) The near coincidence in the number of returnees which Josephus gives for both the first return (42,462 [Antiq. 11:18]) and the second return (48,462 [202] [Antiq. 11:69] or 40,742 women and children [ibid.]) arouses suspicion, especially since all the figures seem to be variants of the one given in Ezra 2:64 (42,360).

2) Josephus's presentation doesn't allow a sufficiently meaningful role for Sheshbazzar. In order to highlight Zerubbabel's role as the leader of the first immigration wave in the first year of Cyrus, Josephus makes a valiant attempt to separate Sheshbazzar from the movement by portraying him as the (apparently non-Jewish) governor of Syria and Phoenicia who was already stationed in Judea, and whose role was limited to safeguarding the temple vessels which were carried over from Babylon by Mithredath and Zerubbabel (Antiq. 11:11, 13, 14, 92, 101). But ultimately, Josephus still cannot avoid the evidence of Ezra 5:16, which as we have often noted, specifically identifies Sheshbazzar as the one who led the first immigration wave and who first attended to the temple's foundations (Antiq. 11:93).[203]

3) Josephus's presentation ultimately doesn't resolve the issue of when the temple vessels were brought back (cf. chart above, p. 132, section A, inconsistency 1).

4) Josephus's sundry modifications of Ezra and 1 Esdras which are necessitated by his reconstructed sequence of events, all too often give the impression of being ad hoc harmonizations. For example, the original version of the three guardsmen story represents Zerubbabel as a young man (1 Esd. 3:4; 4:58), who had probably not yet seen much public ser-

---

[202] This is the number yielded by an emendation of the impossible text "myriads four hundred sixty-two and eight thousand." See Marcus's note c in Loeb Classics ed., Vol. 6, 346–47.

[203] As with the Ezra material itself, we must avoid the urge to read into Josephus an identification of Sheshbazzar with Zerubbabel (thus Bartal, "And Again—Who is Sheshbazzar?" [Hebrew], 364; Blenkinsopp, Ezra-Nehemiah, 104). See Ben-Yashar, "On the Problem of Sheshbazzar and Zerubbabel" (Hebrew), 48–49.

vice, let alone served as governor of the Jews in a faraway province (as Josephus would have it). Evidently, this problem led Josephus to represent the position of the king's bodyguard as an honor worthy of older and distinguished persons (Antiq. 11:32). Other modifications in Josephus which occasion similar critical skepticism have already been mentioned above (pp. 119–20), namely his textual pluses to Ezra 3:7 and 4:3 (Antiq. 11:78, 86), and his rationale for Tattenai's appeal to Darius (Antiq. 11:89).

Equally grave doubt sets in concerning the historical authenticity of Josephus's identification of Cambyses as the recipient of the letter written by the Jews' adversaries. To be sure, this identification succeeds in preserving a straight chronological sequence for the narrative at hand.[204] However, not only is Cambyses unknown in the previous textual traditions, but Josephus himself does not again refer directly to Cambyses' supposed prohibition except in Antiq. 11:97, where he mentions it almost as an afterthought in explaining why Darius might have considered reversing his favorable attitude towards the Jews' efforts at building the temple.

All in all, Josephus's divergencies from both Ezra and 1 Esdras can safely be treated as secondary in origin and exegetically motivated. That is to say, they represent Josephus's attempt as an historian to engage his sources, and synthesize the seemingly conflicting data. If this process of disambiguation wasn't foolproof, it still provided for a smoother historiographic record than either the Biblical or the apocryphal versions alone.

C. Methods

Although Josephus took wider liberties with his source material than is usually evidenced by redactions of the Biblical text, his methodology provides a striking analogy to how ancient tradents could bring together sources which originally spoke in more than one voice. In order to uphold the notion of Zerubbabel's presence in Jerusalem from the earliest period of return onwards despite the contrary testimony of 1 Esdras, Josephus splices a version of Cyrus's command concerning the temple from Ezra 6:3–5 into Ezra 1:8, making sure to expand the command so that it explicitly mentions Zerubbabel (Antiq. 11:12–18). Josephus

---
[204] Cf. also the reasoning of Blenkinsopp, Ezra-Nehemiah, 106.

doesn't hesitate to do this despite the fact that he also uses the same text in its original context (i.e., upon Darius's later discovery of Cyrus's edict) without mentioning Zerubbabel (*Antiq.* 11:99–103), although even there, unlike Ezra 6:3–5, he does mention Sheshbazzar. This method of expanding one context from another while modifying both is reminiscent of the Samaritan Pentateuch's treatment of narratives which are alluded to in more than one place (e.g., the episode of Jethro's advice to Moses, which the Samaritan Pentateuch fills out in Exod. 18 from Deut. 1).[205] Josephus's harmonistic expansions of Ezra 3:7 and 4:3, designed to have the narrative encompass the first two years of Darius (above, p. 119), are in consonance with this same harmonization process.

Josephus's identification of Cambyses as the king to whom Rehum and Shimshai sent correspondence is bolder still. Rather than attempting to integrate diverse sources, Josephus exercised his personal historical judgement by switching the name of the later king Artaxerxes to one whose period of reign corresponded more smoothly to the sequence and circumstances suggested by the account of the correspondence in 1 Esdras.

V. Summary of the sequence differences in Ezra 1–6 and related post-Biblical material

The preceding four sections have demonstrated a number of chronological displacements which are found both in MT Ezra 1–6 and the parallel post-Biblical accounts. The clearest case of displacement in MT Ezra 1–6 is the relocation of the correspondence directed to the fifth-century Persian king Artaxerxes to a sixth-century context between the reigns of Cyrus and Darius (Ezra 4:7–24). This displacement has an ideological motivation, namely to excuse the delays in the building of the temple by appealing to historical analogy. Just as documented evidence showed that the later building of Jerusalem's city wall was delayed by external interference, so the same could be inferred for the original delays in the temple building project.

1 Esdras places the correspondence to Artaxerxes in an even earlier context, namely before the arrival of Zerubbabel in Jerusalem. This could very well be explained as reflecting 1 Esdras's desire to concentrate the

---

[205] Tigay, "An Empirical Basis," 333–34. See also above, n. 153.

setbacks suffered by the Jewish community in Judah to before Zerubbabel's immigration. The same desire probably lies behind 1 Esdras's incorporation of the three guardsmen story, which results in the displacement of Zerubbabel's immigration (vis-a-vis MT Ezra) from the early years of Cyrus to the second year of Darius. At the same time, 1 Esdras's placement of the correspondence to Artaxerxes (though not its inclusion of the three guardsmen story; see above, pp. 134–35) may also derive from an attempt to clearly separate the periods of activity of Sheshbazzar and Zerubbabel which are artificially fused by MT Ezra 2:1– 4:5.

Josephus's reassigning of the correspondence to Cambyses as well as his suggestion that Zerubbabel came to Jerusalem twice (both during Cyrus's reign and Darius's reign) represents a secondary exegetical exercise to salvage the historical trustworthiness of both MT Ezra and 1 Esdras. However, the basic underlying problem in both of the latter sources, namely to what extent are Zerubbabel's return and activities to be separated from those of Sheshbazzar (in the early years of Cyrus), still remains a matter whose basis and resolution lack firm empirical documentation. For that reason, I shall be returning to this issue in the final chapter of the book, which deals with cases of displacement that are recognizable only through equivocal indirect evidence, such as hints within the very text under scrutiny (see below, pp. 167–74).

Esther 2:21–23 and Addition A to Esther

Setting

The six additional passages which were appended to the Greek translation of Esther[206] represent primarily an attempt to overlay the

---

[206] The colophon to the additions (Addition F:11) mentions that "the above book of Purim" was translated into Greek by one Lysimachus of Jerusalem and was brought to Egypt in the fourth year of Ptolemy and Cleopatra. Depending on the royal pair intended, this could come out to either 114 B.C.E. or 78 B.C.E. (see Moore, *The Additions*, 161; Eissfeldt, *Introduction*, 592). On the surface, "the above book of Purim" would appear to refer to the entire Greek version as we now have it, including the additions. However, it is not out of the question that Lysimachus' translation did not yet include all of the material presently found in the additions. Additions A:12– 17 and C:17–23, in particular, appear to be quite late, since unlike the other additional material, they do not appear in Josephus or the Old Latin (Moore, *The*

book with specifically religious elements. This is accomplished by frequently invoking God's name (which is not mentioned in the MT at all and only sparingly in the LXX's parallel portions) and by portraying Mordechai and Esther as offering prayers to him (e.g., Additions A, C, F).[207] The additions also intend to provide the book with a greater stamp of authenticity (e.g., Additions B and E, which give the texts of Ahasuerus's decrees concerning the Jews).[208] These concerns point to the secondary nature of the additions, as does the fact that the additions are not found in any of the standard Semitic translations based on the Hebrew text.[209] The presumption that the additions are secondary applies as well to the analysis of a notable sequence difference from the MT.

Toward the end of Addition A (vv. 12–17),[210] we find what constitutes a rough parallel to the section in the MT which narrates Mordechai's uncovering of a plot against the king (Esther 2:21–23). According to Addition A, after experiencing a dream which foreshadowed an upcoming struggle, Mordechai overheard and reported a plot to kill the king. Because of his role in exposing the plotters, Mordechai was rewarded by the king but was marked for destruction by Haman. Now, since Addition A was inserted in the slot before MT Esther 1:1–3:13, two oddities result: a) The additional section A:12–17 tells of the plot in an earlier chronological context than does MT Esther. Instead of occurring after Esther's coronation in the king's seventh year (Esther 2:16–17), it is now related in a context preceding the opening of the Esther narrative in the king's second year (A:1; cf. Esther 1:3). b) Far from replacing the original section Esther 2:21–23, Addition A:12–17 is merely appended to the existing text, with the result that the two corresponding passages are left standing in fairly close proximity. This is a similar situation to what we found in 1 Esdras, where the author essentially retained the MT tradition even when it created inconsistencies with his own presentation.

Additions, 166, 179–80). We shall sidestep the complex issues of origin and authorship by referring simply to the (final) editor of the Greek version of Esther, who was, after all, responsible for the form of the text as we now have it.
[207] Moore, *The Additions*, 158.
[208] Ibid., 159.
[209] Ibid., 153–54.
[210] Following Moore's numeration.

An internal literary examination of Addition A also betrays its secondary nature. A:2 states that Mordechai was serving in the king's court from the outset of the narrative. Yet, according to A:16, the king first appointed Mordechai to serve in the court as a reward for uncovering the plot. Each of these conflicting statements in turn goes against the MT Esther narrative (retained by the editor of the additions) according to which Mordechai was not rewarded promptly for his loyalty to the king (Esther 6:3) and was not appointed to serve in the court until after Haman's downfall (Esther 8:1–2). In addition, the implication of A:17, namely that Haman's sympathy toward the plotters was the cause of his hatred toward Mordechai, conflicts with Esther 3:5 according to which Haman's antagonism was rooted in Mordechai's refusal to bow down to him. The question thus arises what would have brought the (final) editor of the Greek version of Esther to insert the section A:12–17, thereby disturbing the sequence of the original narrative as well as producing the other inconsistencies just noted?

Motivation

The motivation guiding the editor of Greek Esther in this instance was thematic. Addition A opens with Mordechai's dream which serves as a portentous sign of the upcoming struggle between Mordechai and Haman. As if to focus immediately on the dynamics of this struggle, the editor of Greek Esther continues with his version of the plot episode, in which Mordechai and Haman are set up against each other both personally and politically. Thus, the titanic clash between the two main protagonists of the book is followed up on immediately instead of being delayed until ch. 3 as it is in the MT. Both the notice of Mordechai's reward (A:16) and the mention of Haman's position regarding the court intrigue (A:17) serve to place the two men in their respective antagonistic positions from the outset. The fact that each of these details conflicted with other data in the book (see above) was not as important as the thematic focus which they provided.

Method

Even as the editor of Greek Esther introduced elements which conflicted with the original story, he was also careful to eliminate flagrant inconsistencies which his rearrangement could have produced. For example, since Esther had not yet come onto the scene at this early stage of the narrative, Addition A could hardly have her report Mordechai's findings to the king (as stated in Esther 2:22). In an effort to smooth out this glaring problem, the editor of Greek Esther states that Mordechai personally informed the king of the plot (A:13). In fact, the need to allow for Mordechai's personal access to the king is probably what prompted the editor of Greek Esther to identify Mordechai as a court servant from the outset (A:2), despite the internal inconsistency that this created with the notice of Mordechai's reward in A:16 (see above, p. 144). The editor of Greek Esther also attempted to smoothen out gross inconsistencies in his presentation in an additional way. Having included the names of the conspirators (Bigtan and Teresh) in A:12–17, he (or his Hebrew *Vorlage*) eliminated those names from the text of 2:21–23, so that the two episodes would not, strictly speaking, be mutually exclusive.[211]

Summary of Chapter Three

The results obtained from the study of chronological displacement in post-Biblical sources can be outlined in chart form as follows:

Text	Type of Displacement	Motivation	Method
Jubilees 35–41	a) postdates Isaac's death to after the sale of Joseph b) postdates Judah's family affairs to the seven years of plenty in Egypt	a) exegetical: correcting a perceived displacement b) literary: filling in missing narrative detail	a) precise dating of all events by Jubilees b) reinterpretation of the vague *wayĕhî bāʿēt hahî'* of Gen. 38:1

Chart continues

---

[211] Tigay, "Conflation," 60.

Text	Type of Displacement	Motivation	Method
Tôseftā' Sôṭāh 8; Jer. Tal. Sôṭāh 7:3; Josephus, Antiq. 5:68–70	antedates blessing and curse ceremony of Josh. 8:30–35 to the day of crossing the Jordan OR postdates it to the end of the conquest period	a) exegetical: harmonizing Josh. 8:30–35 with the strictest reading of Deut. 27 OR b) historical: arriving at a more logical geo-military picture	a) forced explanations of either Deut. 27 or the 'āz of Josh. 8:30 OR b) recasting the time frame of the commands of Deut. 27
S.O. ch. 12; Josephus, Antiq. 5:134–135	antedates the Danite migration and concubine incident to the beginning of the Judges period	a) exegetical: making explicit what is seemingly implicit in the Bible itself through attention to the details of specific verses OR b) thematic: setting up a cause-and-effect cycle characteristic of the beginning of the period	a) fitting undated events into any open spot in the chronographic scheme b) use of thematic links and analogies
LXX 3 Reigns 12:24g–n	antedates the story of Jeroboam's sick child and Jeroboam's rejection to before Jeroboam assumes the kingship	ideological (political-religious): anti-Jeroboam	a) highlighting links between the birth of the child in Egypt and his subsequent fate b) selective use of the original text, e.g., omitting Dtr. portions inappropriate to an earlier context
MT 1 Ki. 21	postdates the Naboth incident to after the first round of wars with Aram	thematic: closing the account of Ahab's sins and sealing the fate of his dynasty with a paradigmatic example of his evil	vague formula 'aḥar haddĕbārîm hā'ēlleh; fitting the story into the three-year gap presupposed by 22:1
MT Ezra 4:6–24	antedates documents from the times of Xerxes and Artaxerxes concerning the wall building to a context between Cyrus and Darius concerning the temple building	ideological (cultic): strengthening the explanation for the delays in the temple building	a) use of the "sacred precinct" motif b) vague term bē'dayin = 'āz c) creative historical speculation

Text	Type of Displacement	Motivation	Method
1 Esdras 2–7	a) postdates arrival of Zerubbabel from the early years of Cyrus to the second year of Darius b) antedates document from the time of Artaxerxes even earlier than the MT to the time before Zerubbabel's arrival	a) ideological (political): attaching Zerubbabel's mission to a period of success b) ideological (political) & exegetical: separating the returns and activities of Sheshbazzar and Zerubbabel more explicitly	a) incorporation of additional material (story of 3 guardsmen) at the least inappropriate point in the existing narrative b) inserting specific references to the temple building, either intentionally or through a misinterpretation of Ezra 4:14
Josephus, Antiq. 11:1–113	Zerubbabel comes to Jerusalem twice; the king of the correspondence is identified as Cambyses and the setting is between the two missions of Zerubbabel	exegetical: harmonizing the conflicting accounts of Ezra and 1 Esdras	splicing in a text from a later context referring to an earlier setting (Ezra 6:3–5); harmonistic expansions of the text in Ezra 3:7 and 4:3 to include Darius
Addition A: 12–17 to Esther	antedates the conspiracy of Bigtan and Teresh by at least five years to before the opening of the Esther narrative	thematic: setting up the great clash between Mordechai and Haman from the outset	making appropriate alterations to the original story, e.g., having Mordechai report the plot himself

In this chapter, which afforded us the most examples so far of chronological displacement, we encountered the greatest variety of variables in terms of each of the categories, namely types of displacements, motivations, and methods. For example, we came across more cases of postdating than in the materials examined previously. The span of some of the displacements involved encompassed not only a few years (e.g., Addition A to Esther) but even a few generations (e.g., *Sēder ʿÔlām* and Josephus on Judges 17–21; MT Ezra 4:6–24 and parallels). As can be expected, the post-Biblical material contains a fair number of exegetical motivations, since some of this material, particularly the Rabbinic sources and Josephus, had as one of its guiding forces the elucidation of received traditions. Examples of thematic motivations also continue to surface with the ubiquitous integration of historical writing and literary artistry. However, the greatest variety of all relates to the methods employed. Besides the familiar methods of vague chronological formulae (e.g., 'aḥar haddĕbārîm hā'ēlleh in the Masoretic text of 1 Ki. 21) and selective use of an original text (e.g., the omission of inappropriate Deuteronomistic material in LXX 3 Reigns 12:24g–n), there are other, bolder methods in evidence. Josephus goes so far as to reword the commands of Deut. 27 in order to have them conform to his chronological conception. The same applies to his glosses of Ezra 3:7 and 4:3. But Josephus is not alone in introducing substantive alterations to a pre-existing text. For example, Addition A to Esther has to have Mordechai himself report the plot to the king rather than Esther (as in Esther 2:22), since Esther has not yet made her appearance in the narrative to that point. 1 Esdras 2:15–30 inserts specific references to the temple building, as opposed to Ezra 4:6–23 which speaks just of the city walls (although this might be the result of misguided interpretation rather than intentional alteration, see above, pp. 137–38).

We have thus arrived at a turning point in the present study. After assembling much data concerning chronological displacement in its various aspects (type, motivation, and method), the question remains to what extent the conclusions arrived at from an empirical perspective can be applied to the study of cases for which the basis for identifying a displacement is wholly internal or non-empirical. This question will underlie the next part of the book, in which we will attempt to demonstrate that speculative interpretations of Biblical material can be strengthened through the force of "empirical models" emanating from within the Bible itself or from cognate literatures.

Chapter IV

Chronological Displacements Inferred from Internal Evidence

Introduction

Up until now, we have analyzed cases of chronological displacement which derive from an empirical basis. That is, the arguments pointing toward displacement were based either on alternative chronological frameworks present in two or more texts relating to the same events, or on general historical data which suggested a particular chronological framework that the author/editor chose to ignore. Cases of this variety put us on relatively firm ground in tracing the development of and reasons for the displacement. In the present chapter, however, the apparent displacements which we shall be studying are recognizable only through hints emerging from the same material in which the displacement occurs. Since, in such cases, we cannot definitively point to a prior text from which the author/editor deviated, nor can we confidently state that the author/editor steered away from external historical data known to him, the grounds for identifying and explaining such displacements are by definition "non-empirical" or conjectural. Nevertheless, the patterns identified and conclusions drawn from the material in chapters 1–3 can serve as guideposts in the exegetical tasks facing us in the present chapter.

It ought to be stated clearly that the absence of empirically-based evidence for the proposed cases of displacement in this chapter necessarily precludes the definitive conclusion that displacement actually occurred, at least in the most literal sense. In other words, even if our arguments showing that a given event appears to be presented outside of its natural chronological context seem reasonable, it cannot be proven that there actually existed an earlier rendition reflecting the original sequence, from which the author/editor of our received text consciously deviated. Nor can internally-derived arguments for displacement carry the same weight as evidence adduced from external historical data of which we can reasonably assume that the author/editor was aware. The most that internally-derived arguments for displacement can show is that an author/editor may have presented a given event as occurring in a chronological context other than where hints in his own work intimate that the event belongs sequentially. Thus, in the present chapter, I shall be using the term "displacement" in a somewhat looser sense to refer simply to an author/editor's presentation of an event as if it occurred in a context which he himself inadvertantly suggests is sequentially inaccurate. In theory, then, we can still postulate that the editor dislocated a given event from a previous written context. However, since we lack the empirical evidence which would prove that such a process actually occurred, we must also be open to the possibility that the event in question was narrated in the text from the outset in a non-sequential manner. This particular uncertainty regarding the literary "pre-history" of a text in which the case for displacement can only be made on internal grounds is one of the inherent limitations of the examples to be taken up in this chapter. As in the previous two chapters, I shall present the examples following the order of the Biblical text, beginning with Genesis 35:27–29.

Genesis 35:27–29

We have already taken note of the internal chronological displacement surrounding the notice of Isaac's death in our discussion of its placement in the Book of Jubilees (above, chapter 3, pp. 80–81). There we saw how Rashi correctly concludes that Gen. 35:27–29 is an example of 'ên mûqdām ûmĕ'ûḥār battôrāh ("there is no earlier or later in the Torah") based on the combined evidence of Gen. 25:26; 37:2; 41:46; 45:6; and 47:9. According to the chronological data obtained from those verses, Jacob was 108 years old when Joseph was sold, making Isaac 168 years old at the time. Thus, Gen. 35:27–29, which records Isaac's death at the age of 180 but precedes the account of Joseph's sale in Gen. 37, appears to describe Isaac's death in a context at least twelve years earlier than its actual date of occurrence.[1]

Analysis of documentary sources in Genesis such as that offered by Westermann and Speiser does not provide a specific explanation for the phenomenon in question although it does suggest by implication a particular view of the issue. Both of these scholars note how Gen. 35:27–29 (P), which tells of Isaac's surviving until after Jacob's return from a lengthy twenty-year stay in Haran, appears to be inconsistent with the description of Gen. 27:1–45 (J), in which Isaac is already hovering near death before Jacob sets out for Haran. In light of this apparent discrepancy, Westermann concludes: "The only explanation is that there are two different conceptions of the patriarchal story,"[2] while Speiser writes: "P's chronology is self-consistent, but it cannot be integrated with the data of J and E."[3] Now, since Speiser (along with most scholars) views ch. 37 (the account of Joseph's sale) as reflecting a patchwork of J and E, one is led to believe that Speiser would view the chronological displacement which we have noted for Gen. 35:27–29 (P) as no more than the inevitable clumsy result of two (or more) sources being interwoven in close proximity.

However, without necessarily denying the presence of various sources, the whole burden of our work has attempted to point the way toward understanding the final redactor's purposeful and judicious arrangement of whatever sources came down to him. It is for this reason that we can subscribe to the topical explanation offered by Sarna to the effect that the positioning of the notice of Isaac's death is intended to close the circle of Isaac's life before moving on to the detailed personal accounts of the next generation (chaps. 36, 37f.).[4] Sarna's explanation is supported by the fact that the same structure is found elsewhere in Genesis itself. For example, the notice of Abraham's death in 25:7–10 precedes the *tôlĕdôt* (genealogical listings) of his eldest son Ishmael (25:12–18) and the extended *tôlĕdôt* account of Isaac (25:19f.), just as Gen. 35:27–29 is followed by the *tôlĕdôt* of Esau (ch. 36) and Jacob (37:2).[5] Similarly, Ibn Ezra notes how Terah's passing is noted already in

---

[1] Rashi to Gen. 35:29 (in Rosenbaum and Silbermann, *Pentateuch*, Vol. 1, 173).
[2] Westermann, *Genesis 12–36*, 557.
[3] Speiser, *Genesis*, 274–75.
[4] Sarna, *Genesis*, 246.
[5] Ibid.

Gen. 11:32 before the text moves on to tell in detail of Abram's sojourns (chaps. 12f.), even though the chronological data would suggest that Terah survived into the lifetime of Isaac.[6]

Ramban makes the interesting observation that if anything, topical arrangement would have demanded that the notice of Isaac's death be placed even earlier, namely before any of the lengthy episodes concerning Jacob (from ch. 28 and following). He therefore concludes that the present positioning of the notice was also meant to demonstrate how Isaac in fact lived to a ripe old age until such time that his sons could participate together in burying him honorably.[7]

Exodus 18

Setting

One of the most celebrated cases of apparent chronological displacement in the Pentateuch concerns Exodus 18, the chapter dealing with the arrival and stay of Moses's father-in-law Jethro in the Israelite camp. The rabbis of the Midrash and Talmud debated the question of whether Jethro's visit preceded the giving of the law at Sinai (Exod. 19ff.), as per the given order of the Scriptures, or followed it, in which case, the present order would reflect antedating of the visit.[8] Unfortunately, the exegetical reasoning behind the various positions taken by the rabbis is not completely spelled out. All that one can infer from the give and take in the Mĕkiltāʾ[9] and B. Zĕbāḥîm 116a is that the rabbis were divided on what particular news would have induced Jethro to make the journey from Midian. Evidently, those rabbis who explained Jethro's arrival as the result of his hearing about the splitting of the sea or the war with Amalek held the position that the episode is written in its original sequence. Contrariwise, those who held that the episode is displaced felt that only the news of the revelation at Sinai would have moved Jethro to call upon Moses. However, since the latter position is

---

[6] Ibn Ezra to Gen. 6:3.
[7] Ramban to Gen. 35:28 (Chavel English ed., Vol. 1, 431).
[8] The Midrashic sources are Mĕkiltāʾ, Yitro, sec. 1 (Horovitz-Rabin ed., 188) and *Numbers Rabbāh* 13:2 (Freedman English ed., Vol. 6, 498–99). The Talmudic sources are B. Zĕbāḥîm 116a and B. ʿĂbôdāh Zārāh 24b.
[9] See previous note.

clearly precluded by the text, in which only the exodus is mentioned without any reference to the revelation (18:1, 8–10), the arguments in favor of displacement must be sought elsewhere.

Ibn Ezra systematically spelled out the internal textual indications which support the notion that ch. 18 has been displaced from a later context. Ibn Ezra's points are summarized by Sarna in his recent commentary on Exodus as follows:[10]

1) 18:5 records that the people were encamped at "the mountain of God," which presupposes that the journey between Rephidim (17:8) and Sinai (19:2) had already taken place.

2) 18:16 refers to the adjudication of "the laws and the teachings of God." This would have far more relevance after the giving of the law at Sinai than before it.

3) If Jethro's departure in 18:27 is to be viewed as identical with Num. 10:29–32, which tells of Moses sending away his father-in-law in the second month of the second year after the exodus, the time-frame of the narrative in Exod. 18 is set almost one full year after the revelation at Sinai (cf. Exod. 19:1).

4) Deut. 1:9–19, which repeats the story about the establishment of the judicial system (though without mentioning Jethro), states explicitly that the people were already at, and in fact preparing to leave Horeb (Sinai), at the time of the judicial restructuring.

On the opposite side of the debate, Ramban[11] insists that had Jethro indeed arrived after the revelation at Sinai, some recognition of that event would certainly have been present in the text. As for Ibn Ezra's claims, Ramban argues that "the mountain of God" (18:5) refers not to the site of the Israelite encampment, but to the place in the wilderness from where Jethro sent a message to Moses (18:6). Ramban also supposes that 18:27 refers not to Jethro's final departure for home but only to a temporary leave of absence for the purpose of proselytizing his family. The dialogue in Num. 10:29–32 is to be understood as occurring later, following Jethro's rejoining the Israelite community after his temporary absence. Ramban does not relate to the problems arising from the mention of the laws in 18:16 or from Deut. 1. However, other commentators come to his defense by pointing out that some laws had indeed

---

[10] Ibn Ezra to Exod. 18:1. See Sarna, *Exodus*, 97–98.
[11] Ramban to Exod. 18:1 (Chavel English ed., Vol. 2, 251–56).

been given prior to the revelation at Sinai (e.g., some Sabbath restrictions in Exod. 16:23, 26, 29).[12] Moreover, Deut. 1 refers only to the period in which Jethro's advice was put into practice rather than to the time of his initial arrival. Thus, the most one could say regarding displacement in Exod. 18 is that vv. 24–27 jump ahead to a later point in time simply for the purpose of rounding out the narrative framework.[13]

In my estimation, the latter two points raised by Ibn Ezra are inconclusive, since Num. 10:29 may not be referring to Jethro at all but to his son, and Deut. 1 makes no mention of Jethro whatsoever. However, Ibn Ezra's first two points, which emanate from the narrative itself, are clearly strong enough to carry the debate and the explanations of Ramban and his supporters to these points are unconvincing. Ramban's major objection to the idea of chronological displacement in Exod. 18, namely the omission of any reference to the revelation at Sinai, is somewhat tempered by the similar omission of the events at Sinai from other accounts of Israel's "sacred history" (e.g., Deut. 26:5–9; Josh. 24:2–13; Ps. 105).[14] Besides, midrashic conceptions notwithstanding, the revelation at Sinai is never spoken of in the Bible as attracting the same attention from gentiles that attended the exodus (cf. Exod. 15:14–15; Josh. 2:10–11). It appears, then, that the narrative in Exod. 18 can indeed be viewed as having occurred in a later context than that in which it is set. Explanations for the editor's antedating of the narrative must therefore be sought.

Motivation

Explanations which have been offered are predominantly of the topical-thematic variety. According to Rashbam, Exod. 18 was relocated to an earlier chronological point so that the legal sections following the account of the revelation at Sinai would not be interrupted by a prosaic narrative.[15] Childs explains the literary context of Exod. 18 as a kind of parallel with Exod. 2. Both chapters appear immediately before momen-

---

[12] Bahye, *Bē'ûr ʿal Hattôrāh*, Vol. 2, 161.
[13] Abravanel, *Pērûš ʿal Hattôrāh*, Vol. 2, 152–53. Cf. the approach of Rabbi (Judah the Prince) to Exod. 16:35 in *Sifrê Numbers* 64 (Horovitz ed., 61).
[14] Cf. von Rad, "The Form-Critical Problem," 3–26, 53–54.
[15] Rashbam to Exod. 18:13 (Rozen ed., 107).

tous events of revelation at the mountain of God (Exod. 3 and 19) and purport to portray the serene but fleeting moments in Moses's family life which preceded his great undertakings.16 As such, the placement of Exod. 18 before Exod. 19 can be viewed as deriving from a conscious imitation of the juxtaposition of Exod. 2 and 3.

Neither of the above explanations is particularly satisfactory; Rashbam's because it doesn't delve deeply enough into the particular function of Exod. 18 in its present location and Childs's because the "idyllic family scene" which he imagines can hardly be identified as a major concern of Exod. 18. To be sure, Moses's wife and children return to him after an undefined period of separation, but following this reunification, they drop from the scene and the focus is clearly on Jethro in his role as a gentile acknowledger of YHWH and advisor to Moses.

The best explanation for the displacement of Exod. 18 is still that suggested by Ibn Ezra[17] and Radak,[18] namely that the juxtaposition of Jethro's visit with the Amalekite war in the preceding chapter (Exod. 17:8–16) is designed to contrast the opposing attitudes of the Kenites' ancestor Jethro (see Jud. 1:16) and their neighbors, the Amalekites, toward Israel. Whereas Amalek displayed unbridled antipathy toward YHWH's chosen people, Jethro was eager to acknowledge and celebrate YHWH's saving power. It therefore comes as no surprise that in a later period, Saul singled out the Kenites for special favorable treatment when he embarked on his campaign against the Amalekites (1 Sam. 15:6). The use of displacement to achieve a contrasting effect is somewhat reminiscent of the case in Addition A to Esther (above, p. 144). There, Mordechai's reporting of the plot against the king is moved up to the beginning of the book where it serves to focus on the herculean struggle between the forces of good (represented by Mordechai) and evil (represented by Haman) as foreshadowed by the dream which opens the (Greek) book. The approach of Ibn Ezra and Radak to the placement of Exod. 18 is further strengthened by the seemingly deliberate links between Exod. 17 and 18 recognized by Cassuto which will be noted in the upcoming paragraph.

---

[16] Childs, *The Book of Exodus*, 327.
[17] Commentary to Exod. 18:1.
[18] Commentary to Jud. 1:16.

Methods

The use of associative links to anchor a displaced text in its given location is a technique with which we have already come across in connection with 1 Chr. 13-14 (above, p. 60) and LXX 3 Reigns 12:24g-n (above, p. 109). In the context of Exod. 17-18, Cassuto does a great service in spelling out the verbal similarities which are found specifically between the section dealing with Amalek (17:8-16) and the Jethro episode.[19] These include: "Choose for us men" (17:9)//"Moses chose men of valor" (18:25); "Moses's hands were heavy" (17:12)//"The matter is too heavy for you" (18:18); "until sunset" (17:12)//"from morning until evening" (18:13). Descriptions of Moses as he was preparing for and overseeing a war against a foreign foe (ch. 17) find their mirror image in descriptions of Moses engaging in peaceful activites suggested by a foreign friend (ch. 18). To be sure, no one of these and other proposed links makes a strong impression on its own. However, the cumulative effect is sufficient to bear out the conclusion that the juxtaposition of the episodes concerning Jethro and Amalek reflects an intentional editorial design which highlights the contrast between the two protagonists. Still another associative feature of Exod. 18, this time with the following chapter, is pointed out by Sarna, who notes that the focus of 18:13-26, namely the administration of God's laws and teachings, leads smoothly into the chapters dealing with the giving of the law (Exod. 19-20).[20] Thus, even though the cart is put before the horse sequentially (with the administration of the law preceding its formal enactment), the latter half of Exod. 18 still serves to bring us into the orbit of the legal material which is to follow.

The presence of verbal links between two juxtaposed units does not necessarily indicate either that the units were originally written in their present sequence or that the editor *created* these links in order to juxtapose units that were once separated from each other. Although both of these possibilities must be entertained, a third possibility is that two units which were once separated from each other happened to share a common stock of narrative vocabulary. Recognizing these verbal similarities,

---

[19] Cassuto, Pērûš ʿal Sēper Šĕmôt, 146.
[20] Sarna, *Exodus*, 98.

the editor, who was looking for a precise location in which to displace one of these units, chose to juxtapose them. In our case, for example, the editor who set out to narrate Jethro's visit in conjunction with the Amalekite war could also have arranged the former unit *ahead* of the latter unit. However, the links which the Jethro narrative exhibited not only with ch. 17 but also with ch. 19 (as noted above) induced the editor to (re)arrange the Jethro episode precisely as he did.

Judges 17–21

Setting

The last five chapters in Judges are commonly referred to as an appendix to the book.[21] In terms of style and content, these chapters do indeed stand apart from the body of the book. No longer do we find the familiar pattern consisting of the Israelites' sin, punishment, crying out to God, and deliverance through a "judge" (e.g., 3:12–15) or the formula "After him, so-and-so led Israel" (e.g., 12:8, 11, 13). Rather than relating the activities of a particular judge, chaps. 17–21 cover major incidents such as the Danite migration and the civil war against Benjamin, both of which are said to have taken place during a time when "there was no king in Israel, each man did what was right in his eyes" (17:6; 21:25; cf. 18:1; 19:1). In addition to the break in style and content which occurs beginning with ch. 17, there is reason to believe, as we have already discussed in chapter three (above, pp. 93–97) that chaps. 17–21 are chronologically displaced and belong, sequentially speaking, at the beginning of the book. The most salient points in favor of this conclusion can be briefly recapped as follows:

1) The genealogies of both 18:30 ("Jonathan son of Gershom son of Moses"[22]) and 20:28 ("Phinehas son of Elazar son of Aaron") identify protagonists in the episodes who lived only one or two generations after the exodus.

2) The Danites' search for a permanent inheritance seems to fit better in the period immediately following the early conquests when the

---

[21] See, for example, Soggin, *Judges*, 261; Rudin-O'brasky, "The Appendices" (Hebrew).

[22] See above chapter 3, n. 44.

individual tribes were faced with the situation of the remaining militant Canaanite enclaves in their midst (as opposed to the period slightly later when the Canaanites were subdued into forced labor; see in particular 1:34–35.)

Admittedly, these arguments are not air-tight and some of the other points advanced in support of the case for chaps. 17–21 having been displaced are even more tenuous (above, pp. 93–97). However, cases in which the arguments for chronological displacement are "non-empirical," i.e., where the evidence is drawn solely from an internal examination of the material in question, are by definition, bound to be lacking firm substantiation. At the same time, as long as there exists even a chance of displacement having occurred, it behooves us to suggest appropriate motivations for this possibility, particularly in a case like this in which there is an ancient precedent stemming from exegetical considerations for treating the material as chronologically displaced (viz. the *Sēder ʿÔlām*, see above, pp. 90–91).

Motivation

Among the medieval commentators who offered explanations for the location of chaps. 17–21 in a displaced context, Rashi points to the silver that plays a woeful role in the stories of both Micah (17:3) and Delilah (16:5), thus creating an associative link between the two. Rashi notes that there are even those who would identify Delilah and Micah's mother as one and the same person in light of the identical amount of money (1100 silver pieces) mentioned in both contexts. In Rashi's opinion, this particular conclusion is precluded by the assumption that Micah preceded Samson by many years. However, the general similarity between the impious use of silver in both episodes was sufficient reason to place the Micah narrative in its present location.[23]

Ralbag elaborates upon Rashi's explanation, expanding the mere associative link into a more meaningful thematic connection. He notes that both of the "silvers of woe" brought troubles specifically upon the tribe of Dan. In the Delilah episode, the silver led to the downfall of Samson, who was a Danite. In the Micah episode, the silver was used to

---

[23] Rashi to Jud. 17:3.

form the idol which ultimately led the Danites astray from the proper service of God.[24]

Abravanel approaches the issue topically. In his words:

> The author of this book saw fit to tell first without interruption of all the judges that arose in Israel one after the other, and what happened to them in the wars with the nations after the death of Joshua. And after he completed the story of Samson who was the last of the judges in this book, he went back to tell of the things which occurred amongst the children of Israel between Joshua and the judges.[25]

However, none of the above explanations is satisfactorily convincing. Rashi's explanation relates only to the first section of the Micah story (17:1–4) rather than to the sequels which form the crux of the narrative. Furthermore, in our analysis of cases for which empirical evidence was available, isolated associative links have served only as a method to bind two units once displacement has occurred (e.g., the *pereṣ* motif in 1 Chr. 13–14, above p. 60) rather than as a motivation for the use of displacement in the first place. Ralbag's explanation only slightly mitigates the latter problem and leaves one wondering why the connections between ch. 16 and chaps. 17f. are still rather shaky (e.g., the Philistines, who play such a dominant role in the Samson story, are not referred to at all in chaps. 17–18, even though the setting of 18:1 would have been a most opportune spot for them to be mentioned). Abravanel's approach essentially begs the question of why the material in chaps. 17–21 couldn't have been placed at the beginning of the book, given the fact that the stories of the judges per se do not begin until 3:7.

Modern scholars who attempt to account for the positioning of chaps. 17–21 at the end of the book are not necessarily claiming that the chapters are chronologically displaced. Nevertheless, the same explanations they offer would also hold true were the case for displacement proven correct. The common denominator of the various explanations is that they are thematically oriented. One variation of the thematic approach holds that the chronological fuzziness inherent in chaps. 17–21 is

---

[24] Ralbag to Jud. 17:1.
[25] *Pērûš ʿal Nĕvîʾîm Riʾšônîm*, 141–42.

symbolic of the cyclical nature of the entire period of the judges. Quoting Y. Amit:

> In the case before us, the end of the judges period, like its beginning, is a return to the reality of lack of leadership and breaking of treaties. Therefore, the chronological break not only gives the end of the work a circular character, but it also fits with the idea of historical cycles, and hints thereby at the limited accomplishnemts of the judges' rule and their inability to change the negative tone of the period... The reader becomes convinced that all the heroic acts of the judges were of exceedingly limited value, and when all is said and done, the end of the judges period is similar to its beginning.[26]

In other words, in chaps. 17–21, one still comes across the same state of anarchy and religious waywardness for which the opening chapters of the book set the tone (viz. the lack of a nationally recognized leader following Joshua's death and the motif of covenant-breaking alluded to in Jud. 2:2). Thus, chaps. 17–21 function as a grand summary of the book by invoking paradigmatic examples of the types of ills which plagued the entire period of the judges. This purpose could indeed have served as a motivation for the chapters' displacement in the same way that the MT transferred the Naboth incident (1 Ki. 21) to the last possible position in the stories about Ahab in order to highlight Ahab's shortcomings in climactic summary form (see above, pp. 112–13).

A different emphasis in the thematic approach perceives chaps. 17–21 to function primarily as leading into the period still to come. The editor of the book placed these stories in their present position in order to underscore how desparately the Israelites were in need of a strong, central monarchy.[27] This too is a legitimate dimension of the thematic aspect of displacement (cf. the displacement of David's testament in 1 Chr. 22 which serves as an introduction to the subsequently unfolding events; see above p. 64).[28]

---

[26] Amit, "The End of the Book of Judges" (Hebrew), 74–75.

[27] Buber, *Kingship of God*, 77–78; Uffenheimer, *Ancient Prophecy* (Hebrew), 300.

[28] The only specific claim of scholars who view chaps. 17–21 as anticipatory (of the monarchial age) which I find problematic is that chaps. 19–21, in particular, are meant to express a pro-Davidic and anti-Saulide stance. This proposal was first suggested by M. Güdemann ("Tendenz und Abfassungszeit der letzten Kapitel des

In sum, the postdating of chaps. 17–21 to their present location enabled the editor of Judges to poignantly characterize the entire period as one of continuous moral decline which is attributed to the lack of strong leadership, a lack which was to be addressed in the not-too-distant future.

Methods

Chaps. 17–21 display two familiar methods which, although they are not unique to chronologically displaced materials, are certainly characteristic of them. One is the use of an ambiguous chronological formula, in this case the statement *bayyāmîm hāhēm 'ên melek bĕyiśrā'ēl*, "In those days there was no king in Israel" (17:6; 18:1; 19:1; 21:25). Various opinions have been offered which seek to delimit the time frame to which this statement refers. For example, Radak limits the scope of *'ên melek bĕyiśrā'ēl* to the period between Samson and Eli, when there was no recognized ruler at all in Israel.[29] On the opposite extreme, Talmon limits the statement to the period between Joshua and the first of the judges.[30] However, the genius of the formula is that technically speaking, *'ên melek bĕyiśrā'ēl* can apply to any point prior to Saul, in other words the entire period of the judges. Thus, the editor could present the events of chaps. 17–21 as if they took place later than their true setting (by relating them at the end of the book) without committing himself to an absolute date.

Buches der Richter," *MGWJ* 18 [1869], 357–68). Recent adherents include Uffenheimer, *Ancient Prophecy* (Hebrew), 300; Rudin-O'brasky, "The Appendices" (Hebrew), 158, 161, 164; Brettler, "The Book of Judges," 412–13. The claim is generally based on the negative portrayal of the people of Saul's home town, Gibeah, the unfavorable portrayal of the roots of the Benjamin-Jabesh Gilead connection (21:8–15; cf. 1 Sam. 11:1–11), and the active role taken by David's tribe, Judah, in the campaign (20:18; cf. 1:2). However, the concubine incident, which just happened to occur in Benjaminite territory, is actually a reflection of the general state of anarchy into which the people had sunk. Under the circumstances, the arrangement made with the Jabesh Gilead virgins was the best that could be concocted. Finally, Judah's role can hardly be described as active, given the fact that 20:18 constitutes the sole mention of that tribe's participation.

[29] Radak to Jud. 18:1.
[30] "In Those Days There Was No King" (Hebrew), 144. Talmon agrees with Radak that *melek* refers to any recognized ruler, whether judge or king, but he accepts the notion that chs. 17–21 are displaced from the beginning of the book.

The second method in evidence is the highlighting of associative links which serve to define the precise point at which the displaced material is to be relocated. In this regard, much can be made of the links between chaps. 20–21 and chaps. 1–2. For example, in both 20:18 and 1:1–2, a divine oracle is consulted as to which tribe shall lead the Israelites in battle and in both instances, Judah is designated.[31] The weeping and sacrifice at Bethel in 20:23, 26 and 21:2–4 is reminiscent of the similar scene at Bochim (Bethel in the LXX) in 2:1–5.[32] Such links can be said to anchor chaps. 20–21 in their position at the end of the book by means of literary "enveloping" with the beginning of the book.[33]

However, given the almost "natural" connection between the displaced material in chaps. 17–18 (assuming that it is indeed displaced) and its preceding context (both dealing with the Danites), it was a foregone conclusion that the editor would arrange each of the displaced narratives, chaps. 17–18 and chaps. 19–21, as he did. The links between chaps. 20–21 and the beginning of the book certainly facilitated the editor's task. However, his *active* decision-making process with regard to the precise points at which the displaced narratives in chaps. 17–18 and chaps. 19–21 should be located was determined first and foremost by the topical link between chaps. 16 and 17–18, with chaps. 19–21 following in their present location accordingly.

1 Kings 11

Setting

This chapter, which closes the account of Solomon's reign, is a particularly fruitful source for the study of internally derived chronological displacement, since it quite noticeably attempts to blend earlier events into a later time frame. The chapter's literary structure is defined by the three main topics which it covers, namely Solomon's love of foreign

---

[31] Brettler, "The Book of Judges," 399.
[32] Mayes, *The Story of Israel*, 79; Talmon, "In Those Days There Was No King" (Hebrew), 140.
[33] In addition to these links with the beginning of the book, Rudin-O'brasky ("The Appendices" [Hebrew], 143) points out a couple of associative links between ch. 21 and the immediately following 1 Sam. 1, namely the mention of Shiloh and the term *miyyāmîm yāmîmāh* ("each and every year") in both chapters (Jud. 21:19; 1 Sam. 1:3).

women which led to his religious apostasy and elicited Yahweh's censure (vv. 1–13), the activities of the foreign foes, Hadad and Rezon, who cast a shadow over Solomon's kingdom (vv. 14–25), and the internal threat to Solomon posed by Jeroboam who received the prophetic approbation of Ahijah the Shilonite (vv. 26–40). The time frame for the climax of the first unit (i.e., Solomon's apostasy and Yahweh's rebuke) is explicitly put by v. 4 in the period of Solomon's old age. Thus, the remaining two units, which contextually are set forth as part of Solomon's unfolding punishment, would also appear to have as their setting Solomon's old age. Nevertheless, the text itself hints at much earlier dates for the rebellious activities of Solomon's adversaries. Regarding Hadad, vv. 21–22 state that he returned from his exile in Egypt to his native Edom (where presumably he started fomenting trouble against the Israelite kingdom) as soon as David and Joab had died, in other words in the very early days of Solomon's reign (cf. 1 Ki. 2:10–12, 28–35).[34] Similarly, v. 24 traces Rezon's rise to the aftermath of David's battle against Hadadezer (cf. 2 Sam. 8:3–8) and v. 25 states explicitly that Rezon acted as "an adversary of Israel *all the days of Solomon*."[35]

The blending of time frames regarding Jeroboam's rebellion is a little more complex. V. 27 mentions rather cryptically that Jeroboam's rebellion had something to do with Solomon's building of the *millô´*.[36] Now according to 1 Ki. 9:24, the *millô´* was built around the time that Pharaoh's daughter moved from the city of David into her new home. 1 Ki. 3:1 informs us that Pharaoh's daughter remained in the city of David until Solomon had completed building both his palace and the temple. The chronological data of 1 Ki. 6:37–38; 7:1; and 9:10, in turn, bring Solomon's completion of these projects to his twenty-fourth year. Thus, we can infer that the queen's move as well as the building of the *millô´*

---

[34] See Noth, *Könige*, 245, 253.
[35] Cf. Montgomery, *The Books of Kings*, 241.
[36] The precise connection between the building of the *millô´* and Jeroboam's rebellion is unclear. Rabbi Yohanan fancifully depicts Jeroboam as accusing Solomon of closing off the breaches which David had left in the city wall in order to raise funds (through the collection of entry tolls) for the building of Pharaoh's daughter's palace (B. *Sanhedrîn* 101b). More plausibly, it was Jeroboam's elevation to chief of the House of Joseph labor force during the *millô´* construction which spurred him to react to the burden that was being exacted on his fellow tribesmen (see Montgomery, *The Books of Kings*, 243). For theories regarding the etymology and meaning of *millô´* (usually taken as "fortress" or "rampart"), see Burney, *Notes*, 136; McCarter, *II Samuel*, 141.

and the rebellion which it inspired occurred in the vicinity of Solomon's twenty-fourth year.[37] Nevertheless, Ahijah's oracle, which is said to have been delivered around the time of Jeroboam's rebellion (11:29) brings the time frame of the rebellion into a later context by referring to Solomon's geriatric apostasy (v. 33).[38] The conclusion that two time frames have been blended together is borne out by the fact that Solomon reigned for a total of forty years (11:42) and it is difficult indeed to think of his twenty-fourth year as already coming within the period of his old age, especially if Solomon began his reign as a young man.[39]

In sum, it would appear that the editor of Kings[40] has chosen to intentionally focus Solomon's woes on his latter years, even as references or chronological data pointing to much earlier settings are left intact.

Motivation

1 Ki. 11, like Jud. 17–21 (see above, p. 157) stands at the end of a major historiographic unit describing a particular period, in this case the period of Solomon's kingdom. By virtue of its literary position, 1 Ki. 11 carries the dual function of evaluating the period that it is closing, as well as looking ahead to the period which lies beyond. A greater contribution by the editor is to be expected in a literary unit such as our chapter, which serves as an historiosophic bridge, than in the core account of the period in question, where the editor will lean more heavily on previous sources. Indeed, modern commentators postulate that ch. 11, at least in its present form, does not derive from the same ancient sources such as the "Book of the Acts of Solomon" which appear to be reflected in chaps. 3–10, but rather expresses the particular viewpoint of the editor of

---

[37] See Malamat, "The Contact of the Kingdom of David and Solomon" (Hebrew), 81; Halpern, *The First Historians*, 264, n. 3.

[38] The widespread notion that Ahijah's oracle is a later (Deuteronomistic) supplement to the original history (e.g., Benzinger, *Könige*, 83; Noth, *Könige*, 258) does not affect the argument here which is concerned with the impression of displacement which has been left by the redactor of the book.

[39] To be sure, Solomon's age at the time of his accession to the throne is never stated explicitly and the language of 1 Ki. 3:7 ("but I am a young lad") may be no more than humble formulaics. At the same time, post-Biblical traditions tend to assign a young age to Solomon at the time of his accession (e.g., *Sēder ʿÔlām* ch. 14, which has his age at 12; Josephus, *Antiq.* 8:211 who has it at 14.)

[40] See above, note 38.

Kings regarding Solomon's legacy.[41] This thesis is supported both by the clear Deuteronomistic imprint on ch. 11, especially discernable through much of the phraseology in vv. 1–13 and 31–39,[42] and by the radical shift in content between ch. 11 and the preceding chapters. What has been described as a glorious kingdom led by a God-fearing king full of vitality and wisdom is portrayed as a kingdom beset by external and internal tensions with a religiously wayward and frivolous old king at its helm. This dichotomy appears to reflect the Deuteronomist's need to account for the breakup of the monarchy. In this light, the chronological displacements which we have outlined above can be seen as the result of the Deuteronomist intentionally concentrating all of Solomon's faults and woes at the end of his reign. Thus, Liver states: "This difficulty in the evaluation of Solomon's ambiguous image resulted in the solution which he [the editor of Kings] reached; namely that of postponing those of Solomon's actions which according to him, caused the disruption until his old age."[43]

This approach, which straddles both the ideological and thematic impetuses for displacement, is highly persuasive, particularly in light of the overall literary position of ch. 11. At the same time, since there is a possibility that the information concerning Solomon's "adversaries" (though not its present literary form) was derived from trustworthy historical records,[44] it is not out of the question that the editor of Kings (alongside his primary motivations) was simultaneously attempting to reconcile the data emerging from these records with information which he had recorded previously. Specifically, the statement in 11:25 that Rezon was "an adversary of Israel all the days of Solomon...and reigned over Aram" is inconsistent with 4:4 which states: "For he [Solomon] controlled the whole region west of the Euphrates—all the kings west of the Euphrates, from Tiphsah to Gaza—and he had peace on all his borders roundabout."[45] Also, the trouble which ch. 11 implies that Hadad

---

[41] See in particular Liver, "The Book of the Acts," 91. The approach which views ch. 11 as distinctive from the material preceding it was already anticipated by Abravanel who concluded that the account of Solomon's reign is derived from separate sources, one of which told of his great successes, and the other of which told of his apostasy and troubles during his old age (Pērûš ʿal Nĕvîʾîm Riʾšônîm, 550).
[42] See Burney, Notes, 152–53, 170–71.
[43] "The Book of the Acts," 96.
[44] Ibid., 92; Montgomery, The Books of Kings, 241; Gray, I and II Kings, 280.
[45] Abravanel already raises this question, Pērûš ʿal Nĕvîʾîm Riʾšônîm, 538.

was stirring up in the Edom region is somewhat inconsistent with the notice of Solomon's unchallenged control of the Red Sea trade route (1 Ki. 9:26).[46] By placing the problematic notices concerning Rezon and Hadad precisely at the end of the account of Solomon's reign, the editor of Kings appears to be resolving the tensions they create with previous sources by intimating that although the seeds of the various disturbances may have been planted early on, they only fully blossomed toward the end of Solomon's reign. This reasonable historical explanation[47] dovetailed with the editor's theological agenda as described above.

Methods

The distinction just mentioned between the early beginnings of Solomon's troubles and their later mushrooming fit the editor's scheme admirably. Indeed, the opening unit of the chapter, describing Solomon's marriages to foreign wives (vv. 1–10), serves as a literary model for the following units. Undoubtedly, many of Solomon's political marriages were entered into during a relatively early part of his reign,[48] a fact which the editor does not seek to deny. The only chronological indicator has to do with the statement in v. 4 that over the course of time when Solomon reached old age, his wives induced him to stray from Yahweh. Just as the mention of Solomon's (earlier) marriages was only deemed relevant in the context of the deplorable (later) results to which they led, so the editor could justifiably first incorporate the earlier machinations of Hadad and Rezon at the point where they could serve as background to a later exacerbated situation (following Solomon's apostasy). Thus, the editor is able to maintain an attractive theological scheme, while at the same time expressing an acceptable historical progression which reconciles seemingly inconsistent source material.

---

[46] This problem is made especially acute according to the LXX's reading of 11:25b, "This is the mischief which Ader [Hadad] did, and he was a bitter enemy of Israel, and he reigned in the land of Edom." This reading reflects a *Vorlage* zō't hārā'āh 'ăšer hădad wayyimlōk 'al 'ĕdôm. According to this version, Hadad achieved full official control over the Edom region, which is more than what is implied by the MT.

[47] Cf. Mazar's similar reconstruction regarding Rezon in "The Era of David and Solomon," 98, and Benzinger's explanation regarding Hadad in *Könige*, 80.

[48] Liver, "The Book of the Acts," 91.

The editor strengthens the coherence of his presentation even further by refraining from mentioning a particular date within Solomon's reign at which the adversaries wrought harm on the Israelite kingdom and by omitting any details of the troubles which they instigated. This vagueness enables the editor to focus attention on the period of Solomon's old age while not technically denying the chronological anteriority of the adversaries' designs.[49]

Vague chronology and scarcity of details also figure in the editor's handling of Jeroboam's rebellion. As noted above (p. 163), a date for the building of the *millô'* can only be garnered from the combined evidence of several scattered verses, and even then the date is only an approximation. Technically, then, the editor is not overlooking an historical certitude by omitting a specific date for Jeroboam's rebellion. By glossing over the details of precisely what happened at the *millô'*, the editor strengthens the link between Jeroboam's (earlier) act of rebellion and Ahijah's (later) justification thereof (cf. our remarks above, p. 164, on the chronological implications of 11:33). However, the editor avoids expressing this link in precise chronological terms, employing only the pliable formula *wayĕhî bā'ēt hahî'* ("at about that time") at the transition point between the *millô'* events and Ahijah's encounter with Jeroboam (11:29),[50] thereby dulling the sense of chronological displacement which could emerge from a scrupulous analysis of the data.

Ezra 2:1–4:5

Setting

The evidence pointing to the chronological displacement of this section has already been taken up in detail in our discussion of post-Biblical treatments of Ezra 1–6 (above, chapter 3, pp. 120–25). To briefly recapitulate, Ezra 2:1–4:5 appears to artificially push back the arrivals and activities of Zerubbabel and Jeshua to the time of the earliest wave of immigration under Sheshbazzar in Cyrus's first year. Support for the supposition that Ezra 2:1–4:5 in fact reflects the events of a later time frame than the earliest return can be found in the prophecies of Haggai, which

---

[49] See Halpern, *The First Historians*, 153.
[50] Cf. Liver, "The Book of the Acts," 93.

set the temple-related activities of Zerubbabel and Jeshua squarely in the second year of Darius (Hag. 1; 2:1–9, 15, 18; cf. Zech. 4:9). The harmonistic approach, which assumes either that the participation of Zerubbabel and Jeshua in the temple project encompassed the early years of Cyrus (in cooperation with Sheshbazzar) as well as the early years of Darius,[51] or that Zerubbabel is to be equated with Sheshbazzar,[52] is severely weakened by the testimony of Ezra 1–6 itself. Ezra 5:14, 16 in particular, intimates a clear distinction between the persons and periods of activity of Sheshbazzar and Zerubbabel by having the elders contemporary with Zerubbabel and Jeshua (in Darius's second year, see Ezra 4:24) refer to Sheshbazzar in the third person and as one who had laid the temple foundations at some point beyond the very recent past. The notable absence of Sheshbazzar in Ezra 2:1–4:5 and the assumption of his role by Zerubbabel only heightens one's suspicions that the author of Ezra is silently acknowledging an indeterminate lapse between the events of ch. 1 and chaps. 2f., even as he seeks to give the impression of chronological continuity. We now turn to examine what indeed motivated the author of Ezra to give such an impression.

Motivations

In discussing the motivations behind the chronological displacement which exists in Ezra 2:1–4:5, it is good to keep in mind that this section represents perhaps the most pronounced instance of internally derived displacement taken up so far. As opposed to a particular event or even a particular trend being transposed to a chronological point later (or earlier) than its historical point of occurrence (cf. Jud. 17–21; 1 Ki. 11), our chapters actually telescope the entire sweep of two originally distinctive periods. This phenomenon has not escaped the notice of recent interpreters. A common theme in the scholarly discussion, whether expressed directly or less so, is the tendency of Ezra-Nehemiah toward what we may refer to as "periodization." The author constructs his history around major epochs, with the result that the events and figures of specific historical sub-divisions within the larger blocs may be combined.

---

[51] See above, chapter 3, n. 166.
[52] See above, chapter 3, n. 170.

An illustrative example of this approach is Japhet's analysis of the periodization process in Ezra-Nehemiah in which she identifies two major historiographic blocs.[53] The first runs from Ezra 1–6, the second stretches from Ezra 7–Neh. 13. Japhet adds the observation that each of the two blocs portrays two leading personalities acting side by side. Ezra and Nehemiah themselves, of course, are the dominant figures from Ezra 7–Neh. 13. The prominent pair in Ezra 1–6, then, are Zerubbabel and Jeshua. Viewed in this light, the confluence of the Cyrus and Darius periods comes as no surprise. Quoting Japhet:

> Within such a hard and set historical conception, Sheshbazzar becomes a sort of "survival"—a name passed on by tradition but whose exact role in Israel's history is becoming blurred. Accordingly, Zerubbabel's activity is stretched out over the whole length of the first period, from the Return and the beginning of the building after the decree of Cyrus until its resumption in the days of Darius.[54]

Now, Japhet's position presupposes that over the course of time, Zerubbabel's reputation loomed much larger than Sheshbazzar's, so that by the time Ezra 1–6 was composed,[55] Zerubbabel was still remembered as the towering figure who embodied the nationalist aspirations of the people (cf. Hag. 2:20–23), while Sheshbazzar was viewed as no more than a footnote in history.[56] However, in view of the actual course of events during the sixth and fifth centuries, which did not witness a real revival of the Davidic dynasty, Japhet's supposition is not inevitable.

---

[53] Japhet, "Sheshbazzar and Zerubbabel," 94.
[54] Ibid.
[55] According to Japhet, ibid., 89, n. 55, the date of Ezra-Nehemiah's composition would be no later than the first quarter of the fourth century B.C.E. (some 150 years after Zerubbabel), based on the latest possible date for Ezra's arrival in Jerusalem (397) and on the last-mentioned high priest in the book, namely Jaddua son of Johanan (Neh. 12:11) whose activity fell at the beginning of the fourth century.
[56] Similarly Williamson, "The Composition of Ezra i–vi," 26, who states: "The author [of Ezra 3] may have been attracted by their [Zerubbabel's and Jeshua's] prominence in the later rebuilding and have wanted a member of the Davidic family to be involved from the start." The statements of both Japhet and Williamson contrasting Zerubbabel and Sheshbazzar are somewhat perplexing in view of the good possibility that Sheshbazzar himself was a scion of the Davidic royal family (see above, chapter three, n. 160). Japhet, recognizing this problem, is forced to speculate that Sheshbazzar's (supposed) less glamorous legacy was due to an untimely death or to undefined "historical circumstances" ("Sheshbazzar and Zerubbabel," 93).

That pro-Davidic sentiments could still have been nurtured is demonstrated by 1 Esdras (above, pp. 135–36), but in the presence of a better explanation for the phenomenon of chronological displacement in our chapters (see presently), the possibility should not be pressed.

It is here on the question of motivation that we can endorse one of the main thrusts of Halpern's "historiographic commentary" to Ezra 1–6.[57] Halpern emphasizes time and again the theme of swift and ardent execution of the temple-building project from start to finish. By removing the boundaries between the events and figures of the Cyrus and Darius periods, the author is able to portray the temple-building project as an effort which commanded the community's full attention from the beginning, and which was interrupted only by hostile external forces.[58] For this reason, it is a matter of great importance to the author that the group which ultimately finished the temple-building (i.e., those under Zerubbabel and Jeshua) was the same one that started it. In this light, the placement of ch. 2 in its present location is designed to give the impression that great multitudes of people (over 40,000) returned to Jerusalem as soon as possible (even though in reality, the return of these masses occurred some years after that of Sheshbazzar's original group). The fortunes of the original wave of returnees led by Sheshbazzar are omitted, since that group was not the one which ended up drawing the temple-building process to its conclusion. For that same reason, Sheshbazzar is not allowed a role in ch. 3, which also represents more of a "paradigmatic" source, i.e., things as they should have been, than an "historical" source, i.e., things as they actually were.

The strength of Halpern's argument lies in the fact that it treats Ezra 1–6 in line with comparable literature of the recognized genre of temple-building accounts, most notably the Sippar cylinder of Nabonidus[59] (cf. our discussion above, pp. 36–37). Furthermore, the bending of precise chronology in order to conform to the ideal of expeditious attention to cultic matters is a phenomenon attested to elsewhere in the Bible itself, as we have seen in our discussions of 1 Chr. 13–15 and 2 Chr. 34 (above, pp. 60, 71). There is no doubt, then, that Halpern's conception of the factors motivating the author is the correct one, even if we take issue with some of his exegetical circumlocutions (see below, n. 63). Indeed,

---

[57] Halpern, "A Historiographic Commentary."
[58] Ibid., 109, 115–16, 123–24.
[59] Ibid., 113–14, 128–29.

Japhet too, in a more recent study, puts greater emphasis on the theme of swift temple construction. In her words: "The point which our author [of Ezra 1–6] wishes to make is that the delays in the building of the Temple had only one cause: interruptions from without, enforced by the authority of the Persian government."[60]

Methods

The author's task in 2:1–4:5 was essentially to present a picture of how the early return was supposed to have been without straying too far from his known historical data. Practically, this involved: a) pushing back the arrivals and activities of Zerubbabel and Jeshua without losing sight of their central roles in the Darius years. b) pushing back the disturbances of the "adversaries" to the earliest point within reason. A number of specific methods for accomplishing these goals are in evidence, all of which exhibit an ingenious evasiveness.

The beginning point of our section (2:1), by virtue of its location and subject matter, is intended to come across as a sequel to ch. 1 (cf. also 2:68). Yet, here it can truly be said that silence is louder than words, and the reverberations of the great vacuum occasioned by the disappearance of Sheshbazzar are absolutely resounding. By passing over any follow-up information on Sheshbazzar's fortunes following ch. 1 (save for 5:16) while leading straightaway into Zerubbabel's return (ch. 2), the author succeeds in setting the latter event during the reign of Cyrus with-

---

[60] Japhet, "History and Literature," 183–84. Williamson mentions one more consideration for why the author of Ezra set at least 3:1–6 (in Williamson's opinion) within Cyrus's reign, namely the need to combine the evidence of Haggai "with the contradictory assertion of Ezra 5:16 which suggested that some early work was done on the temple site. He [the author] compromised by having the altar built and dedicated immediately after the initial return." ("The Composition of Ezra i–vi," 25). However, it seems to me that this cannot be regarded as a motivation in and of itself, or else the author would have done even better by bringing Sheshbazzar himself into 3:1–6. Williamson evidently recognizes this problem, and therefore has to fall back on the explanation of Zerubbabel's supposed later prominence (see above, n. 56). Williamson (ibid.) also touches upon the issue of genre, stating that the author of Ezra 1–6 juxtaposed events from the reigns of Cyrus and Darius in order "to write a typological account of the founding of the second temple." However, unlike Halpern who develops this point vis-a-vis the overall blurring of chronology in our chapters, Williamson uses the point primarily to call attention to small details (e.g., the motif of importing fine wood in 3:7, which has parallels in other temple-building accounts).

out, however, stating explicitly that Zerubbabel's group was part of the very first wave of returnees. Interestingly, the possibility of Zerubbabel's *immigration* (though not his temple-related activities) during the reign of Cyrus is historically quite conceivable.[61] Thus, in ch. 2 the author goes beyond his data only in making Zerubbabel appear as the ostensible leader of the *earliest* wave instead of Sheshbazzar. In sum, the historiographic method employed here is the intentional suppression of pertinent data, namely the fate of Sheshbazzar's group of returnees, in the absence of which a bridge is formed automatically between two originally distinct movements.[62]

Consistent with the author's objective of linking Zerubbabel's group with the early Cyrus period without explicitly violating the historical data is the use of loose dating formulae. No specific regnal years are found anywhere in our section. The dates in 3:1 and 3:8 relate most naturally to Zerubbabel's group of returnees. Taken together with the great silent divide between chapters 1 and 2, these dates allow themselves, at least in theory, to be placed at any point during Cyrus's reign. At the same time, the literary continuity of chapters 1–3 invites one to understand them as following immediately upon the heels of the original return under Sheshbazzar. There is no need to see veiled references to Darius's years lurking in the background.[63] It is sufficient for the author

---

[61] See above, chapter 3, p. 123.

[62] See especially Halpern, "A Historiographic Commentary," 108–09. An alternative explanation for the disappearance of Sheshbazzar after ch. 1 is offered by Eskenazi (*In An Age of Prose*, 50, 52, 173). In her view, the disappearance of Sheshbazzar, along with the comparatively limited role allotted to Zerubbabel (as compared with 1 Esdras) and the "disappearance" of Ezra after his initial activities, represents an intentional tendency of the author to downplay the roles of central authoritative figures in favor of popular community influence. I find this approach unconvincing, since while the theme of public participation at momentous occasions is certainly present in Ezra-Nehemiah, the contrast between central authority and "people power" seems too colored by modern outlooks. There are a host of other possibilities as to why leaders appear to be on the sidelines (e.g., Ezra, due to his timid personality and/or the failure of his mission), none of which are any less compelling than Eskenazi's approach. Eskenazi's contention that Nehemiah, who spares no opportunity to emphasize his own role (e.g., Neh. 13:14), is to be viewed as a negative figure in the book (ibid., 144–52) is questionable. Even the contrast between the figure of Zerubbabel in Ezra and in 1 Esdras is only one of degree. The book of Ezra may not build up Zerubbabel as an ideal Davidic ruler, but neither does it downplay his position to the extent suggested by Eskenazi.

[63] On this score, I am somewhat skeptical of Halpern's hairsplitting comments regarding Ezra 3. For example, Halpern feels that by invoking the date "the seventh month" in 3:1, the author was intentionally siezing upon a documented date (Neh.

to bring us into an unspecified chronological zone during the Cyrus years, while inviting us to opt for the earliest setting within this time frame.

Intentional vagueness also comes into play in the author's presentation of the confrontation between Zerubbabel's group of returnees and the "adversaries" (4:1–3). An accomodation of the paradigmatic ideal (what should have been) with the historical reality (what actually was) dictated that the long delay in completing the temple project be attributed solely to forces beyond the people's control (contra Hag. 1:3–11). Now, even though the Tattenai correspondance (Ezra 5:3–6:12) and the silence of Haggai and Zechariah regarding external impediments point to a date no earlier than the second year of Darius as the real historical setting for the major conflicts between the Judeans and their neighbors, it was not unreasonable for the author to suppose that some xenophobically motivated rumbling on the part of the local population had greeted the returning Judeans right from the start of the mass immigration movement. Already in 3:3, the author plants the seeds of such a scenario. In 4:1–3, the author simply takes the next step of expanding the general aggressiveness of the "peoples of the land" to incorporate a specific demand for participation in the temple building. But even here, the author presents the "adversaries" as completely anonymous figures, without identifying them either by name, position, or any other means of association, with the historical persons of the later (Darius) period.[64] Thus, we see that alongside lack of commitment on absolute dates, the non-specification of characters is an effective means of softening the fusion of one chronological time frame with another.

Each one of the methods identified here has some form of analogy with examples derived from "empirically" based cases. For example, the suppression of information (in our case, the omission of Sheshbazzar's activities) which would upset the newly devised chronological framework is a device which we saw reflected in the omission of Jeroboam's

---

7:73) which in his mind could be linked with the "sixth month" of Darius' second year, during which Zerubbabel and Jeshua actually started clearing the temple grounds (Hag. 1:13–15). Of course, one problem with this theory is that the verses which supposedly mirror the activities of the sixth month, namely 3:2–3a, appear subsequent to the opening date of the seventh month in 3:1 (see Halpern, "A Historiographic Commentary," 93–94, 97). Cf. also Halpern's labyrinthian explanation of 3:8 (ibid., 102).

[64] Cf. Halpern, ibid., 117.

wife's disguise by the LXX's alternative version to 1 Ki. 14 (above, pp. 105, 109). The strong implication of an earliest possible date without its explicit formulation is most conspicuous in Nabonidus's Sippar cylinder, which invites us to understand Nabonidus's fulfillment of Marduk's charge regarding the building of the Ehulhul as taking place within three years (even though the precise chronological span between the command and its fulfillment remains rather fuzzy, see above, pp. 38–39).[65] Finally, the speculation which the author of Ezra could have legitimately entertained regarding the existence of early (albeit undocumented) cases of enemy interference in the temple project is basically analogous to his evident supposition of early attempts at building Jerusalem's walls, a supposition which helped to effect the chronological displacement of Ezra 4:6–24 (see above, p. 130).

1 Chronicles 11:4–9

Setting

This small unit narrating David's conquest of Jerusalem corresponds to the parallel unit in 2 Sam. 5:6–10. In both texts, the conquest of Jerusalem is placed immediately after the notice of David's coronation at Hebron (2 Sam. 5:1–5; 1 Chr. 11:1–3). Nevertheless, the placement of the conquest account in Chronicles raises the possibility of an internal chronological displacement. For whereas in the Samuel text, the conquest of Jerusalem is followed immediately by the sections describing David's further activities *there* such as the building of his palace and his battles with the Philistines (2 Sam. 5:11–25), 1 Chr. 11:4–9 is followed by a long parenthetical section that describes matters pertinent to the coronation *at Hebron* and culminating in that event (11:10–12:41).[66]

---

[65] On the links between Ezra 1–6 and Nabonidus's Sippar cylinder, see Halpern, ibid., 113–14, 128–29.

[66] A good portion of the parenthetical section (1 Chr. 11:11–41) parallels the list of David's warriors in 2 Sam. 23. Since the establishment of David's core warrior group (the "thirty") probably goes back to his days as a roving band leader (see especially Mazar, "David's Warriors" [Hebrew], 188–90), both 2 Sam. 23 and 1 Chr. 11 (and 12:1–23) can actually be viewed, sequentially speaking, as extended flashbacks (e.g., 1 Chr. 12:17–19, which evidently refers to the period when David was encamped at Adulam [1 Sam. 22:1–2], see Mazar, ibid.). However, while in Samuel the list of warriors appears as an appendix to the book, the framework and position of the

Internal Evidence 175

The sequential differences between Samuel and Chronicles can be outlined in chart form as follows:

2 Samuel 5–6		1 Chronicles 11–13	
5:1–3	Hebron coronation	11:1–3	Hebron coronation
5:6–10	David's conquest of Jerusalem	11:4–9	David's conquest of Jerusalem
5:11–25	David's activities in Jerusalem	11:10–12:40	list of David's warriors and others who joined his forces in advance of the Hebron coronation
6:1–11	David's bringing of ark to Jerusalem (first stage)	13:1–14	David's bringing of ark to Jerusalem (first stage)

Since the scene in Chronicles shifts back to Hebron and fills in the details of the coronation that took place there, one is led to believe that in terms of internal sequence, David's conquest and settlement of Jerusalem ought to *follow* 11:10–12:41 rather than *preceding* it.[67] This impression is highlighted by the fact that 11:4–9 read as a description of David's first act in the *aftermath* of his coronation, whereas 11:10–12:41 are presented against the backdrop of the Hebron coronation while it is still in progress. Indeed, 12:24 *lĕhāsēb malkût šā'ûl 'ēlāyw kĕpî YHWH* ("to transfer Saul's kingdom to him [David], in accordance with the word of the Lord") harks back to 10:14 *wayyassēb 'et hammĕlûkāh lĕdāwîd ben yišāy* ("He [Yahweh] transferred the kingdom to David son of Jesse") which introduces the Hebron gathering.[68] Similarly, 12:39–41 which wraps up the section, recapitulates the events already related in brief in 11:1–3.[69] From a sequential standpoint, then, the presence of 11:4–9 in

---

list(s) in Chronicles show a greater concern for bringing the time frame of David's organizational buildup right up to the climactic Hebron coronation (see Garsiel, *The Kingdom of David* [Hebrew], 36–40).

[67] Cf. Japhet, "Conquest and Settlement," 208, n. 13. Josephus (*Antiq.* 7:53–64) as is his wont, attempts to combine the reports of Samuel and Chronicles and indeed ends up placing the conquest of Jerusalem following his version of 1 Chr. 12:24–41.

[68] See Rothstein and Hänel, *Das erste Buch der Chronik*, 238.

[69] See Curtis and Madsen, *The Books of Chronicles*, 200.

its current location is anomalous, in that these verses jump beyond a narrative point which has still not been completely rehearsed.[70]

An additional reason for regarding 11:4–9 as being displaced according to the internal structure of the Chronicles account is that the given arrangement casts a shadow of ambiguity on the venue of 13:1–5. On the one hand, the juxtaposition of chapters 12 and 13 might suggest that David's consultation with his military officers and his exhortation to the "whole congregation of Israel" regarding the proposal to transfer the ark (13:1–4) took place while the above groups were still gathered in Hebron. If that were the case, the conquest of Jerusalem would not yet have taken place. Yet on the other hand, Jerusalem would have to have already been conquered in order for David to bring the ark there, and the term *ēlênû* (to us) in 13:3 implies that Jerusalem was already under Israelite control (the ark, after all, was not to be brought to Hebron).[71] Only if 11:4–9 were placed at the end of chapter 12, that is between the coronation and David's proposal, would the above ambiguity have been removed unequivocally. We must assume, therefore, that the Chronicler deliberately chose to present the conquest of Jerusalem where he did, despite creating, or perhaps precisely in order to create, the murky sequence resulting from this arrangement (see below).

Motivation

On the surface, one could argue that in placing the account of Jerusalem's conquest in its present location, the Chronicler was simply adhering to a *Vorlage* represented by 2 Sam. 5:1–10. However, as we saw above in chapter two (pp. 57–58), the Chronicler did not hesitate to rearrange the order of Samuel even in the very chapters under discussion (e.g., in 1 Chr. 13–14, the Chronicler delayed the section parallel to 2 Sam. 5:11–25 until after the section parallel to 2 Sam. 6:1–11).

---

[70] The points raised by Mazar ("David's Reign in Hebron") for claiming that historically speaking, the conquest of Jerusalem actually *preceded* the coronation at Hebron are too subtle for one to assume that the editors of Samuel or Chronicles were aware of this alleged course of events.

[71] Cf. the equivocation of Kil, *Dibrê Hayyāmîm*, 294, on 13:1: "It would appear that David spoke about this matter to the heads of Israel when they came to crown him in Hebron," alongside his explanation of *wayyaʿal* ("went up") in 13:6: "It is possible that the writer used the term 'going up' since Kirjath Jearim is higher (more than 750 meters) than the city of David" (ibid., 298).

Therefore, the motivation for the arrangement of 1 Chr. 11–12 in general and 11:4–9 in particular could lie in considerations beyond the purely editorial. In all likelihood, the reason for the location of the unit concerning the conquest of Jerusalem in both Samuel and Chronicles is to demonstrate how, with God's help, the new king proved himself as an able fighter. The theme of a candidate for leadership or a new king proving himself in battle is quite widespread in the ancient Near East. The best known example is probably in *Enuma Elish* tablet IV, where Marduk attains sole dominion by routing the forces of Tiamat.[72] Biblical attestations include the story of Jephtath (Jud. 11) and the story of Saul's victory over the Ammonites (1 Sam. 11).[73] The commentator on Chronicles known as pseudo-Rashi[74] spells out the significance of the literary pattern found in our passage:

> He (David) went to war immediately when they crowned him over Israel, so that Israelites would not say "All the wars which David waged and won in the days of Saul were due to Saul's good fortune, but now he is hesitant to fight." For that reason, he went immediately to war.[75]

Still, the question remains as to why the Chronicler did not fully conclude his description of the Hebron coronation before bringing in the paragraph on the battle for Jerusalem, i.e., why the latter paragraph didn't follow ch. 12. In our discussion in chapter two of 1 Chr. 13–15 (above, p. 60), we concluded that the Chronicler's rearrangement of 2 Sam. 5:11–6:23 reflected his wish to emphasize David's concern for the cult. In examining the present structure of chaps. 11–13, we can take this thought one step further by positing that the Chronicler was indeed trying to set up two "firsts" for David's nascent kingship, one being the conquering of Jerusalem, and the other being the campaign to transfer the ark. In order for each of these events to come out in slot number one, the Chronicler had to finish the description of the Hebron coronation twice, even though this produced the sequential vagueness pointed out above. Thus, the motivations suggested here are roughly akin to those

---

[72] *ANET*, 66–67.
[73] See Halpern, *The Constitution of the Monarchy*, 113–15, 95.
[74] For the reasons for attributing the commentary to someone other than the historical Rashi, see Kil, *Dibrê Hayyāmîm*, Vol. 2, appendix section, 89–90.
[75] Pseudo-Rashi to 1 Chr. 11:4.

Methods

The author's task of shifting the scene back to Hebron after 11:9 is facilitated by his use of a literary "enveloping" technique in order to parenthetically frame the long section 11:10–12:41. Actually, it is 12:39 which closes out the digression begun back in 11:10. The latter verse commences with the words, "these were David's chief warriors who strongly supported him in his kingdom, together with all Israel to make him king" (*lĕhamlîkô*). 12:39, with its mention of the "fighting men" and "all the rest of Israel," along with the twice repeated term *lĕhamlîk* ("to make king"), clearly echoes the main elements of 11:10a. A framing repetition such as this can be used to mark off a given section and lift it from the flow of the surrounding narrative.[76] If this were the author's intention here, then the following material—ch. 13—would have to be read sequentially as a direct sequel to the conquering of Jerusalem in 11:4–9. However, the fact that two more verses follow after the end of the frame (12:40–41), as well as the close identity of the groups in 13:1–2 and 12:39–41, points to the likelihood that the author's use of framing repetition here was more probably an attempt at creating a relationship of simultaneity between the Hebron coronation and the ark movement,[77] with the conquering of Jerusalem stuck in conveniently through the back door. Thus, the Chronicler managed to blur the precise temporal boundaries between coronation, conquering, and ark movement, all for the purpose of commencing the description of David's kingship in the best possible terms, both militarily and spiritually. The muddling of strict sequence is of course the hallmark of many of the specific methods we saw above in chaps. 1–3 (cf. in particular Nabonidus's Sippar cylinder).

---

[76] See Long, "Framing Repetitions," 385.
[77] See Talmon, "The Presentation of Synchroneity" for this use of a framing repetition.

2 Chronicles 20:1–30

Setting

We have already seen in chapter two (above, p. 65) how 2 Chr. 20:35–37 displaces the point of contact between Jehoshaphat and Ahaziah as compared to the parallel version in Kings (1 Ki. 22:49–50). Here, I wish to point out an internal displacement regarding the Chronicler's location of the narrative appearing before the ship-building story within his overall presentation of Jehoshaphat's reign. As in Kings, the Chronicler places the notice about the shipping enterprise in the closing summary section of Jehoshaphat's reign. However, unlike in Kings where the notice fits in sequentially, following shortly after the account of Jehoshaphat's joint campaign with Ahab, in Chronicles it appears after the lengthy story, unique to Chronicles, of Jehoshaphat's battle against the Transjordanian invaders (2 Chr. 20:1–30). Now, the historical value of the latter account is disputed by scholars, with some viewing it as a "midrashic" reflex of 2 Ki. 3, which tells of the joint campaign of Jehoshaphat and Joram son of Ahab against Moab,[78] and others taking it as preserving an historical recollection of the weakened position of Judah in the aftermath of the latter campaign.[79] Either way, though, the story appears to reflect a period in Jehoshaphat's reign after the southern kingdom had lost its tight grip on the Edom region. The attacking multitude is said to emerge from Aram (2 Chr. 20:2), but this is most likely to be read "from Edom."[80] 20:10, 22–23 specifically mention the participation of Mt. Seir residents in the alliance fighting against Jehoshaphat. Thus, the Transjordanian attack would necessarily postdate the time of the maritime venture (i.e., Jehoshaphat's seventeenth or eighteenth year, during which Ahaziah was reigning in Samaria; see 1 Ki. 22:52), when Jehoshaphat was still in control of the Edom region (see 1 Ki. 22:48—"There was no king in Edom; a viceroy acted as king"). Therefore, one can conclude that despite the chronological anteriority of the events of 20:1–30 (the Transjordanian invasion) to those of 20:35–

---

[78] E.g., Benzinger, *Die Bücher der Chronik*, 107; Curtis and Madsen, *The Books of Chronicles*, 404–05.
[79] E.g., Mazar, "Yĕhôšāpāṭ," 570; Yeivin, "King Yehoshaphat" (Hebrew), 16.
[80] See BHS ad loc.

37 (the ship-building story), the Chronicler has chosen to narrate the episode of the Transjordanian invasion in an earlier context rather than transposing it to a more chronologically accurate spot after 20:35–37.

Motivation

As with our previous example (1 Chr. 11:4–9), a surface explanation can be offered that the Chronicler was simply adhering to a *Vorlage* like Kings, in which the shipping episode appears at the very end of the account of Jehoshaphat's reign.[81] However, there is more to the Chronicler's arrangement than imitative editorial practice. For as a closing statement on Jehoshaphat's reign, the ship-building episode indeed provided a fitting epitome of the Chronicler's evaluation of Jehoshaphat—a king who measured up in almost every respect, save for his attraction to the allurement of alliances with the wicked northern kingdom. This failing had almost brought Yahweh's wrath (*qeṣep*) upon Jehoshaphat on an earlier occasion (2 Chr. 19:2), and thereafter, Jehoshaphat was careful to avoid the looming divine wrath (2 Chr. 19:10). Indeed, Jehoshaphat's attitude of complete trust in Yahweh during the Transjordanian invasion represented the pinnacle of his spiritual growth, in that he recognized his exclusive dependence on Yahweh to the exclusion of all human confederations (see in particular 2 Chr. 20:12). Nevertheless, in the final analysis, Jehoshaphat's legacy, according to the Chronicler, was less than perfect. By inserting the account of the Transjordanian invasion before its true chronological context while retaining the ship-building episode in the summary section, the Chronicler closes the Jehoshaphat cycle with a bittersweet effect, symbolizing the vacillations of that king in pursuing a Godly foreign policy. This thematically motivated presentation (i.e., displacing a chronologically later event to an earlier point in the narrative cycle in order to sound a closing tone) is thus a variation of the cases discussed above of MT 1 Ki. 21 (pp. 112–13) and MT Jud. 17–21 (p. 160), in which chronologically earlier events are postdated for the same purpose.

---

[81] Cf. Myers, *II Chronicles*, 116.

Methods

Although strict chronological presentation was secondary to the Chronicler's purpose, he still attempted to lessen the conspicuousness of the displacement brought about by the location of the Transjordanian war account. For one, he did not take over the notice of 1 Ki. 22:48 stating that Edom was still a Judean protectorate, which would have unnecessarily overemphasized the tension with the overall context detailing the Transjordanian invasion against Jehoshaphat. Moreover, the Chronicler introduced the shipping incident with the vague formula *wĕ'aḥărê kēn*, "afterward" (20:35). Interestingly, the same formula is used at the beginning of ch. 20, but in v. 35, the antecedent reference is even more open-ended. The "afterward" cannot be said to refer back to the victory over the Transjordanian invaders,[82] in view of the four verses of general summary which separate the end of the war account from v. 35. Indeed, *wĕ'aḥărê kēn* refers back to nothing in particular, and perhaps is best taken, in line with the intention of the Chronicler as argued above, as meaning "after all this," Jehoshaphat did not attain the level of complete trust in Yahweh which would have precluded alliances with the idolatrous northern kingdom.[83]

2 Chronicles 25:25–27

Another case of apparent chronological displacement which is unique to the Chronicler's version of a passage parallel with Kings is found in the account of the plot against Amaziah, king of Judah. The parallel passages from Kings and Chronicles, respectively, read as follows:

> King Amaziah son of Joash of Judah lived fifteen years after the death of King Jehoash son of Jehoahaz of Israel. The other events of Amaziah's reign are recorded in the Annals of the Kings of Judah. A conspiracy was formed against him in

---

[82] So Keil, *The Books of the Chronicles*, 393.
[83] *wĕ'aḥărê kēn* is also used in 2 Chr. 33:14 to introduce Manasseh's final activities, although there the narrative is concluded on a fairly positive note.

Jerusalem and he fled to Lachish; but they sent men after him to Lachish, and they killed him there (2 Ki. 14:17–19).

King Amaziah son of Joash of Judah lived fifteen years after the death of King Joash son of Jehoahaz of Israel. The other events of Amaziah's reign, early and late, are recorded in the book of the kings of Judah and Israel. From the time that Amaziah turned from following the Lord, a conspiracy was formed against him in Jerusalem, and he fled to Lachish; but they sent men after him to Lachish and they put him to death there (2 Chr. 25:25–27).

The major difference between the two versions is that the Chronicler links the conspiracy to "the time that Amaziah turned from following the Lord." In light of the Chronicler's presentation of Amaziah's reign, this can only refer to Amaziah's adoption of Edomite gods following his successful campaign against Seir (25:14). According to the Chronicler, Amaziah's rash and humiliating encounter with Joash, king of Israel, was already meant as a divine punishment meted out to Amaziah for having worshipped the gods of Edom (25:20). Now, since the Chronicler notes that Amaziah outlived Joash by fifteen years (25:25), while alloting Amaziah a total of twenty-nine regnal years (25:1), the faceoff between Joash and Amaziah (following Amaziah's apostasy) would have had to occur no later than the latter's fourteenth year. This conclusion is borne out by the synchronism of 2 Ki. 14:23, which has Jeroboam son of Joash ascending to the throne of Samaria in Amaziah's fifteenth year (cf. also 2 Ki. 12:2; 13:10; 14:1). For our purposes, this means that the Chronicler tacitly admits that the apostasy which supposedly led to the conspiracy against Amaziah occurred prior to Amaziah's fourteenth year even though Amaziah survived until his twenty-ninth year. In other words, Amaziah's actual death is separated from his "turning from the Lord," which occasioned the conspiracy, by fifteen years! Thus, the focal point of the displacement falls out on v. 27, which by linking Amaziah's violent death with his apostasy, appears to telescope over the last fifteen years of Amaziah's life.

Some commentators do indeed suppose a fifteen year lapse between the outbreak of the conspiracy and its consummation. According to this view, Amaziah fled to Lachish following his release by Joash, and lived there for fifteen years before being put to death.[84] However, the wording of v. 27—"and he (Amaziah) fled to Lachish; but they sent men after him to Lachish"—hardly allows for the passage of so much time, and as Keil notes, "the conspiracy cannot possibly have lasted fifteen years or more before it came to a head."[85] Nevertheless, Amaziah's adoption of strange gods and his miscalculation in challenging Joash probably did, in fact, help to lay the groundwork for the discontent, which after festering for a long while, ultimately blossomed into a full-grown conspiracy.[86] The Chronicler was obviously interested in providing a religious explanation for Amaziah's downfall. If the author of 1 Ki. 11 saw fit to bring some of Solomon's early troubles into a later context, the Chronicler took the opposite tack of pushing back at least the roots of Amaziah's ultimate undoing into an earlier context. But as in so many other cases of intentional displacement, the Chronicler tried to keep the precise chronological indicators as loose as possible. Halpern, in noting the displacement under discussion, labels the chronological terminology employed here (25:27) "elastic."[87] Actually, in the only other Biblical occurrence of $ûmē^cēt$ ("from the time," Dan. 12:11), the term is used with an intentional exactitude. Nevertheless, our case would probably still be more comparable to the loose $bā^cēt\ hahî'$ ("at that time") of the historical narrative genre[88] than to the apocalyptic genre as represented by Daniel. Thus, $ûmē^cēt$ could be taken to mean here "at some (undefined) point subsequent to."[89] The term would thereby enable the Chronicler to maintain the linkage between Amaziah's apostasy and his bloody fate without sacrificing chronological credibility.

---

[84] E.g., Pseudo-Rashi to 2 Chr. 25:27; Malbim to 2 Chr. 25:27 who modifies the lapse to twelve years; Kil, *Dibrê Hayyāmîm*, 780–81.
[85] Keil, *The Books of the Kings*, 384.
[86] Ibid.; Myers, *II Chronicles*, 145–46. Cf. also the chronological reconstructions which suppose that Uzziah was made acting king in the wake of Amaziah's adverse encounter with Joash, e.g., Tadmor, "*kěrônôlôgiyāh*," 282.
[87] Halpern, "A Historiographic Commentary," 132.
[88] Cf. Cogan and Tadmor, "Ahaz and Tiglath-Pileser in the Book of Kings" (Hebrew), 57. They comment that the use of the terms $'āz$ ("then") and $bā^cēt\ hahî'$ ("at that time") in 2 Ki. 16:5–6 is designed to create a cause-and-effect connection between Ahaz' cultic sins and his military setbacks, even though the individual notices (of vv. 5 and 6) are chronologically indeterminate.
[89] Cf. Josephus (*Antiq.* 9:203) who leaves the time of the conspiracy unspecified, stating only that it was sometime after Amaziah's fourteenth year.

Summary of Chapter Four

The results obtained from our analysis of internally derived chronological displacements are outlined in the following chart:

Text	Type of Displacement	Motivation	Method
Gen. 35: 27–29	antedates context of Isaac's death to before the sale of Joseph	thematic (editorial): to close cycle of Isaac's life before detailing lives of his descendants	use of *tôlĕdôt* (generational) formula to separate life accounts of Isaac and his descendants
Exod. 18	antedates context of Jethro's visit to before Sinai lawgiving	thematic: to contrast behavior of Jethro and Amalekites who appear in previous unit	highlighting links between Jethro episode (ch. 18), Amalekite war (ch. 17), and Sinai lawgiving (ch. 19).
Judges 17–21	postdates context of Danite migration and concubine episode to end of Judges period	thematic: to have stories serve as barometer of entire Judges period and to lead into following period	a) ambiguous chronological formula *'ên melek bĕyiśrā'ēl* b) highlighting topical link with preceding material (both dealing with Danites)
1 Ki. 11	postdates context of rebellious activities against Solomon to his later years	ideological (religious):to connect Solomon's political set-backs with his apostasy in old-age	a) avoidance of explicit details of and chronological dates for various rebellions b) use of formula *wayĕhî bāʿēt hahî'*
Ezra 2:1–4:5	antedates context of activities of Zerubbabel and Sheshbazzar to earliest return in Cyrus's reign	ideological (cultic): to show that building of temple was undertaken and accomplished in smoothest possible manner	a) passing over actual chronological gap between arrivals of Sheshbazzar and Zerubbabel b) avoidance of specific regnal years c) creative historical speculation

Text	Type of Displacement	Motivation	Method
1 Chr. 11:4–9	antedates context of David's conquest of Jerusalem to before end of Hebron coronation	ideological (military and cultic): to open account of David's reign with both military and spiritual accomplishments	blurring of precise sequence between events in Hebron and Jerusalem by implying (through use of framing repetition) that they were roughly simultaneous
2 Chr. 20:1–30	antedates context of Transjordanian invasion to before Jehoshaphat's shipping venture	thematic: to have shipbuilding incident serve as final evaluation of Jehoshaphat's reign	a) omission of additional historical data (1 Ki. 22:48) which could highlight tension inherent in given literary arrangement b) use of vague formula wĕ'aḥărê kēn to introduce final passage
2 Chr. 25:25–27	antedates context of Amaziah's assassination to discontent which sprouted fifteen years previously	ideological (religious): to connect Amaziah's ultimate fall with his mid-reign apostasy	use of loose chronological term ûmēʿēt

The examples of chronological displacement studied in this chapter bear out our original hypothesis, namely that the features which are characteristic of empirically-based displacements are recognizable in cases of internally-derived displacements as well. As with the former group, we found a greater number of cases of antedating than postdating, although this does not appear to carry decisive significance. The spans of time which the internally-derived displacements telescope are generally quite long (e.g., 1 Ki. 11 attempts to telescope most of Solomon's forty-year reign; Ezra 2:1–4:5 telescopes the eighteen years between Cyrus's decree [538] and Darius's second year [520]). This is similar to the trend found in some of the post-Biblical examples (e.g., Sēder ʿÔlām and Josephus on Judges 17–21).

The internally-derived displacements attest to two out of the three categories of motivations for displacement found in the empirically-derived examples, namely the ideological and the thematic. The religiously oriented explanations for displacement that we found for 1 Ki. 11 and 2 Chr. 25:25–27 share the same spirit as the motivation for displacement in 2 Chr. 20:35–37 (cf. 1 Ki. 22:49–50). In each of these cases, events which had a negative outcome are brought into an earlier or later context so that they coincide with the religious failings of the king. The cultic motif of expediting the building of a temple, which is part and parcel of the non-chronological presentation in Ezra 2:1–4:5, is the same dominant factor behind the displacements in Esarhaddon's Babylon inscription and Nabonidus's Sippar cylinder (cf. also 2 Chr. 34). Examples of thematic motivations in the internally-derived cases of displacement also overlap with the results obtained from the empirically-based cases. The postdated material in Jud. 17–21 serves as a climactic conclusion to the entire period in the same way as the postdated narrative in the MT to 1 Ki. 21 (cf. also the antedated material in 2 Chr. 20:1–30 which allows 2 Chr. 20:35–37 to function as a concluding piece). The contrast between the forces of good and evil which is inherent to the antedating in Exod. 18 is roughly similar to the antedating in Addition A to Esther which pits Haman against Mordechai from the very outset of the narrative. The lack of exegetical motivations in the examples from this chapter of our study can be accounted for either by the relatively small number of cases studied or by the nature of the internally-derived examples. The latter group, by definition, does not provide us with previous written versions which might have contained features that the later versions (in this case, the Biblical texts) sought to explicate.

Our analyses in this chapter also identified many of the outstanding methods that we previously found in the empirically-derived examples for anchoring displaced material. The highlighting of associative links which resulted from arranging Exod. 18 and Jud. 17–18 in their precise new contexts is reminiscent of the placement of the narrative concerning Abijah's illness precisely after the story of his birth in Egypt (LXX 3 Reigns 12:24g–n). The use of ambiguous chronological formulae in Jud. 17–21 (bayyāmîm hāhēm 'ên melek bĕyiśrā'ēl); 1 Ki. 11:29 (wayĕhî bā'ēt hahî'); and 2 Chr. 25:25–27 (ûmē'ēt) parallels the same technique in Assurbanipal's annals (ina ūmēšu) and MT 1 Ki. 21 ('aḥar haddĕbārîm hā'ēlleh). The omission by 2 Chr. 20 of written data (i.e., 1 Ki. 22:48) which could upset its new non-chronological scheme lines up with the omission by the LXX's alternative version to MT 1 Ki. 14:1–18 of certain verses which would be problematic for its particular non-chronological presentation. Finally, the general muddling of precise sequence found in 1 Chr. 11:4–9 corresponds to the murky chronological framework found in Nabonidus's Sippar cylinder.

Concluding Remarks

Our primary task in this study was to collect and analyze cases of chronological displacement scattered throughout the Bible and kindred literature. Underlying this endeavor was the opportunity to achieve greater methodological corroboration than is normally available for topics in the Biblical field. This opportunity presented itself because of the presence of "empirical models," that is to say, cases of displacement which could be documented through the existence of external textual and/or historical evidence and which could thus serve to illuminate cases in which the presence of displacement was more conjectural. While allowing for the fact that not even all of our "empirical" examples could reach the same level of decisiveness and clarity (due to the inevitable "subjective" stands that have to be taken, for example, with regard to the relationship between two extant texts), the available evidence still enabled us to put our conclusions on surer ground than would have been the case in the absence of parallel texts or pertinent historical data which may have confronted the author/editor responsible for a particular displacement.

In the first three chapters, we analyzed cases of empirically-based chronological displacement taken from Mesopotamian material, Biblical material, and post-Biblical material, respectively. We saw definite similarities emerging with regard to the arrangement of the displaced materials, the motivations for those arrangements, and the methods through which the displaced materials were set in their present literary locations. The arrangements themselves consisted of two categories, namely antedating and postdating. The motivations could be classified into three broad categories, namely ideological, thematic, and exegetical. The various methods, including the use of vague chronological formulae and the omission of specific chronological data, shared the common denominator of attempting to gloss over the conspicuousness of the displacement in question.

In the last chapter, we assembled cases of chronological displacement in the Bible which were based only on hints and intimations provided by the same text in which the displacement was identified. We demonstrated that the patterns pertaining to the cases of empirically-derived displacement were indeed applicable to the internally-derived cases as well. This conclusion confirms the value of the "empirical models" theory and provides fresh impetus for the intensive study of extra-Biblical sources which might provide the empirical basis necessary for further advances in understanding the literary and historiographic character of the Hebrew Bible.

APPENDIX

Historical Order of Persian Kings	Kings as listed in Ezra-Neh.	Standard Interpretation of S.O. 29–30	Torrey's Interpretation of S.O.,Ez.-Neh.
Cyrus 539–530	Cyrus	Cyrus (2 years)	Cyrus (2 years)
Cambyses 530–522	—	—	—
		Ahasuerus of Ezra 4:6 = Artaxerxes of Ezra 4:7–23. (14 years)	
Darius I (Hystaspis) 522–486	Darius of Ezra 4:5; 4:24–6:15, completion of temple.	Darius of Ezra 4:24–6:15, completion of temple	—
Xerxes 486–464	Ahasuerus of Ezra 4:6	—	Ahasuerus of Ezra 4:6
Artaxerxes I (Longimanus) 464–423	Artaxerxes of Ezra 4:7–23; 6:14; Ezra 7–Neh. 13.	=(same person) Artaxerxes of Ezra 6:14; Ezra 7–Neh. 13 (and Darius of Neh. 12:22) (36 years)	=(same person as) Artaxerxes I of Ezra 4:7–23 (1 Esd. 2:15–29); Ezra 6:14 (14 years)
Darius II (Nothos) 423–404	possibly Darius of Neh. 12:22		Darius II of Ezra 4:24–6:15 (1 Esd. 3:1–5:6; 6–7, completion of temple (6 years)

Chart continues

Historical Order of Persian Kings	Kings as listed in Ezra-Neh.	Standard Interpretation of S.O. 29–30	Torrey's Interpretation of S.O., Ez.-Neh.
Artaxerxes II (Mnemon) 404–358	possibly Artaxerxes of Ezra 7–8		Artaxerxes II of Ezra 7–Neh. 13 (32 years)
Artaxerxes III (Ochos) 358–338			
Arsas 338–336			
Darius III (Codomanus) 336–331			Darius III of Neh. 12:22 (2 years)
		total 52 yrs.	total 56 yrs.

In Torrey's opinion, the author of Ezra, like the *Sēder ʿÔlām*, considered the Darius in whose days the temple was completed (Ezra 4:24–6:15) to be Darius II Nothos, who was preceded by Artaxerxes I (he being the same as Ahasuerus—Ezra 4:6–23), and was followed by Artaxerxes II (Ezra 7–Neh. 13).

Now, it is true that *Sēder ʿÔlām* reflects an order Cyrus-Ahasuerus-Darius, with Artaxerxes (Artahshastah) serving as a generic throne name for any one of them (chs. 29–30, Milikowsky ed., pp. 543–44). However, according to *Sēder ʿÔlām*'s midrashic scheme, which requires compressing the entire Persian period to a mere 52 years (not 56 as Torrey would have it—see S.O. ch. 30, Milikowsky ed., pp. 544, 546; the period of 52 years is part of the 490 allowed for by the S.O. between the destructions of the first and second temples, see Torrey, "Medes and Persians," 3, contra Lauterbach, "Misunderstood Chronological Statements"), the Persian period *ends* with Darius who is to be equated with the Artaxerxes of Ezra 7–Neh. 13 (as well as the Darius of Neh. 12:22). This scheme certainly cannot be brought to bear on the Ezra material, which not only clearly recognizes some historical distance between Darius and the Artaxerxes who sponsored Ezra's mission (7:1), but also distinguishes between Ahasuerus (4:6) and Artaxerxes (4:7), and places the latter *following* Cyrus and Darius in 6:14. It should be noted here that Torrey's own reconstruction, which requires that the Artaxerxes of 6:14 be equated with that of 4:7 (see chart), creates an internal inconsistency in his position. For if ch. 4 does indeed reflect a conception of straight chronological sequence (however historically inaccurate that conception may be), we would have expected the order of 6:14 to be Cyrus-Artaxerxes-Darius. Now, in all fairness to Torrey, it should be noted that his position, which separates the Artaxerxes of Ezra 4:6; 6:14 from that of Ezra 7ff., avoids having to take the mention of Artaxerxes in 6:14 itself (as one of the sponsors of the temple building) as a proleptic statement. However, this phenomenon has a satisfactory explanation, namely to include the building of the city and its wall, which was to take place during the reign of Artaxerxes, under the rubric of the temple project (see above, pp. 129–30).

BIBLIOGRAPHY

Aberbach, Moses and Smolar, Levi. "Jeroboam's Rise to Power." JBL 88 (1969), 69–72.

Abramsky, Shmuel. "Artistry and Historiography in the Story of David's Kingdom" (Hebrew). Beth Mikra 22 (71) (1976–77), 453–72.

Abravanel, Don Isaac. *Pērûš ʿal Hattôrāh*. Jerusalem: Bnei Arbel, 1964.

———. *Pērûš ʿal Něvîʾîm Riʾšônîm*. Jerusalem: Torah VaDaat, 1954.

Ackroyd, Peter R. "The Historical Literature." In *The Hebrew Bible and its Modern Interpreters*. Ed. Douglas A. Knight and Gene M. Tucker. Chico, Ca.: Scholars Press, 1985, 297–323.

Aharoni, Yohanan. *The Land of the Bible: A Historical Geography*. Translated from the Hebrew by A.F. Rainey. Philadelphia: Westminster, 1979.

———. "The Settlement of Canaan." Chapter 6 in Vol. III of *The World History of the Jewish People*. Ed. Benjamin Mazar. Israel: Jewish History Publications/ Rutgers University, 1971, 94–128, 308–13.

———. "The Stories of Samson and the Danite Inheritance" (Hebrew). In *ʿIyûnîm Běsēper Šôpěṭîm*. Publications of the Society for Biblical Research in Israel, book 10. Jerusalem: The Society for Biblical Research in Israel and Kiryat Sefer, 1971, 435–62.

Albright, W.F. "The Judicial Reform of Jehoshaphat." In *Alexander Marx Jubilee Volume*. Ed. Saul Lieberman. New York: The Jewish Theological Seminary of America, 1950, 61–82.

———. *The Biblical Period from Abraham to Ezra*. Harper Torchbook ed. New York: Harper & Row, 1963.

Alt, A. "Die Heimat des Deuteronomiums." In *Kleine Schriften zur Geschichte des Volkes Israel*. Munich: C.H. Beck, 1953, Vol. 2, 250–75.

Alter, Robert. *The Art of Biblical Narrative*. New York: Basic Books, 1981.

Amit, Yaira. "The End of the Book of Judges." *Proceedings of the Ninth World Congress of Jewish Studies* (Hebrew section). Jerusalem: World Union of Jewish Studies, 1986, Part 1, 73–80.

Attridge, Harold W. *The Interpretation of Biblical History in the Antiquitates Judaicae of Flavius Josephus*. Harvard Dissertations in Religion, 7. Missoula, Mt.: Scholars Press, 1976.

Bacher, Binyamin Zeev. ᶜerkê midrāš. vol. 1 (*Tannāʾîm*). Translated from the German by A.Z. Rabinowitz. Tel Aviv: 1923, repr. Jerusalem: 1970.

Bahye (ben Asher). *Bēʾûr ᶜal Hattôrāh*. Ed. by Chaim Dov Chavel in 5 vols. Jerusalem: Mossad Harav Kook, 1966–68.

Bar-Efrat, Shimeon. *The Art of the Biblical Story* (Hebrew). Israel: Sifriyat Poalim, 1979.

Bartal, Aryeh. "And Again—Who is Sheshbazzar?" (Hebrew). *Beth Mikra* 24 (79) (1979), 357–69.

Batten, Loring W. *A Critical and Exegetical Commentary on the Books of Ezra and Nehemiah*. ICC vol. 11. New York: Charles Scribner's Sons, 1913.

Beaulieu, Paul-Alain. *The Reign of Nabonidus King of Babylon 556–539 B.C.* Yale Near Eastern Researches, 10. New Haven and London: Yale University, 1989.

Benito, Carlos A. "*Enki and Ninmah* and *Enki and the World Order*." Unpublished PhD dissertation, University of Pennsylvania, 1969.

Ben-Yashar, Menahem. "On the Problem of Sheshbazzar and Zerubbabel" (Hebrew). *Beth Mikra* 27 (88) (1981), 46–56.

Benzinger, I. *Die Bücher der Könige.* KHAT, Vol. 9. Freiburg: J.C.B. Mohr, 1899.

———. *Die Bücher der Chronik.* KHAT, Vol. 20. Tübingen and Leipzig: J.C.B. Mohr, 1901.

Berlin, Meir and Zevin, Shlomo Zevin (eds.). *'Enṣiqlôpediyāh Talmûdît.* Vol. 1. Jerusalem: Talmudic Encyclopedia Publications, 1955.

Bickerman, Elias. *From Ezra to the Last of the Maccabees: Foundations of Post-Biblical Judaism.* Schocken paperback ed. New York: Schocken, 1962.

Blenkinsopp, Joseph. *Ezra-Nehemiah: A Commentary.* OTL. Philadelphia: Westminster, 1988.

Boling, Robert G. *Judges: Introduction, Translation, and Commentary.* AB, Vol. 6A. Garden City, N.Y.: Doubleday, 1975.

———. *Joshua: A New Translation with Notes and Commentary.* AB, Vol. 6. Garden City, N.Y.: Doubleday, 1982.

Borger, Riekele. *Die Inschriften Asarhaddons Königs von Assyrien.* AfO Beiheft 9. Graz: 1956.

———. *Einleitung in die assyrischen Königsinschriften: Erster Teil, Das zweite Jahrtausend v. Chr.* Handbuch der Orientalistik, Erste Abteilung, Ergänzungsband V. Leiden and Köln: E.J. Brill, 1961.

Braun, Roddy L. "Solomonic Apologetic in Chronicles." *JBL* 92 (1973), 503–16.

Brettler, Marc. "The Book of Judges: Literature as Politics." *JBL* 108 (1989), 395–418.

Bright, John. *A History of Israel.* 3rd ed. Philadelphia: Westminster, 1981.

———. *The Book of Joshua: Introduction and Exegesis.* In *IB* vol. 2. Commentary editor, George Arthur Buttrick. New York and Nashville: Abingdon, 1953, 539–673.

Brinkman, J.A. *A Political History of Post-Kassite Babylonia: 1158–722 B.C.* Analecta Orientalia 43. Rome: Pontificum Institutum Biblicum, 1968.

Buber, Martin. *Kingship of God.* 3rd ed. Translated by Richard Scheimann. London: George Allen and Unwin, 1967.

Burney, C.F. *Notes on the Hebrew Text of the Books of Kings.* Oxford: Clarendon, 1903.

———. *The Book of Judges with Introduction and Notes and Notes on the Hebrew Text of the Book of Kings.* The Library of Biblical Studies ed. New York: KTAV, repr. 1970.

Cassuto, Umberto. *Pērûš ʿal Sēper Šĕmôt.* 2nd ed. Jerusalem: Magnes, 1954.

———. *Biblical and Canaanite Literatures: Studies on the Bible and Ancient Orient, Volume 1* (Hebrew). Jerusalem: Magnes, 1972.

Charles, R.H., ed. *The Apocrypha and Pseudepigrapha of the Old Testament.* Oxford: Clarendon, 1913.

Childs, Brevard S. *The Book of Exodus: A Critical, Theological Commentary.* OTL. Philadelphia: Westminster, 1974.

Cogan, Morton. *Imperialism and Religion: Assyria, Judah and Israel in the Eighth and Seventh Centuries B.C.E.* SBL Monograph Series, 19. Missoula, Mt.: Scholars Press, 1974.

———. "Omens and Ideology in the Babylon Inscription of Esarhaddon." In *History, Historiography, and Interpretation: Studies in Biblical and Cuneiform Literatures.* Ed. H. Tadmor and M. Weinfeld. Jerusalem: Magnes, 1983, 76–87.

———. "The Chronicler's Use of Chronology as Illuminated by Neo-Assyrian Royal Inscriptions." In *Empirical Models for Biblical Criti-*

cism. Ed. J.H. Tigay. Philadelphia: University of Pennsylvania, 1985, 197–209.

——— and Tadmor, Hayim. "Gyges and Ashurbanipal: A Study in Literary Transmission." *Orientalia* 46 (1977), 65–85.

——— and Tadmor, Hayim. "Ahaz and Tiglath-Pileser in the Book of Kings—Historiographic Considerations" (Hebrew). *Eretz Israel* 14 (H.L. Ginsberg Volume). Ed. Menahem Haran. Jerusalem: Israel Exploration Society, 1978, 55–61.

Coggins, R.J. *The First and Second Books of the Chronicles*. Cambridge Bible Commentary. Cambridge: Cambridge University, 1976.

Cohen, Shaye J.D. *Josephus in Galilee and Rome: His Vita and Development as a Historian*. Columbia Studies in the Classical Tradition, Vol. VIII. Leiden: E.J. Brill, 1979.

Cooper, Jerrold S. *The Curse of Agade*. Baltimore and London: Johns Hopkins, 1983.

Cross, Frank Moore, Jr. "The History of the Biblical Text in the Light of Discoveries in the Judaean Desert." *HTR* 57 (1964), 281–99.

———. "The Contribution of the Qumran Discoveries to the Study of the Biblical Text." *IEJ* 16 (1966), 81–95.

———. *Canaanite Myth and Hebrew Epic: Essays in the History of the Religion of Israel*. Cambridge, Ma. and London: Harvard University, 1973.

——— and Freedman, D.N. "Josiah's Revolt Against Assyria." *JNES* 12 (1953), 56–58.

Curtis, E.L. and Madsen, A.A. *A Critical and Exegetical Commentary on the Books of Chronicles*. ICC, Vol. 10. New York: Charles Scribner's Sons, 1910.

Dalley, Stephanie. "Yahweh in Hamath in the Eighth Century B.C." *VT* 40 (1990), 21–32.

Day, John. *God's Conflict with the Dragon and the Sea: Echoes of a Canaanite Myth in the Old Testament.* Cambridge: Cambridge University, 1985.

Debus, Jörg. *Die Sünde Jerobeams: Studien zur Darstellung Jerobeams und der Geschichte des Nordreichs in der deuteronomistischen Geschichtsschreibung.* FRLANT 93. Göttingen: Vandenhoeck & Ruprecht, 1967.

Demsky, Aaron. "The Age of Ezra and Nehemiah." Ch. 4 in *The History of the Jewish People: The Age of the Return to Zion* (Hebrew). Ed. Benjamin Mazar. Tel-Aviv: Massada, 1983, 40–65.

Dijk, J. van. "Einige Bemerkungen zu sumerischen religionsgeschichtlichen Problemen." *OLZ* 62 (1967), 230–44.

Diodorus (of Sicily). Books 1 and 2:1–34. Translated by C.H. Oldfather. Loeb Classical Library, Vol. 1. New York: G.P. Putnam's Sons, 1933.

Drews, Robert. "Sargon, Cyrus and Mesopotamian Folk History." *JNES* 33 (1974), 387–93.

Driver, S.R. *A Critical and Exegetical Commentary on Deuteronomy.* 3rd ed. ICC. Edinburgh: T.& T. Clark, 1901.

Eissfeldt, Otto. *The Old Testament: An Introduction.* Translated from the 3rd German edition by Peter R. Ackroyd. Oxford: Basil Blackwell, 1965.

———. "Gilgal or Shechem?" In *Proclamation and Presence: G.M. Davies Volume.* Ed. J.J. Durham and J.R. Porter. Richmond: John Knox, 1970, 90–101.

Elitzur, Yehuda. *Sēper Šôpĕṭîm.* Daʿat Miqrā´ series. Jerusalem: Mossad Harav Kook, 1976.

Elliger, K. and W. Rudolph (eds.). *Biblia Hebraica Stuttgartensia.* Stuttgart: Deutsche Bibelgesellschaft, 1983.

ʾEnṣiqlôpediyāh Miqrāʾît. 9 vols. Jerusalem: Bialik Institute, 1950–1988.

Eskenazi, Tamara C. *In An Age of Prose: A Literary Approach to Ezra-Nehemiah*. SBL Monograph Series, 36. Atlanta: Scholars Press, 1988.

Falkenstein, A. "Fluch über Akkade." ZA 57 (1965), 43–124.

Feldman, Louis H. *Josephus and Modern Scholarship (1937–1980)*. Berlin and New York: Walter de Gruyter, 1984.

———. "Josephus' *Jewish Antiquities* and Pseudo-Philo's *Biblical Antiquities*." In *Josephus, the Bible and History*. Ed. Louis H. Feldman and Gohei Hata. Detroit: Wayne State University, 1989, 59–80.

Fendel, Zechariah. *Legacy of Sinai*. New York: Hashkafah, 1981.

Finkelstein, J.J. "Mesopotamian Historiography." PAPS 107 (1963), 461–72.

Freedman, D.N. "The Chronicler's Purpose." CBQ 23 (1961), 436–42.

Friedman, R.E. *The Exile and Biblical Narrative: The Formation of the Deuteronomistic and Priestly Works*. HSM 22. Chico, Ca.: Scholars Press, 1981.

———. *Who Wrote the Bible?* New York: Summit, 1987.

Frymer-Kensky, T. "The Atrahasis Epic and its Significance for our Understanding of Genesis 1–9." BA 40 (1977), 147–55.

Gadd, C.J. "The Harran Inscriptions of Nabonidus." *Anatolian Studies* 8 (1958), 35–92.

———. "The Dynasty of Agade and the Gutian Invasion." Ch. 19 in *The Cambridge Ancient History*. Vol. 1, pt. 2, 3rd ed. Ed. I.E.S. Edwards, et al. Cambridge: Cambridge University, 1971, pp. 417–63.

Garsiel, Moshe. *The Kingdom of David: Studies in History and Inquiries in Historiography* (Hebrew). Tel Aviv: Don Publishing and The Israel Society for Biblical Research, 1975.

Gelb, I.J. *Old Akkadian Writing and Grammar*. Materials for the Assyrian Dictionary no. 2. 2nd ed., revised and enlarged. Chicago: University of Chicago, 1961.

Gerardi, Pamela D. "Assurbanipal's Elamite Campaigns: A Literary and Political Study." Unpublished PhD dissertation, University of Pennsylvania, 1987.

Gesenius, W., Kautzch, E., Cowley, A.E. *Gesenius' Hebrew Grammar*. 2nd English ed. Oxford: Clarendon, 1910.

Gevaryahu, H.M.I. "Micah's House of God in Mt. Ephraim and the Danite Expedition" (Hebrew). In *ʿIyûnîm Bĕsēper Šôpĕṭîm*. Publications of the Society for Biblical Research in Israel, book 10. Jerusalem: The Society for Biblical Research in Israel and Kiryat Sefer, 1971, 547–84.

Ginsburg, C.D. *Introduction to the Massoretico-Critical Edition of the Hebrew Bible*. Prolegomenon by Harry M. Orlinsky. New York: KTAV, 1966.

Ginzberg, Louis. *The Legends of the Jews*. Vols. 4 and 6. Philadelphia: The Jewish Publication Society of America, 1913 and 1928.

Gooding, D.W. "Ahab According to the Septuagint." *ZAW* 76 (1964), 269–79.

———. "The Septuagint's Version of Solomon's Misconduct." *VT* 15 (1965), 325–35.

———. "The Septuagint's Rival Versions of Jeroboam's Rise to Power." *VT* 17 (1967), 173–89.

———. "Problems of Text and Midrash in the Third Book of Reigns." *Textus* 7 (1969), 1–29.

———. *Relics of Ancient Exegesis: A Study of the Miscellanies in 3 Reigns 2*. Society for Old Testament Study Monograph Series, Vol. 4. Cambridge: Cambridge University, 1976.

Gordon, R.P. "The Second Septuagint Account of Jeroboam: History or Midrash?" VT 25 (1975), 368–93.

Gray, John. I and II Kings: A Commentary. 2nd ed. OTL. Philadelphia: Westminster, 1970.

Grayson, A. Kirk. Assyrian and Babylonian Chronicles. Texts from Cuneiform Sources, Vol. 5. Locust Valley, N.Y.: J.J. Augustin, 1975.

———. "Assyria and Babylonia." (Histories and Historians of the Ancient Near East). Orientalia 49 (1980), 140–94.

———. "The Chronology of the Reign of Ashurbanipal." ZA 70 (1981), 227–45.

——— and Sollberger, E. "L'Insurrection Générale contre Naram-Suen." RA 70 (1976), 103–28.

Greenstein, Edward L. Essays on Biblical Method and Translation. Brown Judaic Studies, 92. Atlanta: Scholars Press, 1989.

Gurney, O.R. "The Sultantepe Tablets." Anatolian Studies 5 (1955), 93–113.

Güterbock, H.G. "Die historische Tradition und ihre literarische Gestaltung bei Babyloniern und Hethitern bis 1200." ZA 42 (1934), 1–91.

Hallo, William W. and Simpson, William Kelley. The Ancient Near East: A History. New York: Harcourt Brace Jovanovich, 1971.

Halpern, Baruch. The Constitution of the Monarchy in Israel. HSM 25. Chico, Ca.: Scholars Press, 1981.

———. The First Historians: The Hebrew Bible and History. San Francisco: Harper & Row, 1988.

———. "A Historiographic Commentary on Ezra 1–6: Achronological Narrative and Dual Chronology in Israelite Historiography." In The Hebrew Bible and its Interpreters. Ed. W. H. Propp, et al. Winona Lake, In.: Eisenbrauns, 1990, 81–142.

Heinemann, Joseph. "210 Years of Egyptian Exile: A Study in Midrashic Chronology." *JJS* 22 (1971), 19–30.

Heinemann, Y. "Josephus's Method in the Description of the Antiquities of the Jews" (Hebrew). *Zion* 5 (1940), 180–203.

———. *Darkê Ha'aggādāh*. Jerusalem: Magnes and Massada, 1970.

Herodotus. Books 1 and 2. Translated by A.D. Godley. Loeb Classical Library, Vol. 1. Cambridge, Ma.: Harvard University, 1921.

Heschel, Abraham Joshua. *Theology of Ancient Judaism* (Hebrew). 2 vols. London and New York: Soncino, 1962–65.

Hirsch, Hans. "Die Inschriften der Könige von Agade." *AfO* 20 (1963), 1–82.

Ibn Ezra (Rabbi Abraham ben Ezra). See *Miqrā'ôt Gĕdôlôt*.

Jacobsen, Thorkild. *The Sumerian King List*. Oriental Institute of the University of Chicago Assyriological Studies, 11. Chicago: University of Chicago, 1939.

———. "*Iphur-Kīshi and His Times*." *AfO* 26 (1978–79), 1–14.

Japhet, Sara. *The Ideology of the Book of Chronicles and its Place in Biblical Thought* (Hebrew). Jerusalem: Mossad Bialik, 1977.

———. "Conquest and Settlement in Chronicles." *JBL* 98 (1979), 205–18.

———. "Sheshbazzar and Zerubbabel—Against the Background of the Historical and Religious Tendencies of Ezra-Nehemiah." *ZAW* 94 (1982), 66–98.

———. "The Historical Reliability of Chronicles—A History of Investigation of the Problem and its Place in Biblical Research." In *I.L. Seeligmann Volume* (Hebrew section). Ed. Y. Zakovitz and A. Rofé. Jerusalem: Elhanan Rubinstein, 1982, Vol. 2, 327–46.

———. "History and Literature in the Persian Period: The Restoration of the Temple." In *Ah, Assyria...Studies in Assyrian History and*

Ancient Near Eastern Historiography Presented to Hayim Tadmor. SH 33. Ed. M. Cogan and I. Eph'al. Jerusalem: Magnes, 1991, 174–88.

Jepsen, Alfred. "Israel und Damaskus." AfO 14 (1942), 153–72.

Josephus, Flavius. *The Life and Works of Flavius Josephus*. Translated by William Whiston. Philadelphia: John C. Winston, n.d.

———. *Antiquities of the Jews*. Books 1–11. Translated by H. St. John Thackeray and Ralph Marcus. Loeb Classical Library, Vols. 4–6. Cambridge, Ma.: Harvard University, 1930–37.

Kahana, Avraham. *Hassĕpārîm Haḥîṣônîm*. Jerusalem: Makor, 1978.

Kaufmann, Yehezkel. *Sēper Yĕhôšuʿa*. Jerusalem: Kiryat-Sefer, 1959.

———. *Sēper Šôpĕṭîm*. 2nd printing. Jerusalem: Kiryat Sefer, 1964.

———. "The Book of Deuteronomy and the Story of Josiah's Actions" (Hebrew). In his *Mikkibšônāh šel Hayyĕṣîrāh Hammiqrāʾît*. Tel-Aviv: Dvir, 1966, 161–68.

———. *Tôlĕdôt Hāʾĕmûnāh Hayyiśrĕʾēlît*. 8 vols. in 4. 8th printing. Tel-Aviv: Dvir, 1966.

Keil, Karl Friedrich. *Commentary on the Book of Joshua*. Clark's Foreign Theological Library New Series, Vol. 14. Translated by James Martin. Edinburgh: T.& T. Clark, 1857.

———. *The Books of the Kings*. Commentary on the Old Testament by C.F. Keil and F. Delitzsch. Translated from the German by James Martin. Grand Rapids, Mi.: William B. Eerdmans, repr. 1978.

———. *The Books of the Chronicles*. Commentary on the Old Testament by C.F. Keil and F. Delitzsch, Vol. 3. Translated from the German by Andrew Harper. Grand Rapids, Mi.: William B. Eerdmans, repr. 1978.

Keller, Carl A. "Über einige alttestamentliche Heiligtumslegenden I." ZAW 67 (1955), 141–68.

Kil, Yehuda. *Sēper Dibrê Hayyāmîm. Daʿat Miqrā'* series. Jerusalem: Mossad Harav Kook, 1986.

Kittel, Rudolph. *Die Bücher der Könige.* HKAT Ser. 1, Vol. 5. Göttingen: Vandenhoeck & Ruprecht, 1900.

———. *Geschichte des Volkes Israel.* Vol. 2. 5th ed. Gotha: Friedrich Andreas Perthes, 1922.

Kôhelet Rabbāh. Vol. 8 in *The Midrash.* Translated under the editorship of H. Freedman and Maurice Simon. London: Soncino, 1939.

Kraft, Robert A. "Septuagint, Earliest Greek Versions." In *IDB Supplementary Volume.* General ed. Keith Crim. Nashville: Abingdon, 1976, 811–15.

Kramer, Samuel Noah. *Sumerian Mythology: A Study of Spiritual and Literary Achievment in the Third Millenium B.C.* Revised paperback edition. Philadelphia: University of Pennsylvania, 1972.

Lambert, W.G. "The Creation of Man in Sumero-Babylonian Myth" (resume). In *Compte Rendu de l'onzième Rencontre Assyriologique Internationale, 1962.* Leiden: 1964, 101–02.

———. "A New Source for the Reign of Nabonidus." AfO 22 (1968–69), 1–8.

——— and Millard, A.R. *Atraḫasis: The Babylonian Story of the Flood.* Oxford: Clarendon, 1969.

Landsberger, B. and Bauer, Th. "Zu neuveröffentlichen Geschichtsquellen der Zeit von Asarhaddon bis Nabonid." ZA 37 (1926), 61–98.

Langdon, Stephen Herbert and Zehnpfund, Rudolf. *Die neubabylonischen Königsinschriften.* VAB 4. Leipzig: J.C. Hinrichs, 1912.

Lauterbach, Jacob Z. "Misunderstood Chronological Statements in the Talmudical Literature." *PAAJR* 5 (1933–34), 77–84.

Legrain, Leon. *Royal Inscriptions and Fragments from Nippur and Babylon.* PBS, Vol. XV. Philadelphia: University Museum, 1926.

Leiman, Sid Zalman. *The Canonization of Hebrew Scripture: The Talmudic and Midrashic Evidence*. Transactions of the Connecticut Academy of Arts and Sciences, Vol. 47. Hamden, Ct.: The Connecticut Academy of Arts and Sciences, 1976.

———. "Josephus and the Canon of the Bible." In *Josephus, the Bible, and History*. Ed. Louis H. Feldman and Gohei Hata. Detroit: Wayne State University, 1989, 50–58.

Lemke, Werner E. "The Synoptic Problem in the Chronicler's History." *HTR* 58 (1965), 349–63.

Levenson, J.D. *Sinai and Zion: An Entry into the Jewish Bible*. San Francisco: Harper & Row, 1985.

Licht, J.S. "Yôblîm" *E.M.*, Vol. 3, 582–90.

———. "Sĕpārîm Ḥîsônîm Ûgĕnûzîm" *E.M.*, Vol. 5, 1103–21.

———. "'Ezrā', 'Ezrā' Haḥîṣônî" *E.M.*, Vol. 6, 152–55.

Liddell, Henry George and Scott, Robert. *A Greek-English Lexicon*. Revised and augmented by Sir Henry Stuart Jones, with a supplement. Oxford: Clarendon, 1968.

Lie, A.G. *The Inscriptions of Sargon II, King of Assyria*. Part I: The Annals. Paris: P. Geuthner, 1929.

Lipinski, E. "An Assyro-Israelite Alliance in 842/841 B.C.E.?" *Proceedings of the Sixth World Congress of Jewish Studies* (August, 1973). Jerusalem: World Union of Jewish Studies, 1977, Vol. 1, 273–78.

Liver, J. "The Book of the Acts of Solomon." *Biblica* 48 (1967), 75–101.

———. "The Order of Persian Kings in the Books of Ezra and Nehemiah." In *Studies in Bible and Judean Desert Scrolls* (Hebrew). Jerusalem: Bialik Institute, 1971.

———. "Nāśî'." *E.M.*, Vol. 5, 978–83.

Liverani, Mario. "Critique of Variants and the Titulary of Sennacherib." In *Assyrian Royal Inscriptions: New Horizons in Literary, Ideological, and Historical Analysis*. Orientis Antiqus Collectio XVII. Ed. F.M. Fales. Rome: Istituto Per L'Oriente, 1981, 225–57.

Long, Burke O. *I Kings with an Introduction to Historical Literature*. The Forms of the O.T. Literature, Vol. IX. Ed. Rolf Knierim and Gene M. Tucker. Grand Rapids, Mi.: William B. Eerdmans, 1984.

———. "Framing Repetitions in Biblical Historiography." *JBL* 106 (1987), 385–99.

Longman, Tremper. *Fictional Akkadian Autobiography: A Generic and Comparative Study*. Winona Lake, In.: Eisenbrauns, 1990.

Luckenbill, Daniel David. *Ancient Records of Assyria and Babylonia* (ARAB). Vol. 2. Chicago: University of Chicago, 1927.

Luria, Ben-Zion. "The Settlement of the Tribe of Dan" (Hebrew). In ʿIyûnîm Bĕsēper Yĕhôšuʿa. Publications of the Society for Biblical Research in Israel, 9. Jerusalem: The Society for Biblical Research in Israel and Kiryat Sefer, 1971, 248–78.

Malamat, Abraham. "The Contact of the Kingdom of David and Solomon with Egypt and Aram Naharayim" (Hebrew). In *Sēper Tur-Sinai*. Publications of the Society for Biblical Research in Israel, 8. Ed. M. Haran and B.Z. Luria. Jerusalem: The Society for Biblical Research in Israel and Kiryat Sefer, 1960, 77–85.

———. "The Danite Migration and the Pan-Israelite Exodus-Conquest: A Biblical Narrative Pattern." *Biblica* 51 (1970), 1–16.

———. "The Period of the Judges." Chapter 7 in The *World History of the Jewish People*, Vol. III: Judges. Ed. Benjamin Mazar. Israel: Jewish History Publications/Rutgers University, 1971, 129–63, 314–23.

Malbim, Rabbi Meir ben Leibush. *Nakh ʿim Malbim*. 10 vols. New York: M.P. Press, 1974.

Mayes, A.D.H. *The Story of Israel between Settlement and Exile: A Redactional Study of the Deuteronomistic History*. London: SCM, 1983.

Mazar, Benjamin. "Yĕhôšāpāṭ ben ʾĀsāʾ." E.M., Vol. 3, 565–70.

———. "David's Reign in Hebron and the Conquest of Jerusalem." In *In the Time of Harvest: Essays in Honor of Abba Hillel Silver on the Occasion of his 70th Birthday*. Ed. Daniel Jeremy Silver. New York and London: Macmillan, 1963, 235–44.

———. "David's Warriors" (Hebrew). In *Canaan and Israel: Historical Essays*. Jerusalem: Mossad Bialik and the Israel Exploration Society, 1974, 183–207.

———. "The Era of David and Solomon." Chapter 5 in Vol. IV/1 of *The World History of the Jewish People*. Ed. Abraham Malamat. Israel: Jewish History Publications/Rutgers University, 1979, 76–100, 326.

McCarter, P. Kyle, Jr. *II Samuel: A New Translation with Introduction, Notes and Commentary*. AB, Vol. 9. Garden City, N.Y.: Doubleday, 1984.

McKenzie, Steven L. *The Chronicler's Use of the Deuteronomistic History*. HSM 33. Atlanta: Scholars Press, 1985.

Mĕkiltāʾ de-Rabbi Ishmael. Ed. H.S. Horovitz and I.A. Rabin. 2nd ed. Jerusalem: Wahrmann, 1970.

Melammed, Ezra Zion. *Bible Commentators* (Hebrew). 2 vols. Jerusalem: Magnes, 1975.

Metzger, Bruce M. *An Introduction to the Apocrypha*. New York: Oxford University, 1957.

———. (ed.). *The Oxford Annotated Apocrypha of the Old Testament*. Revised Standard Version. New York: Oxford University, 1965.

Metzudat David (Rabbi David Altschuler). See *Miqrāʾôt Gĕdôlôt*.

Michaeli, Frank. *Les Livres des Chroniques, D'Esdras et de Néhémie*. Commentaire de L'Ancien Testament XVI. Paris: Delachaux & Niestle, 1967.

Midrāš Haggādôl on the Pentateuch: Genesis (Hebrew). Ed. Mordecai Margulies. Jerusalem: Mossad Harav Kook, 1967.

Midrāš Těhillîm. Ed. Solomon Buber. Vilna: 1891. repr. Jerusalem: 1966.

Milikowsky, Chaim Joseph. "Seder Olam: A Rabbinic Chronography." Unpublished PhD dissertation, Yale University, 1981.

Miller, James Maxwell. "The Elisha Cycle and the Accounts of the Omride Wars." *JBL* 85 (1966), 441–54.

———. "The Fall of the House of Ahab." *VT* 17 (1967), 307–24.

———. "The Rest of the Acts of Jehoahaz (1 Kings 20; 22:1–38)." *ZAW* 80 (1968), 337–42.

Miqrā'ôt Gĕdôlôt (Rabbinic Bible). Pentateuch, 5 vols. New York: Friedman, n.d.

———. Prophets and Writings, 4 vols. Jerusalem: Books Export Enterprises, 1982.

Mišnat Rabbi Eliezer. Ed. H.G. Enelow. New York: Bloch, 1933.

Montgomery, James A. *A Critical and Exegetical Commentary on the Books of Kings*. ICC. New York: Charles Scribner's Sons, 1951.

Moore, Carey A. *Daniel, Esther, and Jeremiah: The Additions: A New Translation with Introduction and Commentary*. AB, Vol. 44. Garden City, N.Y.: Doubleday, 1977.

Moore, George F. *A Critical and Exegetical Commentary on Judges*. ICC. Edinburgh: T.& T. Clark, 1895.

Moran, W.L. "Notes on the New Nabonidus Inscriptions." *Orientalia* 28 (1959), 130–40.

Myers, Jacob M. *Ezra-Nehemiah: Introduction, Translation, and Notes*. AB, Vol. 14. Garden City, N.Y.: Doubleday, 1965.

———. *I Chronicles: Introduction, Translation, and Notes*. AB, Vol. 12. Garden City, N.Y.: Doubleday, 1965.

———. *II Chronicles: Translation and Notes*. AB, Vol. 13. Garden City, N.Y.: Doubleday, 1965.

Napier, B.D. "The Omrides of Jezreel." *VT* 9 (1959), 366–78.

Nelson, Richard D. *The Double Redaction of the Deuteronomistic History.* JSOT Supplement Series, 18. Sheffield: JSOT, 1981.

Nicholson, E.W. *Deuteronomy and Tradition.* Philadelphia: Fortress, 1967.

Nielsen, Eduard. *Shechem: A Traditio-Historical Investigation.* Copenhagen: G.E.C. Gad, 1955.

Noth, Martin. *Das Buch Josua.* HAT, Vol. 7. Tübingen: J.C.B. Mohr, 1953.

———. *Könige.* BKAT, Vol. 9/1. Neukirchen-Vluyn: Neukirchener Verlag, 1968.

———. *The Deuteronomistic History.* Translated from the 2nd German edition, 1957. JSOT Supplement Series, 15. Sheffield: JSOT, 1981.

———. *The Chronicler's History.* Translated by H.G.M. Williamson. JSOT Supplement Series, 50. Sheffield: JSOT, 1987.

Olmstead, A.T. "Source Study and the Biblical Text." *AJSL* 30 (1913–14), 1–35.

Oppenheim, A. Leo. *Ancient Mesopotamia: Portrait of a Dead Civilization.* Chicago and London: University of Chicago, 1964.

Pfeiffer, R.H. "Chronicles, I and II." *IDB*, Vol. 1. Ed. George Arthur Buttrick. New York and Nashville: Abingdon, 1962, 572–80.

Piepkorn, Arthur Carl. *Historical Prism Inscriptions of Ashurbanipal: Editions E, B1–5, D, and K.* AS 5. Chicago: University of Chicago, 1933.

Plein, Ina. "Erwägungen zur Überlieferung von I Reg. 11:26–14:20." *ZAW* 78 (1966), 8–24.

Poebel, Arno. *Historical Texts.* PBS, Vol. 4, no. 1. Philadelphia: University Museum, 1914.

Pritchard, James B. (ed). *Ancient Near Eastern Texts Relating to the Old Testament* (ANET). 3rd ed. with supplement. Princeton: Princeton University, 1969.

Rad, Gerhard von. "The Form-Critical Problem of the Hexateuch." In his *The Problem of the Hexateuch and Other Essays*. Translated by E.W. Trueman Dicken. Edinburgh and London: Oliver & Boyd, 1965.

———. *Deuteronomy: A Commentary*. Translated from the 1964 German edition by Dorothea Barton. OTL. Philadelphia: Westminster, 1966.

Radak (Rabbi David Kimhi). See Miqrā'ôt Gĕdôlôt.

Rahlfs, Alfred (ed.). *Septuaginta*. 6th ed. Stuttgart: Privilegierte Wurttembergische Bibelanstalt, 1959.

Rainey, A.F. "ʿĒber Hannāhār." E.M., Vol. 6, 43–48.

Ramban (Rabbi Moses ben Nachman). *Commentary on the Torah* (Hebrew). Translated and annotated by Charles B. Chavel. 5 vols. New York: Shilo, 1971–76.

Rashbam (Rabbi Samuel ben Meir). *Pērûš HaRashbam Haššālēm ʿal Hattôrāh*. Ed. David Rozen. Breslau: 1882.

Rashi (Rabbi Solomon ben Isaac). See Rosenbaum and Silbermann, *Pentateuch*, for commentary on Torah; Miqrā'ôt Gĕdôlôt for commentary on Prophets and Writings.

Reade, Julian. "The Accession of Sinsharishkun." JCS 23 (1970), 1–9.

Rofé, Alexander. *Introduction to Deuteronomy: Part I and Further Chapters* (Hebrew). Jerusalem: Akademon, 1988.

Röllig, W. "Erwägungen zu neuen Stelen König Nabonids." ZA 56 (1964), 218–60.

Rosenbaum, M. and Silbermann, A.M. *Pentateuch with Targum Onkelos, Haphtaroth and Rashi's Commentary Translated into English and Annotated*. 5 vols. New York: Hebrew Publishing Company, n.d.

Rothstein, J. Wilhelm and Hänel, Johannes. *Das erste Buch der Chronik.* KAT, Vol. 18, pt. 2. Leipzig: A. Deichertsche Verlagsbuchhandlung, 1927.

Roux, Georges. *Ancient Iraq.* 2nd ed. London: George Allen & Unwin, Ltd., 1980.

Rowley, Henry Harold. "Nehemiah's Mission and its Background." In *Men of God: Studies in Old Testament History and Prophecy.* London and Edinburgh: Thomas Nelson and Sons, 1963, 211–45.

———. "The Chronological Order of Ezra and Nehemiah." In *The Servant of the Lord and Other Essays on the Old Testament.* 2nd revised ed. Oxford: Basil Blackwell, 1965, 135–68.

Rudin-O'brasky, Talia. "The Appendices to the Book of Judges (Judges 17–21)" (Hebrew). *Beer-Sheva* 2 (1985), 141–65.

Rudolph, Wilhelm. *Esra und Nehemiah.* HAT, Vol. 20. Tübingen: J.C.B. Mohr, 1949.

———. *Chronikbücher.* HAT, Vol. 21. Tübingen: J.C.B. Mohr, 1955.

Sarna, Nahum M. *The JPS Torah Commentary: Genesis.* Philadelphia: Jewish Publication Society, 1989.

———. *The JPS Torah Commentary: Exodus.* Philadelphia: Jewish Publication Society, 1991.

Sēder ʿÔlām Rabbāh. Ed. with notes and introduction by Ber Ratner. Vilna: 1890. Repr. New York: Talmudical Research Institute, 1966.

Sēder ʿÔlām Zûṭāʾ. Ed. with notes and introduction by Menashe Grossberg. Lundris: 1910. Repr. Israel: 1970.

Seebass, H. "Zur Königserhebung Jerobeams I." *VT* 17 (1967), 325–33.

———. "Die Verwerfung Jerobeams I und Salomos durch die Prophetie des Ahia von Silo." *WO* 4 (1968), 163–82.

Seeligmann, I.L. "The Beginnings of Midrash in the Books of Chronicles" (Hebrew). *Tarbiz* 49 (1979–80), 14–32.

Segal, M.Z. "'Ezrā' ûNěḥemyāh." E.M., Vol. 6, 143–51.

Seters, John van. *In Search of History: Historiography in the Ancient World and the Origins of Biblical History*. New Haven and London: Yale University, 1983.

Shenkel, James Donald. *Chronology and Recensional Development in the Greek Text of Kings*. Cambridge, Ma.: Harvard University, 1968.

Sifrê d'Bê Rāb (Numbers). Ed. H.S. Horovitz. Leipzig: 1917. Repr. Jerusalem: Wahrmann, 1966.

Smith, Mark S. *The Early History of God: Yahweh and the Other Deities in Israel*. San Francisco: Harper & Row, 1990.

Smith, Sidney. *Babylonian Historical Texts Relating to the Capture and Downfall of Babylon*. London: Methuen & Co., 1924.

———. "Notes on the Gutian Period." *Journal of the Royal Asiatic Society* 1932, 295–308.

Soggin, J. Alberto. "Zwei umstrittene Stellen aus dem Uberlieferungskreis um Schechem." ZAW 73 (1961), 78–87.

———. *Joshua: A Commentary*. Translated from the French by R.A. Wilson. OTL. Philadelphia: Westminster, 1972.

———. *Judges: A Commentary*. Translated from the Italian by John Bowden. OTL. Philadelphia: Westminster, 1981.

Speiser, E.A. "Some Factors in the Collapse of Akkad." JAOS 72 (1952), 97–101.

———. *Genesis: Introduction, Translation, and Notes*. AB, Vol. 1. Garden City, N.Y.: Doubleday, 1964.

———. "Ancient Mesopotamia." In *The Idea of History in the Ancient Near East*. Ed. Robert C. Dentan. New paperback ed. New Haven: Yale University, 1967, 35–76.

Spiro, Abram. "Manners of Rewriting Biblical History from Chronicles to Pseudo-Philo." Unpublished PhD dissertation, Columbia University, 1953.

Sternberg, Meir. *Expositional Modes and Temporal Ordering in Fiction*. Baltimore: Johns Hopkins, 1978.

———. *The Poetics of Biblical Narrative: Ideological Literature and the Drama of Reading*. Bloomington, In.: Indiana University, 1985.

Streck, Maximilian. *Assurbanipal und die Letzten Assyrischen Könige bis zum Untergange Ninivehs*. Part 2. VAB 7. Leipzig: J.C. Hinrichs, 1916.

Tadmor, Hayim. "The Campaigns of Sargon II of Assur: A Chronological-Historical Study." *JCS* 12 (1958), 22–40.

———. "kĕrônôlôgiyāh." *E.M.*, Vol. 4, 245–310.

———. "The Inscriptions of Nabunaid: Historical Arrangement." In *Studies in Honor of Benno Landsberger on his Seventy-fifth Birthday*. AS 16. Ed. Hans G. Güterbock and T. Jacobsen. Chicago: University of Chicago, 1965, 351–63.

———. "Observations on Assyrian Historiography." In *Essays on the Ancient Near East in Memory of J.J. Finkelstein*. Memoirs of the Connecticut Academy of Arts and Sciences, Vol. XIX. Ed. Maria de Jong Ellis. Hamden, Ct.: Connecticut Academy of Arts and Sciences, 1977, 209–13.

———. "History and Ideology in the Assyrian Royal Inscriptions." In *Assyrian Royal Inscriptions: New Horizons in Literary, Ideological, and Historical Analysis*. Orientis Antiqus Collectio XVII. Ed. F.M. Fales. Rome: Istituto Per L'Oriente, 1981, 13–33.

Talmon, Shemaryahu. "In Those Days There Was No King in Israel." In *Proceedings of the Fifth World Congress of Jewish Studies* (Hebrew section). Jerusalem: World Union of Jewish Studies, 1969, Vol. 1, 135–44.

———. "The Presentation of Synchroneity and Simultaneity in Biblical Narrative." *SH* 27 (1978), 9–26.

Talmud, Babylonian. New York: Pardes, 1954.

Talmud, Palestinian. New York: M.P. Press, 1976.

Talshir, Zipporah. "The Description of the Second Temple's Foundation in its Stages" (Hebrew). In *Sēper Yitzhak Aryeh Zeligman*. Ed. Y. Zakovitz and A. Rofé. Jerusalem: Rubinstein, 1982, Vol. 2, 347–59.

———. *The Duplicate Story of the Division of the Kingdom (LXX 3 Kingdoms XII 24a–z)* (Hebrew). Jerusalem Biblical Studies. Jerusalem: Simor, 1989.

Targum Jonathan (Rabbi Jonathan ben Uziel). See *Miqrā'ôt Gĕdôlôt*.

Thackeray, H. St. John. "The Greek Translators of the Four Books of Kings." *JTS* 8 (1907), 262–78.

Tigay, Jeffrey H. "An Empirical Basis for the Documentary Hypothesis." *JBL* 94 (1975), 329–42.

———. "Conflation as a Redactional Technique." In *Empirical Models for Biblical Criticism*. Ed. J.H. Tigay. Philadelphia: University of Pennsylvania, 1985, 53–95.

Torrey, Charles C. "A Revised View of First Esdras." In *Louis Ginzberg Jubilee Volume* (English section). Ed. Alexander Marx et al. New York: The American Academy for Jewish Research, 1945, 395–410.

———. "Medes and Persians." *JAOS* 66 (1946), 1–15.

———. *Ezra Studies*. Library of Biblical Studies edition with a Prolegomenon by William F. Stinespring. New York: KTAV, 1970.

Tôseftā'. Ed. Moshe Shmuel Zuckermandel. Jerusalem: Wahrmann, 1970.

Tov, Emanuel. "The LXX Additions (Miscellanies) in 1 Kings 2 (3 Reigns 2)." *Textus* 11 (1984), 89–118.

———. "The Composition of 1 Samuel 16–18 in the Light of the Septuagint Version." In *Empirical Models for Biblical Criticism*. Ed. J.H. Tigay. Philadelphia: University of Pennsylvania, 1985, 98–130.

———. "Some Sequence Differences between the MT and LXX and Their Ramifications for the Literary Criticism of the Bible." *JNWSL* 13 (1987), 151–60.

Uffenheimer, Benjamin. *Ancient Prophecy in Israel* (Hebrew). 2nd ed. Jerusalem: Magnes, 1984.

Ungnad, A. "Eponymen." *RLA*, Vol. 2, 412–57.

Vansina, Jan. *Oral Tradition as History*. Madison, Wi.: University of Wisconsin, 1985.

Vaux, Roland de. *The Early History of Israel*. Translated by David Smith. Philadelphia: Westminster, 1978.

Weidner, E.F. "Šilkan(ḫe)ni, König von Muṣri, ein Zeitgenosse Sargons II." *AfO* 14 (1941), 40–53.

Weissbach, Franz Heinrich. "Sardanapallus." *Paulys Real-Encyclopädie der classischen Altertumswissenschaft*. Series 2, Vol. 1, pt. 2. Stuttgart: J.B. Metzler Verlagsbuchhandlung, 1920, 2436–75.

Westenholz, Aage. "The Old Akkadian Empire in Contemporary Opinion." In *Power and Propaganda: A Symposium on Ancient Empires*. Mesopotamia (Copenhagen Studies in Assyriology), Vol. 7. Ed. Mogens Trolle Larsen. Copenhagen: Akademisk Forlag, 1979, 107–24.

Westermann, Claus. *Genesis 12–36: A Commentary*. Translated by John J. Scullion. Minneapolis: Augsburg, 1985.

Wevers, J.W. "Exegetical Principles Underlying the Septuagint Text of 1 Kings ii 12–xxi 43." *Oudtestamentische Studiën* 8 (1950), 300–22.

Whitley, C.F. "The Deuteronomic Presentation of the House of Omri." *VT* 2 (1952), 137–52.

Williamson, H.G.M. "The Accession of Solomon in the Books of Chronicles." VT 26 (1976), 351–61.

———. "The Composition of Ezra i–vi." JTS n.s. 34 (1983), 1–30.

———. Ezra, Nehemiah. Word Biblical Commentary, Vol. 16. Waco, Tx.: Word, 1985.

Winckler, Hugo. Alttestamentliche Untersuchungen. Leipzig: Eduard Pfeiffer, 1892.

———. Sammlung von Keilschrifttexten. Vol. 2. Leipzig: Eduard Pfeiffer, 1893.

Wright, G. Ernest. "The Literary and Historical Problem of Joshua 10 and Judges 1." JNES 5 (1946), 105–114.

Yeivin, Shmuel. "Dān, Dānî." E.M., Vol. 2, 678–83.

———. "King Yehoshaphat" (Hebrew). Eretz Israel 7 (L.A. Mayer Memorial Volume). Ed. M. Avi-Yonah, et al. Jerusalem: Israel Exploration Society, 1964, 6–17.

Zalewski, Saul. Solomon's Ascension to the Throne: Studies in the Books of Kings and Chronicles (Hebrew). Jerusalem: Y. Marcus, 1981.